BECOMING A
MASTER MANAGER

A COMPETENCY
FRAMEWORK

BECOMING A MASTER MANAGER

A COMPETENCY FRAMEWORK

Robert E. Quinn
University of Michigan

Sue R. Faerman
State University of New York at Albany

Michael P. Thompson
Brigham Young University

Michael R. McGrath
University of Southern California

WILEY

JOHN WILEY & SONS
New York · Chichester · Brisbane · Toronto · Singapore

Library of Congress Cataloging-in-Publication Data

Becoming a master manager: a competency framework/Robert E. Quinn
    . . . [et al.].
        p.   cm.
    Includes bibliographical references.
    ISBN 0-471-51577-9
    1. Leadership.   2. Executive ability.   3. Management.
4. Organizational behavior.   I. Quinn, Robert E.
HD57.7.B43   1990
658.4—dc20   89-29742
                                                              CIP

Printed in the United States of America
10 9 8 7 6 5 4 3

PREFACE

A CHANGING WORLD

In a global economy characterized by fierce competition, organizations that hire the graduates of management schools are raising uncomfortable questions about the education process. The business community is questioning whether management schools are really "close to the customer," and they are taking a new perspective on how they evaluate management schools. The media is also taking a more critical perspective. In November of 1988, for example, *Business Week* published an evaluation of the top business schools. The evaluation was based, not on academic publications, but on the assessments of recent graduates and of the companies that recruit the graduates. The results were dramatic. Several prestigious schools fell sharply from their normal lofty rankings and, as a result, suffered considerably in terms of lost resources. In that article much was made of the failure to teach leadership. In a similar vein, our own professional associations are forming task forces and evaluating traditional approaches. Last year the AACSB released the Porter and McKibbon Report, *Management Education and Development: Drift or Thrust into the 21st Century?*, which assessed our educational practices; it too called for a greater emphasis on human skills. The top accounting firms recently concluded that accounting students need a much greater emphasis on human skills and dedicated $4 million to stimulate changes in educational practices.

These concerns are not, we think, merely short-term preoccupations. They reflect a serious questioning of what management students need to be learning in school and throughout their lives. All of these groups are concluding that what is now available in management education is necessary but insufficient. All agree that modern organizations, as never before, and even at the lowest levels, are in need of competent managerial leaders. They want technical ability but they also want more. They want people who can survive and help the organization prosper in a world of constant change and intense competition. This means both technical competence and interpersonal excellence. Management is both a technical *and* a social enterprise.

These new demands are profound because they are revolutionary. The management school in the early 1990s is very much like the American auto companies in the early 1980s. Then, the customer made it clear that the new demand was for small cars of high quality. On the surface, this seemed a minor change. It was not. It required an organizational revolution. The most fundamental norms, values, and assumptions had to be modified. The cost was so high that the intense resistance was most understandable. But also understandable was the loss of market share and near collapse of the companies.

Although universities are organized to inform, the new demands call for us to transform our students. To inform is to give the student additional information. To transform is to help the student discover and become a new self, to be more capable of understanding and leading change. Transforming involves more than traditional information dissemination. Shifting from the values of informing to both informing and transforming will not be easy. The change, however, need not be overwhelming. Informing and transforming are not mutually exclusive.

For these reasons, we present yet another textbook on management. We believe this book will add something significant to an already distinguished list of texts on this important subject. This book's significance is grounded in a model of leadership competency, the Competing Values Model. The model is used now in management education and in management and executive development across the nation, with impressive results.

OVERVIEW

The book is organized around the meta-theory in Chapter 1. The theoretical framework integrates four contrasting perspectives on organizing. It suggests that to accomplish the productive functions that are necessary in any organization, a managerial leader must play both a director and a producer role. On the other hand, to accomplish the human relations functions that are necessary, a managerial leader must play both a mentor and a facilitator role. Although these two sets of roles are highly contrasting, there is another set of contrasts. To accomplish the organizing or stabilizing function that is necessary in any organization, a managerial leader must play both a coordinator and a monitor role. In contrast, to accomplish the adaptive function, one must play both an innovator and a broker role. The model makes the complex nature of managerial work very clear. It also makes clear the bias that most people have for or against the values, assumptions, and theories that are associated with each of the above areas. It makes clear the need to appreciate competing values and the need to master and then to balance competencies from each area. The evolution of the model is traced and developed in Chapter 1.

Chapters 2 to 9 of the book are each dedicated to one of the eight roles. Each chapter is broken into three sections, and each section is dedicated to a particular competency associated with the role. In the chapter on the producer role, for example, the three sections respectively cover personal productivity and motivation, motivating others, and time and stress management. Each section or competency is presented around a five-step learning model: Assessment, Learning, Analysis, Practice, and Application.

The roles are presented in the historical order suggested in Chapter 1.

There are many reasons why an instructor might desire to present the roles in a different order or, indeed, to focus on different competencies. In the instructor's manual, a number of alternatives are explored.

Between each of every two skills chapters is an integration. The integration reviews the two roles in a given quadrant of the original model and helps the student to put the roles in the more general perspective. The final chapter of the book returns to the overall model. It provides an integrative perspective and helps the student to consider the process of lifelong learning and development.

This particular approach has grown out of eight years of research and instructional experimentation. All four authors of this text have been involved in writing various papers that have helped to shape the meta-theory. We have experimented with these materials in our classrooms at the University of Michigan, the State University of New York at Albany, Brigham Young University, and the University of Southern California. We have also used this approach in large-scale programs that are designed to improve the competencies of professional managers. Several thousand professional managers have completed programs sponsored by the government of New York State, by the Ford Motor Company, and by the University of Michigan. The results have been gratifying and instructive—gratifying because our students were transformed as well as informed and instructive because we as well as the students were transformed. We hope that the publication of this textbook will lead to similar outcomes for others.

HOW TO USE THIS BOOK

This book may be used in several ways. It can be employed alone as the main text in a course specifically designed to develop competencies, or it can be used with a more traditional text to accomplish the same objective. It can accompany more traditional texts in either an organizational behavior or a management principles course. The instructor's manual includes several papers written by colleagues in these fields that propose alternative uses of this book. The prospective user may find them to be stimulating in considering new approaches. We would like to thank the contributors to the Instructor's Manual who responded to our request for alternative teaching methods with creativity and enthusiasm: Dan Denison, University of Michigan; Bill Metheny, North Texas State University; Larry Michaelsen, The University of Oklahoma; Deborah L. Wells, Creighton University.

Developed along with the book is a pre- and post-course self-assessment for the student, available in software or hard-copy form. The assessment instrument is based directly on the material in this volume and creates two profiles. The first is a general profile across the eight roles. The second is a more specific profile across the 24-skills. Because of the one-to-one relationship between the assessment and the text material, the student should find this tool to be especially helpful.

APPRECIATION

This book began as a project in professional development for New York State. Funding for the project and for this book was provided by the negotiated agreements between the state of New York and the Civil Service Employees Association, Inc., and the Public Employees Federation, AFL–CIO, and made available through New York State's Governor's Office of Employee Relations, Program Planning and Employee Development Division. The project was initially housed at the State University of New York at Albany. All of these organizations should be recognized for their vision and cooperation as well as their funding efforts.

Many people have played critical roles in the development of this book. We particularly thank Don Giek, Director of the Program Planning and Employee Development Division in New York State. Don truly is a master manager, and we respect and appreciate the enormous efforts he has made for us and for so many people in and outside of New York State.

Several others have played key roles in this project. Laurie Newman Di-Padova not only co-authored the innovator chapter but she played several other key roles. During the absence of one of the authors she did much to facilitate the coordination of the overall project. She also took on the formidable task of authoring the instructor's manual. During all of this time she always has remained her continuously upbeat and professional self. We are most appreciative of her efforts.

Few authors could hope for a more involved, inspirational, and talented publishing team. Cheryl Mehalik, our acquisition editor, and Barbara Heaney, our developmental editor, have been magnificent. From the beginning Cheryl caught the vision of this project. She was excited about the notion of producing a text that was truly different. She also recognized the risks involved in leaving the beaten path. While she probably did not recognize the risks of working on a project with four authors, she suffered through the enormous problems of coordination in an admirable manner. Meeting us in cities all over the country, she provided continuous and caring guidance.

Barbara Heaney was the ultimate developmental editor. She too had the vision of this project and maintained her enthusiasm throughout. Her attention to detail and clarity was unending. She went the extra mile in finding additional illustrations of our points and challenged us constantly to provide more examples. We thank her for her energy and encouragement.

A number of people were asked to review this book. They are Meg G. Birdseye, University of Alabama; David E. Blevins, University of Mississippi; Kent D. Carter, University of Maine at Orono; Paul D. Collins, Purdue University; Daniel Denison, University of Michigan; Dennis L. Dossett, University of Missouri-St. Louis; Stuart C. Freedman, University of Lowell; Esther E. Hamilton, Pepperdine University; Marcia Kassner, University of North Dakota; William E. McClane, Loyola College; Edward J. Morrison, University of Colorado at Boulder; Paula C. Morrow, Iowa State University; Ralph F. Mullin, Central Missouri State University;

William E. Stratton, Idaho State University; Charles N. Toftoy, Golden State University; Mark Wellman, Bowling Green State University; and Barry L. Wisdom, Southwest Missouri State University. We appreciate their many helpful comments and insights.

Many others also contributed, and we would like to thank Debbi Berg, Bill Bywater, Bill LaFleur, Chris Dammer, Bruce Hamm, Steve Simons, Onnolee Smith, Chuck Klaer, Warren Ilchman, Tom Kinney, Kary Jablonka, Norma Riccucci, David McCaffrey, Ted Peters, Dianne Haft, Margaret Oberle, Eugene Thompson. All contributed significantly and we are grateful. Finally we thank our families for their continuous support.

Robert E. Quinn
Sue R. Faerman
Michael P. Thompson
Michael R. McGrath

BRIEF CONTENTS

CONTENTS

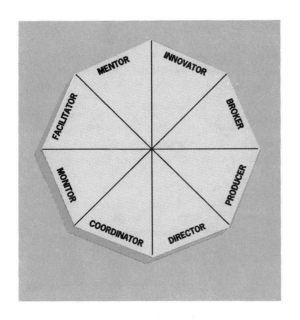

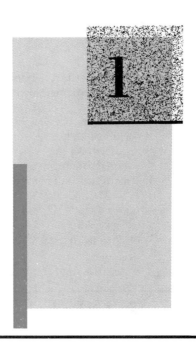

THE EVOLUTION OF MANAGEMENT MODELS A New Approach

LEARNING THE HARD WAY The Case of a Limited Model

We all have beliefs and we all make assumptions about the right way of doing things. This is certainly true when it comes to managerial leadership. Although our beliefs and assumptions can make us effective, they can sometimes make us ineffective. When they do make us ineffective it is hard to understand why. We are not usually very experienced at examining our basic beliefs and assumptions. Nor are we very experienced at adapting new assumptions or learning skills and competencies that are associated with those new assumptions. Often it takes a crisis to stimulate such change. Consider the following case.

I have always seen myself as a woman who gets things done. After 17 years with a major pharmaceutical company, I was promoted to general manager in the international division. I was put in charge of all Southeast Asian operations. The unit seemed pretty sloppy to me. From the beginning I established myself as a tough, no-nonsense leader. If someone came in with a problem, he or she knew to have the facts straight or risk real trouble. After three months I began to feel like I was working myself to exhaustion, yet I could point to few real improvements. After six months or so, I felt very uneasy but was not sure why.

One night I went home and my husband greeted me. He said, "I want a divorce." I was, shocked and caught off balance. To make a long story short, we ended up in counseling.

Our counselor taught me how to listen and practice empathy. The results were revolutionary. I learned that communication happens at many levels and that it's a two-way process. My marriage became richer than I had ever imagined possible.

I tried to apply what I was learning to what was going on at work. I began to realize that there was a lot going on that I didn't know about. People couldn't tell me the truth because I would chop their heads off. I told everyone to come to me with any problem so that we could solve it together. Naturally no one believed me. But after a year of proving myself, I am now known as one of the most approachable people in the entire organization. The impact on my division's operation has been impressive."

MODELS OF MANAGEMENT

The woman in the preceding story had a problem of real significance. The lives of many people, including subordinates, superiors, customers, and even her family members, were being affected by her actions. She was less successful than she might have been because of her beliefs about what a leader is supposed to do. For her, good management meant tight, well-organized operations run by tough-minded, aggressive leaders. Her model was not at all wrong—but it was inadequate. It limited her awareness of important alternatives and, thus, kept her from performing as effectively as she might have.

It turns out that nearly everyone has beliefs or viewpoints about what a manager should do. In the study of management, these beliefs are sometimes referred to as **models.** There are many different kinds of models. Although some are formally written or otherwise explicit, others, like the assumptions of the general manager, are informal. Because models affect what happens in organizations, we need to consider them in some depth.

Models are representations of a more complex reality. A model airplane, for example, is a physical representation of a real airplane. Models help us to represent, communicate ideas about, and better understand more complex phenomena in the real world.

In the social world a model often represents a set of assumptions for, or a general way of thinking about or seeing, some phenomenon. It provides a particular perspective about the more complex reality. Although models can help us to see some aspects of a phenomenon, they can also blind us to other aspects. The general manager mentioned before, for example, had such strongly held beliefs about order, authority, and direction that she was unable to see some important aspects of the reality that surrounded her.

Unfortunately, our models of management are often so tied to our identity and emotions that we find it, as in the preceding case, very difficult to learn about and appreciate different models. Because of the complexity of life, we often need to call upon more than one model; thus we can see and evaluate more alternatives. Our degree of choice and our potential effectiveness can be increased.

The models held by individuals often reflect models held by society at large. During the twentieth century a number of management models have emerged. Understanding these models and their origins can lead managers to a broader understanding and a wider array of choices.

AN EVOLUTIONARY PERSPECTIVE

Our models and definitions of management keep evolving. As societal values change, existing viewpoints alter and new models of management emerge. These new models are not driven simply by the writings of academic or popular writers; or by managers who introduce an effective new practice; or by the technical, social, or political forces of the time. These models emerge from a complex interaction among all these factors. In this section, we will look at the four major management models and how they evolved from the conditions in each of the first three quarters of the twentieth century. In doing this we draw upon the historical work of Mirvis (1985). Keep in mind as you read that the emergence of each new model did not mean that old models were swept away. The choice of 25-year periods is arbitrary; we use them to simplify the discussion.

1900–1925: THE EMERGENCE OF THE RATIONAL GOAL MODEL AND THE INTERNAL PROCESS MODELS

The first 25 years of this century were a time of exciting growth and progress that ended in the high prosperity of the roaring twenties. As the period began, the economy was characterized by rich resources, cheap labor, and *laissez-faire* policies. In 1901, oil was discovered in Beaumont, Texas. The age of coal became the age of oil, and soon after, the age of inexpensive energy. Technologically, it was a time of invention and innovation as tremendous advances occurred in both agriculture and industry. The work force was heavily influenced by immigrants from all over the world and by people leaving the shrinking world of agriculture. The average level of education for these people was 8.2 years. Most were confronted by serious financial needs. There was little, at the outset of this period, in terms of unionism or government policy to protect workers from the demanding and primitive conditions they often faced in the factories.

One general orientation of the period was social darwinism: the belief in "survival of the fittest." Given this orientation, it is not surprising that *Acres of Diamonds,* by Russell Conwell, was a very popular book of the time. The book's thesis was that it was every man's Christian duty to be rich. The author amassed a personal fortune from royalties and speaking fees.

These years saw the rise of the great individual industrial leaders. Henry Ford, for example, not only implemented his vision of inexpensive transportation for everyone by producing the Model T, but he also applied the principles of Frederick Taylor to the production process. Taylor was the father of **scientific management** (see Theoretical Perspective 1.1). He introduced a variety of techniques for "rationalizing" work and making it as efficient as possible. Using Taylor's ideas, Henry Ford, in 1914, introduced the assembly line and reduced car assembly time from 728 hours to 93 minutes. In six years Ford's market share went from just under 10% to just under 50%. The wealth generated by the inventions, production methods, and organizations themselves were an entirely new phenomenon.

Rational Goal Model.   It was in this historical context that the first two models of management began to emerge. The first is the **rational goal model.** The symbol that best represents this model is the dollar sign because the ultimate criteria of organization effectiveness are productivity and profit. The basic means-ends model theory in this approach is based on the belief that clear direction leads to productive outcomes. Hence there is a continuing emphasis on processes such as goal clarification, rational analysis, and action taking. The organizational climate is rational economic and all decisions are driven by considerations of "the bottom line." If an employee of 20 years is only producing at 80% efficiency, the appropriate decision is clear: Replace the employee with a person who will contribute at 100% efficiency. In the rational goal model the ultimate value is achievement and profit maximization. The manager's job is to be a hard-nosed director and producer.

Stories abound about the harsh treatment that supervisors and managers inflicted on employees during this time. In one manufacturing company, for example, they still talk today about the toilet that was once located in the center of the shop floor and was surrounded by glass windows so that the supervisor could see who was inside and how long the person stayed.

THEORETICAL PERSPECTIVE 1.1

TAYLOR'S FOUR PRINCIPLES OF MANAGEMENT

1. Develop a science for every job, which replaces the old rule-of-thumb method.

2. Systematically select workers so that they fit the job, and train them effectively.

3. Offer incentives so that workers behave in accordance with the principles of the science that has been developed.

4. Support workers by carefully planning their work and smoothing the way as they do their jobs.

Adapted from: Frederick W. Taylor, *The Principles of Scientific Management* (New York: Harper and Brothers, 1911), p. 44.

Internal Process Model.   The second model, the **internal process model,** began to emerge during the first quarter of the twentieth century, but it would not be fully codified until the writings of Max Weber and Henri Fayol were translated in the middle of the next quarter century. It was already in practice, however, and was highly complementary to the first. Here the symbol is a pyramid, and the criteria of effectiveness are stability and continuity. The means-ends theory is based on the belief that routinization leads to stability. The emphasis is on processes such as definition of responsibilities, measurement, documentation, and record keeping. The organizational climate is hierarchical, and all decisions are colored by the existing rules, structures, and traditions. If an employee's efficiency falls, control is increased through the application of various policies and procedures. In this model the ultimate value is efficient work flow, and the manager's job is to be a structured monitor and coordinator.

1926–1950: THE EMERGENCE OF THE HUMAN RELATIONS MODEL

The second quarter of the century brought two events of enormous proportions. The stock market crash of 1929 and World War II would affect the lives and outlook of generations to come. During this period the economy would boom, crash, recover with the war, and then, once again, offer bright hopes. Technological advances would continue in all areas, but particularly in agriculture, transportation, and consumer goods. The rational goal model continued to flourish. With the writings of Henri Fayol, Max Weber, and others, the internal process model (see Theoretical Perspectives 1.2 and 1.3) would be more clearly articulated. Yet, even while this was being accomplished, it started to become clear that the rational goal and internal process models were not entirely appropriate to the demands of the times.

Some fundamental changes began to appear in the fabric of society during the second quarter of the century. Unions, now a significant force, adhered to an economic agenda that brought an ever larger paycheck into the home of the American worker. Industry placed a heavy emphasis on the production of consumer goods. By the end of this period, new, labor-saving machines were beginning to appear in homes. There was a sense of prosperity and a concern with recreation as well as survival. Factory workers were not as eager as their parents had been to accept the opportunity to work overtime. Neither were they as likely to give unquestioning obedience to authority. Hence, managers were finding that the rational goal and internal process models were no longer as effective as they once were.

Given the shortcomings of the first two models, it is not surprising that one of the most popular books written during this period was Dale Carnegie's *How to Win Friends and Influence People*. It provided some much desired advice on how to relate effectively to others. In the academic world, Chester Barnard pointed to the significance of informal organization and the fact that informal relationships, if managed properly, could be powerful tools for the manager. Also during this period Elton Mayo and Fritz Roethlisberger carried

THEORETICAL PERSPECTIVE 1.2

FAYOL'S GENERAL PRINCIPLES OF MANAGEMENT

1. *Division of work.* The object of division of work is to produce more and better work with the same effort. It is accomplished through reduction in the number of tasks to which attention and effort must be directed.

2. *Authority and responsibility.* Authority is the right to give orders, and responsibility is its essential counterpart. Whenever authority is exercised, responsibility arises.

3. *Discipline.* Discipline implies obedience and respect for the agreements between the firm and its employees. Establishment of these agreements binds a firm and its employees from which disciplinary formalities emanate should remain one of the chief preoccupations of industrial heads. Discipline also involves sanctions judiciously applied.

4. *Unity of command.* An employee should receive orders from one superior only.

5. *Unity of direction.* Each group of activities having one objective should be unified by having one plan and one head.

6. *Subordination of individual interest to general interest.* The interest of one employee or group of employees should not prevail over that of the company or broader organization.

7. *Remuneration of personnel.* To maintain their loyalty and support, employees must receive a fair wage for services rendered.

8. *Centralization.* Like division of work, centralization belongs to the natural order of things. The appropriate degree of centralization, however, will vary with a particular concern, so it becomes a question of the proper proportion. It is a problem of finding the measure that will give the best overall yield.

9. *Scalar chain.* The scalar chain is the chain of superiors ranging from the ultimate authority to the lowest ranks. It is an error to depart needlessly from the line of authority, but it is an even greater one to keep it when detriment to the business could ensue.

10. *Order.* A place for everything, and everything in its place.

11. *Equity.* Equity is a combination of kindliness and justice.

12. *Stability of tenure of personnel.* High turnover increases inefficiency. A mediocre manager who stays is infinitely preferable to an outstanding manager who comes and goes.

13. *Initiative.* Initiative involves thinking out a plan and ensuring its success. This gives zeal and energy to an organization.

14. *Esprit de corps.* Union is strength, and it comes from the harmony of the personnel.

Abridged from: Henri Fayol, *General and Industrial Administration* (New York: Pitman, 1949), pp. 20–41.

out their work in the famous Hawthorne studies. One well-known experiment carried out by these two researchers concerned level of lighting. Each time they increased the level of lighting, employee productivity went up. However, when they decreased the lighting, productivity also went up. They eventually concluded that what was really stimulating the workers was the attention being shown by the researchers. The results of these studies were also interpreted as evidence of a need for an increased focus on the power of relationships and informal processes in the performance of human groups.

Human Relations Model. By the end of the second quarter of the century, the emerging orientation was the **human relations model.** In this model, the key values are commitment, cohesion, and morale. The means-ends theory is

THEORETICAL PERSPECTIVE 1.3

CHARACTERISTICS OF WEBERIAN BUREAUCRACY

Elements of Bureaucracy:

1. There is a division of labor with responsibilities that are clearly defined.

2. Positions are organized in a hierarchy of authority.

3. All personnel are objectively selected and promoted based on technical abilities.

4. Administrative decisions are recorded in writing and records are maintained over time.

5. There are career managers working for a salary.

6. There are standard rules and procedures which are uniformly applied to all.

Adapted from: A. M. Henderson and Talcott Parsons (eds.), and Max Weber (trans.), *The Theory of Social and Economic Organizations* (New York: Free Press, 1947), pp. 328–337.

that involvement results in commitment. Because the central processes are participation, conflict resolution, and consensus building, the appropriate symbol for this model is a circle. The organization takes on a clanlike, team-oriented climate in which decision making is characterized by deep involvement. Here, if an employee's efficiency declines, managers take a developmental perspective and look at a complex set of motivational factors. They may choose to alter the person's degree of participation or opt for a host of other social psychological variables. The manager's job is to be a sensitive mentor and facilitator.

In 1949, this model was far from crystalized, and it ran counter to the assumptions in the rational goal and internal process models. Hence it was difficult to understand and certainly difficult to practice. Attempts often resulted in a kind of authoritarian benevolence. It would take well into the next quarter century for research and popular writings to explore this orientation, and for managerial experiments to result in meaningful outcomes in large organizations.

1951–1975: THE EMERGENCE OF THE OPEN SYSTEMS MODEL

The period 1951 to 1975 began with the United States as the unquestioned leader of the capitalist world. It ended with the leadership of the USA in serious question. During this period the economy experienced the shock of the oil embargo. Suddenly assumptions about cheap energy, and all the life patterns upon which they were based, were in danger. By the late seventies the economy was staggering under the weight of stagflation and huge government debt. At the beginning of this period, "made in Japan" meant cheap, low-quality goods of little significance to Americans. By the end, Japanese quality could not be matched, and Japan was making rapid inroads into sectors of the economy thought to be the sacred domain of American companies. Even such traditionally American manufacturing areas as automobile production were dramatically affected. There was also a marked shift from a clear product economy to the beginnings of a service economy.

Technological advances began to occur at an ever-increasing rate. At the outset of the third quarter of the century, the television was a strange device. By the end of this period, television was the primary source of information, and the computer was entering the life of every American. At first NASA plotted to accomplish the impossible dream of putting a man on the moon, but then Americans were bored with the seemingly commonplace accomplishments of the space program.

Societal values also shifted dramatically. The fifties were a time of conventional values. Driven by the Vietnam War, the sixties were a time of cynicism and upheaval. Authority and institutions were everywhere in question. By the seventies the difficulty of bringing social change was fully understood. A more individualistic and conservative orientation began to take root.

In the work force, education jumped from the 8.2 years, at the beginning of the century, to 12.6 years. Spurred by considerable prosperity, workers in the United States were now concerned not only with money and recreation, but also with self-fulfillment. Women began to move into professions that had been closed to them previously. The agenda of labor expanded to include social and political issues. Organizations became knowledge intense, and it was no longer possible to expect the boss to know more than every person he or she supervised.

By now the first two models were firmly in place, and management vocabulary was filled with rational management terms, such as management by objectives (MBO) and management information system (MIS). The human relations model, however, was also now familiar. Many books about human relations became popular during this period, further sensitizing the world to the complexities of motivation and leadership. Experiments in group dynamics, organizational development, sociotechnical systems, and participative management flourished.

In the mid-sixties, spurred by the ever-increasing rate of change and the need to understand how to manage in a fast-changing, knowledge-intense world, a variety of academics began to write about still another model. People such as Katz and Kahn at Michigan, Lawrence and Lorsch at Harvard, as well as a host of others, began to develop the open systems model of organization. This model was more dynamic than others. The manager was no longer seen as a rational decision maker controlling a machinelike organization. The research of Mintzberg, for example, showed that in contrast to the highly systematic pictures portrayed in the principles of administration (see Theoretical Perspective 1.2), managers live in highly unpredictable environments and have little time to organize and plan. They are, instead, bombarded by constant stimuli and forced to make rapid decisions. Such observations were consistent with the movement to develop contingency theories (see Theoretical Perspective 1.4). These theories recognized the oversimplicity of earlier approaches.

Open Systems Model.   In the **open systems model,** the organization is faced with a need to compete in an ambiguous as well as competitive environ-

THEORETICAL PERSPECTIVE 1.4

CONTINGENCY THEORY

Appropriateness of Managerial Actions Vary with Key Variables:

1. *Size.* Problems of coordination increase as the size of the organization increases. Appropriate coordination procedures for a large organization will not be efficient in a small organization, and vice versa.

2. *Technology.* The technology used to produce outputs varies. They may be very routine or very customized. The appropriateness of organizational structures, leadership styles, and control systems will vary with the type of technology.

3. *Environment.* Organizations exist within larger environments. These may be uncertain and turbulent or predictable and unchanging. Organizational structures, leadership styles, and control systems will vary accordingly.

4. *Individuals.* People are not the same. They have very different needs. Managers must adjust their styles accordingly.

ment. The key criteria of organizational effectiveness are adaptability and external support. Because of the emphasis on organizational flexibility and responsiveness, the symbol here is the amoeba. The amoeba is a very responsive, fast-changing organism that is able to respond to its environment. The means-ends theory is that continual adaptation and innovation lead to the acquisition and maintenance of external resources. Key processes are political adaptation, creative problem solving, innovation, and the management of change. The organization has an innovative climate and is more of an "adhocracy" rather than a bureaucracy. Risk is high and decisions are made quickly. In this situation common vision and shared values are very important. An employee's efficiency tends to be very high over extended periods; a drop off would usually suggest an overload of stress and perhaps a case of burnout. The manager is expected to be a highly adaptable innovator and a broker (someone who uses power and influence in the organization).

1976–THE PRESENT: THE EMERGENCE OF "BOTH/AND" ASSUMPTIONS

In the final quarter of the century, it became fully apparent that American organizations were in deep trouble. Innovation, quality, and productivity all slumped badly. Japanese products made astounding advances as talk of U.S. trade deficits became commonplace. Reaganomics and conservative social and economic values fully replaced the visions of the Great Society. In the labor force, knowledge work became commonplace and physical labor rare. Labor unions experienced major setbacks as organizations struggled to downsize their staffs and increase quality at the same time. The issue of job security became increasingly frequent in labor negotiations. Organizations faced new issues, such as takeover and downsizing. One middle manager struggled to do the job previously done by two or three. Burnout and stress became hot topics.

Peters and Waterman published a book that would have extraordinary popularity. *In Search of Excellence* attempted to chronicle the story of those few organizations that were seemingly doing it right. It was really the first attempt to provide advice on how to revitalize a stagnant organization and move it into a congruent relationship with an environment turned upside down. Like Carnegie's book, long before, it addressed, and in so doing, made clear the most salient unmet need of the time: how to manage in a world where nothing is stable.

In a world of intense competition and change, the new buzzwords were *excellence, quality, customer driven, urgency, continuous improvement, culture, transformational leadership,* and *integrity.* These all reflected the challenge of revitalizing the still bureaucratic orientations of the 1951 to 1975 period to an orientation of continuous responsiveness in a highly ambiguous and fast-changing environment.

In such a world, simple solutions became suspect. None of the four models, summarized in Table 1.1, offered a sufficient answer. Even the more complex open systems approach was not sufficient. Sometimes we needed structure, sometimes we needed change—more and more we needed both at the same time. Today, for example, many organizations find themselves both downsizing and expanding simultaneously. Managing such a process is difficult.

TABLE 1.1 Characteristics of the Four Management Models

	Rational Goal	*Internal Process*	*Human Relations*	*Open Systems*
Symbol	$	△	○	⟨⟩
Criteria of effectiveness	Productivity, profit	Stability, continuity	Commitment, cohesion, morale	Adaptability, external support
Means-ends theory	Clear direction leads to productive outcomes	Belief that routinization leads to stability	Belief that involvement results in commitment	Continual adaptation and innovation lead to acquiring and maintaining external resources
Emphasis	Goal clarification, rational analysis, and action taking	Defining responsibility, measurement, documentation	Participation, conflict resolution, and consensus building	Political adaptation, creative problem solving, innovation change management
Climate	Rational economic: "the bottom line"	Hierarchical	Team oriented	Innovative, flexible
Role of manager	Director and producer	Monitor and coordinator	Mentor and facilitator	Innovator and broker

In the academic world Quinn and Rohrbaugh (1983) discovered that the four models need not be seen independently, but rather as competing or complementary elements in a larger model of management. It is around this larger model that this book is organized.

THE FOUR MODELS IN A SINGLE FRAMEWORK

A SINGLE FRAMEWORK

At first the models discussed seemed to be four entirely different perspectives or domains. However, they can be viewed as closely related and interwoven. They are four important subdomains of a larger construct: managerial leadership. Each model within the construct of managerial leadership is related insofar as the models both contrast and complement each other, as we will see. Thus, depending on the models and combinations of models we choose to use, we can see managerial leadership as simple and logical, as dynamic and synergistic, or as complex and paradoxical. Taken alone, no one of the models allows us the range of perspectives and the increased choice and potential effectiveness provided by considering them all as part of a larger framework. As we'll explain soon, we call this larger framework the **competing values framework.**

The relationships among the models can be seen in terms of two axes. In Figure 1.1 the vertical axis ranges from flexibility at the top to control at the bottom. The horizontal axis ranges from an internal organization focus at the left to an external organization focus at the right. Each model fits in one of the four quadrants.

The human relations model, for example, stresses the criteria shown in the upper left quadrant: participation, openness, commitment, and morale. The open systems model stresses the criteria shown in the upper right quadrant: innovation, adaptation, growth, and resource acquisition. The rational goal model stresses the criteria shown in the lower right quadrant: direction and goal clarity, and productivity and accomplishment. The internal process model, in the lower left quadrant, stresses documentation, information management, stability, and control.

As can be.seen in Figure 1.2, some general values are also reflected in the framework. These appear on the outer perimeter. Expansion and change are in the upper right corner and contrast with consolidation and continuity in the lower left. On the other hand, they complement the neighboring values of decentralization and differentiation at the top and competitive position of the overall system to the right. Each general value statement can be seen in the same way.

Each model has a perceptual opposite. The human relations model, defined by flexibility and internal focus, stands in stark contrast to the rational goal model, which is defined by control and external focus. In the first, for example,

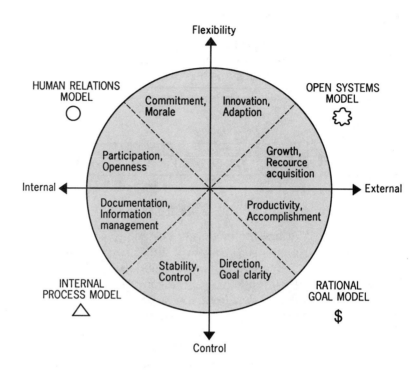

FIGURE 1.1 *The competing values framework: effectiveness criteria.* Each of the four models of organizing in the competing values framework assumes different criteria of effectiveness. Here we see the criteria in each model; the labels on the axes show the qualities that differentiate each model. *Source:* R. E. Quinn, *Beyond Rational Management.* San Francisco: Jossey-Bass Inc., 1988, p. 48. Used with permission.

people are inherently valued. In the second, people are of value only if they contribute greatly to goal attainment. The open systems model, defined by flexibility and external focus, runs counter to the internal process model, which is defined by control and internal focus. While the open systems model is concerned with adapting to the continuous change in the environment, the internal process model is concerned with maintaining stability and continuity inside the system.

Parallels among the models are also important. The human relations and open systems models share an emphasis on flexibility. The open systems and rational goal models share an emphasis on external focus. The rational goal and internal process models emphasize control. And, the internal process and human relations models share an emphasis on internal focus.

THE USE OF OPPOSING MODELS

We will use this framework of the four opposing models throughout the book as our management model. We call this framework the **competing values framework** because the criteria within the four models seem at first to carry a conflicting message. We want our organizations to be adaptable and flexible, but we also want them to be stable and controlled. We want growth, resource acquisition, and external support, but we also want tight information management and formal communication. We want an emphasis on the value of human

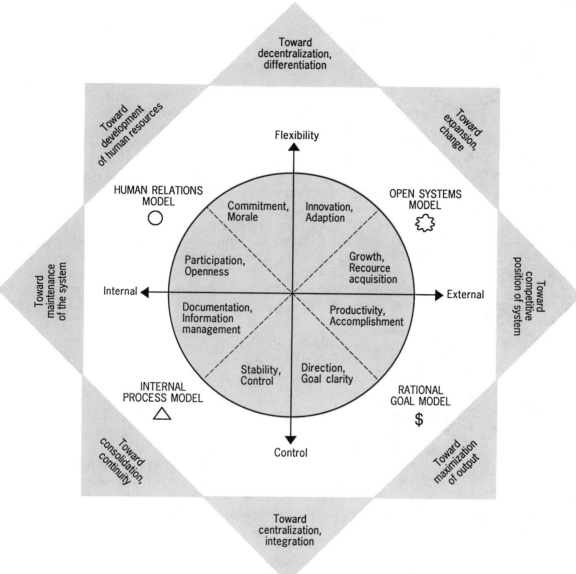

Source: R. E. Quinn, *Beyond Rational Management*. San Francisco: Jossey-Bass Inc., 1988, p. 48. Used with permission.

FIGURE 1.2 *Eight general orientations in the competing values framework. The eight general values that operate in the competing values framework are shown in the triangles on the perimeter. Each value both complements the values next to it and contrasts with the one directly opposite it. Some of these values are shared among roles; these are shown in color.*

resources, but we also want an emphasis on planning and goal setting. In any real organization all of these are, to some extent, necessary.

The framework does not suggest that these oppositions cannot mutually exist in a real system. It does suggest, however, that these criteria, values, and assumptions are at opposites in our minds. We tend to think about them as mutually exclusive; that is, we assume we cannot have two opposites at the same time.

The four models in the framework represent the unseen values over which people, programs, policies, and organizations live and die. Like the pharmaceutical executive at the outset of this chapter, we often blindly pursue values in one of the models without considering the values in the others. As a result, our choices and our potential effectiveness are reduced.

For managers the world keeps changing. It changes from hour to hour, day to day, and week to week. The strategies that are effective in one situation are not necessarily effective in another. Even worse, the strategies that were effective yesterday may not be effective in the same situation today. Managers tend to become trapped in their own style and in the organization's cultural values. They tend to employ very similar strategies in a wide variety of situations. The overall framework, consisting of the four models described here, can increase effectiveness. Each model in the framework suggests value in different, even opposite, strategies. The framework reflects the complexity confronted by people in real organizations. It therefore provides a tool to broaden thinking and to increase choice and effectiveness. This, however, can only happen as three challenges are met.

Challenge 1 To appreciate both the values and the weaknesses of each of the four models.
Challenge 2 To acquire and use the competencies associated with each model.
Challenge 3 To dynamically integrate the competencies from each of the models with the managerial situations that we encounter.

The abilities needed to meet these challenges will be discussed in greater detail in Chapter 10 of this text, after you have encountered the competencies associated with each model.

For someone just entering a management position, the dynamics associated with these seemingly competing models are difficult to conceptualize. It is not easy to think about opposites. The failure to understand them, however, can hinder the development you need as a manager.

BECOMING A MANAGER   THE NEED FOR NEW COMPETENCIES

When people take on a position of leadership, they must operate effectively in all areas of the competing values framework. Conceptualization is not enough; they must be able to act. That is, they must have the behavioral competencies that allow them to operate in each of the four quadrants. **Competency** is the knowledge and skill necessary to perform a certain task or role.

First we will describe the competing roles managers play in their organization. We will then turn to the specific competencies that are embedded in each role. Finally we will describe a process for developing each of the competencies.

EIGHT ROLES

The competing values framework is helpful in pointing out some of the values and criteria of effectiveness by which work units and organizations are judged. It is also useful in thinking about the conflicting roles that are played by managers (Quinn 1984, 1988). Figure 1.3 shows a second version of the competing values framework. The structure of Figure 1.3 is very similar to the structure of Figure 1.1, but this time the figure focuses on *leadership* effectiveness, rather than organizational or work-unit effectiveness. This framework specifies competing roles or expectations that might be experienced by a manager.

Rational Goal Model: The Director and Producer Roles. In the lower right quadrant are the director and the producer roles. As a **director,** a manager is expected to clarify expectations through processes, such as planning and goal setting, to be a decisive initiator who defines problems, selects alternatives, establishes objectives, defines roles and tasks, generates rules and policies, and gives instructions.

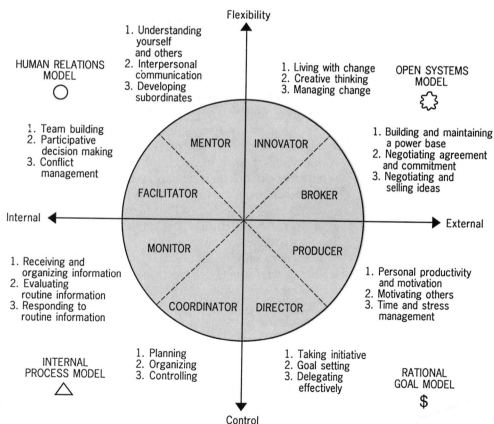

FIGURE 1.3 *The competencies and the leadership roles in the competing values framework. Each of the eight leadership roles in the competing values framework contains three competencies. They, like the values, both complement the ones nest to them and contrast with those opposite to them.*

Source: R. E. Quinn, *Beyond Rational Management*. San Francisco: Jossey-Bass Inc., 19? 86. Used with permission.

When someone is playing the director role, there is no question about who is in charge. Consider, for example, the following statement made about a particularly directive manager:

She is everywhere. It seems as if she never goes home. But it is not just her energy; she, is constantly reminding us why we are here. I have worked in a lot of organizations, but I have never been so clear about purpose. I know what I have to do to satisfy her and what the unit has to do. In some units around here, the employees really don't care; she has caused her people to care about getting the job done.

When people think about the director role, they often cite hard-driving athletic coaches like Bobby Knight, the basketball coach at the University of Indiana—people who are known for their no-nonsense, take-charge attitude. In considering large organizations we think of the clear direction given by people like Jack Welch at General Electric. Another excellent example is provided by the opening scene of the movie *Patton*. When George C. Scott, portraying General Patton, addresses his soldiers prior to entering battle, they absolutely know what the objective is and how they are to obtain it. Thornton Wilson was the chief executive at Boeing for 17 years. A highly competitive, swift-acting decision maker, he did very well in playing the director role. One of the first acts in taking over a faltering company was to cut 95,000 people, nearly two-thirds of the work force. Making such decisions, he managed to make an impressive organizational turnaround. When it came to communication, expectations were clear. The people around him indicate that when someone talked to Wilson, they walked away knowing exactly what they were to do. Wilson argues that there are times when people simply must be kicked around or even removed from their jobs. In such situations he never hesitates to act decisively.

Interestingly, Patton, and many of the others mentioned, also serve as excellent examples of the producer role. **Producers** are expected to be task oriented and work focused and to have high interest, motivation, energy, and personal drive. They are supposed to accept responsibility, complete assignments, and maintain high personal productivity. This usually involves motivating members to increase production and to accomplish stated goals.

Stereotypes of this role often have a fanatic desire to accomplish some objective. Like Captain Ahab in the novel *Moby Dick*, they drive themselves and their crews unrelentingly toward a stated objective. Harold Geneene of ITT and Ross Perot, formerly of Electronic Data Systems, are examples from the world of business. No one who has read the book *On Wings of Eagles*, portraying Perot's determined efforts to rescue his employees from their imprisonment in Iran, can have trouble understanding what it means to be a producer.

Internal Process Model: Monitor and Coordinator Roles. In the bottom left quadrant are the monitor and coordinator roles. As a **monitor** a manager is expected to know what is going on in the unit, to see if people are complying with the rules, and to see if the unit is meeting its quotas. The monitor knows all the facts and details and is good at analysis. Characteristic to this role is a zeal for handling paperwork, reviewing and responding to routine information, conducting inspections and tours, and authoring reviews of reports and other documents.

Consider, for example, this description of a manager:

She has been here for years. Everyone checks with her before doing anything. She is a walking computer. She remembers every detail, and she tracks every transaction that occurs. From agreements made eight years ago, she knows which unit owes equipment to which other unit. Nothing gets past her. She has a sixth sense for when people are trying to hide something.

The monitor role suggests a care for details, control, and analysis. Robert Crandall, chairman of AMR Corp, the parent of American Airlines, is someone who plays the monitor role in a very effective manner. He loves to study every alternative in the finest detail. Indeed, some argue that he has an obsession for detail which is reflected in the constant probing questions that he unleashes on everyone around him. In meeting with managers from even the smallest cities served by American Airlines, he will hold nonstop, eight-hour meetings going over every line in the manager's budget. In staff meetings he dominates each session, demanding facts from everyone present. He knows every aspect of what's going on in his organization. He does not let anything slip by unnoticed. Another particularly good example of someone who exemplifies this role is Robert McNamara, first at Ford Motor Company and then later at the U.S. Department of Defense. McNamara was a genius at creating control systems. He could find ways to quantify nearly any activity. At Ford, he developed extensive information systems and was able to bring new levels of control to a company that desperately needed it. Later, at the Department of Defense, he again went to great lengths to introduce such measurement and control systems.

As a **coordinator,** a manager is expected to maintain the structure and flow of the system. The person in this role is expected to be dependable and reliable. Behavioral traits include various forms of work facilitation such as scheduling, organizing, and coordinating staff efforts; crisis handling; and attending to technological, logistical, and housekeeping issues.

An excellent example of someone who plays the coordinator role well is Jim Manzi, the CEO at Lotus Development Corporation. He took over the company in 1984 when Lotus was growing with enormous speed. The obvious need was to control the growth in a positive way. He popularized the quotation from Edward Abey: "Growth for growth's sake is the ideology of the cancer cell." Always looking for applications of computer technology, he regularly has people experiment with new ways to communicate and coordinate efforts within the company. His overall coordinating efforts have clearly held the fast-growing company together.

Human Relations Model: The Facilitator and Mentor Roles. The **facilitator** is expected to foster collective effort, build cohesion and teamwork, and manage interpersonal conflict. In this role the manager is process oriented. Expected behaviors include intervening into interpersonal disputes, using conflict reduction techniques, developing cohesion and morale, obtaining input and participation, and facilitating group problem solving.

Consider, for example, this description of a public manager:

> *It is like any company. The finance people and the operations people are always at war. He brings people like that into a room, hardly says a word, and walks out with support from both sides. Same with subordinates, he brings us together, asks lots of questions, and we leave committed to get the job done. He has a gift for getting people to see the bigger picture, to trust each other, and to cooperate.*

A particularly outstanding example of the facilitator role is Suzanne de Passe, the president of Motown Productions. A highly energetic manager, she is recognized as having many skills, yet the one that stands out the most is her incredible ability for team building. With her, no subject is taboo. Her staff are free and safe in raising any issue, including the shortcomings of the boss, herself. She refuses to let any conflict stay hidden. All issues are raised and worked on until there is a resolution and consensus. Her people have a sense of involvement and influence. The level of openness and cohesiveness astounds most newcomers. Many comment that the organization is the only one they have ever seen where the truth is always told and potentially divisive political issues are immediately confronted and resolved. The sense of openness and cohesiveness creates an exciting and productive organizational context.

A **mentor** is engaged in the development of people through a caring, empathetic orientation. This might be called the concerned human role. In this role the manager is helpful, considerate, sensitive, approachable, open, and fair. In acting out this role, the manager listens, supports legitimate requests, conveys appreciation, and gives compliments and credit. People are resources to be developed. The manager helps with skill building, provides training opportunities, and plans for their individual development.

Ed Lundy, the former controller of the Ford Motor Company, was known as a master of this role. He would carefully select graduates from the best business schools, bring them into Ford, train them, and then watch over every aspect of their career development. To be one of Lundy's protégés was to be on the sure track to success at Ford.

Open Systems Model: The Innovator and Broker Roles. The innovator and broker roles, in the upper right quadrant of the framework, reflect the values of the open systems model. As an **innovator,** a manager is expected to facilitate adaptation and change. The innovator pays attention to the changing environment, identifies important trends, conceptualizes and projects needed changes, and tolerates uncertainty and risk. In this role, managers must rely on induction, ideas, and intuitive insights. They are expected to be creative, clever dreamers who see the future, envision innovations, package them in inviting ways, and convince others that they are necessary and desirable.

Consider, for example, this description:

> *In a big organization like this, most folks do not want to rock the boat. She is always asking why, looking for new ways to do things. We used to be in an old,*

run-down wing. Everyone accepted it as a given. It took her two years, but she got us moved. She had a vision, and she sold it up the system. She is always open, and if a change or a new idea makes sense, she will go for it.

Many innovators have gained attention in recent years. Bill Gates of Microsoft; Steve Jobs, first of Apple Computer and then of Next; and Don Burr of People Express exemplify this role. Another good example is Frances Lear, a woman who walked away from a 28-year marriage to the famous television producer, Norman Lear, to found a new magazine designed to help women live happier lives. *Lear's,* started in 1988, was an almost immediate success, reaching a circulation of over 350,000 copies, larger then the circulation of many well-established magazines. Aimed at women over 40, the periodical has picked up astounding levels of advertising revenues. Despite a lack of experience, her vision led her to reach an untapped market. In running her company she is intense, passionate, and somewhat unpredictable as she explores new ideas and strategies.

Innovators need not all be entrepreneurs, nor do they need to be only in the private sector. Quinn and Cameron (1983), for example, describe the case of a psychiatrist who shaped a new vision of how mental health services should be delivered. Within the huge New York State bureaucracy, he shaped a highly responsive system that received worldwide acclaim.

The **broker** is particularly concerned with maintaining external legitimacy and obtaining external resources. Image, appearance, and reputation are important. Managers as brokers are expected to be politically astute, persuasive, influencial, and powerful. They meet with people from outside the unit to represent, negotiate, and to acquire resources; they market, act as a liaison and spokesperson. The broker role is played very well by Katherine Graham, chairman and chief executive officer of the Washington Post Company. Graham is known as a patient opportunist who has been very successful in growing her already large company. Well-known people all over Washington consider Graham a most important contact. It is a recognized fact that Graham can move political deals in ways that other executives can hardly understand. With an astute understanding of the dynamics of power, Graham is careful not to abuse the influence she holds.

IDENTIFYING THE CORE COMPETENCIES

The eight roles help us to organize our thoughts about what is expected of a person holding a position of leadership. In addition, recent empirical studies have found support for the validity and the importance of the eight roles. In a study of over 700 managers, Quinn, Denison, and Hooijberg (1989) found that measures of the eight roles met standard tests of validity and that the eight roles do indeed appear in the four indicated quadrants. In a study of over 900 managers, Pauchant, Nilles, Sawy, and Mohrman (1989) not only found support for the eight roles, but also reported that of 36 possible roles, these eight were "rated by the sample as the most important ones to be performed in their organizations." Quinn, Faerman, and Dixit (Quinn 1988) found that people who do not play these roles well are considered ineffective managers, whereas people who play them all are believed to be very effective managers.

Although the eight roles are a useful organizing structure, we have not as yet specified what competencies are necessary in order to be productive. It is to that issue that we now turn.

Several years ago a group of experts, consisting of 11 nationally recognized scholars and 11 prominent administrators and union representatives, were brought together to identify key competencies associated with each role in the competing values framework (Faerman, Quinn, and Thompson 1987). Participants were chosen based on their experience and expertise as practitioners or scholars in the field of management. Over 250 competencies were identified and given to this group. Their task was to identify the most important competencies in each of the eight roles. Based on the results of this exercise, this book is organized around the most important competencies in each role. These are shown in Table 1.2.

Each of the chapters is divided into three sections, and each section is organized around one of the three competencies in the role. Thus the next eight chapters cover 24 key competencies. The competencies are highly consistent with the existing literature (Ghiselli 1963, Livingston 1971, Miner 1973, Katz 1974, Mintzberg 1975, Flanders 1981, Yukl 1981, Boyatzis 1982, Luthans and Lockwood 1984, Whetten and Cameron 1984). Completion of the next eight chapters is likely to greatly broaden your skills and increase your capacities. The balanced set of competencies that you master in this text will allow you to operate well in a world of competing values.

ORGANIZING THE LEARNING PROCESS

A competency suggests both the possession of knowledge and the behavioral capacity to act appropriately. To develop competencies you must be both introduced to knowledge and have the opportunity to practice your skills. Many textbooks and classroom lecture methods provide the knowledge but not the opportunity to develop behavioral skills.

In this book, we will provide you with both. The structure we will use is based on a five-step model developed by Whetten and Cameron (1984). We have modified the labels for one of the components in the five-step model and call it the ALAPA model. The components are as follows.

Step 1: Assessment   Helps you discover your present level of ability in and awareness of the competency. Any number of tools, such

TABLE 1.2 The Eight Managerial/Leadership Roles and Their Key Competencies

Director Role	1. Taking initiative 2. Goal setting 3. Delegating effectively
Producer Role	1. Personal productivity and motivation 2. Motivating others 3. Time and stress management
Coordinator Role	1. Planning 2. Organizing and designing 3. Controlling
Monitor Role	1. Reducing information overload 2. Analyzing information with critical thinking 3. Presenting information; writing effectively
Mentor Role	1. Understanding yourself and others 2. Interpersonal communication 3. Developing subordinates
Facilitator Role	1. Team building 2. Participative decision making 3. Conflict management
Innovator Role	1. Living with change 2. Creative thinking 3. Managing change
Broker Role	1. Building and maintaining a power base 2. Negotiating agreement and commitment 3. Presenting ideas

as questionnaires, role plays, or group discussions, might be used.

Step 2: Learning Involves reading and presenting information about the topic using traditional tools, such as lectures and printed material. You can use these to learn from each other, as well as from the professor.

Step 3: Analysis Explores appropriate and inappropriate behaviors by examining how others behave in a given situation. We will use cases, movies, role plays, or other examples of behavior.

Step 4: Practice Allows you to apply the competency to a worklike situation while in the classroom. It is an opportunity for experimentation and feedback. Again, exercises, simulations, and role plays will be used.

Step 5: Application Gives you the opportunity to transfer the process to real-life situations. Usually assignments are made to facilitate short- and long-term experimentation.

In working with the model, we discovered that the five components, and the methods normally associated with each component, need not be mutually exclusive. A lecture, for example, does not need to follow an assessment exercise and precede an analysis exercise; a lecture might be appropriately combined with a role play in some other step. The methods can be varied and even combined in the effective teaching and learning of a given competency. In the following chapters, the presentation of each of the 24 competencies will be organized according to the ALAPA model.

Using the competing values model, eight roles are presented and illustrated. In each role there are many competencies. Chapters 2 through 9 are each organized around one of the eight roles. The three sections in each chapter are organized around the three most important competencies in each role.

In turn, each competency is presented in a five-step learning model: Assessment, Learning, Analysis, Practice, and Application. The five-step ALAPA model takes learning from an instructional approach (an expert giving a lecture) to an instructional-developmental approach (an expert giving a lecture plus students experimenting with new behaviors).

CONCLUSIONS

People have models. These models sensitize us to some things and blind us to others. When acting as a leader in an organizational unit, our models greatly affect our level of effectiveness. In this chapter we have traced the evolution of four basic models in management thinking: rational goal, internal process, human relations, and open systems. Each model is based on assumptions that lead to different sensitivities, decisions, and behaviors.

In recent years, world conditions have made it increasingly obvious that there is a need for "both/and" thinking. As we increase the number of models that we can use to assess a situation, we increase our array of choices.

In this chapter we considered the competing values model. It suggests that the four basic models can be integrated into a comprehensive whole. The model is called the "competing values" model because we tend to see the oppositions as conflicts. They are not, however, mutually exclusive. In fact, they need to be complementary. We can use the model to get out of a single mind-set and to increase choice. In our most creative moments, we might even be able to use, simultaneously, two seemingly opposite approaches. Think, for example, of the leader who practices "tough love." This person is effectively integrating or making complementary domains that we normally keep separate.

The competing values model suggests three challenges: to use multiple mind-sets in viewing the organizational world; to learn to use competencies associated with all four models; and finally, to integrate the diverse competencies in confronting the world of action.

We use the ALAPA model in presenting these competencies. Although the book allows the instructor to follow traditional instruction methods, it also allows a second phenomenon to occur. It allows you to develop, grow, and internalize new competencies. The emphasis, then, is not on traditional social science theory, but on those aspects of the social science literature that facilitate acquisition of competencies.

ASSIGNMENT Course Preassessment

There is an instrument that will allow you to do a preassessment of yourself on the eight roles and the 24 skills in the competing values framework. This preassessment is available in two forms: as a software package and as a written questionnaire. Either may be used. If your instructor desires that you do this preassessment, the instructor will direct you in how to proceed.

REFERENCES

Boyatzis, R. E. *The Competent Manager.* New York: John Wiley and Sons, 1982.

Daft, R. L. *Management.* Chicago: Dryden Press, 1988.

Faerman, S. R., R. E. Quinn, and M. P. Thompson. "Bridging Management Practice and Theory." *Public Administration Review* 47(3) (1987): 311–319.

Flanders, L. R. Report 1 from the Federal Manager's Job and Role Survey: Analysis of Responses by Washington, D.C.: U.S. Office of Personnel Management, 1981.

Ghiselli, E. E. "Managerial Talent." *American Psychologist* 18 (1963): 631–642.

Katz, R. L. "Skills of an Effective Administrator." *Harvard Business Review* 51 (1974): 90–102.

Livingston, J. S. "Myth of the Well-Educated Manager." *Harvard Business Review* 49 (1971): 79–89.

Luthans, F., and D. L. Lockwood. "Toward an Observational System for Measuring Leader Behavior in Natural Settings" in H. G. Hunt, R. Stewart, C. Schriesheim, and D. Hosking (eds.) *Managers and Leaders: An International Perspective.* New York: Pergamon, 1984.

Miner, J. B. "The Real Crunch in Managerial Manpower." *Harvard Business Review* 51 (1973): 146–158.

Mintzberg, H. "The Manager's Job: Folklore and Fact." *Harvard Business Review* 53 (1975): 49–61.

Mirvis, P. H. *Work in the 20th Century: America's Trends and Tracts, Visions and Values, Economic and Human Developments.* Cambridge, Mass. Revision, Rudi Press, 1985.

Pauchant, T. C., J. Nilles, O. E. Sawy, and A. M. Mohrman. "Toward a Paradoxical Theory of Organizational Effectiveness: An Empirical Study of the Competing Values Model." Working paper. Laval University, Administrative Sciences, Quebec City, Quebec, Canada, G1K 7P4, 1989.

Quinn, R. E. "Applying the Competing Values Approach to Leadership: Toward an Integrative Framework" in J. G. Hunt, D. Hosking, C. Schriesheim, and R. Stewart (eds.), *Leaders and Managers: International Perspective on Managerial Behavior and Leadership.* Elmsford, N.Y.: Pergamon Press, 1984.

————. *Beyond Rational Management: Mastering the Paradoxes and Competing Demands of High Performance.* San Francisco: Jossey-Bass, 1988.

Quinn, R. E., and K. S. Cameron. "Organizational Life Cycles and Shifting Criteria of Effectiveness: Some Preliminary Evidence." *Management Science* 29 (1983): 33–51.

Quinn, R. E., D. Denison, and R. Hooijberg. "An Empirical Assessment of the Competing Values Leadership Instrument." Working paper. The University of Michigan, School of Business, 1989.

Quinn, R. E., and J. Rohrbaugh. "A Spatial Model of Effectiveness Criteria: Towards a Competing Values Approach to Organizational Analysis." *Management Science* 29(3) (1983): 363–377.

Robins, S. P. *Management,* 2d ed. Englewood Cliffs, N.J.: Prentice-Hall, 1987.

Whetten, D. A., and K. S. Cameron. *Developing Management Skills.* Glenview, Ill.: Scott, Foresman, 1984.

Yukl, G. A. *Leadership in Organizations.* Englewood Cliffs, N.J.: Prentice-Hall, 1981.

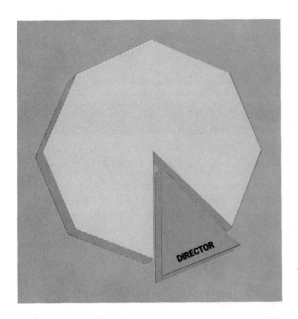

COMPETENCIES

- **Taking Initiative**
- **Goal Setting**
- **Delegating Effectively**

THE DIRECTOR ROLE

We begin our study of the eight roles a manager must play by looking first at the director role contained in the rational goal model. In the director role, the manager is expected to clarify expectations through processes, such as planning and goal setting, and to be a decisive initiator who defines problems, establishes objectives, defines roles and tasks, generates rules and policies, and gives instructions. In this chapter, we will focus on three core competencies of the director role:

> ***Competency 1***   Taking Initiative
> ***Competency 2***   Goal Setting
> ***Competency 3***   Delegating Effectively

These three competencies are all very much of the same cloth. Together, they constitute the most basic activities of managing and organizing—namely, catalyzing action; setting a clear, challenging and yet attainable direction and vision; and empowering and enabling organizational members to carry out and implement that vision.

Competency 1 Taking Initiative

ASSESSMENT Rowe Decision Style Inventory

Directions The Decision Style Inventory[1] (Rowe and Mason 1987) consists of 20 questions, each with four responses that relate to typical situations facing executives. Although each response to a question may appear equally desirable or undesirable, the instrument is intentionally designed to force individuals to "rank," or differentiate among them. There are no "correct" or "incorrect" answers; the scores reflect your individual preferences for the different responses.

Rank each set of four using the following scale. You must use all four numbers within each set of four responses.

Scale

1	Do not prefer at all
2	Would consider on occasion
4	Consider often
8	Most often prefer

	I	*II*	*III*	*IV*
1. My prime objective is to	Have a position with status __1__	Be the best in my field __8__	Achieve recognition for my work __4__	Feel secure in my job __2__
2. I enjoy jobs that	Are technical and well defined __1__	Have considerable variety __4__	Allow independent action __8__	Involve people __2__
3. I expect people working for me to be	Productive and fast __1__	Highly capable __4__	Committed and responsive __8__	Receptive to suggestions __2__
4. In my job I look for	Practical results ____	The best solutions ____	New approaches or ideas ____	Good working environment __8__
5. I communicate best with others	In a direct one-to-one basis __8__	In writing __2__	By having a group discussion __4__	In a formal meeting __1__
6. In my planning I emphasize	Current problems ____	Meeting objectives ____	Future goals ____	Developing people's careers ____
7. When faced with solving a problem, I	Rely on proven approaches ____	Apply careful analysis ____	Look for creative approaches ____	Rely on my feelings ____

[1] Reproduced by permission of Alan J. Rowe.

	I	II	III	IV
8. When using information, I prefer	Specific facts ____	Accurate and complete data ____	Broad coverage of many options ____	Limited data which is easily understood ____
9. When I am not sure about what to do, I	Rely on intuition ____	Search for facts ____	Look for a possible compromise ____	Wait before making a decision ____
10. Whenever possible, I avoid	Long debates ____	Incomplete work ____	Using numbers or formulas _1_	Conflict with others ____
11. I am especially good at	Remembering dates and facts _4_	Solving difficult problems _2_	Seeing many possibilities _1_	Interacting with others _3_
12. When time is important, I	Decide and act quickly ____	Follow plans and priorities ____	Refuse to be pressured ____	Seek guidance or support ____
13. In social settings, I generally	Speak with others ____	Think about what is being said ____	Observe what is going on ____	Listen to the conversation ____
14. I am good at remembering	People's names ____	Places we met ____	People's faces ____	People's personality ____
15. The work I do provides me with	The power to influence others ____	Challenging assignments ____	Achieving my personal goals ____	Acceptance by the group ____
16. I work well with those who are	Energetic and ambitions ____	Self-confident ____	Open minded ____	Polite and trusting ____
17. When under stress, I	Become anxious ____	Concentrate on the problem ____	Become frustrated ____	Am forgetful ____
18. Others consider me	Aggressive ____	Disciplined ____	Imaginative ____	Supportive ____
19. My decisions typically are	Realistic and direct ____	Systematic or abstract ____	Broad and flexible ____	Sensitive to the needs of others ____
20. I dislike	Losing control ____	Boring work _1_	Following rules ____	Being rejected ____
Total	____	____	____	____

Scoring   1. Add the points in each of the four columns—I, II, III, IV (numbered left to right).

2. The sum of the four columns should be 300 points. If your sum does not equal 300 points, check your addition and your answers.

3. Place your scores in the appropriate box—I, II, III, IV.

ANALYTIC **II**	**CONCEPTUAL** **III**
DIRECTIVE **I**	**BEHAVIORAL** **IV**

LEARNING Taking Initiative

Taking initiative is very much the "take charge . . . take the bull by the horns . . . I'm in control here . . ." competency that you as a manager must often use as a director. This "shooting from the hip," act first–think later competency directly competes, and sometimes conflicts, with the competency of deliberate, rational, logical problem solving that you must also possess as a director. This overlapping, competing, and conflicting of competencies and roles is not a function of poorly or loosely defined terms. Rather, it is the reality of the leadership world that you as a manager, particularly as you enact the director role, must face.

READY, FIRE, AIM!

No, this is not a misstatement of the command typically given to a firing squad when it's time for the execution. It's part of the new conventional wisdom for supervisors, managers, and leaders of all kinds that is found in books like Peters and Waterman's *In Search of Excellence* (1982). These authors, like many others, are telling us that we spend too much time planning, analyzing, gathering information, and number crunching and not enough time *doing* and *acting*. They advise us that "management is not a passive art." Rather, being a manager means being an activist, focusing on results, and making things happen—not being a passive keeper of administrative rules and procedures.

The activist manager must be able to maintain optimism in the face of the inertia of bureaucratic rules and procedures, possess a good knowledge of his or her people in order to motivate them to maximum productivity, and maintain a hardened stance in demanding high standards of performance from others (Odiorne 1982, 32–33).

One of the classic examples of the activist, results-oriented leaders of our times is General George Patton. In 1942, after assuming command of the First Armored Corps, amid a setting that included blasting sirens, gleaming helmets, shining rifles, and dozens of flags—along with tanks and troop carriers—Patton stated:

> *We are in for a long war against a tough enemy. We must train millions of men to be soldiers. We must make them tough in mind and body, and they must be trained to kill. As officers we must give leadership in becoming tough physically and mentally. Every man in this command must be able to run a mile in fifteen minutes with full military pack! ... Damn it! I mean every man! Every officer and enlisted man, staff and command, every man will run a mile! We will start running from this point in exactly thirty minutes! I will lead!* [2]

Patton was clearly an activist, results-oriented leader. He was directive (clearly, a *very dominant* directive in Rowe's language of style!) and took the initiative.

One of the outstanding activist leaders of recent times is John F. Welch, Jr., chairman and chief executive officer of General Electric Company. In a recent *Fortune* article entitled "The Mind of Jack Welch," the CEO articulated his six rules for effective management:

1. Face reality as it is, not as it was or as you wish it were.
2. Be candid with everyone.
3. Don't manage, lead.
4. Change before you have to.
5. If you don't have a competitive advantage, don't compete.
6. Control your own destiny, or someone else will. [3]

TAKING INITIATIVE AND BEING DECISIVE

From our discussion of the results and interpretation of Rowe's Decision Style Inventory, you have some sense of the extent to which you can take initiative and be decisive. Your score on the "directive" style gives you this sense. If you are a very dominant or dominant directive, then you probably have little trouble with these competencies. If your "directive" score falls in the backup range, it suggests that you are capable of taking initiative and being decisive in certain situations. If you have a least preferred "directive" score and a very strong "behavioral" score, then you most likely find taking initiative and being decisive difficult and very uncomfortable.

Whatever your scores, we believe the following suggestions will help you become better at taking initiative and being decisive (Rowe and Mason, 1987).

---

[2] Cited in Rowe and Mason, 1987; original source, Williamson, 1979.
[3] S. P. Sherman, "The Mind of Jack Welch," *Fortune* (March 27, 1989), p. 50.

TAKING INITIATIVE: AN EXAMPLE

One of the most famous examples of a leader taking initiative and being decisive can be found in Johnson & Johnson's CEO James Burke. Burke has always supported the contention that the best leaders hire energetic individuals who can take initiative and are rarely satisfied with the status quo. Burke states: "My style is to encourage controversy and encourage people to say what they think." Burke saw this style pay off during the long crisis over Tylenol poisoning. Relying on the sometimes boisterous counsel of his staff, Burke took the initiative in 1982 after seven people died from cyanide-laced Tylenol capsules. He recalled approximately 30 million Tylenol packages and replaced them with new ones packaged with elaborate safety seals. When poisoning occurred again in 1986, Burke removed *all* capsules off the market and sold the product only in tamper-resistant tablet and caplet forms. Both these initiatives were taken in the midst of extreme contention and with significant financial consequences.[4]

Five Steps for Taking Initiative[5]

1. *Draw on your inner drive.*   Keeping a positive mental attitude is the beginning. Make a habit of taking energetic and positive approaches to tasks. Never be satisfied with "good enough."

2. *Focus on the most important tasks.*   We will talk more about this later when we discuss time management in the producer role, but suffice it to say, learn to separate the trivia, distortion, and opportunities to slack off from the really important tasks that must be done first.

3. *Be tough-minded.*   Persistence and patience in the face of inertia are crucial. This patience is not passivity, however. The extreme of being tough-minded might be seen as ruthlessness.

4. *Be a positive Pygmalion—instill a desire for excellence.*   Again, we will discuss this in much greater depth in Chapter 3, Competency 2: Motivating Others, but the bottom line here is to use the initiative that *others* possess.

5. *Catalyze "smart" action.*   Activating and doing must be centered around clearly specified and attainable goals and objectives. See Competency 2: Goal Setting below for more details.

Keys to Decisiveness[6]

1. *Know that you might fail.*   Every decision contains some element of risk, and that implies the potential for failure. If we spend all our time worrying about not failing, we're going to have a difficult time making decisions. In their study of 90 leaders, Bennis and Nanus (1985) found a striking consistency in individual attitudes toward mistakes, errors, and failure. Almost without

---

[4] K. Labich, "The Seven Keys to Business Leadership," *Fortune* (October 24, 1988), p. 62.

[5] *Adapted from How Managers Make Things Happen* by George S. Odiorne, Copyright © 1982. Reprinted by permission of the publisher, Prentice Hall, Inc., Englewood Cliffs, New Jersey.

[6] *Adapted from Careertracking.* Copyright © 1987 by Jim Calano and Jeff Salzman. CAREERTRACK is a registered trademark of Career Track Seminars, Inc. Reprinted by permission of Simon & Schuster, Inc.

exception, the leaders believed that mistakes and failures were a natural part of the process of leading.

2. *Know that you can change your decision.*   This realization alone can remove much of the tension around decision making. Many decisions are not only changeable, but revocable. When confronting a decision, realize that you can't always have certainty.

3. *Don't overemphasize facts and data.*   Don't make analysis the end instead of the means! This problem stems from formal education, where facts were what we memorized and upon which we were tested. In the real world, we almost never have *enough* information to make a decision.

4. *Trust your gut feel, intuition, and sense of what's right.*   Intuition is often given a bad rap. In fact, managers should take intuition quite seriously. Hunches are not random; they're based on our experiences and our decision-making styles. Ask yourself if this feels like the "right thing to do."

5. *Get input from colleagues and others whose input you respect.*   Ask others (e.g., associates, co-workers, bosses, and friends) what they think of your decision. As long as you make the decision and accept responsibility for it, knowing the opinions of others can be helpful.

6. *Use outside experts when required.*   In serious matters, when there's a great deal at stake, don't shoot from the hip with a quick decision. A quick call to the right professional (e.g., a mentor, accountant, or other advisor) could give you information that will help make the right decision more obvious.

7. *Generate as many solutions as possible.*   Pull out a pad, get into a brainstorming mode, and list every possible solution, no matter how unlikely, that you can think of.

8. *Play devil's advocate.*   Eliminate all the middle-ground outcomes, and focus on extremes. Think of the worst and the best possible outcome of your decision. What is the most you are willing to risk?

9. *Postpone the decision.* If the situation calls for it, don't be afraid to delay making the decision. This is not a sign of weakness. It is very decisive to respond, "I'm not going to decide right now." What's important here, though, is to be aware of the costs of delaying the decision.

ANALYSIS   The Case of The Eccentric Programmer[7]

Directions   Read the case of The Eccentric Programmer. In small groups assigned by your instructor, consider the questions that follow the case, and be prepared to discuss your answers with the class.

[7]*From* Francis J. Bridges, Kenneth W. Olm, and J. Allison Barnhill, *Management Decisions and Organizational Policy*, 2nd edition. Needham Heights, MA: Allyn & Bacon Publishers, 1977, p. 618. Used with permission.

Wilfred Nortz, computer programmer with the Electronics Testing Corporation, walked into Project Manager Fred Wilson's office and announced that he was "through," "finished," and "absolutely compelled to resign from the company." With the conclusion of that statement, he headed out the door with the announcement that he would be back in an hour to pick up his final paycheck.

Wilson reflected on his problem. Nortz had been sent to this project facility some 200 miles from the home office to run tests on a new computer that had been installed recently. The outcome of the tests was most significant because the future work of this project group could not proceed much more until Nortz completed his tests. However, Nortz was accountable to Sid Young, who had been sent to Wilson's facility along with Nortz. Sid Young's job was to supervise Nortz and coordinate his work with that of Wilson's project group. On several occasions in the past two weeks, Nortz had told Wilson that Sid Young was demanding too much of him, motivating him through undue pressure, and having him work overtime and on weekends. Nortz said that Young hardly knew a computer when he saw one and had little appreciation of the stress and strain he (Nortz) was under. Wilson also reflected that he had talked with Sid Young about this matter just two days before and had been told that Nortz was one of those eccentric, specialized staff people who had been "babied" in his jobs all his working life. Young had stated that with the deadline to complete the tests less than a week away, Nortz was going to finish these tests on schedule if he had to sleep beside the computer and be spoon-fed.

Discussion Questions   1. Which of the five steps for taking initiative are illustrated in this case?
2. Which are used effectively/successfully? Why?
3. Which could have been used more effectively? How?

PRACTICE   Role Play

Directions   In groups formed by your instructor, *role play* the characters and situation described in the case of the eccentric programmer. After the roles for Nortz and Young have been assigned, the remaining group members should form a subgroup and collectively brainstorm how to play out the role of Fred Wilson. One actual player should then be selected. (Special instructions to the Fred Wilson character: Consider how the 11 keys to decisiveness can help.)

APPLICATION   Interviewing a Decision Maker

Select the most decisive person you know and conduct an hour-long interview with that individual. Include in your interview protocol questions around the keys to decisiveness discussed in this competency.

Competency 2 Goal Setting

ASSESSMENT Personal and Organizational Goal Setting

Directions   The following questions are designed to help you assess how well goal-setting processes are working in your personal and work lives. Indicate how much you agree or disagree with each statement. When you finish, review the items that received the lowest scores.

Scale

Strongly disagree 1	Disagree 2	Neutral 3	Agree 4	Strongly agree 5

At School and in My Personal Life

__4__ 1. I am proactive rather than reactive.
__2-3__ 2. I set aside enough time and resources to study and complete projects.
__5__ 3. I am able to budget money to buy the things I really want without going broke.
__4__ 4. I have thought through what I want to do in school.
__5__ 5. I have a plan for completing my major.
__5__ 6. My goals for the future are realistic.

At Work (complete only if you have work experience)

_____ 1. We are proactive rather than reactive.
_____ 2. Policies, programs, and procedures are developed in an integrated fashion.
_____ 3. Time and resources are committed to set goals and objectives.
_____ 4. We work on forecasting future opportunities and threats.
__3__ 5. The overall mission is clear to all.
_____ 6. Goal-setting processes take place at the organizational, unit, and individual level.
__3__ 7. There are written goals and objectives.
__2__ 8. There are long-range goals and objectives.
__4__ 9. There is short-range objective setting.
__3__ 10. Goals and objectives are realistic.
__2__ 11. Goals and objectives are challenging.
__3__ 12. Goals and objectives are reviewed and modified on a regular cycle.
__2__ 13. Accomplishment of goals and objectives is tied to a reward system.
_____ 14. Pursuing goals and objectives is a productive activity.

Interpretation   The goal setting assessment helps you focus on basic aspects of goal setting processes in your personal and professional or school life. There are several keys to making *any* goal setting process effective and we discuss those throughout the Learning section below. Our intent with this brief assessment is to get you thinking about goal setting as it relates to your school, personal, and work settings.

In the first part of the assessment, we focus on whether your personal goal setting is *passive* or *active*. Question 1 queries your general tendency around "action" and questions 4 and 5 select a specific example of proaction vs. reaction (i.e., having a plan for completing your major). *Allocating "resources"* for the completion of goals is queried in questions 2 and 3. Question 6 focuses on a cornerstone of effective goal setting: creating goals that are *attainable,* yet *challenging.* If your score on any of these questions is "3" or less, you should pay particular attention to the corresponding material in the Learning section below.

In the second part of the assessment we ask you to focus on the goal setting processes of an organizational unit that you may work in or have knowledge about. Questions 1, 6, and 12 focus on the extent to which goal setting is an *integral part* of a work unit's operation (i.e., proactive, at all organizational levels, predictable, periodic intervals). The extent to which goal setting processes are *supported by other organizational* factors is queried in questions 2, 3 and 13 (i.e., consistent policies, procedures; appropriate allocations of time and resources, goal setting linked to reward systems). The *comprehensiveness* of organizational goal setting is the focus of questions 4, 5, and 7–9 (i.e., goal setting proceeds from a clear mission, includes short- and long-range considerations, formalized or written). Questions 10, 11 and 14 address the *appropriateness* of goals (i.e., attainable, challenging, worthwhile).

If the organizational unit you assessed scored low in any of these areas, you may want to pay special attention to the corresponding discussions in the Learning section below for potential improvement suggestions.

LEARNING Goal Setting

What is goal setting, and why should the manager be concerned about it? The classic response to these questions can be found in Lewis Carroll's classic tale *Alice's Adventure in Wonderland:*

Alice:	Would you tell me, please, which way I ought to walk from here?
Cheshire Cat:	That depends a good deal on where you want to go.
Alice:	I don't care where.
Cheshire Cat:	Then it doesn't matter which way you walk.

Without knowing where it is you want to go, you won't know how to get there and may wind up somewhere else! Likewise, if you don't articulate what it is you want and need to accomplish, you won't be able to determine how best to get it done.

Definition: Tactical Goal Setting

1. Formulation of objectives.
2. Definition of action plans (i.e., strategies, policies, and detailed plans to accomplish objectives).
3. Establishment of an organization to implement decisions.
4. Review of performance and feedback initiating a new cycle of the process.

Experts in the planning and goal-setting field tell us that formalized planning and goal-setting processes have been used by managers and supervisors since the turn of the century. Hundreds of research studies on goal setting have been conducted with 90% of them reporting positive results. These results suggest that a median improvement of 16% in performance (with minimum and maximum ranging from 2% to 58%, respectively) can be attained through the use of goal-setting techniques. (Locke and Latham 1985, 6).

GOAL SETTING AT DIFFERENT ORGANIZATIONAL LEVELS

Goal setting takes place at all levels in an organization. The focus, purpose, and kinds of activities that take place as part of the process, however, vary with the level of the organization within which they take place. At the CEO or vice president/general manager level, for example, goal setting tends to be more *"strategic"* or *directional*. That is, it involves an organization's most basic and fundamental decisions: the choice of missions, strategies, objectives, policies, programs, goals, and major allocations of resources. Statements of these are found in most corporate annual reports, as the following example from 3M Corporation. These strategic choices, taken together, will generally shape the organization's overall future. Individual managerial decisions, especially if made within the context of the broader strategy that is set, often affect only a particular or specific aspect of that future.

3M
CORPORATE GOALS AND OBJECTIVES

3M is an organization of employees and stockholders who have combined their resources to pursue common goals in providing useful products and services, creating rewarding employment, assuring an adequate return to investors and contributing toward a better social and economic environment for the public generally.

In pursuing these goals, certain fundamental principles of management characterize 3M.

The first principle is the promotion of entrepreneurship and insistence upon freedom in the work place to pursue innovative ideas. Policies, practices and organizational structure have been flexible and characterized by mutual trust and cooperation.

Second is the adherence to uncompromising honesty and integrity. This is manifested in the commitment to the highest standards of ethics throughout the organization and in all aspects of 3M's operations.

Third is the preservation of individual identity in an organizational structure which embraces widely diverse businesses and operates in different political and economic systems throughout the world. From this endeavor, there have developed an identifiable 3M spirit and a sense of belonging to the 3M family.

It is upon these principles that the following objectives are based:

Profits/Growth: 3M Management will endeavor to maintain optimum profit margins in all product lines in order to finance 3M's future growth and to provide an adequate return to stockholders. Expansion will not be an end in itself, but dictated by needs and requirements of the marketplace for new and useful products and services. In meeting this objective, 3M management will work for the preservation and improvement of the profit system. It advocates free market principles.

Human Resources: 3M Management believes that it is essential to provide an organizational structure and work climate which respect the dignity and worth of individuals, encourage initiative, challenge individual capacities, provide equal opportunity for development, and equitably reward effort and contribution. It will endeavor to provide a stable work environment which promotes career employment. It believes 3M employees are the corporation's most valuable resource.

Products/Customers: It is 3M Management's objective to develop and sell unique products and services of high quality and reliability that are genuinely useful to customers and consumers. In this mission, 3M contributes to a better quality of life and a higher standard of living for its employees and the public generally.

Citizenship: 3M Management recognizes that 3M's business operations have broad societal impact. It will endeavor to be sensitive to public attitudes and social concerns in the work place, the community, the environment and within the different political and economic systems where 3M conducts business. It will strive to keep the public, employees, and investors well informed about 3M business operations.[8]

At middle management and supervisory levels, goal setting tends to be more *tactical,* with a primary emphasis on *implementing* and carrying out decisions made as a part of strategic or directional planning. Here, the process involves:

1. Formulating specific objectives, targets, or quotas that need to be achieved by a certain time.
2. Developing an action plan to be followed and identifying specific steps to be taken in order to meet or exceed those objectives.
3. Creating a schedule showing when specific activities will be started and/or completed.
4. Developing a "budget" (including any type of necessary resources).
5. Estimating or projecting what will have happened at certain points during the life span of the plan.
6. Establishing an organization to implement decisions.
7. Setting standards against which performance will be evaluated.

[8] *From 3M Annual Report,* 1981.

LESSONS LEARNED FROM GOAL-SETTING RESEARCH AND PRACTICE[9]

Our focus in this section on goal setting will be on that process as it most affects the manager. We will begin by reviewing the lessons learned about that process from research and practice. We will then move to an examination of a set of techniques that have been developed to increase the effectiveness of tactical goal setting—management by objectives (MBO).

1. *Specific, challenging goals tend to result in better performance than vaguely specified, easily attained goals.* Goal setting is more effective when goals are clearly defined in terms of what needs to happen, how often, in what quantity and by when. Clear, specific goals reduce the probability of miscommunication or misunderstanding and provides a clearer "target" to work toward. Generally, more challenging goals result in higher levels of performance—within certain constraints. Goals should be perceived as attainable given a reasonable "stretch" of effort.

2. *Feedback on goal attainment progress enhances the process.* Feedback on progress toward the desired objective is essential. When individuals are told how well they are performing against some expected standard, they can make changes in their efforts, if necessary, or continue unchanged if their actions have proven to be effective. The source of feedback and its timing are also important variables.

3. *Goals should be prioritized if there are more than one.* Using the relative importance of a goal or objective to rank it enables individuals to direct their actions and efforts in proportion to the importance of each goal. This ranking also serves to verify both the manager's and the subordinates' expectations.

4. *Informal competition among employees produced by goal setting and feedback can enhance the benefits of the process.* Informal competition often arises spontaneously when performance is evaluated and fed back to individuals in quantitative terms. Excitement, challenge, and pride in accomplishment can result from constructive peer pressure. However, too much "formal" competition can lead to unproductive rivalry.

5. *Goal accomplishment and performance should be rewarded.* Later in this chapter, we will discuss a variety of incentives available for use by the manager to reward goal accomplishment. These incentives cover the gamut from monetary incentives to various forms of nonmonetary reward.

---

[9] *Adapted from* E. A. Locke and G. P. Latham, *Goal Setting: A Motivational Technique That Works.* Englewood Cliffs, NJ: Prentice-Hall, Inc. 1984. Used with permission.

6. *Goal setting can be an important part of performance management.* Performance appraisal processes serve several intended and sometimes unintended functions in organizations. Ideally, appraisals lead to the identification of strengths and weaknesses in individual performance and, consequently, improved individual and hence organizational performance. Some performance appraisal processes, however, lead to a decline in performance when individuals are criticized and respond defensively. One key way to avoid this unintended outcome is to evaluate a person's performance against preset goals.

7. *Individuals need to develop action plans to carry out their goals.* Action plans detail the specific tasks and schedules required to accomplish goals. The development of an effective plan presupposes that the goal or objective has been clearly defined.

8. *Organizational policies need to be reviewed for consistency and complementarity with goal accomplishment.* Organizational policies exert a tremendous influence over the effectiveness of goal accomplishment. Typically, policies related to decision-making processes and speed, communication, and productivity have the greatest impact.

9. *The climate within which goal setting occurs should be a supportive one in which managers help and encourage their employees to succeed.* Results suggest that individuals whose managers behave supportively during the goal-setting processes accept or set much higher goals than those whose managers are nonsupportive. Managerial support gives people confidence and trust, which leads to higher levels of performance.

10. *Depending on how they are used, goals can decrease or increase the amount of stress perceived by subordinates.* The goal-setting process generates negative stress when goals are too difficult (have a high risk of failure) or when there is goal overload, goal conflict, or goal ambiguity. The process can reduce or prevent negative stress by making certain expectations are clear.

These 10 lessons on planning and goal setting suggest that the processes involved, although only a part of the manager's function, are tied to and intimately relate to almost *all* aspects of management and organization. They have an *impact on* subordinate understanding and communication, motivation, performance appraisal processes, and reward systems. The 10 lessons cited also suggest that planning and goal-setting processes are *affected by* broader organizational policies and processes, and the specific "climate" within which those processes take place.

Instead of looking at all of these, let's focus on one key management tool: the use of objectives. We'll emphasize developing and articulating clear goals and objectives, and tracking performance against them as a key stone in a management system.

USING OBJECTIVES AS A MANAGEMENT TOOL: MBO-TYPE APPROACHES

Management by objectives (MBO) is a term used to describe a broad array of systems, procedures, and programs. What may be called MBO in one organization may not exactly match what you find in another organization. But, generally speaking, all MBO programs share the following characteristics:

Characteristics of MBO-Type Processes[10]

1. Joint goal setting between members of two consecutive levels of supervision.
   - Managers provide subordinates with a framework reflecting their own purposes and objectives.
   - Subordinates propose objectives for themselves.
   - Managers and subordinates discuss, sometimes modify, and eventually agree upon a set of objectives for the subordinates.

2. Periodic measurement and comparison of actual performance against agreed-upon goals and objectives.
   - Subordinates review their own progress and describe it periodically (as agreed) to their managers.
   - (This sequence is repeated as necessary.)

3. Objectives, whenever and wherever possible, are stated in quantifiable terms like units, dollars, percentages, and so on.

WHAT MAKES A GOOD MBO

Well-written and formulated goals and objectives can serve as the cornerstone of an MBO system. There is, however, an art and science to the process. Take New Year's resolutions as an example. Two out of three people you query on January 1 about resolutions or objectives for the coming year will identify the following as one of their top two or three: "I want to lose weight this year." Consider this personal example of an objective for its utility in an MBO-type system. In and of itself, the objective of "losing" weight is not very informative. It gives no indication of *how much weight* (quantity), no sense of how fast the weight is to be lost (time), or any indication of the "processes" to be used in losing the weight (quality). It also gives no indication of attainability (hence, not allowing for any health challenge), or any sense of flexibility to allow for changes or midcourse corrections.

Consider some examples that are work related:

- To work on my interpersonal skills.
- To purchase a computer-based system.

[10] Filley, House, and Kerr, 1976.

■ To improve the file system so that it's easier to find things.

■ To reduce the daily entry error rate.

■ To make better decisions.

How can we improve these goals and objectives to make them more useful in an MBO-type system? Doran[11] has suggested that meaningful objectives are "smart"—that is:

Specific	A specific area of improvement is targeted.
Measurable	Some indicator of progress is established.
Assignable	Ability to specify an individual or group who will be responsible to accomplish the goal.
Realistic	Given available resources, state what can realistically be achieved.
Time Related	Specification of when the result(s) can be achieved.

WRITING AN MBO

Let's revisit the weight loss example already cited and apply what we have just presented.

Old Objective	Lose weight this year.
New Objective	Lose 30 pounds by June 15 so that I can wear a size 39 suit to my twentieth high school reunion.
Action steps	To accomplish this, I must

1. Cut my calories to 1500 per day.
2. Eliminate beer from my diet beginning immediately.
3. Eat fruit or nothing between meals beginning next week.
4. Reduce consumption of sweets to one serving per week beginning in two weeks.
5. Begin a regular exercise program (alternating jogging and aerobics).

ANALYSIS   MBO Is Not for Me[12]

Directions   Read this case of Don Smith's objection to objectives, and then answer the questions that follow the case.

You are Nancy Stuart, plant personnel manager for Countrywide Manufacturing Company's local plant in Jamestown, Ohio, a city of about 17,000 people. The plant is the principal employer in the area.

---

[11] "There's a S.M.A.R.T. Way to Write Management's Goals and Objectives" by George T. Doran, Nov. 1981, from *Management Review*. Reprinted, by permission of publisher, from *Management Review*, November/1981 © 1981. American Management Association, New York, All rights reserved.

[12] "Don Smith's Objection to Objectives" from *Behavior in Organizations: An Experiential Approach*, 4th edition, by J. B. Lau and A. B. Shani, 1988, pp. 364–366. Reprinted by permission of Richard D. Irwin, Inc. and the authors.

During the past two years, the personnel division (see Figure 2.1 for the organization chart) in the central headquarters of Countrywide has been quite successful in helping line managers learn and implement a new management by objectives (MBO) program throughout the company. The vice president for personnel of Countrywide was recently embarrassed when the company president asked him, "If MBO is improving effectiveness in the line divisions through-

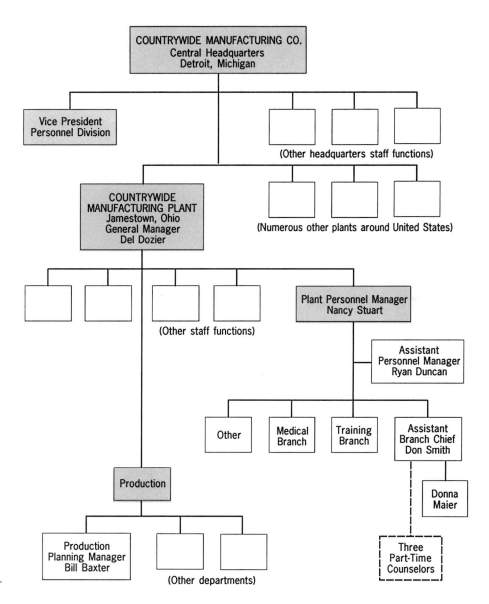

FIGURE 2.1
Organization chart for the Countrywide Manufacturing Company.

out all the plants, why haven't you used it more in your own personnel area?" This resulted in a directive to you and all plant personnel officers to come up immediately with a five-year plan applying the MBO approach. You wrote a memorandum to your branch chiefs asking them to submit a first draft of a plan to include objectives and how they are to be implemented and evaluated. This would provide data for a planning conference of your branch chiefs.

Don Smith is the chief of your counseling branch. He was hired two years ago to replace an employee who was retiring. Don was right out of college, having completed a masters in counseling. He has proved himself to be highly successful in getting the line managers in the plant to use counseling services. The quality of his branch's service is recognized throughout the plant. Last year, Don recruited Donna Maier, who had just completed her graduate work. Don has trained her well, and the two of them are a great team.

In addition, Don employs on a part-time basis three counselors (they work full-time for the public health office, but are allowed to work for Countrywide in their free time). Don and Donna are the only regular employees in the branch.

The following is an informal memorandum you received from Don in answer to yours:

MEMORANDUM
To: Nancy Stuart
From: Don Smith
Re: MBOs

I am scheduled to leave on my two-week vacation tonight, so I am writing you about my views on MBO. I am sure you will understand when I say MBO seems to apply to production areas very well and to areas of personnel such as wage and salary administration, but it really does not apply to counseling services. Last week, Donna and I saw a total of 25 employees for counseling and had 8 interviews with managers about problem people. The three part-time counselors each worked two hours last week, and their caseload was 4 each, for a total of 12. Compare this with the situation two years ago when I came aboard and the one-person counseling service was handling only 4 to 5 cases a week.

Our business is so pressing that the obvious objective is to get another full-time counselor. We find that more and more we have to book appointments for a week or two ahead. The people who need several sessions with a counselor because of the seriousness of their cases are being assigned whenever possible to the part-timers from Public Health. We are getting more and more calls from managers asking for help in handling nonproductive employees. One has asked us to work with him on a motivation program for his section that would help raise the production of all eight of his people. We have been able to do nothing so far on the program to help alcoholics and problem drinkers, which central headquarters thinks we should be doing. I am really not sure this is a problem here; we have had no referrals. Managers seem more interested in problems of pregnant women than social drinkers. We ought to also get started on a policy guidance statement for work-related stress illness.

Do you agree with me when I say that in a service area like counseling the main objective is to get enough qualified counselors to handle the employee problems that already exist? So the objectives of my branch are (1) more personnel and (2) a bigger budget. If you need anything else on MBO for our branch, ask Donna. She knows our work as well as I do.

See you in two weeks,

Don Smith

Don's answer is the first you receive from your branch chiefs. You are a little taken aback and wonder if the rest of your team is going to be as flippant, and apparently perplexed, in trying to formulate their objectives. The chiefs of your medical and training branches were making snide remarks about MBO at lunch yesterday. This could prove embarrassing because the vice president of Personnel is the executive who brought MBO programs into the organization. You become vaguely aware that you are not sure how Don should go about defining his objectives. You decide, in view of Don's vacation, to write his objectives yourself.

Discussion Questions

1. Based on the limited evidence presented, what are the factors you, as Nancy Stuart, will have to consider before working out the objectives for Don Smith's branch? (Use Figure 2.1 to generate ideas.)
2. Prior to sitting down to write, is there any action you could take that would help you get started?

PRACTICE   Write Your Own MBO

Directions

Restate each of the following in a manner that will allow them to be pursued using an MBO progress.

1. Be a better manager.
2. Be a more supportive friend.
3. Be a more successful student.
4. Increase my attractiveness in the job market.
5. Get more organized.

APPLICATION   Setting Your Goals[13]

1. Choose a goal for your schoolwork, job, or personal life, and develop an implementation plan. Include:
   - *Smart* objectives.
   - Outside factors that might affect the objective.
   - Steps necessary to achieve the goal. By when?

[13] *Adapted from* an exercise used in *Getting Work Done Through Others: The Supervisor's Main Job,* Advanced Human Resources Development Program, New York State Governor's Office of Employee Relations and CSEA, Inc., 1987.

2. Evaluate the possible results:
   - What would be a *good* result?
   - What would be a *satisfactory* result?
   - What would be a *poor* (unacceptable) result?

3. Include any other comments or explanations about your plan.

COMPETENCY 3 Delegating Effectively

ASSESSMENT To Delegate or Not To Delegate[14]

Directions   Record how you feel about the following statements by using the scale shown.

Scale

Strongly disagree 1	Disagree 2	Neutral 3	Agree 4	Strongly agree 5

__2__ 1. Most of the time subordinates are too inexperienced to do a job, so I prefer to do it myself.

__4__ 2. It takes more time to explain the job than to do the job myself.

__3__ 3. Mistakes by subordinates are too costly, so I don't assign work to them.

__4__ 4. In my position, I get quicker action by doing a job myself rather than having a subordinate do it.

__4__ 5. Some things simply should not be delegated.

__2__ 6. Many subordinates are detail specialists and lack the overall knowledge required for a job out of their specialty; thus, they cannot be assigned additional job responsibilities.

__2__ 7. Subordinates are usually too busy to take on any more work.

__2__ 8. Most subordinates just aren't ready to handle additional responsibilities.

_____ 9. As a manager, I should be entitled to make my own decisions about my doing detail work rather than administrative work.

_____ TOTAL

Scoring and Interpretation   Your responses to the nine items above, when totalled, will result in a score that ranges between 9 and 45. Each of the questions represents one of the commonly used reasons or "excuses" for not delegating. Those reasons include lack of subordinate experience, amount of time delegation takes, costliness of errors, and the appropriateness of dele-

[14] From *First Line Management,* 4th edition, by L. Steinmetz and R. Todd, Homewood, IL: Business Publications, 1986, pp. 64–67. Reprinted by permission of Richard D. Irwin, Inc.

gating in general. The more strongly *you personally* agree with each of these, the less likely you are to delegate (i.e., the larger your score, the less likely you are to delegate).

In the Learning section below, we suggest some ways that these arguments against delegation can be turned into reasons for delegating.

LEARNING   Delegating Effectively

Managers who are most strongly opposed to delegation often use variations of arguments included in the assessment above. Frequent responses by these managers to the topic of delegation include: "Delegation, I tried that once and the employee fouled things up royally," or "Delegate my authority? Why? I'm the manager, that's my job." A striking contrast to this viewpoint can be found in Beth Pritchard, head of S. C. Johnson Wax's insect control division, a unit that markets such products as "Off" mosquito repellent and "Raid" insect spray. Pritchard became head of the division in 1986 when it was the leader in its field. Since then, she has contributed to increased success by altering key product formulas, redesigning packages, and refocusing top staffers so as to make them more customer-focused. Pritchard attributes *all* these accomplishments to her recognition of the potential of the individuals working for her and delegating as much authority as possible. She states her beliefs thusly: "My philosophy is that you can't do anything youself. Your people have to do it."[15]

The ability *and* willingness to delegate effectively are essential to successfully carrying out the director role. In the previous section, we focused on the importance of generating clear and attainable goals and objectives. Now we will focus on the importance of knowing when, how, and how much to delegate to others.

Delegation is typically defined as a rather simple process of giving assignments to subordinates. It is touted for its significant payoffs of providing the manager with more time and allowing him or her to focus attention on more rather than less significant issues. It is also viewed as a key to the training and development of subordinates as well as the wise allocation of organizational resources. Why, then, are managers so reluctant to delegate? Why does delegation tend to be a misunderstood, inappropriately used, or under-utilized tool? As you review your score on the self-assessment, how do you explain *your* attitude toward delegation?

Consider the most commonly offered reasons for *not* delegating more listed on the left side of Table 2.1. Which of these are your "top 3"? To the right of each reason for not delegating more in Table 2.1 is a corresponding counterargument. How persuaded are you by each of the counterarguments?

Now that we have addressed some of the psychological barriers to delegating, let's talk about *how* delegation ought to take place.

[15] Labich, p. 59.

TABLE 2.1 Delegation: Point—Counterpoint

Reasons for Not Delegating	*Counterarguments*
1. I feel uncomfortable asking subordinates to do my tasks.	1. Effective managers tend to delegate everything they do not absolutely have to do themselves. If subordinates understand this principle, they will not be offended by your requests.
2. My subordinates lack the appropriate knowledge.	2. If subordinates lack the appropriate knowledge, you are failing in at least one important responsibility you have to them.
3. I can do some tasks quicker than it would take to explain them.	3. This may be true and even a wise strategy, but how many tasks fall in this category?
4. My subordinates lack the appropriate skills and experience, I can do it better than they can.	4. If they lack the knowledge and skills, are they getting appropriate training and development?
5. My subordinates are too busy already.	5. Delegating to busy subordinates will force them to learn to delegate or better manage time.
6. If someone else does it, it may weaken my control.	6. Your control may weaken, but you are free to do more strategic and more influential things in the organization, which is what you should be doing.
7. If someone makes a mistake, I am responsible.	7. Learning to live with risk and to allow failure and learning in others is an ability you need in order to move to higher levels where the ability is even more needed.
8. I feel better if people see me as an extraordinarily hard worker.	8. You are working hard but ineffectively. People will eventually see your overcommitment as a weakness.
9. I am uneasy relying on the judgment of subordinates around delegated tasks. I no longer know what is going on.	9. Trusting subordinates is a skill that is increasingly necessary as you move up. In the meantime, you are undermining their development.
10. I do not understand some tasks well enough to delegate them.	10. This may be a legitimate argument. How many of your tasks does it really apply to?
11. It is not appropriate for subordinates to do some of my tasks.	11. This is sometimes true, but usually it is greatly exaggerated. Why is it inappropriate?

Keys to Effective Delegation

1. In your own mind, clarify what it is that you want done. Writing it down can be helpful.

2. Match the desired task with the most appropriate employee.

3. In assigning the task, be sure you communicate clearly. Ask questions to see if the task is fully understood. Be sure that deadlines and time horizons are clear.

4. Keep the communication channels open. Make it clear you are available for consultation and discussion.

5. Allow employees to do the task the way they feel comfortable doing it. Show some trust in their abilities. Do not hold such high expectations that they can only fail.

6. Check on the progress of the assignment, but do not rush to the rescue at the first sign of failure.

7. Hold the person responsible for the work and any difficulties that may emerge, but do this as a teacher, not a police officer. Explore what is going wrong, and help them to develop their own solutions.

8. Ignoring an employee's efforts can be devastating to motivation. Recognize what has been done, and show appropriate appreciation.

POTENTIAL "PITFALLS" OF DELEGATION

The eight keys to effective delegation will not always result in a successful outcome, even if followed to the letter. Occasionally, a subordinate will receive an assignment and then fail to perform it properly. This can be frustrating to both a manager and the subordinate. Before taking action, it might be useful to try to discover *why* the subordinate has failed to perform the delegated task.

One of the most common explanations for failed delegation is misunderstanding the assignment and the manager's expectations. Both the manager and the subordinate must examine their roles in the communication "breakdown." The manager can reduce the frequency of miscommunication by asking the subordinate to repeat or feedback his or her understanding of the delegated assignment.

A related course of delegation failure is also based in the communications process. Subordinates may feel that the assignment surpasses their ability, and they fear being embarrassed by failure. This, however, is not communicated to the manager at the time of the initial delegation. The manager may be able to avoid this problem by asking subordinates about how confident they are in their ability to complete the assigned task.

A classic reason for failed delegation is being given the responsibility for an assignment without being given the authority to complete the assignment or the appropriate discretion in choosing the manner of completion. Another simple, but often overlooked, course of delegation failures is the lack of time for subordinates to complete the task. Some subordinates just can't say "no," even when they should (i.e., when they just don't have enough time). Still another reason might be the subordinate's giving the assignment a lower priority than the one assigned to it by the manager. Again, these can be avoided by proactive communication by the manager from the start.

The causes for failure of delegation cited above by and large are a function of the subordinate's *ability* to complete an assigned task or the manner in which the task was communicated. There is a second type of reasons that generally are a function of the subordinate's *motivation* to complete the assigned task. Failure to complete the task may reflect rebelliousness, seeing the delegated task as inappropriate to their "status," or no perceived "pay off" in completing the task. These and countless other motivational causes for failed delegation should be treated as motivational problems. (Please see the Producer chapter for a discussion of motivation.)

ANALYSIS   The Storm Window Assignment[16]

Directions   Read the instructions for George Brown. Assume that you are George Brown and that you have the conversation with Jack that appears in script II. Script I is a conversation among the work crew that is going on when you arrive.

Instructions for George Brown   You are a manager in the plant department in the telephone company and have your headquarters in a small town. The department is located in a two-story frame building that contains the operation equipment. Your crew is required to maintain the central office equipment, repair lines, install phones, and so on. A total of four people report to you, and this number is entirely adequate. There is no maintenance worker or janitor in the group because there are practically no upkeep problems. When a door lock needs repairing, someone fixes it when he or she has a spare moment. Often you fix little things if everyone is busy. However, now and then certain jobs have to be assigned. The accepted practice you have followed is to give these assignments to the person with least seniority. This procedure is followed quite generally in the company, and no one has even questioned it as far as you know. You put in your share of dirty work when you were new. One of the special jobs that comes up periodically is the washing and putting up of storm windows in the fall and taking them down in the spring. There are 12 windows on the first floor and 12 windows on the second. The windows are stored in the

[16] *From N. R. F. Maier, A. R. Solem, and A. A. Maier, Supervisory and Executive Development: A Manual for Role Playing.* New York: John Wiley & Sons, 1957, pp. 167–170. Used with permission.

basement. There is a new aluminum ladder that you just got. That ought to make the job easier.

The time is late October. It's getting chilly, but today is a nice day. It is a good day to put up the storm windows. Jack, Steve, Dave, and Bill are in the other room having lunch. They bring their lunches and have coffee in thermos bottles. You got them this table, and they seem to like eating together. It's time for everybody to get back to work, so it's a good time to assign the job. Steve, Dave, and Bill have just left for work, so Jack is now available.

Jack has the least seniority, so you are going to ask him to do the job. Since you have had no replacements for some time, Jack has done this job for several years and knows the ropes. He is a good fellow and cooperates nicely.

Scene   Telephone crew work out of a small building which contains central office equipment serving the community.

Although Jack has been on his job five years, he has the least seniority of anyone in his group. Many of the unpleasant jobs around the place fall to him because he is the newest man. One of these is washing and putting up the storm windows each year. There are 12 windows on the first floor and 12 on the second. Jack has never complained about this assignment.

However, after lunch one day when he is sitting around with other members of the group, the conversation takes an interesting turn. Let's listen in.

Script: Part I

Jack: Boy, that hot coffee really tastes good.

Steve: Yeah, it's getting chilly outside. Almost had a frost last night.

Dave: Yeah! Time to finish my fall plowing in the south forty.

Bill: (*reading from the paper*) Here's a special on storm windows that looks good. It's time to start thinking of them. By the way, Jack, it seems to me that we ought to be getting them put up here, too, shouldn't we?

Steve: Sure, Jack, get out the Glasswax and shine 'em up.

Jack: Aw, quiet—you guys are always riding somebody.

Dave: What's the matter, don't you like the job?

Bill: Takes all your brains to do it, doesn't it, Jack?

Steve: That's a real stiff job! You have to figure which one to wash first and which end is up.

Jack: Why don't you dry up?

Dave: What's the matter, Jack? Don't you like the job?

Bill: Aw, it can't be that! He's been doing it for years. He must like it.

Jack: You know well enough I don't like it.

Steve: Well, you keep doing it, don't you?

Jack: I'm going to get out of it, though.

Dave: This I must see!

Bill: What are you gonna do—jump the seniority list?

Jack: I don't know, but I think it's time somebody else did it.

Steve: Not me!

Dave: You don't hook me on it either. I had my turn.

Jack: For how long? One time, that's all you ever did it.

Bill: And that was enough, too, wasn't it, Dave?

Steve: What's the matter, Jack, can't you take it?

Jack: Sure I can take it. I have for five years.

Dave: Looks like you're gonna make it six years now.

Jack: Not me—I'm through doing all the dirty work around here.

Bill: What do you mean dirty? You get your hands clean, don't you?

Steve: Who do you think's gonna put 'em up—Brownie himself?

Jack: I don't care who does it, but it's not me any more.

Dave: Aw, you talk big but you can't make it stick.

Bill: Yeah, Jackie, you're just asking for trouble.

Script: Part II

Mr. Brown, the manager, enters.

Brown: Hello, fellows. (*Greetings from the group.*) Say, Jack, could I see you a minute? I don't want to break up the lunch session. (*Looks at some papers in his hand.*)

Dave: Oh no—it's time we were getting back on the job, anyway.

Jack: Yes, sure, Mr. Brown. (*Picks up the paper bag and waxed paper and throws them in the basket.*) Anything wrong?

Brown: No, Jack, not at all. I just wanted to remind you about the storm windows. (*Laugh from group at the table.*)

Jack: What about 'em?

Brown: It's starting to turn cold, Jack. I think we ought to get 'em up. Don't you think so?

Dave: This is where we came in, fellows, let's go. (*All but Jack leave.*)

Jack: Yeah, I guess *somebody* ought to put 'em up.

Brown: Will you take care of that, Jack—anytime this week you can manage it.

Jack: I wanted to talk to you about that, Mr. Brown. I'd rather not do it this year.

Brown: Do what—put up the storm windows?

Jack: Yes, Mr. Brown, I'd rather not do it.

Brown: Well, Jack, it won't take you any time at all. I'll get you some help to get 'em out when you're ready.

Jack: It isn't that—I just don't want to do it again. I've had it for five years. It's not fair!

Brown: Well, now—I know how you feel, Jack. I know it's a chore, but somebody has to do it.

Jack: If you don't mind—count me out this time.

Brown: But I do mind, Jack. We've got to do what's part of our job. And you're the newest one here. Be a good fellow.

Jack: I've been the goat around here for five years. Let somebody else do it for a change.

Brown: Now, Jack, the others had their turn.

Jack: For how long? Dave did it once and so did Bill. I don't think Steve ever had to put 'em up. Why pick on me?

Brown: Nobody's picking on you. We just have to do our jobs, that's all.

Jack: Well, it's not part of my job—it's not in my job description.

Brown: It *is* part of your job, and I think we have a right to expect you to do it.

Jack: Count me out.

Brown: Now, be yourself, Jack. I don't want to be unreasonable about this thing, but after all . . .

Jack: Well, I think I've done my share.

Brown: We can try to work something out on this next year, but suppose you take care of it this time.

Jack: No, Mr. Brown. I just don't feel I ought to do it.

Brown: Jack, I think I'll have to say you've got to do it.

Jack: I'm sorry, but I'm not going to do it this time.

Brown: It's an order.

Jack: Not to me it's not.

Brown: You'll take an order, Jack, or get out.

Jack: You're not firing me. I quit, and you can give your dirty job to some of those other guys. I'm through.

Discussion Questions   1. How did George Brown use the eight keys to effective delegation discussed previously?
2. Which keys did he use effectively?
3. Did he neglect any of the keys?
4. How do you account for Jack's reactions and behavior? Can any of the pitfalls of delegation be used to explain the situation?

PRACTICE   Improvising a Delegation Problem

Directions   In groups formed by your instructor, select half the members to enact the role of George and half to enact the role of Jack.

Each subset of role players should brainstorm how they would carry out their respective role. George Brown role players: Use the keys to effective delegation and your knowledge of the potential pitfalls to change the outcome of the preceding conversation.

APPLICATION   Interviewing a Delegator

1. Conduct a 45-minute interview with a parent, a manager, and a friend who is not taking this course. Pose the storm windows situation (in brief form) to the inverviewees and ask for *their* explanation and solution.

2. Ask the inverviewees to identify three tasks that they do not currently, but could, delegate to someone else. Each task should be defined in terms of:

    ■ Nature of the task.
    ■ Qualities the task requires.
    ■ Individual selected.
    ■ Influence strategy to be used.

REFERENCES

Albrecht, K. *Successful Management by Objectives: An Action Manual.* Englewood Cliffs, N.J.: Prentice-Hall, 1978.

Allison, G. T. *Essence of Decision: Explaining the Cuban Missile Crisis.* Boston: Little, Brown, 1971.

Behn, R. D., and J. W. Vaupel. *Quick Analysis for Busy Decision Makers.* New York: Basic Books, 1982.

Below, P. J., G. L. Morrisey, and B. L. Acomb. *The Executive Guide to Strategic Planning.* San Francisco: Jossey-Bass, 1987.

Benson, H., and M. Z. Kipper. *The Relaxation Response.* New York: Avon Books, 1975.

Calano, J., and J. Salzman. "The Power of Decisiveness." *Careertracking,* New York: Simon & Schuster, 1988.

Doran, George. "There's a S.M.A.R.T. Way to Write Management's Goals and Objectives," *Management Review* (November 1981).

Drucker, P. F. *Managing for Results: Economic Tasks and Risk-Taking Decisions.* New York: Harper & Row, 1964.

Engel, H. M., *How to Delegate: A Guide to Getting Things Done.* Houston, Tex.: Gulf, 1983.

Filley, A. C., R. J. House, and S. Kerr. *Managerial Process and Organizational Behavior* (2d ed.). Glenview, Ill.: Scott, Foresman, 1976.

Huber, G. P. *Managerial Decision Making.* Glenview, Ill.: Scott, Foresman, 1986.

Jenks, J. M., and J. M. Kelly. *Don't Do. Delegate!* New York: Ballantine, 1985.

Keppner, C. H., and B. B. Tregoe. *The Rational Manager: A Systematic Approach to Problem Solving and Decision Making.* New York: McGraw-Hill, 1965.

Labich, K. "The Seven Keys to Business Leadership." *Fortune,* October 24, 1988, pp. 58–66.

Lau, J. B. and A. B. Shani. *Behavior in Organizations: An Experiential Approach,* 4e. Homewood, Ill.: Irwin, 1988.

Locke, E. A., and G. P. Latham. *Goal Setting: A Motivational Technique That Works.* Englewood Cliffs, N. J.: Prentice-Hall, 1984.

———. "Organizational Goal Setting Questionnaire Interpretive Guide." Organization Design and Development, Inc. Copyright © 1985.

Maier, N. R. F., A. R. Solem, and A. A. Maier. *Supervisory and Executive Development.* New York: John Wiley and Sons, 1957.

Mali, P. *MBO Updated: A Handbook of Practices and Techniques for Managing Objectives.* New York: John Wiley and Sons, 1986.

Odiorne, G. S. *How Managers Make Things Happen.* Englewood Cliffs, N. J.: Prentice-Hall, 1982.

Peters, T. J., and R. H. Waterman, Jr. *In Search of Excellence.* New York: Harper & Row, 1982.

Rowe, A. J., and R. O. Mason. *Managing with Style.* San Francisco: Jossey-Bass, 1987.

Selye, H. *The Stress of Life* (2d ed.). New York: McGraw-Hill, 1978.

Sherman, S. P. "The Mind of Jack Welch." *Fortune,* March 27, 1989, pp. 39–50.

Steinmetz, L. and R. Todd, Jr. *First Line Management* (rev. ed.). Dallas, Tex.: Business Publications, 1979.

Williamson, P. B. *Patton's Principles: A Handbook for Managers Who Mean It!* New York: Simon & Schuster, 1979.

Woolfolk, R. L., and F. C. Richardson. *Stress, Sanity, and Survival.* New York: New American Library, 1979.

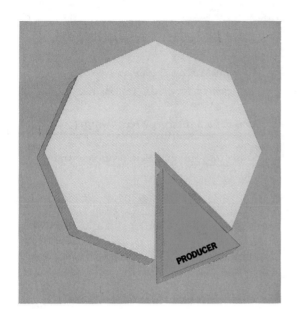

THE PRODUCER ROLE

*T*he second role in the rational goal model is the producer. In this role, managers are expected to be task oriented, work focused, and highly interested in the task at hand. The producer is also expected to exhibit high degrees of motivation, energy, and personal drive. In this chapter, we will examine your role as producer as reflected in three core competencies:

Competency 1 Personal Productivity and Motivation
Competency 2 Motivating Others
Competency 3 Time and Stress Management

Competency 1 Personal Productivity and Motivation

ASSESSMENT Do You Produce?

Directions   Take five minutes to think about a situation during the last month when you were extremely motivated and productive. Write a short, one-paragraph description of that

54

situation. Explain why you were so motivated and productive. Which of these "reasons" were under *your personal, direct* control? Is the situation you described an exceptional one or the norm?

Interpretation In the situation you described, your high level of motivation and productivity was most likely a consequence of a large number of factors. Those which were under your direct and personal control reflect your underlying sources of personal motivation and productivity. Although these factors vary from individual to individual, some factors consistently arise in explanations of very high motivation and productivity. We address these below in our discussion of "personal peak performance." As you read through the Learning section below, compare your contributing factors with those of the peak performers. Are there similarities? Differences? Might your motivation and productivity have been even higher if some of the missing peak performance factors were present?

LEARNING   Personal Productivity and Motivation

The first two competencies in this chapter have a great deal in common. The first competency focuses on how *you,* as a manager, discover the "what, where, why, and how" of motivating yourself to high levels of productivity; and the second competency focuses on how *you* motivate others (i.e., your subordinates) to high levels of productivity and performance. The core competencies of *personal* productivity and motivating *others* in the producer role require you to strive for what has come to be known as "personal peak performance" (Garfield 1986).

The common ground in these two sections is the "theoretical" foundations of motivation. We treat the more esoteric part of that theoretical foundation as historical backdrops and frames of reference and confine them to boxes and charts. Theory is only useful to you, the manager, if it can be readily applied. For that reason, we will elaborately treat expectancy theory in this chapter's second competency because it is the most comprehensive, practical and easily applied framework for understanding and *using* motivation theory. Remember, though, that expectancy theory applies to both competencies.

We began with an assessment that we hope got you started thinking about what really motivates *you* and makes *you* productive. The key question is that assessment was: "Over which of these (i.e., factors, items, etc.) do *you* have direct and personal control?" This question should help you sort out those factors which are a function of *your* own personal motivational needs and work/study habits, and those which are a consequence of external factors (e.g., organizational or school rules and policies, your manager's or teacher's style, resource constraints, work unit climate, etc.). The ability to sort these two out will help managers to maximize both their *own* motivation and productivity and those of their subordinates.

PERSONAL PEAK PERFORMANCE

Earlier we referred to personal peak performance (PPP). Garfield's (1986) research on PPP studied individual high achievement in a wide array of endeavors. The results are truly encouraging for all of us, because the conclusions reached thus far suggest that PPP does not result from a specific innate talent or trait. Nor does it result from a particular set of behaviors. Rather, PPP seems to result from an overall pattern of traits or attributes. A peak performer possessing this pattern of attributes will most likely be

1. *Results-oriented* because of a sense of personal mission.
2. Able to display the dual capacities of *self-management* and *team mastery.*
3. Capable of making course corrections and managing change. (Garfield, pp. 16–17)

We believe the knowledge and experience gained from the study of PPP will be helpful to you in understanding your own motivation/productivity profile.

Six conditions that stimulate PPP appear in Table 3.1 (Adams 1984). Let's take a closer look at each.

COMMITMENT

Several researchers on PPP found a strong sense of commitment to be evident. Among their conclusions and findings on "commitment" were

1. A high level of commitment shields people from the adverse effects of stress load and work loads (Pines, 1980).
2. Significant investments of time and feeling are required if you want to generate high levels of performance in a work group (Vaill, 1982).
3. Peak performers value internal goals and intrinsic rewards most, and care a great deal about the tasks they perform (Garfield 1986).

Commitment can be an outcome of many factors, but one of the most tried and true is the involvement of employees in making decisions that affect them.

TABLE 3.1 Conditions That Stimulate Personal Peak Performance[1]

1. Commitment	4. Control
2. Challenge	5. Transcendence
3. Purpose	6. Balance

[1] *From* J. D. Adams, "Achieving and Maintaining Personal Peak Performance," *Transforming Work,* J. D. Adams (general ed.), (Alexandria, Va.: Miles River Press, 1984), p. 198.

One of the Fortune 500's most ardent supporters of employee involvement is Ford Motor Company CEO Donald E. Petersen.

> *Employee involvement requires participative management.... Anyone who has a legitimate reason, who will be affected by a decision, ought to have the feeling that people want to know how he or she feels.*[2]

Ford's worker involvement program is widely credited as a keystone to Ford's vastly improved product quality in the 1980s and its outstanding financial turn-around.

CHALLENGE

A second characteristic identified in peak performers was a need or desire for an appropriate level of challenge—a consistent search for reasonable risks and opportunities to pursue "stretch" goals. Peak performers respond to challenge by emphasizing outcomes, results, and solutions, rather than ruminating about perfection (Garfield 1986).

Margaret Loesch, CEO of Marvel Productions Ltd., is also known as the "queen of cartoons." Loesch's animation studio is home to such well-known characters as Spiderman, G. I. Joe, Kermit the Frog, and Miss Piggy. She is also the only woman in Hollywood who holds the titles of both president and CEO of a major studio.

When presented with the choice for the helm at Marvel Productions in April 1984, Loesch was in a comfortable position at wealthy, well-established Hanna-Barbera Productions. She describes her decision this way:

> *I did not have a burning desire to become the head of the company. I wasn't that farsighted.... Yet, when the opportunity to run Marvel Productions presented itself, I thought, "This is what I need to do to stretch myself. But it was still a struggle making the decision, because I had a very fulfilling career and a future with Hanna-Barbera. One evening, my secretary walked into my office and said, "I have one thing to say to you: Comfort doesn't mean growth." I made my decision that night.*[3]

PURPOSE

A third condition associated with peak performance is a clear vision or purpose (Vaill 1982). Managers need to know not only the answers to the what and why questions, but also to *agree* with the answers.

Ray Kroc, founder of McDonald's, envisioned his empire long before it was realized, and he knew how to get there—with a clear, compelling, realizable vision. The Kroc vision was reflected in the company's motto, which he invented himself: "Quality, service, cleanliness, and value." Kroc constantly repeated it for the rest of his life (Labich 1988: p. 60).

[2] *From* Kenneth Labich, "The Seven Keys to Business Leadership," *Fortune* (October 24, 1988), p. 59.
[3] Mary Wheeler, "Marvel Woman," *Executive Female* (May/June 1988), p. 64.

CONTROL

Peak performers require a <u>delicate balance between acting autonomously and responding to clear and specific goals.</u> They need to have enough discretion to exercise their judgment while not being left without guidance or standards.

Jan Carlzon, CEO of Scandinavian Airlines Systems Group (SAS), provides an excellent example of control-balancing autonomy and direction. Just after he took the CEO position at SAS, Carlzon attempted a two-week vacation before beginning work, but after three days of constant phone calls about what he considered routine and mundane problems and decisions, he returned to SAS offices to begin his new job. Carlzon's success is now almost legendary. He took over SAS, and within two years (1981–1983) he turned it into a financial and customer-service success. One key to that success, argues Carlzon, was turning SAS's organization chart upside down—empowering frontline workers and middle managers to make decisions on the spot—at the point of customer contact. When Carlzon took his next vacation at SAS, the telephone did not ring *once* (Carlzon 1987).

TRANSCENDENCE

A fifth condition found to be common among peak performers is a drive to <u>transcend previous performance levels</u>. The Japanese call this *Kaizen* (Imai 1986). We, here in the United States, commonly refer to it as "<u>continuous improvement</u>."

Ray Meyer, perhaps the most successful coach in college basketball, led De Paul University to 42 consecutive years of winning seasons. At one point, however, his team lost its first game after 29 consecutive home-court victories. When questioned about his feelings around the loss, he responded, "Great, now we can start concentrating on winning, not on not losing" (Bennis and Nanus 1985).

BALANCE

The sixth condition refers to a sense of perception about the "<u>health</u>" of the total being. Peak performers were able to enjoy and manage work, home, family, friends, and play.

Many large corporations are now taking proactive stances to ensure that their employees do not "burn themselves out." Time Inc. (publisher of *Fortune*), Intel, Apple Computer, and IBM advocate employee sabbaticals as a burnout preventative. Intel suggests a new but job-related course of study; IBM gives workers one year off with pay to teach in an inner-city school, work for a nonprofit organization, and so on.[4]

---

[4] Brian Dumaine, "Cool Cures for Burnout," *Fortune* (June 20, 1988), p. 84.

ANALYSIS   What Motivates You?

Directions   Refer back to your description of the situation(s) when you were most motivated and productive. In groups formed by your instructor, consider and respond to the questions that follow. Appoint a spokesperson in your group to present a five-minute summary of your work.

1. What common factors exist across your group members' descriptions of personal productivity and motivation?
2. What factors seem most unique to individual members? Are these under the direct control of individual members?
3. What key lessons can you generate from the experiences of the group?

PRACTICE   "Feeling Dead-ended"[5]

Directions   Read the following case study and individually answer the questions that follow. Discuss your responses with the other members of your small group. Choose a group spokesperson to present responses to Questions 2, 4, and 6 to the larger group.

Margaret Jardine was sure when she completed her associate's degree in business at Wagner Community College more than eight years ago, that she would go places in her career in the public sector. She had graduated with honors from WCC with an emphasis in Finance and Accounting. She passed the Audit Clerk exam the first time with a grade of 92; she was second on the list, and hired within six months. Within the next 14 months she had taken and passed the Senior Audit Clerk exam. It took two years to be selected from the list.

She felt she had truly made the right decision because she moved so quickly within the first four years. She felt that the Civil Service system was large enough to allow for movement into a variety of areas considering her two year degree, her good work performance and her ability to do well, it seemed, on exams.

She felt that she had been successful in her first four years because she had been able to work closely with good people. She was a hard worker and a fast learner.

Margaret waited almost two years to take the Principal Audit Clerk (grade 11) exam and failed it with a grade of 68. She couldn't believe it. She went to the review to determine what she had done wrong. The answers, though tricky, seemed so clear when the monitor explained them. Now she had to wait between two and three years for the next exam, depending on the need to fill positions. She felt thoroughly discouraged.

[5] *Adapted from* an exercise used in *Getting Work Done Through Others: The Supervisor's Main Job,* Advanced Human Resources Development Program, New York State Governor's Office of Employee Relations and CSEA, Inc., 1987.

What distressed her even more was that she worked with a grade 11 Principal Clerk who "didn't know beans about the work." Margaret was the one who got all the difficult assignments because her accuracy rate was so high and she always met her deadlines.

Margaret felt that given her ability and recent responsibility she should really be in charge of the unit, regardless of her grade on the test.

Recently, she began to wonder about her future in the Tax and Finance Department. She even wondered about staying with government service. She was feeling almost dead-ended and didn't know how or where to move. It seemed, suddenly almost, that there was little or no movement within her area of expertise.

In her years with state government, she felt that she had done well with fairly regular pay increases, promotions, the degree of responsibility held and the expertise gained. Now, however, she felt that she had lost some of her motivation. Now if she put in extra time, it was only out of necessity of getting something done that *had* to be done. It certainly was not voluntary.

Margaret felt trapped, pigeon-holed in some way. She felt like she had no idea where she was going in the state. Others who had come when she did all seemed to be on their way to their goal, so to speak. She thought that perhaps they had chosen a broader, more diversified career path, situations that were easier to promote from. She felt that her work was very good and highly valued, but her salary increases were getting smaller and her options were becoming more limited. Recently, Margaret had turned down a very attractive offer from Northwestern Security and Exchange, a small finance company in Salem, near Albany, New York because she thought there would be too little opportunity for advancement. Now she wondered if it would have been better to take the opportunity.

Still, Margaret was confused about her feelings about the State. She felt that a move elsewhere might not be wise because she'd lose what seniority she had, her retirement benefits, and so on.

After dialing Northwestern's number, only to hang up before it rang, Margaret decided that she would put off any decision for at least a month so she could have plenty of time to think over her situation.

Discussion Questions

1. How would you describe Margaret's motivation level at the present time?
2. What factors contributed to this present situation?
3. What can Margaret do to clarify her options and choices?
4. What specific steps would you suggest to her?
5. Do you see any similarities between Margaret Jardine's situation and situations you have gone through? Explain.
6. With your answers to question 5 in mind, what actions can you identify that help renew enthusiasm and boost motivation?
7. In a structured system, like many state governments, how can you fit in while retaining your enthusiasm to fulfill projected goals?

APPLICATION   Creating Your Own Strategy for Increasing Personal Motivation and Productivity

Throughout this section you have had the opportunity to assess and explore your motivation level and the factors that influence and affect your personal motivation. In this application activity, you will have a chance to plan ways to maintain or increase motivation using those ideas and skills discussed throughout this chapter. Answer the following questions as specifically as possible. Although some responses (for questions 1, 4, and 5) will be voluntarily shared, this information will be seen only by you.

1. What are the major motivating forces in your life? (Consider your work at school, at a job, or at any extracurricular activity in which you're involved.)
2. What are the major blocks or forces that oppose these motivators?
3. How do both positive and negative forces affect your work and the motivational climate in a study group?
4. What resources or ideas could reduce the blocks you have identified?
5. What steps can you take to better use these resources?
6. What resources or ideas will help you maintain or increase your positive energy forces? What motivators could be added?
7. What steps can you take to maintain or increase the motivational factors?
8. How will you know you are successful?
9. How will you feel when you attain success?

Competency 2   Motivating Others

ASSESSMENT   Your Motivating Potential[6]

Directions   Motivation often wanes when people cannot satisfy the needs they have. Here are eight sets of needs that might be considered. Indicate, in the first column, how important you think each need is to employees and in the second column, how much opportunity employees have to satisfy that need.

Scale

Very low		1	2	3	4	5		Very high

Importance   *Opportunity*

$\frac{5}{4}$ _____   1. Direction, purpose, role clarity.

_____   2. Belonging, teamwork, affiliation.

[6] *From* R. E. Quinn. *Beyond Rational Management: Mastering the Paradoxes and Competing Demands of High Performance.* San Francisco: Jossey-Bass Inc., 1988, p. 31. Used with permission.

Importance *Opportunity*

5	____	3. Compensation, recognition, rewards.
4-5	____	4. Productivity, impact, achievement.
3	____	5. Standardization, measurement, objectivity.
4	____	6. Sensitivity, consideration, support.
5	____	7. Challenge, variety, stimulation.
2-3	____	8. Coordination, predictability, control.

Interpretation   Now consider the following in small groups formed by your instructor. Prepare a five-minute summary presentation for the larger group.

1. How do you account for the magnitude of the *difference* between importance and opportunity in each of the eight?

2. Who has more control over (i.e., responsibility for) each, you or your subordinates?

3. What could you, as a manager, do to address these *differences?*

LEARNING   Motivating Others

The director of management information systems for a Fortune 500 company was talking with one of the new programmer-supervisors about his experiences in this company and others like it: "The toughest thing about doing our kind of work for a big company like this is keeping people motivated," observed the director. "If we worked in a smaller company, we could pay our people much more than we do now. We could also promote and move people around more. Between the human resources department's regulations and other controls and constraints on us, it's darned near impossible to keep people excited about their jobs."

Trying to keep employees motivated over time is one of the universal frustrations of all managers. One of the greatest sources of this frustration is the common misconception that people join organizations to pursue the organization's goals. In fact, most people join organizations to pursue their *own* goals.

There are three potential solutions to this dilemma:

1. Select (employ) only those individuals whose goals and motives are wholly consistent and consonant with those of management.

2. Select those whose goals and motives are not immediately *consistent* but which will lend themselves to shaping via training, socialization, or other means.

3. *Motivate* employees to work toward your goals and those of the organization.

The first solution is nearly impossible, given the current state of modern selection techniques, and probably undesirable even if it were possible, given its potential negative impact on creativity and innovation within the organization. The current effectiveness of even the most sophisticated training programs now available makes the efficacy of the second solution doubtful as well. Not surprisingly, we are left with the third solution—motivation: Design and use a reward system that pays off for the behaviors you are seeking. Consider this story often told by Steve Kerr, a professor at the University of Southern California Business School. It concerns an entrepreneurial high school student who was out selling magazine subscriptions on a frigid Minnesota winter's day:[7]

> *This kid rings your door bell and says, "I'm selling magazine subscriptions so that I can win a trip to Florida next month. Would you like to buy some?" Kerr chides, "Why would anyone want to buy magazines so that some kid could enjoy the warmth of Florida while the purchaser continues to get frostbite in Minnesota? This is a simple example of a fundamental principle of motivation, one which the young magazine salesman neglected: Tell them 'what's in it for them!'"*

APPLYING MOTIVATION THEORY

The extent and depth of motivation theory fills literally thousands of books and journal articles. Again, it is our concern to only discuss theory as it informs practice. One of the most comprehensive theories of motivation in use today is **expectancy theory,** which is a motivational theory based on the relationships among job effort, performance, and outcomes of performance. The expectancy framework incorporates the central elements of need and process approaches. Victor Vroom (1964) was the first to conceptualize expectancy theory with the following "equation":

$$\text{Motivation} = \text{Expectancy} \times \text{Valence} \times \text{Instrumentality}$$

or

$$M = E \times V \times I$$

Figure 3.1 graphically depicts expectancy theory.

Vroom's formulation of the theory has been expanded to take into account multiple outcomes.[8] The expanded equation becomes:

$$\text{Motivation} = E \longrightarrow P \times \Sigma\,[(P \longrightarrow O) \times (V)]$$

or

$$\text{Motivation} = \text{Effort to Performance} \times \text{the sum of}$$
$$[(\text{Performance to Outcomes}) \times (\text{Valence})]$$

[7] Kerr, 1975.
[8] Nadler and Lawler, 1977.

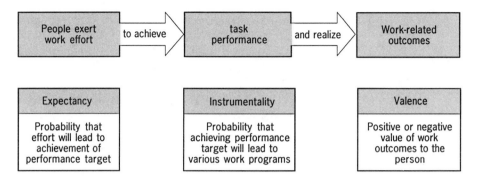

FIGURE 3.1 *Elements in the expectancy theory of motivation. Source: John R. Schermerhorn, Jr.,* Management for Productivity, *3rd ed., New York: John Wiley & Sons, 1989, p. 365. Used with permission*

Note that the fundamental linkages are the same, but the expanded equation allows the consideration of multiple outcomes. Consider the following example: Anne Johnson is the project leader of a group of computer programmers and systems analysts who have been charged with the task of creating a new MIS for one of her company's largest divisions. Johnson is a little disappointed at the rate at which progress has been made. She is considering working on the project during the entire holiday weekend that is coming up.

Applying the multiple outcomes version of the expectancy theory, we can analyze Anne's level of motivation regarding working the holiday weekend. Let's begin with the effort to performance linkage (i.e., expectancy). Here, the consideration is whether or not working the holiday weekend (the "effort" to be expended) will result in her completing the new MIS more quickly. Anne can estimate the probability of this using a number between 0 and 1. If she believes that she personally can be productive and move the project along over the holiday weekend, then she will likely estimate this probability as being relatively high—say 0.9.

Let us now turn to the instrumentality or performance to outcome linkage. Here, the concern is what the probability is that if she does indeed complete the project more quickly, it will lead to certain outcomes. Those outcomes could include a promotion, increased responsibility, a special recognition award, a spat with her husband and family about not being at home over the holiday, exhaustion, fatigue, and so on. Johnson could estimate a probability for *each* of these (e.g., what is the probability that if I complete this project quickly, I will get a promotion?). Johnson must then determine the valence (attractiveness, value) each of these has to her and then include those valences into the equation (using a −1 … 0 … +1 scale for each outcome, with −1 being extremely undesirable and +1 being extremely desirable).

With the multiple outcomes version of the expectancy formulation, Johnson can weigh, balance, and make trade-offs among the various outcomes and their valences.

SUMMARY GUIDE FOR APPLYING THE EXPECTANCY THEORY

How can you, as a manager, apply the expectancy theory? There are three ways for you to tie directly to the three components of the expectancy theory:

1. Tie effort to performance.
2. Link performance to outcomes.
3. Understand valences for desired employee outcomes.

TIE EFFORT TO PERFORMANCE

An employee will ask himself or herself: "If I work hard (exert a certain level of effort), can I attain the level of performance expected by my manager?

Managers can respond in two ways to tie an employee's effort to performance:

1. They can increase the employee's estimate of the effort to performance probability by involving the subordinate in defining what "performance" is. This implies the existence and use of MBO-type processes and performance evaluation systems (see Chapter 2's discussion of goal setting).
2. They can utilize the power of positive expectations with subordinates (see "Be a Positive Pygmalion").

BE A *POSITIVE* PYGMALION

Pygmalion was a sculptor in Greek mythology who created a gorgeous woman who was subsequently brought to life. George Bernard Shaw's play of the same name and the musical "My Fair Lady" are built on the same theme—that through the power of sheer self-effort and will, an individual can transform another person. J. Sterling Livingston, a professor at the Harvard School of Business, believes that supervisors, managers, and executives at all levels in organizations can also play Pygmalion-type roles. He bases this belief on research of his own that suggests:

1. What managers expect of their subordinates and the way they treat them largely determine subordinates' performance and career progress.

2. A unique characteristic of superior managers is their ability to create high performance expectations that their subordinates fill.

3. Less effective managers fail to develop similar expectations, so, as a consequence, the productivity of their subordinates suffers.

4. Subordinates, more often than not, appear to do what they believe they are expected to do.

Source: Reprinted by permission of *Harvard Business Review.* An excerpt from "Pygmalion in Management" by J. S. Livingston, 47:4 (July/August 1969). Copyright © 1969 by the President and Fellows of Harvard College; all rights reserved.

Being a positive Pygmalion is probably the single most important way a manager can motivate his or her subordinates. It does not require large amounts of money or other types of rewards. It does not require dealing with the complexities and contingencies of job design. It is under the complete control of the manager. But it is not easy. Being a positive Pygmalion for your subordinates goes to the very heart of your assumption about people and your own managerial style. It also requires that you be a positive Pygmalion for yourself—that is, believing that you are capable of being a peak performer as we discussed in Competency 1.

LINK PERFORMANCE TO OUTCOME(S)

Employees will ask themselves: "If I, in fact, perform at the level expected by my manager, what is the likelihood that certain outcomes will result?"

The manager can address this concern by making certain that employees are aware of all the possible outcomes that will result from performance. Regular and consistent use of performance appraisals and MBO-type discussions like those discussed earlier are again the most effective means of accomplishing this.

UNDERSTAND VALENCE FOR DESIRED EMPLOYEE OUTCOMES

Employees can evaluate all possible outcomes and the attractiveness or value (i.e., positive or negative) each has to them.

Managers can address this component by making certain that they know what "outcomes" are important to their employees. There's no substitute for knowing your employees. Depending on the size of your group, you can obtain this information either through one-on-one conversations or, if the group is too large, through employee attitude survey processes.

ANALYSIS   The Case of Michael Simpson[9]

Directions   Read the case of Michael Simpson, and answer the questions that follow.

Michael Simpson is one of the most outstanding managers in the management consulting division of Avery McNeil and Co. He is a highly qualified individual with a deep sense of responsibility.

Simpson obtained his MBA two years ago from one of the leading northeastern schools. Before being graduated from business school, Simpson had interviewed

[9] *From* David Nadler, M. Tushman, and N. Hatvany (eds.), *Managing Organizations* (Boston: Little, Brown 1982). Used with permission from the authors.

with a number of consulting firms and decided that the consulting division of Avery McNeil offered the greatest potential for rapid advancement.

Simpson was recently promoted to manager, making him the youngest manager at the consulting group. Two years with the firm was an exceptionally short period of time in which to achieve this promotion. Although the promotion was announced, Simpson had not yet been informed of his new salary. Despite the fact that his career had progressed well, he was concerned that his salary would be somewhat lower than the current market value that a headhunter had recently quoted him.

Simpson's wife, Diane, soon would be receiving her MBA. One night over dinner Simpson was amazed to hear the salaries being offered to new MBA's. Simpson commented to Diane, "I certainly hope I get a substantial raise this time. I mean, it just wouldn't be fair to be making the same amount as recent graduates when I've been at the company now for over two years! I'd like to buy a house soon, but with housing costs rising and inflation following, that will depend on my pay raise."

Several days later, Simpson was working at his desk when Dave Barton, a friend and a colleague, came across to Simpson's office. Barton was hired at the same time as Simpson, and had also been promoted recently. Barton told Simpson, "Hey, Mike, look at this! I was walking past Jane's desk and saw this memo from the personnel manager lying there. She obviously forgot to put it away. Her boss would kill her if he found out!"

The memo showed the proposed salaries for all the individuals in the consulting group that year. Simpson looked at the list and was amazed by what he saw. He said, "I can't believe this, Dave! Walt and Rich are getting $2000 more than I am."

Walt Gresham and Rich Watson had been hired within the past year. Before coming to Avery McNeil, they had both worked one year at another consulting firm.

Barton spoke angrily, "Mike, I knew the firm had to pay them an awful lot to attract them, but to pay them more than people above them is ridiculous!"

"You know," replied Simpson, "if I hadn't seen Walt and Rich's salaries, I would think I was getting a reasonable raise. Hey listen, Dave, let's get out of here. I've had enough of this place for one day."

"Okay, Mike, just let me return this memo. Look, it's not that bad; after all, you are getting the largest raise."

On his way home, Simpson tried to think about the situation more objectively. He knew that there were a number of pressures on the compensation structure in the consulting division. If the division wished to continue attracting MBAs from top schools, it would have to offer competitive salaries. Starting salaries had increased about $3500 during the last two years. As a result, some of the less-experienced MBAs were earning nearly the same amounts as others who had been with the firm several years but who had come in at lower starting salaries, even though their pay had been gradually increased over time.

Furthermore, because of expanding business, the division had found it necessary to hire consultants from other firms. In order to do so effectively, Avery McNeil found it necessary to upgrade the salaries they offered.

The firm as a whole was having problems meeting the federally regulated Equal Opportunity Employment goals and was trying especially hard to recruit women and minorities.

One of Simpson's colleagues, Martha Lohman, had been working in the consulting division of Avery McNeil until three months ago, when she was offered a job at another consulting firm. She had become disappointed with her new job and, on returning to her previous position at Avery McNeil, was rehired at a salary considerably higher than her former level. Simpson had noticed on the memo that she was earning more than he was, even though she was not given nearly the same level of responsibility. Simpson also realized that the firm attempted to maintain some parity between salaries in the auditing and consulting divisions.

When Simpson arrived home, he discussed the situation with his wife. "Diane, I know I'm getting a good raise, but I am still earning below my market value—$3000 less than the headhunter told me last week. And the fact that those two guys from the other consulting firm are getting more than me shows that the firm is prepared to pay competitive rates."

"I know it's unfair, Mike," Diane replied, "but what can you do? You know your boss won't negotiate salaries after they have been approved by the compensation committee, but it wouldn't hurt to at least talk to him about your dissatisfaction. I don't think you should let a few thousand dollars a year bother you. You will catch up eventually, and the main thing is that you really enjoy what you are doing."

"Yes, I do enjoy what I'm doing, but that is not to say that I wouldn't enjoy it elsewhere. I really just have to sit down and think about all the pros and cons in my working for Avery McNeil. First of all, I took this job because I felt that I could work my way up quickly. I think that I have demonstrated this, and the firm has also shown that they are willing to help me achieve this goal. If I left this job for a better paying one, I might not get the opportunity to work on the exciting jobs that I am currently working on. Furthermore, this company has time and money invested in me. I'm the only one at Avery that can work on certain jobs, and the company has several lined up. If I left the company now, they would not only lose me, but they would probably lose some of their billings as well. I really don't know what to do at this point, Diane. I can either stay with Avery McNeil or look for a higher paying job elsewhere; however, there is no guarantee that my new job would be a fast track one like it is at Avery. One big plus at Avery is that the people there already know me and the kind of work I produce. If I went elsewhere, I'd essentially have to start all over again. What do you think I should do, Diane?"

Discussion Questions   1. What are the motivational drivers of Simpson's dilemma?
2. Using the expectancy theory, *define* the dilemmas.
3. If you were Simpson's manager, and he approached you with this problem, how would *you* respond? What would *you* do?

PRACTICE   The Same Old Job[10]

Directions   Read the following case study and answer the questions that follow. When each person has finished answering the questions individually, discuss your answers in your small group. Choose a recorder/reporter to present the small group's findings to the large group.

Helen Ames awoke this morning with another headache. This was the second time in three days. She hadn't been sleeping well for the past four months or so either. When she awoke, a feeling of dread overpowered her again; she thought about going to work. As she sat on the edge of the bed, she thought about the good working conditions, decent pay, and the people with whom she worked. But it didn't seem to matter.

She'd been thinking a great deal recently about how tired and bored she'd become. She'd been on the job now three and a half years, and all the excitement was gone. There was plenty of work to do, but it all seemed routine now. She didn't even get upset or excited about the problems that arose because she felt like "she'd heard it all before."

She was tired of doing "the same old thing, day in and day out." Even though the assignments were different, the tasks seemed almost identical—writing reports, checking quotas, giving the same directions over and over again to the same people—the same problems in the same areas. She could almost describe what would happen every day for each situation.

Helen's friends and family told her how lucky she was to have a job at which she did well, and one that offered security. Some had begun to ask her what it was that she would really like to do or what it was that would make her happy. They suggested that she take some time to think about what was wrong and what she could do about it.

---

[10] *Adapted from* an exercise used in *Getting Work Done Through Others: The Supervisor's Main Job,* Advanced Human Resources Development Program, New York State Governor's Office of Employee Relations and CSEA, Inc., 1987.

She decided to request three days off.

Discussion Questions   1. How would you describe Helen's personal motivation level?
2. What personal conflicts exist for her?
3. What do you think Helen might do during her time off?
4. Do you see any similarities between any of the following? Explain.
   Helen Ames and you, now or at some other time?
   Helen Ames and people you've known?
   Helen Ames and workers you've known or dealt with?
5. If you were supervising Helen Ames and had all this information, how would you try to motivate her?
6. Which of the conditions for PPP presented to you earlier could be used to increase Helen's personal motivation?

APPLICATION   Understanding Organizational Reward Systems

The diagnostic framework that follows will be helpful to you in assessing the overall motivation potential and reward systems in potential job areas. Using the questions as a starting point, interview three potential employers about how they motivate their employees and what their reward systems are.

Motivation and Reward Systems: A Diagnostic[11]

1. What are the rewards offered by your organization that are useful in getting individuals to pursue organizational objectives?

   ■ Consider economic incentives such as pay and benefits.
   ■ Consider symbols of prestige and status.
   ■ Consider informal job content incentives such as freedom, recognition, and interesting work.

2. How is each reward listed in question 1, obtained? Is it for:

   ■ Individual performance.
   ■ Group performance.
   ■ Attendance.
   ■ Fixed membership (the reward is automatically awarded to all organization members).
   ■ Variable membership (the reward is given to long-service members only, or is given in proportion to time on job or years with the company).
   ■ Level (the reward is given automatically to all those who are at a particular organization level).
   ■ Don't know (the reward is given, but it is not clear what recipients do to get it).

[11]*Adapted from* "On the Folly of Rewarding A While Hoping for B" by Steve Kerr, *Academy of Management Journal* 18 (1975): 769–783. Used with permission.

3. Which organization unit or level is primarily responsible for the distribution of each reward listed in question 1?

- Top management/company policy.
- Personnel.
- The union.
- Level of management immediately above your own.
- Yourself.
- Your subordinates.

Competency 3 Time and Stress Management

ASSESSMENT

Directions   Check off each of the following events that you have experienced during the previous year. Total the points for your score. Remember that this score reflects your stress level at this time; in six weeks (or months), your score and your ability to cope may have changed.

Life Event	Mean Value	
Death of spouse	100	_____
Divorce	73	_____
Marital separation from spouse	65	_____
Detention in jail or other institution	63	_____
Death of a close family member	63	_____
Major personal injury or illness	53	_____
Marriage	50	_____
Being fired from job	47	_____
Marital reconciliation with spouse	45	_____
Retirement from work	45	_____
Major change in the health or behavior of a family member	44	_____
Pregnancy	40	_____
Sexual difficulties	39	_____
Gaining a new family member (e.g., through birth, adoption, oldster moving in, etc.)	39	_____
Major business readjustment (e.g., merger, reorganization, bankruptcy, etc.)	39	_____
Major change in financial state (e.g., a lot worse off or a lot better off than usual)	38	_____
Death of a close friend	37	_____
Changing to a different line of work	36	_____
Major change in the number of arguments with spouse (e.g., either a lot more or a lot less than usual regarding child rearing, personal habits, etc.)	35	_____

[12]Reprinted with permission from *Journal of Psychosomatic Research,* Vol. 11, T. H. Holmes and R. H. Rahe, "The Social Readjustment Rating Scale." Copyright © 1967, Pergamon Press, Ltd.

Life Event	Mean Value	
Taking on a mortgage or loan for a major purchase (home, business, etc.)	31	✓
Foreclosure on a mortgage or loan	30	
Major changes in responsibility at work (e.g., promotion, demotion, lateral transfer)	29	✓
Son or daughter leaving home (e.g., marriage, attending college, etc.)	29	
In-law troubles	29	
Outstanding personal achievement	28	
Spouse beginning or ceasing work outside the home	26	
Beginning or ceasing formal schooling	26	✓
Major change in living conditions (e.g., building a new home, remodeling, deterioration of home or neighborhood)	25	✓
Revision of personal habits (dress, manners, associations, etc.)	24	
Troubles with the boss	23	
Major change in working hours or conditions	20	
Change in residence	20	
Changing to a new school	20	
Major change in usual type and/or amount of recreation	19	
Major change in church activities (e.g., a lot more or a lot less than usual)	19	
Major change in social activities (e.g., clubs, dancing, movies, visiting, etc.)	18	
Taking on a mortgage or loan for a lesser purchase (car, TV, freezer, etc.)	17	
Major changes in sleeping habits (a lot more or a lot less sleep, or change in part of day when asleep)	16	
Major change in number of family get-togethers (e.g., a lot more or a lot less than usual)	15	
Major change in eating habits (a lot more or a lot less food intake, or very different meal hours or surroundings)	15	
Vacation	13	
Holidays (Christmas, Chanuka, etc.)	12	
Minor violations of the law (e.g., traffic tickets, jaywalking, disturbing the peace, etc.)	11	

Scoring Add up the numbers you checked to determine your total score. Write the score here: _____. Your instructor will lead a discussion about the meaning and implications of various score ranges.

Interpretation 1. While we often associate stress with major life tragedies, such as the death of one's spouse, many people do not tend to associate stress with positive life events, such as marriage, major purchases or vacations. How many of the items that you checked on the scale were actually positive events in your life? Why do you consider these events to be stressful?

2. As you examine the items you checked, try to consider the feelings you had at the time of each event, and the duration of those feelings. Perhaps for you the values would be slightly different. Try to ascertain common denominators to the stressful experiences which you checked.

LEARNING   Time and Stress Management

Stress is a popular concept these days, usually having negative connotations. While it is important to remember that some stress is positive—that is to say, the complete absence of stress is death—there is ample justification for being concerned about too much stress in our lives. In this discussion we will focus on defining what stress is and how it affects us, as well as outlining stress management techniques. Since we cannot, of course, adequately cover all of the possible stress management techniques, we will list a few and discuss a critical one: time management.

Stress and time management are often discussed in reverse order, and there is little agreement among scholars and practitioners about the direction and nature of the relationship between the two topics. We believe that time management can be an effective tool in stress management. We agree with Oncken (1984), however, that much of the writing on time management misses the point by not clarifying the most important first step in time management: knowing how to leverage your time across high payoff activities. We have addressed this in more detail with our treatment of the preconditions for effective stress and time management. We have also included several specific guidelines and tips that are important for effective time and stress management. We believe that stress in and of itself is not bad. But stress that leads to physical, psychological, and emotional strain can negatively affect the productivity of managers and the people they lead.

The reason we are so concerned about stress is that even when it is based in attitudes and/or emotions, stress is distinctly physiological in its consequences. All of us have perhaps experienced a near-miss while driving or riding in a car. We may have developed sweaty palms, a racing heart, and a breathless feeling long after the split-second had passed. We may even experience some of these physiological symptoms when we recall what happened—and what could have occurred. We have the power to create and recreate these stress symptoms in our bodies with our minds, even in response to memory, our imagination, fiction or horror movies. The important thing is that the body does not distinguish between the real and the imagined threats; the physiological responses are the same.

Furthermore, the body does not distinguish between negative sources of stress and positive ones. Dr. Hans Selye, recognized as the world's foremost authority on stress in human beings, defined stress in terms of the need for the body to adjust to changes. Just as we shiver in response to cold, or perspire in response to heat, the body adjusts to changes, regardless of the sources of those changes. That is to say, the sources may be catastrophic events, or pleasant ones. Adjustment is still required.

More recent research has reinforced the mind-body connection made apparent by stress. The Social Readjustment Rating Scale, which you just took as the assessment, has a medical history. Several physicians noted that their patients often came down with major illnesses after experiencing a high number of stressful events in their lives within a relatively short time. They discovered, for instance, that patients who had come down with a major illness often had a score of over 300 points in a given year, which had occurred 18–24 months before the onset of the illness. Such a score indicates the presence of prolonged stress, or distress, which has been identified as a factor related to the weakening of the immune system and to accelerating the aging process.

As producer, managers must be proactive in assisting their units and departments to maximize positive stress (without physical, psychological, or emotional strain) and minimize negative stress. The manager must not inadvertently fall into the trap of being a negative stress carrier.

THE REALITY OF TIME AND STRESS MANAGEMENT

The tips, tools, and techniques we present assume that you, the manager, live and function in a rational, logical, mundane, orderly world in which the only thing about which you must be concerned is doing your job—your "own" work—for eight hours each day. You know that this is not the case. One of the most insightful and realistic models developed approaches the management of time and stress multidimensionally. It views your world as manager from the perspective of a managerial "molecule" (Oncken 1984). It demonstrates that your attempt to manage time and stress must take into account the expectations, constraints, and demands of all the elements within the molecule, namely *your* supervisor or manager, your peers (defined very broadly), and your subordinates. Oncken proposes several preconditions for effective time (and hence stress) management, and offers them as strategies for avoiding "wheel spinning."

Precondition 1 involves resolution of the following dilemma:

Much of the wheel spinning in management ranks is due to the time that managers spend trying to reconcile management's requirements for compliance and conformity with its expectation of—and the need for—creativity and innovation. (p. 1)

Precondition 2 exhorts you to capitalize on, rather than be sidetracked by, the random and incessant interruptions and intrusions on your time by the other parts of your "molecule"—managers, peers, and subordinates, as well as clients, suppliers, union representatives, and so on.

Precondition 3 forces you to choose a set of *values* appropriate for your career aims. Oncken suggests that the choice boils down to choosing between "what you know" and "whom you know":

A third source of wheel spinning time is an ambivalence, endemic to our industrial culture, between two apparently contradictory sets of values: The so-called Work Ethic epitomized in the familiar "an honest day's work for a fair day's pay" and what I prefer to call the Management Ethic which, however stated, reaffirms the fact that judgment and influence command a higher price than time and effort. (p. 67)

Precondition 4 requires you to develop appropriate strategies for addressing the following:

> *The most significant attribute contributing to a manager's* upward career mobility *is his or her <u>constructive influence with the boss and with higher management</u>; the one contributing most to his or her personal productivity is the ability to get the system working for him or her rather than vice versa; the one contributing most to his or her managerial level is to be accessible to subordinates while leaving adequate time to him- or herself. (p. 103)*

Precondition 5 warns us to <u>know the rules of the road</u>; that is, know when and for whom to yield:

> *More damaging than wheel spinning is slippage of time, caused by collisions between priorities based upon two independent criteria, namely (1) temporal priorities based on <u>relative</u> urgency (often subjectively determined) and (2) logical priorities based on <u>relative</u> importance (usually objectively determined). (p. 139)*

The analysis activity will give you further opportunity to think through these preconditions.

The following are specific actions for effectively utilizing your management molecule.

1. If you have several items of similar urgency and importance, do the hardest one first.
2. Do the most important items during that portion of the day when you perform best.
3. Do the most trivial tasks during that portion of the day when your creative energy is lowest.
4. Never do a task that someone else can do. Do not let guilt, pride, or fear keep you from delegating.
5. Challenge the value of meetings that do not have a clear, useful purpose.
6. Skim all documents before reading them. Do not read documents with low return on investment.
7. Whenever a subordinate presents a problem, require that person to suggest one or more solutions.
8. Accomplish daily at least one significant task that brings a sense of accomplishment and productivity.
9. Do long-range planning and short-range priority setting so as to avoid as many crises as possible.
10. Maintain an organized work space.
11. Have a place where you can work uninterrupted on important tasks.
12. Constantly evaluate your investment—return patterns in the area of time management.

Once you have thought through how you can most effectively leverage your time within the context of your relevant management molecule, the following

10 steps in priority setting can help you and your department or unit be more productive.

1. Begin the day with a short planning session that is protected from interruptions.
2. Briefly review the calendar of commitments for the next reasonable period (a day, week, month, or year, depending on your time horizons).
3. List all your task demands.
4. Prioritize by time pressure (how soon it must be done) and by importance (how significant in terms of import results).
5. Select at least one item that can be completed by the end of the day which, if completed, will provide a sense of satisfaction.
6. Put all the items in order.
7. Set a deadline for each item.
8. Determine what can be delegated, and write in the name of the person to be assigned.
9. Follow the list as closely as possible. Try to avoid distractions so as to work single-mindedly on the important items but try to do more than one routine item at a time.
10. End the day by reviewing the list and evaluating how well you managed your time.

The following are several "tips" that will assist you in being an effective producer by helping you manage your stress (and time).

1. Get regular physical exercise.
2. Learn to use muscle relaxation techniques.
3. Develop a more healthy diet.
4. Find someone you can really talk to.
5. Become part of an interpersonal support group.
6. Learn to use positive thinking techniques.
7. Plan escapes: sabbaticals, leaves, vacations, short breaks.
8. Clarify values. Write 20 answers to the question "Who am I?"; then write a paragraph entitled "What I Really Want."
9. Confront the problem with planned change techniques, such as bargaining and negotiation.
10. Put yourself in situations where people are having fun.
11. Go regularly to places that renew you.
12. Increase spirituality through study, meditation, fasting, or prayer.
13. Write an action plan that will in some way improve your situation.
14. Regularly engage in intense activities that focus your mind off the source of stress.

15. Regularly develop new skills.
16. Regularly explore alternatives to your present form of employment.

ANALYSIS   Job Stress

Directions   After reading the following statements, rate each in terms of job stress. You will be asked to share your responses in a large group discussion.

1. Assign values from 1 to 100 to each stressor mentioned, adding any others you can think of.

2. Indicate whether you have control (C) or no control (NC), or whether you could get more control (MC), over this stressor.

3. Indicate how you usually cope with this stressor (example: avoidance).

Assigned value of stressor	Control, no control, more control	Coping techniques	
_____	_____	_____	1. I feel that the expectations regarding my role are unclear.
_____	_____	_____	2. I sense that various people have different expectations of me.
			3. I am overloaded with work.
_____	_____	_____	4. I feel my relations with the boss are poor.
_____	_____	_____	5. I feel my relations with my subordinates are poor.
_____	_____	_____	6. I sense my relations with my peers are poor.
_____	_____	_____	7. I feel thwarted in my ambitions.
_____	_____	_____	8. I feel the stress of office politics.
_____	_____	_____	9. I am not ready for the promotion given to me.
_____	_____	_____	10. I feel stress from being responsible for my unit.
_____	_____	_____	11. I feel stress from making "gray area" decisions for clients.

Assigned value of stressor	Control, no control, more control	Coping techniques	
			12. I feel stress from problems in delegating work to others.
————	————	————	13. I have no part in making the rules.
————	————	————	14. I cannot consult effectively with anyone about my job.
————	————	————	15. I feel that organizational demands conflict with personal demands.
————	————	————	16. I have insufficient time for decision making.
————	————	————	17. I feel stress from having unequal job titles/paychecks among staff doing similar work.
————	————	————	18. I feel stress from assigning unequal job titles/pay scales among staff doing similar work.
————	————	————	19. I feel stress from unequal working conditions.
————	————	————	20. I feel stress in an organization that has a poor community image.
			Others (any you can think of):
————	————	————	21.
————	————	————	22.
————	————	————	23.

PRACTICE   Wasting Time[13]

Directions   Read the case of Frank Fernandez. In your small group discuss the case, using the questions below as a guide. A large group discussion will follow.

[13] Reprinted from training materials for, *Getting Work Done Through Others: The Supervisor's Main Job,* Advanced Human Resources Development Program, New York State Governor's Office of Employee Relations and CSEA, Inc., 1987.

Wednesday morning Frank Fernandez, a senior clerk, reported to the central office promptly at 9 a.m. After washing out his coffee cup, Frank poured a fresh cup and walked over to Bonnie Wiczarowski's desk. She had been at a training session for the last few days, and they spent several minutes reviewing what had been going on at training and in the office.

Leaving Bonnie's desk, Frank stopped by the washroom before heading to his desk. Back at his desk was a memo detailing new policies concerning non-business or personal use of vehicles while on state business. Friends or spouses could no longer be dropped off or picked up in a state vehicle while the responsible employee is en route to or from a meeting. Frank was surprised by this news, and he asked Ralph Larrowe if he had read the memo. Ralph is a well-liked person in the office, but once you get him talking, you can't get him to stop. It was 9:45 before Frank escaped and returned to his desk.

At 10:30 Frank's boss telephoned and asked him to find a report detailing program expenditures over the last three years. His boss also expressed his disgust with the new vehicle policy and discussed at length its effect on unit morale, not to mention his wife and the issue of the family car. Bonnie, Frank's subordinate, would usually be the one to locate the report, but she was upstairs, coordinating an EAP meeting. Frank did it himself. Trying to understand Bonnie's filing system confused him, though, and after 20 minutes he decided to wait until after Bonnie returned to the office. It was now 11:30, and there was not enough time to begin any major project before lunch. Frank cleaned up his desk instead, preparing himself for an efficient afternoon.

Returning to work at 1:00, Frank quickly glanced over the union newsletter, and then became engrossed in some busy work. It was 1:30 before Frank remembered to have Bonnie find that report.

A couple of minutes later she came back with two reports. One listed program expenditures over the last two years, the other program expenditures over the past five years. There was no three-year report, and Bonnie stated that there never had been one. Frank asked her to look again.

When Bonnie still couldn't find the report, Frank called his boss back. The secretary said the boss was in a meeting and didn't know when the boss would return. After Frank left a message, he and Bonnie returned to what they were doing.

Frank's busy work wasn't really due until the end of the month, but it was nearing 3:00 (actually it was 2:45) and two hours wasn't enough time to begin work on the budget, especially when he knew that Ralph Larrowe would be by in a few minutes. That new vehicle policy had upset him, and he always wanted to talk when he was upset about something. Frank could see Ralph stewing from across the office and knew that sooner or later Ralph would be wandering over. A project like the budget is best accomplished when a large block of time is available and Ralph is not in the picture. Frank made a mental note to reserve such a block of time later in the week.

Discussion Questions **"Wasting Time"**

1. What are some of Frank's time wasters? How could he have avoided them?
2. What behaviors would he have to change to improve his use of time? What steps would he need to take?
3. What is the best way to deal with a boss who (a) interrupts your work with nonwork-related matters? or (b) gives you imprecise information?

APPLICATION Improving Your Time and Stress Management[14]

1. Generate your own list of time wasters.

2. Identify their possible causes.

3. Using the general strategies for effectively using time discussed earlier, develop possible solutions. Make sure that you select realistic and timesaving solutions.

4. In your small group, discuss some of your identified time wasters. Discuss your solutions for making better use of your time. Ask others in your group for other suggestions.

REFERENCES

Adams, J. D. "Achieving and Maintaining Personal Peak Performance." *Transforming Work.* J. D. Adams (general ed.). Alexandria, Va.: Miles River Press, 1984.

Bain, D. *The Productivity Prescription: The Manager's Guide to Improving Productivity and Profits.* New York: McGraw-Hill, 1982.

Bennis, W. and B. Nanus. *Leaders: The Strategies for Taking Charge,* New York: Harper & Row, 1985.

Carlzon, Jan. *Moments of Truth.* New York: Harper & Row, 1987.

Dumaine, B. "Cool Cures for Burnout." *Fortune* (1988): 78–84.

Friedman, M. *Overcoming the Fear of Success: Why and How We Defeat Ourselves and What to Do about It.* New York: Random House, 1985.

Garfield, C. S. *Peak Performers.* New York: Avon Books, 1986.

Grove, A. S. *High-Output Management.* New York: Random House, 1985.

Holmes, J. H., and R. H. Rahe, "Social Readjustment Rating Scale." *Journal of Psychosomatic Research* (1967).

Imai, M. *Kaizen.* New York: Random House, 1986.

Kendrick, J. W. *Improving Company Productivity.* Baltimore, Md.: John Hopkins University Press, 1984.

[14] Reprinted from training materials for *Time Management Training for Income Maintenance Supervisors,* Continuing Education Program, School of Social Welfare, State University of New York at Albany. Used with permission.

Kerr, S. "On the Folly of Rewarding A, While Hoping for B." *Academy of Management Journal* 18 (1975): 769–783.

Kushel, G. *The Fully Effective Executive.* Chicago: Contemporary Books, 1983.

Labich, K. "The Seven Keys to Business Leadership." *Fortune* (October 24, 1988): 58–66.

Livingston, J. S. "Pygmalion in Management." *Harvard Business Review* (July–August 1969).

Mandell, M. *1001 Ways to Operate Your Business More Profitably.* Homewood, Ill.: Dow Jones–Irwin, 1975.

McCoy, J. T. *The Management of Time.* Englewood Cliffs, N.J.: Prentice-Hall, 1959.

Nadler, D. A., and E. E. Lawler (eds.). "Motivation: A Diagnostic Approach." Hackman, J. R., and E. E. Lawler. *Perspectives in Behavior in Organizations,* New York: McGraw-Hill, 1977.

Nadler, D., M. Tushman, and N. Hatvany (eds.). *Managing Organizations,* Boston: Little, Brown, 1982.

Nash, M. *Making People Productive: What Really Works in Raising Managerial and Employee Performance.* San Francisco: Jossey-Bass, 1985.

———. *Managing Organizational Performance.* San Francisco: Jossey-Bass, 1983.

Oncken, W. *Managing Management Time.* Englewood Cliffs, N.J.: Prentice-Hall, 1984.

Philips, J. J. *Improving Supervisors' Effectiveness: How Organizations Can Raise the Performance of Their First-Level Managers.* San Francisco: Jossey-Bass, 1985.

Pines, M. "Psychological Hardiness: The Role of Challenge and Health." *Psychology Today* (December 1980): 34–44.

Sawyer, G. C. *Designing Strategy.* New York: John Wiley and Sons, 1986.

Stankard, M. F. *Productivity by Choice: The 20 to 1 Principle.* New York: John Wiley and Sons, 1986.

Vaill, P. B. "The Purposing of High Performing Systems." *Organizational Dynamics* 11(2) (1982): 23–39.

Vough, C. F. *Productivity: A Practical Program for Improving Efficiency.* New York: AMACOM, 1979.

Vroom, V. H. *Work and Motivation.* New York: John Wiley and Sons, 1964.

Wheeler, Mary. "Marvel Woman." *Executive Female* (May/June 1988): 20ff.

Ziglar, Z. *Top Performance: How to Develop Excellence in Yourself and Others.* New York: Berkeley Book, 1986.

The Director and Producer Roles

We have just completed our discussion of the director and producer roles. Before we move on, let's take a moment to place these roles in the context of the entire model for you. We will do the same as we complete each pair of roles in the competing values model.

A BRIEF REVIEW

When you read the description of each role, you may think we mean to apply it to all situations. You may begin to argue that it is right or wrong, good or bad. Instead, however, we want you to think about a role as being appropriate in some situations and not in others. When a role is not appropriate, we will show you how to use the competing values framework to decide what role might be better to use or develop.

The director and producer roles are part of the rational goal model. In this model the desired ends are productivity, profit, or general goal attainment. The assumed means or processes to these ends have to do with goal clarification and direction. This model says that managers need to take charge, specify the desired outcomes and the alternative strategies for achieving those outcomes, then act decisively in pursuing the strategies and objectives. The model assumes individual action; the manager needs to be independent and strong-willed in the relentless pursuit of the bottom line.

WHEN THE DIRECTOR AND PRODUCER ROLES ARE MOST APPROPRIATE

There are two axes that define the rational goal model. On the horizontal axis the model is defined by an external focus, short time lines, and competitive pressures. On the vertical axis, it is defined by high control, which suggests situations where the basic problems are easily understood. When a situation is pressing and the basic strategies are clearly known, it is appropriate to take charge, to specify direction and push for action. Others accept such behavior in this situation. Here, if the leader stopped and took time for participative decision making, associates would feel it quite inappropriate because it is obvious what should be done and time is critical.

COMPLEMENTARY ROLES

Because some people feel that the rational goal model is inherently "right," they may tend to overuse it. In all situations they believe that they should be in charge. At times, though, acting as a producer or director is not the best course that a manager can take. The failure to balance the director and producer roles with the other roles, particularly the facilitator and mentor roles in the human relations quadrant, can lead to problems. Consider, for example, the following situation.

Roger Smith took over General Motors in 1981. He made huge technical changes as he set out to "reindustrialize" the company. Initially he was seen as a man of vision, a true leader. But then things started to go wrong. Ford outearned GM for the first time since the 1920s. GM's market share slipped from 45% to 36%. The praise of Roger Smith began to turn negative and eventually it became vicious. In 1989, when he reviewed his efforts to rebuild GM, he wrote about the most important lesson he had learned.

> *But I sure wish I'd done a better job of communicating with GM people. I'd do that differently a second time around and make sure they understood and shared my vision for the company. Then they would have known why I was tearing the place up, taking out whole divisions, changing our whole production structure. If people understand the why, they'll work at it. Like I say, I never got all this across. There we were, charging up the hill right on schedule, and I looked behind me and saw that many people were still at the bottom, trying to decide whether to come along.*[1]

Clearly the roles in the rational goal model must be seen in context. They must be balanced with other models.

---

[1] "Roger Smith: The U.S. Must Do as GM Has Done" *Fortune,* February 13, 1989, p. 71.

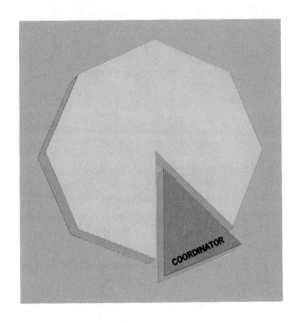

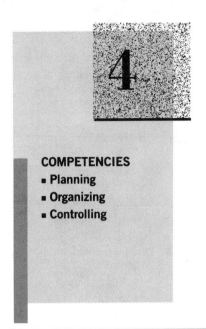

4

COMPETENCIES
- **Planning**
- **Organizing**
- **Controlling**

THE COORDINATOR ROLE

Management is often defined as the process of getting the job done through and with the help of other people. In Chapter 2, we discussed delegation, the process of giving assignments to employees, as a tool for getting the job done through others. In many cases, however, getting the job done involves more than giving assignments to individuals. "Getting the job done" also involves coordinating the work of two or more employees, work groups, or work units that act interdependently.

In this chapter we will explore the **coordinator role,** the first role in the internal process model of the competing values framework. In the coordinator role, the manager's task is to make sure that work flows smoothly and that activities are carried out according to their relative importance with a minimum amount of conflict among individuals, work groups, or work units. That is, the coordinator must see to it that the right people are at the right place at the right time to perform the right task. In addition, managers performing in this role must be concerned with the physical materials that allow employees to do their work. They must make sure that the necessary tools of the job are available, that the physical space where the work is to be done is adequate, and that the output of one work group is available as input for the second work group when that group is ready.

In performing the role of coordinator, the manager relies on three inter-related competencies:

Competency 1   Planning
Competency 2   Organizing
Competency 3   Controlling

As you will see in this chapter, these three competencies are the key to accomplishing the organization's work. They are basic to the day-to-day functioning of the organization and the maintenance of its stability and continuity.

Competency 1 Planning

ASSESSMENT   Planning a Reunion

Directions   All of us have been involved in the planning and coordination of social activities, such as birthday and anniversary parties, church events, family outings, and picnics. In this self-assessment activity, you can begin to focus on your planning skills by thinking about how you would plan a social event: your high school reunion.

Assume that you are the chairperson of this year's reunion committee. Using the following key phrases, describe how you would plan for this reunion.

1. Planning steps.

2. Resources needed.

3. Events and people that require coordination.

After you have completed planning the reunion, answer the following process questions.

1. Which of the following human, material, and financial resources did you consider? What additional details did you consider?

Pre-reunion Activities

_____   Selection of reunion committee.

_____   Reunion committee task coverage and coordination.

_____   Getting names, addresses, phone numbers, and so on.

_____   Method of locating class members.

_____   Reunion site selection.

_____   Availability of secretarial/word processing skills.

_____   Availability of graphics/design skills.

Reunion Activities, Events, and So On

_____   Menu selection.

_____   Decorations, flowers, and so on.

_____   Photographer.

_____ Speakers for reunion/entertainment.

_____ Role of class officers, reunion committee, faculty.

Reunion Budget

_____ Telephone (local/long distance).

_____ Postage (invitations, reminders, etc.).

_____ Printing/photocopying.

_____ Stationery and other office supplies.

_____ Cost of reunion activities, events, and so on.

_____ Ticket price to charge for the event.

2. Did you use any of the following schedules or time lines? Which others did you establish?

_____ Chart of when planning activities should commence.

_____ Chart/list of when to check on progress.

_____ Chart of reunion committee meetings.

_____ Chart of reunion committee members' availability.

3. What events and/or people did you identify as needing coordination? What means, if any, did you identify to coordinate them?

Interpretation   1. Overall, how well did you do in planning this reunion?

2. Did you consider all or most of the needed details, or did you overlook some important details? Was there a pattern in the types of details you overlooked?

3. To what extent did the reunion year affect your planning? Would you have planned differently for a 20-year class reunion, as opposed to a 5-year class reunion?

4. How did your planning for the reunion compare to other planning that you've done? Do you usually tend to consider or overlook the details?

LEARNING Planning

In Chapter 2, we talked about planning and goal setting as important tools for determining where it is you want to go and how you want to get there. We made the distinction between *strategic planning,* or planning directed towards setting an organization's mission, and *tactical planning,* or planning that involves implementing the strategic plan, setting specific objectives for each unit (and for each employee) and indicating how those objectives will be accomplished.

Once we know what we want to accomplish, the objectives must be translated into actions. This translation requires yet a third type of planning: operational planning. **Operational planning** involves preparing and maintaining the work flow of the system. More specifically, it involves deciding how financial, material, and human resources should be used to ensure the most effective delivery of services. Operational planning is the first step in coordinating the work of several people, work groups, or work units.

In order to translate goals into plans, the manager needs to make two changes in focus.

1. Shift from an organizationwide or divisionwide perspective to a perspective that focuses on a particular work unit, functional area, program, or project. Also note how specific resources allocated to complete the work will be used to accomplish desired results.

2. Shift from a long-range to a short-range time frame for planning. Although operational planning still involves thinking ahead, it usually does not involve thinking as far into the future as strategic and tactical planning. Strategic plans usually focus on time frames of 5 to 10 years and tactical plans focus on time frames of 1 to 5 years, but operational plans generally focus on time frames of less than one year, and sometimes as short as one week.

ESTABLISHING STANDARDS AND PRIORITIES

Operational planning is important both for managers and for their employees for three reasons. First, operational planning translates the future into the present by providing a detailed map of how to "get from here to there." If we use maps as a metaphor, we can think of strategic plans as national or global maps, and operational plans as street maps. Each serves its own unique purpose, and neither is dispensable.

Employee participation in operational planning increases employees' understanding of work unit (and organizational) objectives. Involving employees in the operational planning process not only increases their knowledge and understanding of objectives, but also tends to reduce employees' resistance to changes resulting from new or revised plans.

Perhaps more importantly, employees usually have good ideas about how to plan the work more efficiently. In his book *Thriving on Chaos* (1987), Tom Peters argues that *all* employees should be involved in planning at *all* levels.

Roger Smith, retiring CEO of General Motors, has launched an all-out effort to increase employee participation in decision making and planning (*Business Week* 1989). Bob Allen, CEO at AT&T, is trying hard to move decision making further down in the organization because "that's where the best decisions get made for the customer" (Kupfer 1989, 59).

A second reason to engage in operational planning is that it provides a mechanism for setting standards and clarifying what is to be done, and, in some cases, how it is to be done. Once you have set performance standards, you can evaluate how well you are doing or have done. In the last section of this chapter and in Chapter 5, "The Monitor Role," we will discuss further the evaluation process. Before you can evaluate, however, you must set the standard.

Performance standards may be established for human, financial, physical, or technical resources. For example, the standards established in employee performance programs provide employees with knowledge of what behaviors are expected, and they provide the organization with a basis for assessing whether or not employees are appropriately performing their jobs. Similarly, organizations can set standards for physical resources, indicating an "acceptable rate of downtime," or the percentage of time that a piece of equipment can be in need of repair before there is need for corrective action.

Performance standards should be set using an MBO-type approach. That is, you should use the same SMART guidelines (Doran 1981) for establishing standards as you used in Chapter 2 for setting objectives. Standards should be:

- Specific, with respect to what is to be accomplished.

- Measurable, with respect to what progress has been made toward meeting the standard.

- Assignable, with respect to which individual or group of individuals is responsible for performing the task.

- Realistic, with respect to the available resources.

- Time-related, with respect to when results are expected.

The third reason for engaging in operational planning is that it clarifies work unit and organizational priorities. As you will see later, much of operational planning is concerned with scheduling and establishing time tables and milestones for completion. Before setting a schedule, the manager must establish priorities for task completion. Managers at all levels of the organization will find that as long as there are many tasks to perform, it is necessary to set priorities and decide what should happen first.

Four factors influence the establishment of priorities.

1. *External constraints.* What externally imposed deadlines exist? What is the urgency of completing this task, activity, or project?

2. *The overall amount of time required.* If the task is inherently lengthy, the schedule must allow for the necessary time for completion. On the other hand, if the task requires a relatively short period of time for completion, it may be possible to delay the start-up of the task.

3. *The relationship of this task, activity, or project to other tasks, activities, and projects.* How does completion, or lack of completion, affect other plans for project completions? Are other people, work units, or organizations dependent on the output of this project to begin their work?

4. *The relative benefit of completing a task within a given time frame against the penalty of not completing it within that time frame.* What is to be gained by completing the task? What are the consequences of delaying the work by a week, two weeks, or a month?

PLANNING AND SCHEDULING TOOLS

Managers can use various tools to translate strategic and tactical plans into operational plans. These tools involve generating specific descriptions of the work to be done and the time frame for each employee or work group for completing the work.

STATEMENT OF WORK

The statement of work (SOW) is a written description of the work required to complete the project. It includes descriptions of the tasks necessary for project completion, as well as a description, where appropriate, of how individual tasks will be integrated into the whole. It also includes an overall schedule specifying when each task will be completed.

Task descriptions should be sufficiently detailed to allow you to tabulate and summarize human and other resources required to accomplish each task. They should also list specific outputs associated with task completion, such as written reports, recommendations, and other final products.

TASK RELATIONSHIP DIAGRAMS

The people you work with affect your work. Even when you are performing a task essentially on your own, you often rely on others to provide input. For example, office employees usually rely on the office secretary for typing, word processing, photocopying, answering telephones, and making travel arrangements. Managers, however, rarely perform a task on their own. Rather, they rely on each of their employees to get the job done.

Drawing an individual task relationship diagram can help make you more aware of how these relationships affect your work. For each task relationship diagram, put your name in a circle in the middle and the names of all the people involved in completing the task in circles around you. The diagram should include lines between you and each of the people in your task relationship diagram (see Figure 4.1).

Next, identify the kinds of communication that you have with these people (e.g., giving instructions, checking on progress, and asking for information) and the mode of communication (e.g., in person, telephone, or memoranda). Finally, examine the effectiveness of each communication link, identifying persons with whom you may need to communicate more often, or in a different way, in order to improve the task coordination.

Task relationship diagrams can also be used to track the communication necessary to coordinate among several work units. In this case, you would place the name of the focal work group in the middle circle and the names of the other work groups in the surrounding circles. As with the individual task relationship diagrams, you would then identify the kinds and modes of commu-

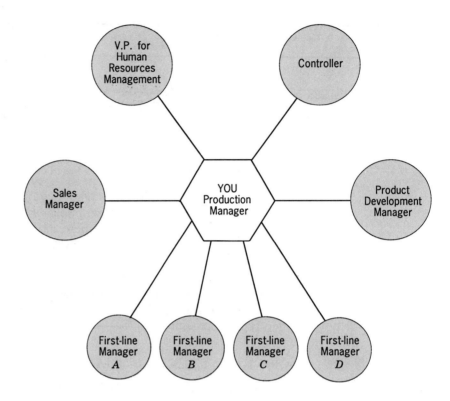

FIGURE 4.1 *Task relationship diagram.*

nication among the different units and examine the effectiveness of the communication links, looking for ways to improve task coordination.

GANTT CHARTS

As mentioned before, a major component of planning is scheduling: that is, setting up the time relationships among the various project tasks within the overall time frame of the project. Gantt charts, developed by Henry L. Gantt in the early part of the twentieth century, allow you to see at a glance how the different tasks fit into the overall schedule.

To develop a Gantt chart, make a list of each of the major tasks or task groups in the sequence in which they will occur. Estimate the time required to complete each task, and determine which tasks can begin before the previous task has been completed and which tasks cannot. Construct the Gantt chart by drawing the time line for the project along the horizontal axis of a graph and placing the list of tasks along the vertical axis of the chart. For each task, draw a bar showing the time commitment (see Figure 4.2). You can also identify specific milestones, or points of accomplishment, within each task by using a circled number within the bar. In Figure 4.2 the milestones represent first drafts of reports due at the end of the task.

The Gantt chart is most useful when there are a limited number of tasks and each task time is long, relative to the units of time drawn on the horizontal

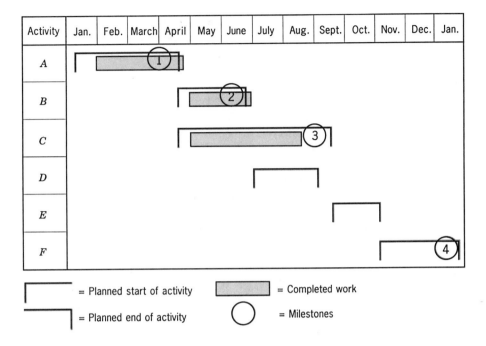

FIGURE 4.2 *Gantt chart.*

axis. That is, if the horizontal axis is drawn in terms of months, most tasks should take at least two months. By using different colors or different symbols, the Gantt chart can track how well you are doing in keeping to the planned schedule. When a given task runs over the allotted time, the Gantt chart can be used to determine whether or not the schedule needs to be rethought. Unfortunately, Gantt charts are not as useful when a project has many separate, but interrelated, tasks. In these cases, network models are more useful.

PROGRAM EVALUATION AND REVIEW TECHNIQUE AND CRITICAL PATH METHOD

Like Gantt charts, networks are graphic tools for planning. Program Evaluation and Review Technique (PERT) was introduced by the Special Projects Office of the United States Navy in 1958 as an aid in planning (and controlling) its Polaris Weapon System, a project that involved approximately 3000 contractors. At virtually the same time, a similar technique, Critical Path Method (CPM), was introduced by DuPont Company.

PERT/CPM analysis allows the manager to see the flow of tasks associated with a project, to estimate the time necessary to complete the overall project given the interdependencies among tasks, and to identify those critical points where a delay in task completion can have a major effect on overall project completion. In performing the PERT/CPM analysis, one assumes that all tasks or activities can be clearly identified and sequenced, and that the time necessary for completing each task or activity can be estimated.

Figure 4.3 shows a simple PERT chart. In it tasks and activities are designated by arrows. The circles at the beginning and end of the arrows are referred to as *nodes;* they designate starting and ending points for tasks and activities. These points in time are called events and consume no time in and of themselves. The numbers along the arrows indicate the expected time for the task to be completed. Expected time for task or activity completion (t_e) is generally calculated using a weighted average of an optimistic time (t_o), a pessimistic time (t_p), and the most likely time (t_m) using the following equation:

$$t_e = (t_o + 4t_m + t_p)/6$$

Note that Activity 3,6 has an expected time of zero weeks. This type of activity is called a **dummy activity,** as used to indicate that Activity 6,7 cannot begin until Activity 1,3 is complete.

CPM analysis involves finding that path, or chain of activities, that takes the longest time through the network. In Figure 4.3 the path is 1–2–4–5–6–7. It indicates the least possible time in which the overall project can be completed, and it is the path that needs to be watched most carefully to ensure that the project stays "on track."

The more specific your plans, the easier it will be to stay "on track." Remember, though, that even specific plans will often need to be modified for unexpected changes. Thus, it is important to allow for flexibility in planning.

ANALYSIS   The Case of Jack Matteson

Directions   As you read the following case, try to think about it from three different perspectives: from that of Jack Matteson, that of his manager, and that of a student of management and organizations. Then, respond to the questions that follow the case.

Jack Matteson feels that his life is a mess right now. Ironically enough, two weeks ago he was on top of the world. He had just been promoted to the position of unit manager and had been given, as his first assignment, a new project that was described as being "of great importance to several of the company's central goals."

Prior to his promotion, Jack had worked in the company for seven years and had consistently received outstanding performance appraisals. He had decided to make his career at this company and had turned down several opportunities to transfer to other companies and one opportunity to work for the industry's leading firm. Jack enjoyed his work, enjoyed the people with whom he worked, and appreciated the strong sense of pride that people felt about the company's work.

When he first learned about his promotion to the position of unit manager, he had been thrilled. He had also been thrilled about the assignment to the new

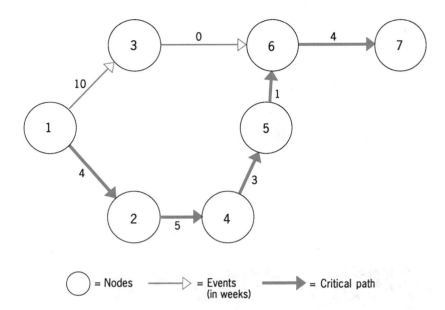

FIGURE 4.3 *PERT network with critical path.*

◯ = Nodes   ——▷ = Events (in weeks)   ➤ = Critical path

project. Jack's manager had recommended Jack's unit for this project because she felt Jack was "well-suited for the assignment." Jack recognized that this assignment was a reward, recognition of the high potential that others saw in him. In his excitement, Jack eagerly accepted the new project, even though he knew little about it and knew that it would be a tremendous challenge, especially for his first assignment.

Two weeks have now passed, and things have changed considerably. Jack is beginning to dread coming to work each day; he can't face the papers and project specifications piled high on his desk. He is simply not sure how to proceed. At the end of last week, he decided to assign three start-up tasks to his three senior employees, but this morning they each came in and reported that they could only go so far before they would need information from reports to be generated by one of the other employees. In addition, a few of the other employees in the unit have begun to ask when there will be a meeting to discuss the new project. He is hoping that they don't speak with the division chief because yesterday, when the division chief asked Jack how everything was going with the special project, Jack responded, "Oh, just fine!"

Jack is afraid to talk to his manager and to let her know that he is feeling overwhelmed and disorganized. He is hesitant to ask her for guidance because she seems to expect him to know what he is doing. He is beginning to suspect, however, that the situation is about to go from bad to worse, and he will have to do something. On top of it all, he has a headache that just won't quit! He wishes the clock would stop so that he can catch up. Better yet, he wishes it was two weeks ago and that he had turned down the special project assignment.

Discussion Questions
1. Looking at the case from Jack's perspective, what do you think the real problem is? What are some of the sources of Jack's frustration? What specific knowledge, skills, or tools could he use to get out of this situation?
2. Looking at the case from Jack's manager's perspective, what do you think the real problem is? What is your responsibility, as Jack's manager, in this situation? If Jack gathers up his courage to come and talk with you, how will you approach the situation? What if he doesn't?
3. Assume that you are a close friend of Jack's. He knows that you are a student of management and organizations and has called you to ask for advice. What advice will you give him? What can Jack do in the short term? What should he do in the long term?
4. Can you personally identify with Jack? Describe a similar situation, preferably a work-related situation. What did you do? Was it effective? Knowing what you know now about planning, what other actions might you have taken?

PRACTICE Planning the Annual Office Picnic

Directions At the beginning of this section you planned a reunion for members of your high school graduating class. It was quite successful, and you are pleased with the results of your hard work and planning. Everyone at work heard about your success with the reunion and has asked you to organize the department's annual summer picnic. You respectfully decline, saying that you have had enough of being in charge for one year. You offer, however, to give the chair some hard-earned advice, based on your experience. As it turns out, the chair of the event is totally inexperienced and at a loss as to what to do. Consequently, he welcomes and seeks your counsel. Since you will be out of town on business for the next two weeks, you decide to write a memo to him. Include in your memo anything you think would be helpful in the successful planning and coordination of the project. Be sure to suggest a list of planning steps, and indicate how he can use the various planning tools you learned in this chapter. Complete your memo by comparing your experience as chair of the high school reunion committee with your current advice to the chair of the picnic. Discuss the differences in the two types of plans and the reasons for the differences.

APPLICATION Getting in (Operational) Gear

Choose a complex project or a program in which you are involved at school or work, or in a community organization to which you belong. If you cannot think of any such projects, think about a project you would like to undertake, such as searching for a job after you graduate.

Write a statement of work for the project. At the end of your statement of work, indicate what you consider to be the most challenging aspects of this project. If the complexity of the project currently makes you feel frustrated or overwhelmed, express those feelings. (The skills and techniques you learn in this chapter should help reduce these feelings.)

1. List the major planning tasks necessary for completing the project.

2. Draw a diagram of your individual task relationships. Identify where coordination can be improved. Describe how you will approach the people involved.

3. If this is a project involving a group or work unit, also draw a diagram of the intergroup or interunit task relationships, if appropriate.

4. Develop a Gantt chart for the project; indicate milestones where you can check on your progress. Also develop a PERT chart; indicate the critical path.

Competency 2 Organizing

ASSESSMENT Analyzing Tasks

Directions   Respond to the following questions concerning your current role as a student or, if you work, on your job.

1. List three major tasks or functions that you perform either routinely or on a periodic basis in this role.

2. Describe each task or function in terms of the steps or components required to complete these tasks.

3. Describe the types of knowledge or skills required to accomplish each task.

4. Compare your answers to questions 2 and 3, and evaluate how well you fit the job.

   If you are currently a manager, also answer question 5.

5. Identify one or two work unit tasks or functions. Repeat questions 2 to 4, focusing on the work unit tasks. Can you identify one or two ideas for reorganizing some of the tasks in a way that would be beneficial to your unit?

Interpretation   After examining the tasks in this manner, you probably are thinking somewhat differently about the tasks or functions you perform.

1. What did you learn by breaking down your tasks and functions into their component parts?

2. Has your perception of these tasks changed? For example, are you more aware of the importance of certain components that you previously did not see as important? Do you see relationships among components on which you previously had not focused?

3. How aware were you before of the importance of matching individual knowledge and skills to task requirements?

LEARNING Organizing

Once organizational and work unit plans are set, a manager must decide how to allocate and coordinate organizational resources in order to accomplish the goals. **Organizing** is the process of dividing the work into manageable components and assigning activities to most effectively achieve the desired results. Said in another way, if planning provides the tools for deciding where "you want to go and how best to get there," organizing provides the tools to actually "get you there."

At the organizational level, organizing involves designing the organizational structure so that the work can be efficiently and effectively allocated across the different departments and work units. At the work-unit level, organizing involves designing jobs and allocating tasks so that the work unit can effectively accomplish its goals in support of the overall organizational mission. In this section we will examine both organizational and job design, focusing on current tools and techniques of organizing that have evolved from ideas first written about by Adam Smith in 1776.

EFFICIENCY AS AN ORGANIZING PRINCIPLE

In his treatise *The Wealth of Nations,* written in 1776, Adam Smith established two management principles which today still stand as guiding principles of organizations. Writing about the manufacture of straight pins, Smith noted that if (1) the work were divided into its component tasks and (2) workers were specialized so that each individual only had responsibility for completing one of the component tasks, the overall job would be accomplished far more efficiently than if each worker performed all tasks associated with the job.

More than 200 years later, the process of organizing is still very much influenced by the principles of **division of labor** (that work should be divided into component tasks) and **specialization** (that each person should only be assigned a small piece of the total job). Although current management thought on how to design organizations and jobs effectively no longer focuses exclusively on efficiency, it remains an important building block in the process of organizing.

Small organizations often remain informal with respect to rules and procedures. They have little need for standardization of jobs and specialization—when a job needs to be done, people share in the work. Large organizations, however, need rules and procedures. Without standardization and specialization there would be chaos. Organizing, then, serves several important functions.

1. Organizing clarifies who is supposed to perform which jobs and how those jobs should be divided among organizational members.

2. Organizing clarifies the lines of authority, specifying who reports to whom.

3. Organizing creates the mechanisms for coordinating across the different groups and levels of the organization.

DESIGNING ORGANIZATIONS THROUGH DEPARTMENTATION

At the organizational level, dividing jobs among organizational members is called **departmentation.** Here employees are grouped into departments according to some logic. Three pure forms of departmentation are departmentation by function, departmentation by division, and departmentation by matrix.

BY FUNCTION

Departmentation by function creates departments based on the specific functions that people perform. For example, financial management offices, engineering departments, and legal offices are grouped by function. All people in these offices perform similar functions.

Organizing by function increases organizational efficiency by having people with similar expertise working together to perform similar functions. Conversely, it decreases organizational efficiency because the structure creates barriers between departments that generally result in increased time to respond to interfunctional problems.

BY DIVISION

Departmentation by division creates departments based on services, clients, territories, or time differences. For example, AT&T reorganized its computer-oriented division from a functional structure to a divisional structure in order to increase coordination. IBM organizes its marketing by geographic region, both domestic and worldwide. In the United States, IBM has two marketing divisions: North–Central and South–West.

Organizing by division increases organizational efficiency because the departments can be more responsive to specific client or regional needs. Conversely it often leads to duplication of effort and makes it more difficult for people who are doing the same type of work, in different departments, to share their ideas and learn from each other.

BY MATRIX

Departmentation by matrix, or matrix organization, attempts to take the advantages and overcome the disadvantages of functional and divisional organizational forms by combining the two. In matrix organizations, employees are assigned (1) to a functional department and also (2) to a cross-functional team that focuses on specific projects or programs. They report to the heads of both the functional department and cross-functional team. For example, an engineer in a manufacturing firm that is organized in matrix form will report to the head of the engineering department and also to the product manager, who also manages marketing, production, and finance specialists assigned to that project or product. Such diverse service and manufacturing organizations as Prudential Insurance, General Mills, and Caterpillar Tractor are organized in matrix form.

CHOOSING A FORM OF DEPARTMENTATION

As discussed previously, each of the pure forms of departmentation has advantages and disadvantages; they are summarized in Table 4.1. In choosing a form of departmentation, organizations often organize according to a mix of these forms. For example, because of the greater flexibility and ability to respond to client needs, many corporations are organized by division with respect to the specific products or services they provide, but they are organized by function with respect to personnel/human resources management, financial management, and legal offices. Similarly some organizations are organized by division with respect to regions, but they are organized by function within each region. Hospitals and psychiatric institutions may have matrix structures for providing services, but they maintain a functional structure for such activities as records management, building maintenance, and nutrition and dietary services.

As the global economy becomes more competitive, many U.S. companies are beginning to organize their units in ways that foster flexibility and innovation over centralized control and standardization. For example, AT&T, America's largest diversified service company, has undertaken a dramatic restructuring in an effort to win more market share in the long distance phone call industry.

Under the new CEO, Bob Allen, AT&T has cut centralized levels of middle management, making the whole organization flatter, and created 19 new business units, organized by product line, such as computer network systems or switching systems. Each business is responsible for its own profits and losses, and has the authority to decide which products to make, and how to make and sell them.

Recently, Joe Nacchio, the head of marketing for the AT&T unit that sells long-distance service to businesses, appeared in a fast-talking ad on national television. Nacchio promised Sprint and MCI customers that if they would switch to AT&T he would pay the reconnection charges if they were in any way disappointed with the new service and wanted to be reconnected to their old company. The ad won AT&T about 30,000 new accounts. Managers at AT&T say this kind of speed and innovation in marketing would never have happened under the old structure. One executive, who left the company just before the reorganization, said, "I was overseeing a construction budget of $150 million, but I had to get central office approval for travel" (Kupfer 1989, 61–62).

TABLE 4.1 Potential Advantages and Disadvantages of Three Pure Forms of Departmentation

Departmentation by Function

Advantages	*Disadvantages*
Allows task assignments to be consistent with technical training	May reduce accountability for total product or service delivery
Allows greater specialization in technical areas of expertise	Promotes overspecialization
Supports in-depth training and development	Breaks down communication across functions
Promotes high-quality technical problem solving	Refers too many problems upward in hierarchy
Reduces technical demands on the manager	Promotes narrow, self-centered perspectives within functions
Provides career paths within areas of technical expertise	Allows slow response to interfunctional problems

Departmentation by Division

Advantages	*Disadvantages*
Allows for flexible response to new developments	May not allow for sufficient depth of technical expertise
Concentrates functional attention on common tasks	May duplicate efforts as personnel assigned to separate work divisions work on similar problems
Improves coordination across functions	May overemphasize division versus organizational objectives
Facilitates growth by adding new divisions	May result in unhealthy competition among divisions

Departmentation by Matrix

Advantages	*Disadvantages*
Allows for efficient use of resources	Allows for potential power struggles between an employee's two bosses
Allows for flexible response to new developments	Allows for confusion regarding which of two bosses has greater authority
Promotes high-quality technical problem solving	May allow program teams to overemphasize team goals versus organizational goals.
Frees top management for long-range planning	May produce prohibitive cost of program manager salaries

Sources: Adapted from John R. Schermerhorn, Jr., *Management for Productivity* (New York: John Wiley and Sons, 1989), pp. 179–185; and John M. Ivancevich and Michael T. Matteson, *Organizational Behavior and Management* (Homewood, IL: Business Publications, Inc., 1987). Reprinted by permission of Richard D. Irwin, Inc.

LINES OF AUTHORITY

In addition to defining how the organization's work is to be divided, departmentation defines the organization's authority relationships—who reports to whom. In designing authority relationships, we often rely on three efficiency principles. First, each person should report to one and only one manager. This is referred to as the **unity-of-command principle.** The principle ensures that employees know from whom they should expect job assignments and reduces the potential for conflicting job assignments. Note that, by definition, matrix organizations violate the unity-of-command principle. In fact, the advantages of matrix organizations are considered to be sufficient to warrant this violation. Managers in matrix organizations, however, should monitor job assignments and communication patterns to check that employees are not receiving conflicting messages from their two bosses.

Building on the principle of unity of command, the **scalar principle** states that there should be a clear line of command linking each employee to the next higher level of authority, up to and including the highest level of management. When the lines of authority are clear, it is easier to know who is responsible for the completion of each job.

Finally, the principle of **span of control** states that a person can effectively manage only a limited number of employees. How many, then? The answer is not clear and may vary with the individuals involved. But the principle recognizes that as the number of individuals reporting to a manager increases, the more difficult it is to coordinate and control individual efforts.

The size of the span of control influences the organization's structure. For a given number of employees, as the span of control decreases, the number of levels in the organizational hierarchy will increase. More managers are needed and, hence, the greater the number of layers in the hierarchy. Conversely, the greater the span of control, the fewer the number of managers needed and, hence, the fewer the number of layers in the hierarchy.

Organizations with many levels in the hierarchy are referred to as **tall organizations;** organizations with fewer levels in the hierarchy are referred to as **flat organizations.** In general, tall organization tend to operate less efficiently than flat ones. Recent trends in both industry and government have been to reduce the number of levels in the hierarchy and to increase the span of control. F. Kenneth Iverson, chairman of NuCor Corporation, said, "The most important thing American industry needs is to reduce the number of management layers" (Peters 1987, 425). Here are factors that should be considered in planning any manager's span of control:

Factor	Effect	Recommendation
Variety of functions	The greater the variety of functions to be managed, . . .	The *smaller* the span of control should be
Physical location of functions	The greater the physical distance between functions managed, . . .	The *smaller* the span of control should be
Complexity of functions	The greater the complexity of the tasks being managed, . . .	The *smaller* the span of control should be

Planning required for functions	The greater the planning required for tasks being managed, . . .	The *smaller* the span of control should be
Coordination required among functions	The greater the amount of coordination required, . . .	The *smaller* the span of control should be
Skill level of subordinates	The greater the skill level of subordinates, . . .	The *greater* the span of control can be
Need for balance between span of control and number of levels of hierarchy	The greater the need for a flatter organization, . . .	The *greater* the span of control should be

CONFLICTS AMONG ORGANIZING PRINCIPLES

The five principles of organizing—specialization, division of labor, unity of command, scalar chain, and span of control—often contradict one another (Simon 1976). There will always be situations where the adherence to one principle of efficiency will result in violation of a second principle. In these situations, trade-offs will be required across different types of efficiency. To decide which trade-offs to make, return to the overall mission of the organization and determine which principle of efficiency serves this mission most efficiently.

DESIGNING SUBSYSTEMS

Up to this point we have discussed the principles of organizational design in relation to the entire organization. Each of these principles, however, is equally applicable to designing the individual work unit. Recall from the discussion of departmentation that an organization can, and most do, have a mix of organizational structures. In fact, the most effective organizational structures are those that consider the design of each department or work unit, sometimes referred to as a *subsystem,* as well as the coordination among them. This type of approach is referred to as a **contingency approach,** meaning that there is no "one best way" for all circumstances. Rather, managers choose the most appropriate design for each specific situation.

ENVIRONMENT AND TECHNOLOGY

How does a manager know which is the most appropriate subsystem design? Research has shown several important factors to consider. Two of the most important factors, at both the organizational and subsystem levels, are environment and technology. Because research has shown that the effects of environment and technology appear most concretely at the subsystem level, however, we consider these factors in this section. The **environment** includes general influences such as the social, legal, political, and economic environment of the organization, as well as specific influences such as the major organizations and constituencies with which the organization or subsystem interacts. The specific influences are said to compose the task environment.

The organization's environment is often characterized along a continuum of **certainty to uncertainty.** Certain environments have high degrees of predictability and low rates of change. For example, the Internal Revenue Service has a fairly predictable environment that changes rather slowly over time (e.g., there will always be a need for tax collection and monitoring of the tax system). Alternatively, most businesses have more uncertain, less predictable environments, in which changes can occur rapidly. Organizations must be alert to actions by their competitors, government agencies, and consumer advocacy groups, as well as to environmental factors that might affect their performance. For example, think about how quickly Johnson & Johnson's environment changed immediately following the Tylenol scare.

Technology refers to the equipment, knowledge, and work methods that are used to perform the organization's tasks. Like environment, technology can be classified according to the degree of certainty (Thompson 1967).

Long-linked technologies are those that have a fixed sequence of repetitive steps, for which each activity is known and specified in advance. These technologies generally exist in organizations performing very standardized tasks, such as assembly-line production.

Mediating technologies are usually associated with organizations that provide services linking parties together. Examples of organizations that use mediating technologies are real estate agencies that link buyers with sellers and employment agencies that link potential employees with employers. The steps in these technologies are not as fixed as those in long-linked technologies and, therefore, have less certainty.

Finally, **intensive technologies** have the greatest degree of uncertainty as to how to produce the desired outcome. Here individuals with different types of knowledge and skills are necessary to solve problems in order to complete the task. In addition, intensive technologies generally involve high degrees of interdependence across work units—the output of one group becomes the input of the next, and vice versa. Research and development laboratories and hospitals are examples of organizations with intensive technologies.

DIFFERENTIATION AND INTEGRATION

When the environments and technologies within a single organization differ, there is greater need for **differentiation** across departments. That is, departments should be structured differently so that they can approach their tasks differently. Departments can be differentiated according to time, goal, and interpersonal orientation.

1. *Time orientation.* Some tasks, such as paper processing, require a shorter time orientation than others, such as planning or research.

2. *Goal orientation.*   Even when organizations have a single organizational mission, the goals of the individual work units will differ to some degree. For example, organizational units closely associated with the organization's mission pursue different goals than organizational units associated with maintaining the organization's structure (personnel, financial management, etc.).

3. *Interpersonal orientation.*   To the extent that the degree of interdependency among employees varies across organizational tasks, patterns and styles of interaction will differ across work units.

Thus, organizational subsystems that must be more responsive to their environments should be organized to allow for greater response. Organizational subsystems that have more uncertain environments must be organized to allow for greater flexibility and adaptability to sudden changes. And organizational subsystems that have more uncertain technologies should be organized to accommodate the greater need for interaction among people.

Returning for a moment to the organizational level, think about the organizational implications of maintaining a highly differentiated organization. If each subsystem is structured differently, the potential exists for the organization to become a "dis-organization." In fact, the greater the differentiation across units, the greater the need for **integration,** or coordination across units (Lawrence and Lorsch 1967). Various mechanisms are available to the organization to achieve effective integration, ranging from basic tools (such as rules and procedures, referral of problems up the hierarchy, and planning) to more complex tools (such as liaison roles, task forces and interunit teams, and matrix organization designs). An in-depth discussion of these mechanisms is beyond the scope of this chapter. Suffice it to say that rules, procedures, and the referral of problems up the hierarchy tend to work best when the need for integration is low. Alternatively, when departments that are highly differentiated have high needs for integration, task forces, teams, and matrix structures are most effective.

DESIGNING JOBS

Just as departmentation provides the logic for allocating jobs across the organization, **job design** provides the logic for allocating work within the work unit. That is, job designs describe what any individual in a specific job area should be doing.

OBJECTIVE JOB CHARACTERISTICS

Job designs usually focus on three objective characteristics of an individual's work: range, depth, and relationships.

1. **Job range** refers to the number of different activities a person performs; the greater the number of different types of work, the wider the job range is said to be.

2. **Job depth** refers to the amount of control the person has in determining what is to be done and how it is to be done. Jobs that are determined by assignment or environmental demands are said to have low depth; jobs that allow for considerable autonomy in deciding job activities or outcomes are said to have high depth.

3. **Job relationships** refers to the number of people with whom the employee comes in contact and the nature of those interactions. The number of job relationships is determined by the span of control and the degree of interdependence among individual workers.

A variety of techniques exist to measure job range, depth, and relationships. These techniques are called *job analysis* techniques and are generally used for writing job descriptions and in performing *job audits* that examine whether, in fact, the individual is performing the job as it is detailed in the job description.

SUBJECTIVE JOB CHARACTERISTICS

Objective job characteristics describe what people do in performing their jobs. In designing jobs, however, it is also necessary to examine the subjective characteristics of the job, or how the individual perceives the job. The most frequently used approach to measuring the subjective characteristics of a job is the job diagnostics survey (Hackman and Oldham 1975). The survey measures five job characteristics that are said to lead to critical psychological states that influence personal and work outcomes (see Figure 4.4). The five job characteristics are:

1. *Skill variety.*   The degree to which the job requires the individual to perform a wide range of tasks.

2. *Task identity.*   The degree to which the job requires completion of a whole piece of work that employees can identify as resulting from their individual efforts.

3. *Task significance.*   The degree to which the job is seen as having an impact on the lives or work of other people.

4. *Autonomy.*   The degree to which employees have discretion in determining work schedules and procedures.

5. *Feedback.*   The degree to which the job provides employees with clear and direct information about job performance.

As shown in Figure 4.4, these five core job dimensions of work influence employees' internal work motivation, work performance, job satisfaction, absenteeism, and turnover. But that influence is moderated by employees' degree of "employee growth-need strength," or their need for personal accomplishment and individual development. That is, the greater the individual's needs for self-actualization through work, the stronger the influence of the job characteristics on personal and work outcomes.

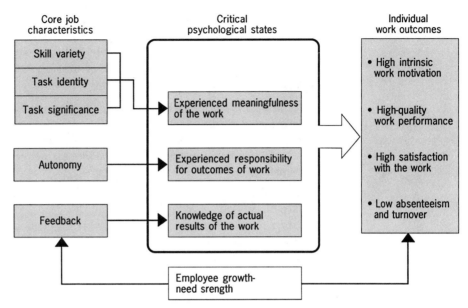

FIGURE 4.4 *Core job characteristics and individual work outcomes in a diagnostic model of job enrichment.* Adapted from: *J. Richard Hackman and Greg R. Oldham, "Development of the Job Diagnostic Survey,"* Journal of Applied Psychology *60 (1975): 161. Copyright © 1975 by the American Psychological Association. Adapted by permission.*

JOB DESIGN STRATEGIES

Over the past 20 years, employment trends have lead organizations to experiment with a variety of job design techniques aimed at increasing both job performance and satisfaction. As workers have begun to expect more from their jobs than a paycheck, strategies for job redesign have focused on changing the subjective characteristics of the job to enhance employees' experiences.

Job Enlargement.   **Job enlargement** increases the skill variety and task identity by redesigning the job to increase its range. Opposite to task specialization, job enlargement requires employees to perform a greater number of tasks, which increases their ability to complete a whole piece of work.

Job Rotation.   Similarly, **job rotation** increases the skill variety by allowing individuals to shift among a variety of tasks, based on some time schedule. Although both job enlargement and job rotation lead to increased skill variety, these job design techniques have been criticized for their limited ability to influence individual and work outcomes. If an employee is performing a boring task, one should not expect to be able to enhance job performance and satisfaction by merely increasing the number of boring tasks.

Job Enrichment.   Alternatively, **job enrichment** has been proposed as a job design technique that can potentially increase all five subjective job characteristics. Whereas job enlargement focuses primarily on job range, job enrichment focuses on range, depth, and relationships. That is, instead of merely increasing the number and variety of job activities, job enrichment practices increase the responsibility and decision making regarding one's work practices, as well as enhance the nature of job relationships with managers, co-workers, and clients.

In a job enrichment project conducted with keypunch operators at the Travelers Insurance Companies, each of the following strategies was implemented (Hackman, Oldham, Janson, and Purdy 1975).

1. *Forming natural work units.* Distributing work according to a logic that is based on work flow and completion of a whole job. By forming natural work groups, jobs potentially have greater task identity and task significance because employees experience their work as a whole, rather than seeing only a small piece.

2. *Establishing client relationships.* Whenever possible, employees should have direct contact with the ultimate user of the product or service provided. Direct contact increases the likelihood of feedback, as well as increasing skill variety and autonomy.

3. *Vertical loading of jobs.* Vertical loading is simply the redesign of jobs so that employees have greater responsibility and control over work schedules, work methods, and quality checks. Vertical loading gives the employee greater discretion over decisions affecting the job and, thus, increases worker autonomy.

4. *Opening feedback channels.* Increasing feedback to employees increases their opportunity to adjust and improve their performance. The more frequent the feedback, the greater the likelihood that job performance will improve. Efforts to open feedback channels should focus on job-provided feedback rather than manager-supplied feedback.

American industry, facing a shortage of skilled labor, is taking job enrichment more seriously than it used to. For example, Lechmere, a retail chain store owned by Dayton Hudson, now offers raises based upon the number of jobs an employee can perform. In 1985, when National Steel lost nearly $150 million, the company struck an agreement with the United Steelworkers Union to consolidate 78 job classifications into 16, and to broaden worker responsibilities and participation. National is again showing very healthy profits, and a more skilled and satisfied work force (Alster 1989, 62–66).

ALLOCATING JOBS ACROSS THE WORK UNIT

Up to this point we have focused on designing jobs in order to allocate work that is performed on a continuous basis. Often work units perform projects that are assigned on a one-time basis. In these cases a team-building technique know as **responsibility charting** (Beckhard and Harris 1977) can also be a useful tool for allocating the work. To create the responsibility chart, the manager needs to make a list of all tasks and activities along the left side of the chart and all employees' names along the top of the chart (see Figure 4.5).

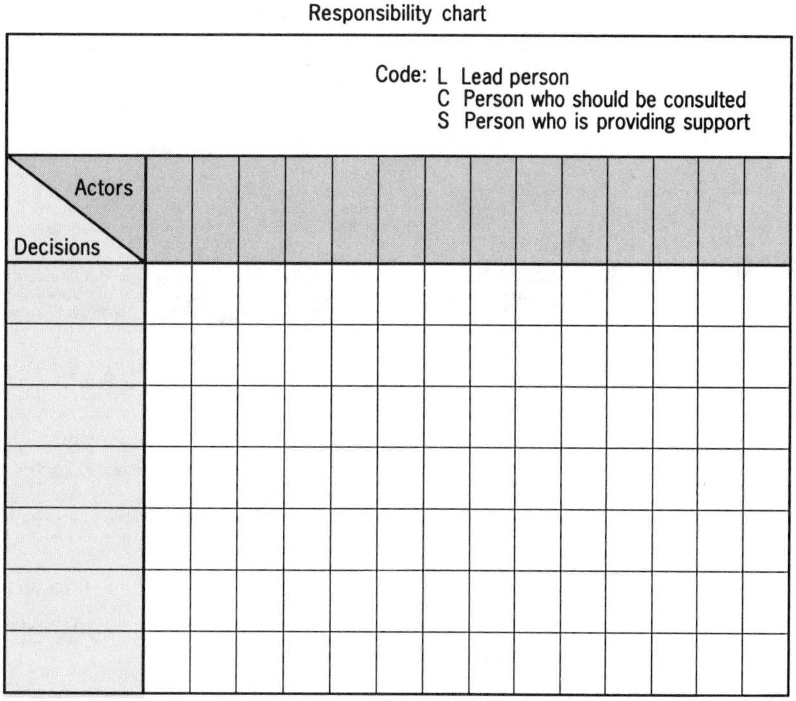

Responsibility chart

Code: L Lead person
C Person who should be consulted
S Person who is providing support

Actors

Decisions

FIGURE 4.5
Responsibility chart.
Adapted from: *R. Beckhard and R. T. Harris,* Organizational Transitions: Managing Complex Change. © 1977, Addison-Wesley Publishing Co., Inc., Reading, Massachusetts. Figure 6.1. Reprinted with permission of the publisher.

When used in team building, the responsibility chart clarifies who is responsible, who needs to be consulted, and who needs to be informed of any particular activity or decision. In allocating work, responsibility charts can be used to clarify who is the lead person on a given task (L), who needs to be consulted (C), and who is providing support (S). By preparing such a chart, the manager can see whether the work is fairly allocated, or whether one person has been assigned all the difficult work whereas others have easier assignments. The manager can also use the chart to monitor employees' opportunities for growth and development through assignment of challenging, new tasks.

ANALYSIS   What's My Job Design?

Directions   Think again about the job that you described in the assessment exercise and examine the job design in terms of the concepts presented in this section. If you have never worked, think of your role as a student as your current job.

1. Describe the job in terms of its range, depth, and relationships.

2. List as many of the component tasks of the job as you can.

3. Describe each of the component tasks in terms of its skill variety, task identity, task significance, autonomy, and feedback.

4. Review the job outcomes of internal work motivation, quality performance, general job satisfaction, absenteeism, and turnover presented in Figure 4.4. How did the five subjective job characteristics described in question 3 affect these outcomes?

PRACTICE   Redesigning Jobs

Directions   For this exercise, work in groups of two. If you described your job as a student, try to find a partner who has held a job in a work organization. Share the results of the previous exercise with your partner. Review the job designs; choose the one that you agree has the greatest need for job redesign, and respond to the following questions.

1. How might you redesign the job to increase the skill variety, the task identity, the task significance, the autonomy, and the feedback?

2. Which of these characteristics seemed easiest to change?

3. Which of these changes would have the strongest impact on employee satisfaction and on employee performance? Why?

4. Which would have the most immediate impact? Why?

5. Which would be the easiest to implement? Which would be the most difficult? Why?

APPLICATION   Identify the Organizational Structure

Identify two organizations with which you are somewhat familiar. Try to identify organizations with very different missions, such as a human service organization and a manufacturing organization. Obtain a copy of each company's organization chart. If they do not have an organization chart, try to interview someone and draw it yourself.

1. Describe the departmentation as presented in each chart.

2. What are the lines of authority presented in the two charts?

3. Choose one subsystem from each of the organizations, and describe the environment of those subsystems. How well does the subsystem structure match the environment?

4. Describe also the technology of those subsystems. How well does the subsystem structure match the technology?

5. What structural changes, if any, would you suggest?

Competency 3 Controlling

ASSESSMENT   In and Out of Control

Directions   Make a list of 5 to 10 areas in your life where you feel that you are in total control. Make a second list of 5 to 10 areas in your life where you feel that you are somewhat in control. Finally, make a third list of 5 to 10 areas in your life where you feel that you have no control. Then respond to the following questions.

1. How easy or difficult was it for you to identify areas in your life where you are in total control and somewhat in control? What does *control* mean to you in these cases?

2. How easy or difficult was it for you to identify areas in your life where you feel you have no control? What does *control* mean to you in these cases?

3. Why do you think it is important for individuals to feel that they are in control?

4. Why do you think it is important for organizations to have controls?

5. What similarities and differences do you see in your answers to questions 3 and 4.

Interpretation   We all have situations in our lives in which we feel more or less in control. Sometimes we feel controlled by others. In some cases we actively resist control, as when we drive faster than the posted speed limit. In order to understand organizational controls, it is important to also understand how individuals react to these controls. As you read through this chapter, think about your responses to this exercise and about your personal response to control.

LEARNING   Controlling

Thus far in this chapter we have discussed planning ("where we are going and how best to get there") and organizing (the mechanisms "to get you where you plan to go"). Now we are ready to complete the cycle and focus on controlling as a process that tells you "whether or not you actually got there." In maintaining the continuity and stability of the organization, the coordinator uses control as a mechanism that provides feedback, which tells you if you have met the goals set in planning. As you will see in Chapter 5, controlling is also part of the monitor role. We begin the discussion of control here, however, so that we may put it in the context of the planning-organizing-controlling cycle.

In point of fact, control is more than a process for determining whether actual performance is consistent with planned performance and whether the organization or work unit has reached its goals. It is also a process for analyzing the discrepancies between planned and actual performance so that future organizational plans and processes can be modified to better meet organizational needs. In fact, the most effective control systems focus on the future, as well as on the past and present.

Implementing and maintaining organizational control systems are often considered to be the more uncomfortable jobs of the manager. Although we recognize the necessity of control in the work unit, we often hesitate to exercise direct control over employees. This is partly because, as individuals, we identify with the human desire for autonomy, as well as with the tendency to resist control. Nevertheless, the effective functioning of all organizations depends on the appropriate institution of control systems.

THE BASICS OF CONTROL

Before we look at organizational control systems, let us look for a moment at one of the most basic control systems with which most people are familiar: the thermostat. Thermostats operate by measuring the room temperature and comparing room temperature against a preset desired temperature. When there is a sufficient discrepancy between desired and actual room temperature, the thermostat acts to correct this discrepancy by turning on the heating or cooling system. Moreover, the thermostat continues to compare desired room temperature against actual room temperature, and when the discrepancy has been reduced, the thermostat turns off the heating or cooling system and the cycle is started anew.

From this example we can define the four basic steps necessary to all control systems.

1. *Setting performance objectives or standards.* Control systems must start with some agreed-upon standard of performance. In the case of the thermostat, the desired temperature is a standard indicating a level of comfort. Similarly, in organizations it is necessary to set objectives or standards that indicate an expected level of performance.

2. *Measuring actual performance.* Once you have set a standard, it is necessary to see if actual performance meets this standard. In the case of the thermostat, the actual room temperature is measured. In organizations, depending on our objective, there may be a variety of ways to measure performance.

3. *Comparing actual performance against objectives or standards.* By comparing actual performance against objectives or standards, you can determine whether action is necessary to correct the discrepancy. In the case of the thermostat, action is not taken until the discrepancy is sufficient to warrant action. Similarly, in organizations we must decide how large a discrepancy can be tolerated before corrective action should be taken.

4. *Taking appropriate action.* When the discrepancy between objectives or standards and actual performance exceeds a tolerable level, we must determine what is the appropriate action to take. In the case of the thermostat,

corrective action simply involves turning the heating or cooling system on or off. In organizations we must first determine whether the discrepancy is positive or negative (i.e., whether actual performance is greater than or less than standards or objectives). When performance is less than the standard, corrective action is required; when performance exceeds the standard, it is important to understand why this situation occurred and determine whether objectives and standards should be set at a higher level.

Often performance can be measured in a variety of ways. Sometimes, these performance measures will conflict with each other, such as when reduced costs result in decreased quality. In taking corrective action or deciding whether to set new, higher standards, it is necessary to consider these potential conflicts. Thus, if performance, measured in terms of quantity, exceeds the standard during a given time period, it may be necessary to examine performance in terms of quality before considering adjusting the standard.

IDENTIFYING CRITICAL CONTROL POINTS

In establishing control systems, it is necessary to decide what will be measured, where in the process it will be measured, how often will measurements be examined, and who will be responsible for taking corrective action.

What will be measured? One of the basic rules of establishing control systems is to ensure that the systems be appropriate, adequate, and economical (Haimann, Scott, and Connor 1978). Thus, in deciding what to measure, it is necessary to examine the expected costs, both monetary and nonmonetary, of establishing a control system, as well as the expected improved performance and the expected consequences of not establishing such a system.

Where in the process will it be measured? All organizational systems have three components: inputs, transformational processes, and outputs. Inputs are the human and material resources available to the organization. Transformational processes are the functions that employees perform in order to create the outputs, or products and services of the organization. Control systems can be established in any of these components.

Control systems that focus on inputs are referred to as **feedforward** systems. These systems are preventive in nature and are designed to reduce the probability of discrepancies between actual outcome performance and standards. In universities, admissions procedures are feedforward control systems. They only allow into the system those students who are expected to pass. Similarly, work organizations use hiring procedures to increase the probability that employees will be able to perform their jobs.

Control systems that focus on transformational processes are referred to as **concurrent** systems. These systems are also preventive in nature. The focus here, however, is on monitoring the transformation process and attempting to predict the outcome if the system continues on its current path.

There are two types of concurrent systems: steering controls and yes/no controls. Steering controls monitor performance continuously and attempt to improve performance in process. Airplane pilots use steering controls to keep planes on course. Similarly, managers who regularly provide employees with information regarding their performance are using steering controls. Yes/no controls monitor performance at specific points in the process and determine whether or not the process can continue. Safety and health inspections, or accreditation procedures that could potentially result in the closing of a facility, are considered to be yes/no controls. Both steering and yes/no controls are designed to identify errors and correct them before they are compounded.

Control systems that focus on outputs are referred to as **feedback** systems. Feedback systems are used to document past performance, most often in order to plan for the future. When students evaluate a course at its completion, they are giving the professor feedback on how well he or she has done in teaching the course, with the expectation that the professor will use this information in planning future courses. When employees receive annual performance evaluations, they are getting feedback about their past performance, with an expectant eye towards what improvements need to be made over the next evaluation period.

How often will measurements be examined? Depending on the specific performance measure, and the type of control system, performance can be measured on a continuous basis or at fixed intervals. As in the case of deciding what should be measured, the frequency of measurement should be decided based on what is adequate and economical. Often it would not be possible to measure each unit, because the act of measurement ruins the product. For example, in order to measure the quality of food served at fast food restuarants, it is necessary to *sample;* that is, examine only a few meals according to some preset schedule.

Who will be responsible for taking corrective action? Often discrepancies between actual performance and objectives or standards can be handled according to an existing rule or procedure. The principle of **management by exception** states that managerial attention should only be drawn to cases of severe discrepancy; that is, only in situations that cannot be handled by the person at the next lowest level of the hierarchy.

EXAMPLES OF ORGANIZATIONAL CONTROL SYSTEMS

In the previous section we raised the question of what should be measured. That is, in what areas is it appropriate for an organization to implement a control system? The answer is simple: Anywhere an organization is interested in measuring performance it should consider implementing a control system. Here we discuss briefly three of the most common types of control systems: performance appraisal systems, financial control systems, and information systems.

Performance appraisal systems are designed to formally evaluate individual performance and to provide feedback to employees so that performance adjustments can be made. Performance appraisal systems often include guidelines for providing both formal and informal feedback, as well as procedures for dealing with employees whose performance does not improve after receiving feedback. In implementing a performance appraisal system, special attention should be paid to make sure that all employees using the system understand the intent, as well as the procedures, of the system.

Financial control systems are designed to evaluate an organization's financial status. *Budgets* are generally considered to be feedforward controls; they indicate what the organization intends to spend. *Financial analyses,* such as financial statements and ratio analyses, are generally considered to be concurrent controls; they focus on how money is being spent and project the financial condition of the organization. Finally, *audits* are generally considered to be feedback controls; they verify that money has been spent according to the budget and that financial statements accurately reflect the flow of financial resources.

Information systems are designed to collect, store, and distribute data in a manner that is useful for decision making. Information systems support other control systems, such as performance appraisal and financial control systems, by providing the mechanism to track data. In addition, other organizational information, such as time and attendance records, inventory records, and service records, may be tracked through these systems. Today, virtually all information systems are computer-based, allowing large amounts of data to be accessed by many people for many different reasons. In designing centralized computer-based information systems, organizations need to pay special attention to the unique needs of different organizational units. That is, systems should be designed to provide information in a way that is useful to those who need and receive the information.

For example, Toyota grew impatient with the slow pace of information between its dealers and its plants, so it created direct computer links to dealers. The company now modifies its production schedule based on daily demand changes. This rich and rapid information flow helps Toyota reduce the costs of large inventories (Ernst 1989, 39).

HUMAN REACTIONS TO CONTROL

Control systems will only work if those people who have the responsibility for implementing the systems have the ability and willingness to carry through. The best performance appraisal systems in the world will not work if they are not properly explained to the managers who must evaluate their employees. Similarly, information systems designed to monitor organizational performance will not work if employees, either intentionally or unintentionally, report incorrect information.

Employees may resist control systems for several reasons. First, they may resent the very act of measurement because they feel it places restraints on their behaviors and limits their ability to act autonomously. Second, employees may disagree with performance standards. They may feel that standards are arbitrary or irrelevant to their actual job performance. Often professionals feel that their performance can only be evaluated subjectively, and that objective standards of performance cannot adequately represent their performance expectations.

A third reason employees, including managers, may resist control systems is that they are defensive about their performance. Individuals may feel that their performance is acceptable and resist being evaluated or having their unit's performance evaluated; they may also disagree with the evaluation. This problem may be magnified when information is available to a manager through a centralized system. Here individuals may feel that the information presented to the manager does not tell the full story and, therefore, is not an adequate representation of individual or work-unit performance.

When employees resist control systems, they are likely to find ways to "get around the system." In some cases, employees will falsify reports or provide inaccurate information about how a task was performed. In other cases, employees may work to the specific standards, rather than work to optimal performance. When performance is only measured along a few dimensions, employees may focus their efforts on those dimensions and ignore other aspects of performance. The shift of focus from organizational or work-unit goals and objectives to the specific aspects of performance that are measured by the control system is referred to as *goal displacement.* Earlier we mentioned the possibility of quality being sacrificed for quantity. If a control system only measures quantity, employees resisting controls will likely focus only on quantity and ignore the quality aspects of their job.

GUIDELINES FOR ESTABLISHING EFFECTIVE CONTROL SYSTEMS

Will control systems always be resisted by employees? Not necessarily. When appropriately designed and implemented, employees will understand the necessity for measuring and evaluating performance. Moreover, when appropriately given, employees often welcome the feedback and the opportunity to learn how to do their jobs better. The following five guidelines can be used for establishing effective control systems.

1. *Wherever possible, control systems should be designed and implemented with employee involvement.* Make certain that employees understand how the system works and what it is supposed to accomplish. Employees should see the control system as worth their effort, rather than as an imposition or negative reflection of their current performance.

2. *Make sure the system focuses on results, rather than on the act of measurement.* Focus on the goals of the organization, and measure as many dimensions of performance as necessary to accurately provide information. Be

sure that the actions to correct discrepancies between actual and desired performance do not contradict organizational goals.

3. *Keep the system as simple as possible.*   Although this guideline may seem to contradict the previous one, remember that a control system should be worth the resources invested in the system. If greater resources are used to measure performance than are the monetary and nonmonetary benefits received from having the system, the organization may want to reconsider establishing such a system.

4. *Make sure the system provides timely information.*   Feedback should provide information that can be used to correct performance. Feedback that is provided too late for action is as good as no feedback at all. For this reason, feedforward and concurrent controls should be implemented, wherever possible and appropriate.

5. *Control systems should be flexible.*   Control systems should be designed to serve the organization and its employees, not vice versa. On both a long-term and short-term basis, systems should be implemented to allow for human judgment. In the short term, they should allow for human input to adjust to specific, exceptional, or unique circumstances. In the long term, they should allow for system adjustments as organizations change and adapt to new and different general circumstances.

ANALYSIS   Computers, People, and the Delivery of Services

Directions   Because of an ever-increasing need for information, computers and management information systems have become common phenomena in organizations. It is important that we know how to develop and manage them rather than have them manage us. At several points in this activity, you will be instructed to stop reading and respond to the questions before proceeding with the case.[1]

A Call for Help   One year ago Brenda Tybe, the director of a university computer services center, received a call from Paul Powers, an executive in charge of evaluation at the local United Way office. He described a meeting he had just had with the directors of various neighborhood centers which they fund. In the meeting, the directors had complained about their paperwork: They fill out forms for United Way, for government agencies, and for other funding sources. Paul suggested the possibility of setting up a consolidated information system. For years he had been trying to obtain good performance data for evaluation. He was excited about the prospect of having a consistent set of objective measures for all the centers so that they could compile longitudinal data and measure changes over time. This would make it possible to link funding to performance. Paul thought,

[1]*Adapted from* Quinn, Robert E. "Computers, People, and the Delivery of Services," © Professional Development Program, Rockefeller College, University of Albany, State University of New York. Reprinted with permission.

"Everyone wins: The directors cut back on paperwork, and we get greater control." Having heard that Brenda was the best person in the region to contact for advice, he called to see if she would set the system up for them.

Stop Reading   Respond to the following questions.

1. Given this brief description of the situation, what would be your concerns if you were the director of one of the neighborhood centers?
2. How likely is it that the directors see the situation differently than Paul does? What are those differences?

Back to the Case   Brenda indicated that she was interested, and a week later she and Paul met with the directors of eight neighborhood centers. She noted that each center had its unique variety of funding sources, and each director was inundated with a different set of paperwork. Still there were a number of similarities; although their services varied widely, they usually included housing, employment, food, clothing, child care, and referrals.

During the discussion, Brenda explained what might be done to reduce the paperwork. She noted that many of the forms, as well as the current narrative reports written by the caseworkers could be reduced to a few standardized forms. From that information, the computer could produce summaries that would eliminate 80% of the paperwork the directors were doing. The presentation generated considerable enthusiasm, and it was agreed that Brenda's staff would begin to wade through the numerous forms used in each of the centers.

Stop Reading   Respond to the following questions.

1. The directors did not raise any concerns in this meeting. What concerns do you think they may have?
2. When the directors present the concept of an information system to their caseworkers, what do you think their reactions will be? Why?

Back to the Case   For the next five months, Brenda's staff conducted over 100 interviews with people at all levels of the eight centers, gathered forms that were currently in use, and sorted and analyzed them. Before beginning the design of a set of standardized forms, they interviewed each of the eight center directors at least twice, for the purpose of presenting initial findings and determining the exact information needs of the directors. Shortly thereafter, Brenda held a staff meeting, during which the project director, Dick Strauss raised some serious concerns.

"Brenda, I've worked on this project for five months and frankly I don't think the center directors have the slightest idea what's happening. They don't seem to understand the first thing about information systems.

"We go in and ask what information they need. They get a shocked look on their face, like they never had thought of such a question. They hem and haw. We try a different tack and ask them what decisions they have to make. Again they are shocked. They have no vision of what an information system is or what it might do for them. No matter how many times we go back, they still cannot deal with the questions we need answered. Whenever we are around, the directors disappear. It's like we have a tacit agreement—we don't bother them with questions and they don't bother us with objections; we show them the forms and they look at them and say 'okay.'"

Stop Reading   Respond to the following questions.

1. What do you think about Dick's assessment of the directors and their behavior? What do you think their behavior indicates?
2. What very valuable information is Dick giving to Brenda in this dialogue? What can she do about it?
3. If you were Brenda, how would you respond to Dick's assertions in front of your staff? What would you recommend that Brenda do next?

Back to the Case   Two months later, all the forms were prepared and the system was ready for a trial run. Brenda met with the directors to discuss the forms and select several sites for the pretest. After presenting the forms, Brenda asked for questions. When no one responded, she pressed the group. Finally, one of the directors raised a concern which took Brenda by surprise.

"You developed all these forms but what about confidentiality? How are the rights of the clients going to be protected? What if the police want the information that is on these forms?"

The question ignited the group, and many specific questions were asked. Finally Brenda agreed to summarize a description of the system on paper, sending them a memo before meeting with them again.

Stop Reading   Respond to the following questions.

1. What do you think of the issue of confidentiality raised by one of the directors? Do you think this is his only concern?
2. What concerns might the directors feel constrained not to express? Why?
3. What advice do you have for Brenda on the content of the memo?

Back to the Case   As promised, Brenda sent the following memo to the directors:

MEMORANDUM
TO: Center Directors and Paul Powers
FROM: Dr. Brenda Tybe, Executive Director,
             University Computer Services Center
SUBJECT: Nature and Purpose of the Information System

I am sending this memo to summarize what the computer system will be like when it is fully implemented this summer.

The purpose of the computer-based information system is: (1) to provide relevant data which will permit each center to conduct an internal audit of its overall performance and (2) to supply summarized data to a central system that will monitor the community change process. The audit information can assist administrators in better understanding their clientele, allowing them to make needed management decisions and evaluate properly the agency's performance. The central system data will provide management reports to show whether or not objectives are being achieved satisfactorily.

The information system will document client involvement with each center, including client registration, service rendered, change in status of the client, and so on.

The computer service center will provide printouts of overall center operations on a regular basis, along with a weekly printout of new client information. When the system is fully operational, center directors, the United Way, and other funding sources, will be able to assess, on a weekly basis, information concerning: (1) the number of clients registered by each center; (2) the major needs of these clients; (3) basic demographic information on each client; (4) the number of referrals made by each center and how long they took, along with the mode and disposition of referrals; (5) the number of clients served by the agency, the type of service, and the length of contact; and (6) the number of clients receiving casework services, the number of times served, the date of each, and problems.

Careful attention will be given to the training of center staff by computer center employees on how to use the system. Because of the confidential nature of the information, completed forms turned over to the computer service center will, of course, not be available to unauthorized persons.

Stop Reading   Respond to the following questions.

1. If you were a director, how would you react to this memo? How would you respond?
2. Do you think that Brenda is yet aware of the possible concerns of the directors? Why?

The Case Concludes   Much to Brenda's surprise, several weeks passed with absolutely no response to the memo, although computer service center staff complained that the directors were less cooperative than ever. Brenda was baffled. Finally at one meeting she reached her breaking point. As Glenn Morgan, one of the directors, complained about confidentiality, Brenda angrily interrupted, "I am tired of hearing that nonsense! We have addressed this issue and have clearly indicated that no unauthorized persons will have access to confidential information. Glenn, I have been at your center a dozen times. Files on clients are lying out on the desks, file drawers are not locked, and a kid could unlock the front door with a hairpin. Do you call that protecting confidentiality? Your people cannot find files when they need them. Half of your workers don't keep their narratives up to date. Most of you can't get a single accurate statistic on what your center is doing. The computerized system will provide information you never had before and will be 10 times safer than the information you have on clients now!"

Brenda's outburst was met with silence and a motion to adjourn the meeting. Brenda and Paul sat down to talk.

Brenda: Paul, I just don't get it. This is very frustrating. Their arguments about confidentiality just do not make sense.

Paul: You know, Brenda, I have been puzzling over this for months, and the more I think about it, the more I think that the issue is not confidentiality at all. Confidentiality may just be a smoke screen. They initially responded well to the reduction of paperwork and other benefits, but as indicated from the beginning, I gain a lot of control. With one sheet I can compare how they are doing—so can other funding sources. This must terrify the directors. For years they have been able to get their funds by showing pictures of handicapped kids in rags. Now we are actually going to assess their performance.

Brenda: Paul, I think you're on the right track. Why didn't we see this before? All of the resistance is not to the computerized system per se, but to what can be done with the information, and to their losing control. I don't blame them.

Paul: If they had just spoken up earlier in the process, it would have saved a lot of time and money.

Brenda: They couldn't have spoken up! You sponsored this project. They probably felt that speaking up would jeopardize their future funding as much as the implementation of the system.

Paul: That's a good point, Brenda. Now the burning question is, what do we do now?

Discussion Questions
1. Do you think that Brenda and Paul have an accurate view of the situation now? What were the barriers to their developing this view earlier? How could these barriers have been avoided?
2. What is your response to Paul's final question: What do we do now? Be specific.
3. Assume that the concluding section transpired *before* the memo was written. Rewrite Brenda's memo in light of this new awareness.
4. What conclusions can you draw on the issue of control and resistance to control as a result of this case?

PRACTICE   Instituting a Control System

Directions   In the previous exercise, the information system was resisted by the center directors. In this exercise you will work in groups of five to seven students to design a basic information system that would meet their needs.

Choose one person to play the role of Paul Powers, and one person to play the role of Brenda Tybe. The rest of the group should play the roles of the different center directors. As you design the information system, think about the guidelines for establishing effective control systems discussed in this chapter.

After you have designed the system, discuss the following questions in your group.

Discussion Questions
1. How were Paul Power's needs met? How much control will he have under the system?
2. How were each of the center director's needs met? How much control will they have under the system?
3. What was the role of Brenda Tybe in your role play? Did anyone feel that Brenda was taking sides? Why or why not?
4. Which of the guidelines for establishing an effective control system were easiest to include in the design? Which were most difficult?
5. If you were actually living the roles you played, what would the next step be for each of you?

APPLICATION Check Your Organizational Control

Choose an organization with which you have some familiarity. You may want to choose one of the organizations you studied in the application exercise in the previous section on organizing, or the organization where you work. Identify several control systems used in that organization, and choose one for further exploration. Write a three- to five-page paper describing this control system. Include in your paper:

1. A description of how the control system works and how effective it is.

2. A discussion of how the system was implemented and what, if any, modifications have been made to the system since its implementation.

3. A suggestion for improving the system and an action plan for implementing the change.

REFERENCES

Alster, Norm. "What Flexible Workers Can Do," *Fortune* (February 13, 1989): 62–66.

Beckhard, R., and R. T. Harris. *Organizational Transition: Managing Complex Change.* Reading, Mass.: Addison-Wesley, 1977.

Business Month "Reeducation of a Company Man," *Business Month* (October, 1989): 78–80.

Doran, George. "There's a SMART Way to Write Management's Goals and Objectives," *Management Review* (November 1981).

Ernst, R. G. "Why Automating Isn't Enough." The *Journal of Business Strategy* (May/June 1989): 37–42.

Hackman, J. Richard, and Greg Oldham. "Development of the Job Diagnostic Survey," *Journal of Applied Psychology* 60 (1975): 159–170.

Hackman, J. Richard, Greg Oldham, Robert Janson, and Kenneth Purdy. "A New Strategy for Job Enrichment," *California Management Review* 17(4) (1975): 57–71.

Haimann, Theo, and Raymond L. Hilgert. *Supervision: Concepts and Practices of Management.* Cincinnati, Ohio: South-Western, 1972.

Haimann, Theo, William G. Scott, and Patrick E. Connor. *Managing the Modern Organization.* Boston: Houghton Mifflin, 1978.

Ivancevich, John M., and Michael T. Matteson. *Organizational Behavior and Management,* Plano, Texas: Business Publications, Inc., 1987.

Jelinek, Mariann. "Organization Structure: The Basic Conformations." In Mariann Jelinek, Joseph A. Litterer, and Raymond E. Miles (eds.), *Organizations by Design: Theory and Practice.* pp. 253–265. Plano, Texas: Business Publications, Inc., 1981.

Kerzner, Harold. *Project Management: A Systems Approach to Planning, Scheduling, and Controlling.* New York: Van Nostrand–Reinhold, 1984.

Koontz, Harold, and Cyril O'Donnell. *Essentials of Management.* New York: McGraw-Hill, 1978.

Kupfer, Andrew. "Bob Allen Rattles Cages at AT&T," *Fortune* (June 19, 1989): 58–65.

Lawrence, Paul R., and Jay W. Lorsch. *Organization and Environment: Managing Differentiation and Integration.* Boston: The Division of Research, Graduate School of Business Administration, Harvard University, 1967.

Peters, Tom. *Thriving on Chaos.* New York: Harper & Row, 1987.

Schermerhorn, John R., Jr. *Management for Productivity.* New York: John Wiley & Sons, 1989.

Simmons, John "The Painful Reeducation of a Company Man," *Business Month* (October, 1989): 78–80.

Simon, Herbert A. *Administrative Behavior.* New York: The Free Press, 1976.

Smith, Adam. *The Wealth of Nations* (1776). New York: Random House, 1937.

Szilagyi, Andrew D., Jr. *Management and Performance.* Glenview, Ill.: Scott, Foresman, 1988.

Thompson, James D. *Organizations in Action.* New York: McGraw-Hill, 1967.

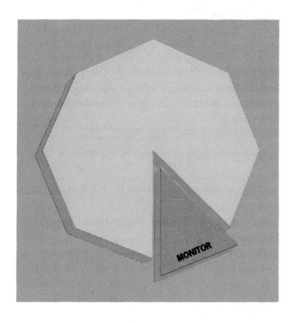

COMPETENCIES
- **Reducing Information Overload**
- **Analyzing Information with Critical Thinking**
- **Presenting Information; Writing Effectively**

THE MONITOR ROLE

*O*f the eight roles described in the competing values model, the monitor role may at first seem the least exciting. But the monitor's tasks cannot be ignored in any organization, or any career. In Chapter 1 we described the monitor's role as "knowing what's going on in the work unit." Monitors watch the vital signs of the work unit and also keep track of their own work. The expert monitor has a clear sense of what is more important and what can be done later.

Believe it or not, many organizations flounder or die because people *simply lose track* of what's going on within the organization. No matter how well a company manages innovation and fosters creativity and teamwork, it still needs to know about and control its operations.

More and more, we are bombarded with all sorts of information, the trivial with the important. Without a system and some principles to help sort it out, you may not be able to wade through the insignificant stuff to find the information you need, when you need it. So the first task a monitor must undertake is information management—setting up a system that:

1. Sorts and channels the information you need, but filters out most of what is unnecessary.

2. Organizes that information into a meaningful form that allows you to plan, make decisions, and present what you think is most important.

That's why the <u>monitor role, which falls into the internal process model</u> of management, is so important. The monitor is responsible for knowing what is actually going on in a work unit. Managers in this role must be able to keep track of the facts, analyze them, and decide which are important. Detail work? Yes. But the payoffs can be big. Some of the best things happening today in quality control, strategic planning, and innovation focus on detail, thousands of details: trying to make a hundred small improvements rather than the one sweeping change that will revolutionize the field (Imai 1986).

How do you make those hundred small improvements? By observing the way things work and asking simple but powerful questions like:

- Where does our work really come from?

- What are our major sources of error and inefficiency?

- If people in my unit could change one thing about our processes, what would that be?

- Of all the mistakes we make, which are insignificant?

- Which mistakes can we not afford to make?

- Exactly how do we know how well we're doing as a work unit?

We'll look at how a monitor operates in three core competencies:

Competency 1   Reducing Information Overload
Competency 2   Analyzing Information with Critical Thinking
Competency 3   Presenting Information; Writing Effectively

Competency 1 Reducing Information Overload

ASSESSMENT   Are You in Information Overload?

Directions   No matter what your work experience, paper probably plays a major role in your daily life. Certainly much of your experience in school has been played out on paper. Think of the forms and records that have followed you to your current situation; think of the handouts and exams, the course outlines, and the book reports. Think of the notes you passed around in the fifth grade—the paper that contained the really vital information. Consider these questions:

1. Has the amount of paper and documents with which you've been confronted at school, work, and in your personal life increased or decreased over the past three years?

2. Do you feel you have become more skillful in sorting, storing, transmitting, and using information via paper?

3. What would you most like to change about the way you handle paper?

4. As a student, what are your major sources of overload in managing information via paper? What can you do about the overload?

Depending on the kind of organization for which you end up working, the paper chase can become even more intense when you leave school.

In the 1970s there was a lot of talk about how computers would create the "paperless" office. Twenty years later we're still talking about it, and in some cases we're closer to making it a reality. Nevertheless, most offices are buried deeper than ever in paper. Procedures, regulations, and office politics all require us to put something in writing, and then put that something into a file—just in case.

We've also been overloaded with the amount of information being generated through databases and electronic systems. The marketers of databases, business journals, computer-based search services, and software want us to believe that we'll be completely uninformed without their million bits of information each morning. The challenge is not in gathering more information but doing a better job of sorting, delimiting, and retrieving information.

That is why most discussions of time management focus so much on paper management.

Unfortunately, much of the information glut in businesses is seen as an American export. Since World War II, American firms have prided themselves on their use of scientific management principles, sophisticated accounting systems, and exhaustive marketing research, but such procedures sometimes stifle innovation and tie the hands of managers with fresh ideas. Don McCrickard of TSB Bank, a major European firm, began his career with American Express's European subsidiary, Amex. McCrickard pushed hard for greater flexibility with the American Express credit card, wanting to allow customers to make payments over a period of time. Amex researched the idea, and proposed a new, flexible payment card, but the idea went nowhere. It was lost on a paper trail of memos, market research and feasibility studies. By the time McCrickard's idea, the Optima Card, was launched, other companies had a big head start in Europe (Guterl 1989, 64).

Now with TSB Bank, McCrickard says many of the big ideas can be launched in months instead of years. For example, TSB decided to try McCrickard's idea of offering mortgages in partnership with life insurance companies. They realized that studying the idea would be about as expensive as trying the idea. They approved the plan, bought the necessary hardware, and trained the people immediately. Within four months they had brought in $3 billion in new mortgages (Guterl 1989, 64).

THE TRAF SYSTEM

Here's a simple but powerful method for processing paper. It's called the TRAF system (think of traffic) (Winston 1983, 40). The benefit of "traffing" is that it forces you to *do something* with every piece of paper that hits your desk. Traffing is the remedy for doing nothing with the same piece of paper many times.

Imagine that you receive in the morning mail a copy of a report from a quality control committee. This report is being circulated to all departments. The document looks interesting, but you're too busy to read it now. You're not even sure why it came to you, but you're intrigued enough to keep it. The quarterly report from the design unit comes with it along with some advertising copy on new office equipment. There's a memo from the vice president for operations on the increase in shop floor accidents. The invitation to the design unit's holiday party is an R.S.V.P., and this list of training films that must be previewed before the end of the month is still stuck on your desk. There are four signed contracts being returned for your final approval, a memo requesting agenda items for the next staff meeting, and a sign-up sheet for the next blood drive.

What do you do with all this stuff? Traffing gives you four options:

1. *Toss* papers into the wastebasket if they are not immediately valuable. Most of us are too conservative when deciding which things to save.

2. *Refer* papers to other people (secretary, staff, colleagues). You should probably set up files for the people you refer things to most. If you're not using routing slips, start immediately. If you're writing a little note on each piece of paper you refer, you're wasting time.

3. *Act* by putting papers requiring your personal action (for example, writing a response letter or a brief report) in an action box or folder.

4. *File* documents by indicating *on the document itself* the name of the file into which it should go. Put the paper in a box or file labeled "to file." Keep in mind that reading, in terms of this system, is a form of acting. If a document takes more than five minutes to read, put it in the "act" box. Don't let reading short-circuit your traffing, or you'll never get the papers sorted.[1]

Make a clear distinction between traffing and acting, and schedule time for doing both. Another tip: *Handle each piece of paper only once.* If you have the habit of taking a paper out of your in-basket, looking at it, and returning it to the same place, start using the "freckle method." Tap your pen point on the paper every time you look at or handle it. If a paper starts getting "freckled," you'll know you're wasting a lot of time fussing with it, and it's time to trash it, refer it, or act on it.

FILING

Having good habits of tracking and transmitting information is not sufficient to make a good manager, but the lack of these competencies can get in the way of your abilities. Unfortunately, "Personal Organization 101" isn't offered in

[1]*Reprinted from The Organized Executive, A Program for Productivity: New Ways to Manage Time, Paper, and People,* by Stephanie Winston, by permission of W. W. Norton & Company, Inc. Copyright © 1983 by Stephanie Winston.

school, so we need to learn on our own. This section shares some advice taught by the experts and learned through experience.

Ninety percent of the problems we have with personal filing systems revolve around three problems:

Problem 1   Creating a system but no logical method to go with it. This leads to the "now where have I filed . . ." syndrome.

Problem 2   Establishing a decent system, but not keeping up with it. If you have more than 10 or 12 pieces of paper sitting in your "to be filed" box, you're already losing control of your system, even if it's a good one.

Problem 3   Filing in perpetuity. Documents that were vital in 1985 might be discarded in 1991 with impunity. The question to ask yourself in deciding whether to file something is not, "will I ever need this again," but "what's the worst that could happen if I throw this out?" (Eisenberg 1986, 44–45).[2]

In order to set up your own filing system, think about the major categories your system would need and what kind of folders and labels your desk and other drawers can accommodate. You'll need to do some experimenting as well as an "audit" from time to time to throw away the papers you haven't looked at for a year or two. Now let's look at three necessary tools for making a record-keeping system complete: the tickler file, a calendar, and a note-keeping system.

The tickler file is a system you set up to "tickle" your memory on projects and deadlines. The simplest method is to create a file for each working day of the week, and one file for each month of the year. If you take work home with you a lot, you might want to create a weekend file as well. That's 18 files total.

The other tools, a calendar and a note-keeping system, can be combined into a planner or kept separate. Planners that provide sections for note taking, addresses and phone numbers, and other important information are becoming increasingly important. More and more students are being asked by interviewers if they keep planners, and how they use their system. Regardless of what system you use, you must also have a way of keeping notes.

THAT'S NOT WHAT WE DECIDED   Taking Good Notes

Dates alone are not sufficient for handling routine information. You need concise but adequately detailed notes to yourself as well. The details of events quickly fade from memory. Good notes can help you avoid serious misunderstandings about who was committed or assigned to do what, or what transactions actually took place and when. The expert monitor can open to a log book with a date on the top right corner that reads, "Reserved five rooms for Quality Control

---

[2]*From Organize Yourself* by Ronni Eisenberg, p. 44. Copyright © 1986 by Ronni Eisenberg and Kate Kelly. Reprinted with permission of MacMillan Publishing Company.

Conference. Reservation # 032266." When the hotel clerk tells you that he's very sorry, but your group has not reserved the room, your log book becomes scripture. You can reply, "I called you on November 18 and made the reservations through David Wise. Here's the reservation number." Sometimes the faintest ink is better than the sharpest memory.

Part of the problem with note taking is grounded in status anxiety. In our society, taking notes is often identified with taking dictation and performing clerical services for someone else. But your own information system revolves around the notes you take, not the notes someone else gives you. Expert monitors are first concerned about monitoring themselves.

Most of the notes you will take will be from meetings or from phone conversations. It's smart to make a few notes of phone conversations. Note the date, the gist of the conversation, and any action items for you or anyone else. For example:

> *Nov. 19. Called Gary W. about lab design. He will contact architect* before next briefing. *I have to forward plans to treatment team before briefing. They respond by Dec. 10, or we live with the plan forever.*

Meetings are of course more complex. An important part of meeting management is note taking. Here's a simple plan that works well. Track the primary features of the meeting by separating your paper into quadrants. Figure 5.1 shows how the paper would look.

The note-taking format shown in Figure 5.1 will help you prepare for meetings and keep track of the transactions, assignments, and dynamics. For example, you should know before going into a meeting what you plan to actually present (top left quadrant). In the bottom left quadrant, note what you're assigned to do during the course of the meeting, but also note what *others* have been handed. People often do not remember these things in the same way. When the cry goes up, "That's not what we decided!" you'll have your notes to refer to. In the bottom right quadrant under "For my information" you can take personal notes on the dynamics of the meeting. Don't assume you'll remember

Subject _____
Present _____   Date _____

Presentation items: Calendar items:
   (Items you plan to present at the
   meeting.)

Action items: For my information:
   (The things you are assigned to do,   (Nonaction information items, per-
   and what other people are to do as   sonal impressions and so forth.)
   well.)

FIGURE 5.1 *A simple note-taking format.*

all these things. Impressions and ideas come quickly, but they quickly disappear. Take a few notes:

- Helen is against the new quality control plan.
- Dave and Sybil don't really agree on the attachments for the proposal.
- Julio Torres (Personnel) is great at logistics.

You don't have to prove or substantiate such impressions, nor do you have to show your notes to anyone. These hunches and catches may prove prophetic and helpful as time goes by.

The other benefit of taking notes is that the process makes you a better listener and observer. The expert monitor is noting not just the surface structure of a work unit—the obvious things that happen—but also the deep structure as well. How are people interacting? What kinds of themes or issues keep resurfacing in meetings? What are we spending most of our time talking about and working on? What are the major interruptions and distracters?

Note taking in school presents a similar challenge. Students have to differentiate between content and process. Some students may take meticulous notes on the content of the course but fail to note the important details and impressions about assignments. They monitor the course content but not the instructor's intentions. Remember, students are more likely to do poorly in a course if they fail to take notes on course assignments than if they neglect to take notes on a particular topic covered in class.

HOW DO WE KNOW HOW WE'RE DOING   External Monitoring

So far we've talked primarily about internal monitoring, or monitoring yourself as an individual unit of productivity and effectiveness. We now need to look at external monitoring—the oversight of work unit performance as a whole.

LOOKING AT THE SYSTEM

First, an axiom about human performance: *People perform better if they know how well they're performing.* What do workers complain about most? In our experience, two things: they don't feel they know exactly what they're supposed to do, and they don't get enough feedback on how well they're doing it.

Feedback is a key concept (see Chapter 6 for more detail on feedback). Managers are the key players in solving these two problems. Managers have to know what their people are supposed to do, but they must also know what performance information or data is significant and helpful to them. The unit manager must begin with good performance objectives for the unit, and then he or she must develop good performance measures or criteria for monitoring performance. Figure 5.2 illustrates this monitoring (or control) process.

FIGURE 5.2 *Four steps in the control process.* Source: *John R. Schermerhorn,* Management for Productivity, *3rd ed., New York: John Wiley & Sons, 1989, p. 425. Used with permission.*

As soon as an organization is created, it contains boundaries. It has an inside and an outside boundary; it has an "up" and a "down" boundary. The boundaries between the organization and its environment, and between managers and workers, can become filters that block information essential to the organization's vitality. Every leader and manager fears being cut off from the important information. Business leaders fear losing touch with both the customer and the company's employees. In leading a work unit, the question every manager should ask is, "How do we know how we're doing?" Here are some key subquestions to it:

- As a manager, do I know what the system (work unit) is supposed to be doing?
- Do my people know individually what to do, and what the system collectively needs to do?
- Do I know what measures and indicators of performance need to be monitored and shared with my people over time?
- Do my people have the skills and knowledge required to do their jobs?
- If not, how can we improve their skills and knowledge?
- Does the system allow them to work at capacity, or is the system a major impediment to performance? How can I know this for certain?
- If the system is unstable, or consistently inefficient, how can we change our procedures, improve our equipment and processing, or restructure the work environment to bring the system to a higher capacity?

As we've heard in recent years, the Japanese excel at high-level technology and quality control. But many Americans do not realize an American industrial consultant, G. Edwards Deming, is considered the father of Japan's quality and productivity miracle. During the post-war reconstruction, Deming was part of Douglas MacArthur's team of advisers. Deming had drawn only a small audience of listeners among managers in the United States, but the Japanese attended carefully to his advice on quality production and the use of statistical methods in monitoring work-unit performance. Deming insisted that managers accept responsibility for performance, and not automatically pass the blame on to workers.

In order to monitor performance, said Deming, we have to observe performance over time and be certain that the system is in statistical control. Managers often make the mistake of dwelling on one data point without tracking total system performance.

Take this example from the experience of a management consultant who was asked by a manufacturing company to work on a problem.

> *I recently spent a day at a plant that produces a consumer good product. The plant manager and his team were asked to identify a set of "things they would like to see different" in the plant if they had the power to cause everyone to behave exactly as they would like them to. The flip chart in front of them was divided down the middle with "nonmeasurable" written on one side of the page and "measurable" written on the other. They had listed eight nonmeasurable things they wanted to see changed in the plant before one of them said, "I guess we should have some measurable objectives too."*
>
> *Then they identified absenteeism as an objective. They all agreed this was a serious problem. I asked them what attendance or absenteeism was running at the plant. Nobody knew. They had no idea whether it ran at 5 percent, 10 percent, 15 or 20 percent. They thought there were records from which they could get this information, but no one had bothered to do this. Yet this turned out to be the only measurable performance they wished to change! (Miller 1984, 102)*

This example may be somewhat unusual, as Miller admits. Most managers and supervisors have some idea what the major performance variables are for their units. But many of them have no idea what the current trend is, whether upward or downward, and what the "variability of performance, or standard deviation is from the mean" (Miller 1984, 102).

Deming says that you need to keep performance figures, but not to tell you when there's a problem. You usually know when there's a problem. You need performance data to help you know when to change the system.

There are many possible examples of this kind of monitoring error. We tend to blame individual errors or "poor performers" when sometimes the system—the procedures and equipment and the collective average rate of error—are the real problems. Here's another way to describe it.

$$\text{Performance} = \text{Ability } (or \text{ Capacity}) + \text{Motivation}$$

In order to improve performance, we want to have the "capacity" of our people to do their jobs at a maximum. But what is capacity? Is it simply their ability or competence as individuals? No. Individual competence is a big part of the variable, but the capacity provided them by the system is a major part as well. The best driver in the world will not be an effective courier if he or she is driving a truck that frequently breaks down. The best warehouse manager will not do "quality" work if the computer inventory system is inadequate.

ANALYSIS Burke Jackson: Information Anxiety

Directions Read the following case and analyze how Burke Jackson is doing with sorting, retrieving, and interpreting information.

Burke Jackson, director of Fleet Management for Stromberg Freight Company, was breathing hard when he walked past his secretary on the way to his office at 8:20 A.M. It's March 13. He had wanted to be in at the officer earlier to avoid traffic and get started on a report, but he had taken time to adjust the derailleur on his son's bike; another "five-minute job" that had taken 40 minutes. Jackson's first love is still mechanics. Fixing things is good therapy for him.

But the heavy traffic, and the nagging worry about a quarterly field report that was due in two days, had put him in a snit. His secretary, Muriel Hausler, read his mood immediately. She had some information for him.

> *Muriel:* Burke, Glenn Jesop called this morning about new truck deliveries. The dealer can't guarantee arrival before May 19 (*nine weeks away*).
>
> *Burke:* It's the same old crap again. We can't keep doing business with a dealer 200 miles away. I'm calling Jesop and telling him to cancel the order and start working with our local people.
>
> *Muriel:* But Glenn says he has an idea about delivering direct to the field, and saving some time with vehicle safety inspections. He wants you to call him. He says he mentioned the idea to George Phillips (*vice president*) and he liked it.
>
> *Burke:* (*looking through the doorway into his own office*) Where's the file I left on my desk last night? I have to have it for the quarterly report. Did the cleaning people strike again, or did I take the damn thing home with me and leave it there?
>
> *Muriel:* It's on the credenza. Are you going to call Glenn back? He sounded anxious.
>
> *Burke:* Jesop's always anxious. That's why Phillips loves him so much. Jesop does the worrying for both of them.

Jackson walks into his office and starts rifling through the stack of mail. With the bundled mail, he pulls a few other documents out of his in basket. Swearing under his breath, he flips through each item:

- A copy of a report from the quality control committee. It was mentioned in last week's management team meeting, but it wasn't discussed much.
- Some advertising copy for new office equipment.
- A memo from the dispatching department on new procedures for tracing lost freight.

- An invitation to the maintenance department's holiday party.
- A list of training films that have to be reviewed by the end of the month or they are automatically returned.
- Two contracts from major accounts, renewing their commitment to Stromberg. The contracts have some changes in conditions and wording, as indicated on their cover letters. Deadline for signature is March 16.
- A four-page report from the maintenance department (*Burke's former home unit*) on fleet performance.

Burke starts reading the fleet performance report. They still haven't matched the record he set seven years ago for consecutive months without a vehicle breakdown. The phone rings. It's Sharon Elwell calling from the dispatching department. They're trying to schedule another meeting to review the new procedures for tracing lost freight. Could he or a representative attend at 10:30 tomorrow morning? Burke looks at his planner for March 14.

He has a meeting with the management team at 2:00 and a 3:30 interview with a manager who has some ideas about the new computer dispatching system. He will probably go to lunch with three people from the maintenance department. Wednesday is their traditional lunch date. He tells Sharon to put him down for the 10:30 meeting and goes back to reading the report.

He's marking some comments in the margins of the report when another phone call prompts him to look at his watch. It's Dave Allison, one of their biggest accounts. Allison needs three Stromberg trucks to make a delivery to Bridgeport, Connecticut, and has been told it will take two days before the trucks and drivers are available. Allison is a little upset and is just checking with Burke about getting some "special help with this one."

Burke solves that problem, but it takes about an hour to do it. Worrying now about the quarterly report, he checks some figures he wrote the night before on the white board in his office. He pulls a file out of the drawer that has dates and figures from the notes he took at the last team meeting and goes through his planner to find out who attended the last meeting on shipment quotas for this quarter. He needs to track those figures down, and someone has to have them. He took notes from that meeting in his planner, but he had two important talks on the phone later with people who had attended, and he can't find those notes.

Muriel, his secretary, pokes her head into his office and asks if he needs anything before she goes to lunch. He waves her off with an attempted smile and the phone rings again. It's his administrative assistant, Craig Sparks. Craig wants to meet with him about a long-term problem of late shipments in region 8. Jackson tells Sparks to meet with him at 4:00 today.

Discussion Questions
1. How well is Burke doing with sorting, retrieving, and analyzing information? Does anything distract him from these tasks?

2. If Burke is not yet a master monitor, how could he improve? Using as many specifics as possible, write your analysis in a memo to your instructor.

PRACTICE   Christine Elm: Is There Safety in Numbers?

Directions   The minicase below describes a fairly typical day at the office for Christine Elm, a 41-year-old middle manager. Assume that you are Christine Elm. Using the information available, write a memo to Stuart Reece giving whatever explanation or analysis you think should be provided to explain what is going on. Write the memo to Stuart Reese, Vice President of Operations.

Christine works for Power Systems, a small manufacturing company that produces capacitors and other electronic components for utility companies and private power plants throughout North America. Power Systems employs 320 people.

Holding a degree in electrical engineering, Christine was one of the first women to break into management in a company that has had, until recently, few women with the technical training and credentials necessary for leadership.

Christine works for Stuart Reese, the Vice President of Operations. Stuart is an intense guy, famous for his habits of meddling and micromanaging. But Stuart is fair and basically good natured. He spotted Christine's talent and initiative the first few months she was with the company, and he has been a big supporter. The two of them work quite well together. Christine's primary task for the past year has been plant safety. This is a pet field of Stuart's, who is active in a national group of business leaders that promotes industrial safety.

She is greeted this morning by a call from Stuart who wants her to "touch base" with him first thing, before the day's interruptions get started. She quickly learns that he's upset about this month's accident report from the "shop floor." The *shop floor* is the term used for all manufacturing operations of the company's three facilities. There were two reported accidents last month, and two more this month.

"The floor's record is going to hell in a basket," Stuart says, looking out his window. "What do we have to do to get these guys to be careful?" Christine remembers a similar conversation last year when there was a rise in accidents. The company launched another safety program and offered a small bonus to units that would go accident-free for a full quarter. The system seemed to work well. Christine volunteers to look into the situation and hold a meeting with all managers.

She returns to her office and starts pulling out the old files. She asks her assistant, Alan Patterson, to gather all monthly accident reports for the past five years and compile the data into one table. She calls the management team members who oversee operations and asks for a special meeting with all managers for Thursday at 5:00. That means overtime for the day shift, but Elm insists it's necessary.

Some new information surfaces the same day. Christine sees a brief article in the local paper about industrial safety, and Power Systems is named as "one of the most exemplary in the northeast." That publicity has probably helped trigger Stuart Reese's anxiety. She also learns from a phone call to Stuart's secretary that he is scheduled to make a presentation on industrial safety programs to a business group in Atlanta—stress factor number two. Christine is concerned that Stuart may be overreacting.

Her perception isn't changed during her discussions with managers on Thursday. They insist that everything is status quo on the floor. "People are careful. They're well trained, and we are on their backs about safety all the time. These things happen sometimes."

Christine isn't an expert on the history of the floor. She's only been with the company two years. She knows 1985 brought a big improvement because new equipment was installed all over the plant. Exposed cables on overhead lifts were covered with metal conduit, and the company imposed hard hat and safety footwear regulations that went beyond federal and state requirements. The equipment improvements had cost $3.5 million.

Since making those changes the company had used "motivational" appeals, such as bonuses and award banquets, to encourage safe work behavior among employees.

Friday morning, Alan Patterson brings Christine Elm the information on accidents. The record is kept according to the unit in which the accident takes place. The plant is divided into five major units:

1. Metal Bending and Extrusion
2. Welding and Soldering
3. Warehouse and Dock Facility
4. Fleet Unit (Transportation)
5. Assembly

All of the units, with the exception of the administrative offices, are part of the shop floor. The list of accidents is as follows:

Metal Bending and Extrusion

1. Manager tripped on cable and broke ankle. Jan. 1986.
2. Machinist cut hand while running high-speed lathe. March 1986.
3. Employee struck by forklift, broken femur and bruised hip joint. April 1987.
4. Employee cut hand on sheet metal; five stitches. Aug. 1988.

Welding and Soldering

1. Employee injured right eye from accidental flash from arc welder. June 1986.
2. Employee's right hand and lower arm burned from hot sheet metal falling from soldering rack. April 1987.
3. Employee tripped on cable; broke ankle. June 1988.

Warehouse and Dock Area

1. Dock worker reported back injury caused by steadying imbalanced load suspended from crane. June 1986.
2. Dock worker struck by falling capacitor box from warehouse shelf. No hard hat. Aug. 1986.
3. Employee injured when foot was run over by forklift tire. Aug. 1987.
4. Employee struck by small crates falling from shelf; right shoulder bruised. Sept. 1987.
5. Employee cut left hand while using wire tightener; nine stitches. Dec. 1987.
6. Employee slipped on ice while unloading crates; left knee and ankle injured. April 1989.
7. Employee struck by crate that fell from poorly secured crane load; shoulder injury. Dec. 1989.

Fleet Unit

1. Employee killed in Dayton, Ohio while driving transport truck. Jan. 1988.
2. Employee fell from dock onto a capacitor crate; neck and back injury. April 1988.
3. Employee slipped on ice while carrying tool box; sprained left ankle and bruised left wrist. Jan. 1990.

Assembly

1. Employee cut right hand on whiskered sheet metal; 18 stitches. Jan. 1987.
2. Employee injured left eye from loose write on capacitor box. Feb. 1987.
3. Employee broke two fingers of right hand while operating extruder. June 1989.
4. Employee cut left hand on whiskered sheet metal, 10 stitches. Oct. 1989.
5. Employee burns right forearm with molten lead. March 1990.
6. Employee bruised right knee by falling from steps. Oct. 1990.

Discussion Questions

1. What kind of information is Christine Elm getting? Is it in the most useful form for her?
2. What kind of information is Christine not getting?
3. How should the company organize this information in the future?
4. How "unstable" is the system that Stuart Reese is so upset about?

APPLICATION   Information Overload or Overdrive?

1. For the next three weeks, analyze yourself as a monitor. Most of the information and performance management you have to do is in your role as student.

2. Observe and assess the way you sort, retrieve, and analyze information. Here are some guidelines.

Task 1: Internal Monitoring

- Are you doing a lot of "straight" line reading, or do you know how to scan, read, and analyze, making notes of significant sections and raising questions as you go?

- Are you discriminating among things that need to be skimmed, read once quickly, or read carefully, and things that must be studied and about which notes should be taken? If you're reading everything the same way, you're probably in information overload.

- How effective are you with note taking? The best method is selective note taking (Gall 1988). Many students try to write everything the instructor says and miss the highlights. Others trust their sharp memories too much and miss some details after a few days or weeks have passed.

- Are you effective at discerning your instructor's intentions? For example, most lectures, demonstrations, and discussion groups held in college classes are designed to do at least one of the following:
  - Present information not in the assigned readings.
  - Explain difficult ideas in the assigned readings.
  - Explain and provide practice in new skills.
  - Conduct demonstrations.
  - Discuss course assignments.

- Are you managing time as well as information effectively?

3. At the end of the three weeks, write a detailed memo to your instructor on your performance as a monitor. Try to be specific and concrete. Give examples as evidence. Share both your successes and failures.

Task 2: External Monitoring

- Find three informative articles on information management in business journals, newpapers, or other published sources. Write summaries of these articles as though they were to be read by the manager of the unit in which you work. (The organization can be imaginary.) Try to focus on a major theme, issue, or trend in information management, and make any recommendations on applying this information that you think would be helpful to your reader. You may want to look at topics such as innovations in software or hardware, the use of databases in making better decisions, how organizations are coping with information overload, the financial issues of managing information, and security and information.

■ With the help of a person in charge, check out a real management information system in an organization—a school, government office, or a business. Talk to the people who use it about its effectiveness and the problems and solutions the system presents. Write the results in a memo to your instructor.

Competency 2   Analyzing Information with Critical Thinking

ASSESSMENT   Who to Send for Training

Directions   Read the following case and answer the questions.[3]

You are a manager in the claims department of Quality Life Insurance Company. You have the opportunity to provide an extensive training program for two of your employees. Below are brief descriptions of six of your employees.

Charles Jefferson   Black male; age 41; Vietnam veteran; married, wife pregnant; with agency one year; good work record so far; capability to be better performer.

Naomi Smith   White female; age 45; recently divorced, supports three children; with agency five years; number of recent absences, fairly good work record otherwise.

Robert Boyd   White male; age 24; unmarried, with agency three years; good performance records; wants to start own business some day.

Ralph Ball   White male; age 45; married; no children at home; with agency 10 years; erratic work record; reputed to be an alcoholic.

Sarah Field   Black female; age 36; husband recently disabled, two children; on the job two months; too early to evaluate performance.

Carmelita Valiquez   Hispanic female; age 41; two children, husband employed intermittently; with agency nine months; steady worker.

Discussion Questions   1. First, assume the role of manager A. You are a white female, age 48, and married with two children, and you are strongly committed to providing opportunities for women to advance to administrative positions.

■ Which criteria would be most important to you in making your decision?   *work record*
■ Whom would you send for training? Why?

[3] *Adapted from* W. F. Glueck and L. Jauch. *The Managerial Experience: Cases, Exercises and Readings.* Hinsdale, IL.: Dryden Press, 1977. Used with permission.

2. Next, assume the role of manager B. You are a minority male, age 25, and single, with a strong interest in a long-term career in the industry. You believe that conscientious hard work is the key to success.

- Which criteria would be most important to you in making your decision?
- Whom would you send for training? Why?

3. Finally, answer the questions for yourself in your present position.

- Which criteria would be most important to you in making your decision?
- Whom would you send for training? Why?

Interpretation   What are the implications of this activity to you? What is the connection between analyzing information from three points of view and critical thinking?

This exercise is similar to the problems you will face as managers. There is such a thing as rationality, and it is possible to be honest and fair. It is important to gather information and consider various alternatives before making a decision. But it is impossible to see everything as it "really is," because we construct reality based upon limited information and through the lenses of our own dispositions, values, experiences, and intellects.

LEARNING   Evaluating Routine Information

Information management can help make sure that the right information gets to you, but then it's time to *analyze* that information. Making the most effective use of information is one of the hallmarks of critical thinking. Critical thinking is usually identified with the attributes of objectivity, balance, an openness to new information, and a methodical or careful manner in studying problems before making a decision. The opportunity for using critical thinking skills is great now, while you are in school, and will be so later when you've joined the work force. You constantly analyze, select, interpret, or recommend in the face of limited information and time. For a manager, some of the most common critical thinking tasks include hiring staff, conducting performance appraisals, purchasing equipment, conducting needs assessments or interpreting their results, responding to budget requirements, allocating resources, analyzing quantitative data, and writing reports or proposals.

In school the problems we were handed are prepackaged and well defined, but at work most of the problems carry no labels and come in mismatched sets. "Real" problems are part technical, part social, and part political.

SEEING THINGS AS WE REALLY ARE

To a great extent, we see things, not as they are, but as we are. For this reason, we began with the exercise for choosing people for a training opportunity. This problem involves a judgment call, a personal decision based upon accurate information and shaped by values and judgment.

Not all problems managers face are as subjective as this one. Some revolve more around the ability to analyze data or separate important information from incidental information. But most problems, even the seemingly straightforward ones, involve judgment, and not simply computation.

Obviously, what we are calling critical thinking can be very creative and inventive. The difference is that creative thinking (covered in Chapter 8, The Innovator Role) focuses on developing *new* ways of doing things—the process of invention in general. The critical thinker is working on doing things better, solving problems more efficiently and accurately.

Each task presents an opportunity for error. Think of the resources and energy wasted and the pain, frustration, and damage caused by ill conceived equipment purchases, inaccurate needs assessments, poor decisions on hiring and promotion, flawed estimates for construction costs, and mistakes in medication dosages, structural design, and inventory control. And these problems occur in the best work units in our best organizations, public and private. Human error, the problem of random mishaps (such as fire and flood), and the unintended results of our best efforts work against us.

WHAT HAPPENS ON THE WAY TO GOOD JUDGMENT?

What gets in the way of good judgment and sound thinking? Here are some gremlins that impede good judgment in dealing with everyday problems. Based on your experience, you should be able to add to the list.

- N.I.H. (Not Invented Here) Syndrome
- Pattern hypnosis
- Denial
- Conformity
- Ego involvement
- Faulty or incomplete analysis

N.I.H.

"Not invented here" is the belief, often unconscious, that "mine is better," or mine is the standard by which others must be judged. N.I.H. is similar to ethnocentrism, which is the tendency of cultures to resist values, practices, or traditions unlike their own, and to judge the unfamiliar by the degree to which it resembles the familiar. Most of us have a natural tendency to resist change. Change is threatening, and we can usually think of reasons to avoid it. The United States automotive industry was, until recently, encased in its own ethnocentrism. American auto executives resisted adopting many of the improvements in design and quality that foreign automakers were introducing, not solely because of financial or technical considerations, but because of a parochial attitude. Detroit assumed that since it had literally invented the automobile and exported cars to the world for three generations, when better cars were built, Detroit would build them.

PATTERN HYPNOSIS

Problem solving often involves formulating lots of minipredictions. We take in only as much information as we need in order to see a pattern forming, and then we construct the whole based on the part we're looking at. The patient's fever and soreness in the neck and throat can probably be attributed to a viral infection, but it might be something else.

Patterns help us think. We like to group things, people, situations, and feelings into sets so that we can deal with them more easily. But it's a trap to draw generalizations and impressions about the whole from small samples of any set. Ethnic groups, religions, people from other regions, or institutions other than our own are often the victims of our stereotypical thinking. Stereotypical thinking is a sink hole for sound judgment because it can reverse cause and effect in our minds without our realizing it. We can think, "He operates that way because he works for the accounting department. All those people have a controlling mentality," but the truth may be that we construct that impression of another person's controlling mentality because we *expect* it. All the stereotypical thinker needs to know about someone is attainable given the department she works for, the religion he belongs to, or his ethnic origin.

Pattern hypnosis can be detrimental to your own career development. After a few years in school, or on the job, everything may start to look like the "same shade of gray." We frame problems in the same way and look at people and work in the same way.

DENIAL

Denial is a problem because there is much of it in the workplace, in families, and in our own lives. Denial is a hallmark of the person addicted to alcohol or drugs, but the problem is not limited to those who suffer from addiction. Denial is wrapped around all the other roadblocks to sound judgment. The mind has an uncanny ability to protect itself against pain and anxiety by fogging over its awareness. A growing number of cognitive researchers believe that 90% of the information processing we do is actually performed at the subconscious level (Goldman 1987). Denial is difficult to detect in ourselves because so much of it is unconscious.

For example, if your company is being taken over, you may well deny that your job could be one of those eliminated and not take precautionary steps to find other options. Poor performance evaluations could be a signal that your organization doesn't value your work, but you could let a personal friendship with your manager convince you that everything is fine. We have seen many instances of companies denying the falling performance of a product line because they had invested so much energy, time, and money into its development.

For example, Roger Smith, retiring CEO of General Motors, says many middle managers refused to believe their jobs were in jeopardy when GM began to streamline the company, and eventually laid off over 40,000 middle managers. Says Smith, "We told people this [that there would be layoffs] more than once, but sometimes people believe what they want to believe. The guy kept saying to himself, 'Well, after this temporary period is over I know I'm still going to have a job.' We had told the guy, 'Hey, you've gotta understand, your assignment will only last for eleven months.' But the guy kept saying, 'Gee, I know something will work out.' " (*Business Month* 1989, 80).

CONFORMITY

We've all heard about groupthink, the tendency to conform to the direction being taken by a group to which we belong and with which we identify. Some of history's biggest disasters were the products of groupthink. The war in Vietnam has provided historians a banquet of cases that demonstrate poor judgment and miscalculation, much of it forced by political and social pressure. The *Challenger* space shuttle disaster is a more recent example of inappropriate risk taking from pressure to conform. Managers at NASA were putting intense pressure on engineers working for companies like Morton Thiakol, which had designed components of the *Challenger*. The need to get the shuttle launched was given precedence over engineers' concerns about product safety.

We tend to seek the advice of those who see the world the same way we do. We can disagree without offending (in most cases), and we can improve the quality of our decisions by not automatically agreeing just to avoid tension. The short-term comfort is often bought with long-term frustration. Good leaders have the ability to work effectively with people who disagree with them.

Groups deceive themselves, much the same way individuals do, by preventing painful or difficult questions from reaching the surface. "The dangers of groupthink," says psychologist Daniel Goldman, "are greatest when there is a leader in charge, and the group feels not only close knit but special. Critical questions then are less likely to come up, since they may diminish the leader's prestige or otherwise challenge the group's feelings of pride and closeness" (Goldman 1987, 30).

As the nation continues to deal with the staggering expense of the savings and loan bailout, many analysts are citing a kind of groupthink as one of the causes for so much poor judgment on approving loans to customers involved in risky speculations. All of the savings and loans are required by a recent federal law to have private auditors review their books and pass judgment on the institutions' financial health each year. Why didn't more auditors express concern and even alarm at the financial risks the S & L's were taking? Some did. But many were distracted and impressed by the short-term success the savings and loans were having. The S & L's were making big loans primarily to finance real estate speculation in an economy that was rapidly expanding. The immediate success created a lot of psychological momentum, and few people wanted to ask how long the boom would last. When the oil bust in the southwestern United States dropped the bottom out of real estate, the loaning institutions were left holding millions of dollars of bad loans and low-priced land (Wayne 1989, 12).

Here are some antidotes for avoiding the pitfalls of groupthink.

- Invite the participation of someone willing to play devil's advocate. Have people put on the "black hat" and tell you why a decision you like may be a bad one.

- If you are uncomfortable with a decision, and aren't sure why, buy time if possible. You may return to the problem tomorrow with a clearer view of it.

- Create diversity in your groups. As a manager, try to avoid surrounding yourself only with people who think like you, and have the same strengths and weaknesses you have.

- Encourage diverse reactions and approaches, as well as a climate of openness and candor.

EGO INVOLVEMENT

The human ego is the biggest roadblock to sound judgment and innovation. At many brainstorming sessions and problem solving meetings, the real game being played is not "How can we solve the problem?" but "Who knows best?" or "Who carries the most weight?" Good managers have to be adept at knowing how to channel and absorb the jet wash of other people's egos *and* put their own egos in a box when they start running away with good judgment.

Edward Beauvais, Chairman of America West Airlines, places great importance on management's ability to nurture the talents of workers and "draw out their ideas." That means the manager's ego has to take a backseat. "When things work right," Beauvais tells his managers, they [the workers] get the credit. When things don't work, you take the blame" (Dumaine 1988, 60). To do that, managers have to be secure in their own abilities and draw satisfaction and legitimacy from helping others succeed. One of the best managers we've ever seen, a quality control engineer with an electronics firm, used to say, "I ask myself, do I want to be right all the time, or do I want my unit to do good work?"

Good managers cannot only accept criticism, but they seek it from the people they respect. They want to improve, and the key to improvement is inviting and reacting to constructive criticism. Many promising young professionals fail this test, as, for example, a brilliant young attorney named Jonathan:

> *When Jonathan started as an associate in a prestigious Chicago law firm, he was highly praised by the firm's partners. He came from a first class law school, and his training and ability showed him to be superior to his peers. Jonathan soaked up the praise like a sponge. When he had been on the job for six months, the partners of the firm began a serious effort to shape the briefs of the associates to fit the style and needs of the firm.*
>
> *Some of the associates eagerly sought the partners' criticism, hoping to improve their work. Jonathan not only did not seek such criticism, he actively avoided it. As*

the work of the other associates greatly improved, Jonathan's did not. The partners became more and more critical of him. Jonathan's avoidance of criticism and failure to seek out advice for constructive change eventually resulted in his dismissal (Sternberg 1988, 81).

FAULTY OR INCOMPLETE ANALYSIS

"If you're going to repair a motorcycle," says Robert Pirsig, "an adequate supply of gumption is the most important tool" (Pirsig 1974, 273). *Gumption* means persistence in the face of aggravation, complexity, and boredom. Gumption has nothing to do with raw intelligence. It's the ability to stay with something, to take a second look before turning it in, and trying one more time to find the problem before giving up.

When Mike Walsh was made CEO of Union Pacific Railroad, he discovered that 18% of the bills the company was sending out contained errors, many of them serious errors in pricing and deadlines. Walsh organized a team of 20 managers from Shipping, Finance, and Scheduling to solve the problem. He challenged them to cut the error in half in six months and to reduce it to zero in one year (Dumaine 1989, 51). In the process, Walsh combined the competencies of the expert monitor (he found the error in billing process himself by ordering a more complete analysis than had ever been done) with the expert mentor (he freed the special team to act on their own as experts to solve the problem).

FLEXIBILITY AND OPENNESS

Managers are leaders, agents of social change and transformation. As a leader, you may need to challenge some of the reactions and perceptions of your people, with sincerity and patience:

> *"I know Headquarters hasn't covered itself with glory on needs assessments, but this time they have some data we shouldn't ignore."*
>
> *"I think we may be moving to a quick, easy reaction to this suggestion. I'm not convinced our resistance is reasonable. Please tell me more about why we know this proposal can't work?"*

Managers and supervisors are in a position to influence the norms organizations develop over time. These norms are seldom written anywhere, but they are real. Norms are like an invisible list of expectations people create for themselves and each other. We have found that people are able to create a long list of norms that exist in their organizations, once individuals feel comfortable enough to talk about them. Here's a partial list:

- Never disagree with your boss.
- Don't rock the boat.

- Treat women as second class citizens—don't take their reactions seriously.
- Look busy even when you're not.
- Cheat a little on your expense records.
- Make fun of new ways of doing things.
- Criticize the organization to outsiders.
- Complain frequently.
- Don't share information with other groups. (Mitroff and Kilmann 1984, 69)

People are not told to act this way in organizations. They are shown how to act this way. These habits of thought and behavior are subtly impressed upon them by the examples of "veterans" who are streetwise and show the new people the ropes. New members conform, often without realizing they are doing so. Furthermore, the more cohesive the group, the greater the conformity to the norms, whether they are positive or negative. Unity, teamwork, and community are good, but not when a group is committed to bad habits or ineffective solutions.

ANALYZING ARGUMENTS

Many of the tasks that require critical thinking confront us in writing. But even those that are created orally—in meetings or in conversations or interviews—are often complex and need more analysis than a cursory listening. Our job may be to react to someone else's recommendation, or to make a recommendation ourselves based upon the available information. The challenge is to identify the gist of an argument and to map its major contours.

Most arguments have three basic elements:

1. The *claim* or conclusion of the argument. (Ask yourself, "What point is being made?")

2. The *grounds,* or the facts, and all other evidence that support the claim. The claim can be no stronger than the grounds that support it. (Ask yourself, "What do you have to go on?")

3. The *warrant,* or bridge between the claim and the grounds. Sometimes the link is obvious. Sometimes it is not. (Ask yourself, "What justifies making the connection between your claim and your grounds?") (Toulmin 1984, 30–34)

Here's a simple example of a claim based upon grounds:

I see smoke. There must be a fire.

The claim here is, "There must be fire." The grounds on which the claim is based is, "I see smoke." But the warrant that makes the connection between them is not stated. It is assumed. That warrant is, of course, "Where there's smoke there's fire." Let's see how we can use this model to map some arguments that managers encounter in reports or meetings. Take this example from a sales report by a sales manager at a manufacturing company.

> *We conclude that the 28% decrease in unit sales for this quarter was caused by a dramatic deterioration in the quality of service provided during the previous quarter.*
>
> *The strongest evidence that poor service is the cause of the lower sales is the fact that over half of our large, regular accounts ordered no new units during the quarter. These are the customers who have a history with our service, and now have reason to be dissatisfied.*
>
> *On the other hand, sales to new accounts were about average during this quarter. These are accounts who have yet had little experience with the quality of our service work.*
>
> *We know the quality of our service has dropped sharply, because the number of complaint calls recorded in the log, as well as repeat calls requesting service, is four times higher than during any other quarter on record.*

The argument here is pretty straightforward. The primary fact (data) being discussed is a 28% decrease in sales for the current quarter. The claim is that the decrease has been caused by a poor service record during the previous quarter. The warrant that ties the data and claim together is that poor service performance over time will have a negative effect on sales. Notice that the author of the report provides backing for his statement that the quality of service has "dramatically deteriorated." He alludes to an official piece of evidence, the service department's log book.

Often, we encounter arguments that are logically consistent, but empirically weak. For example, let's look at another version of the sales report. In the following version the writer gives another explanation for why sales declined sharply in this quarter.

We believe this decrease in sales was brought about by a lackluster performance of our sales representatives. The strongest evidence that poor sales work is behind the problem is the low number of contacts made during this quarter.

We reviewed the sales reports from the field and found that our sales reps had contacted 16% fewer potential accounts during this quarter than they did last quarter.

What is the warrant behind the claim? That a decrease in contacts will result in a decrease in sales. That's certainly a logical argument. In this case, however, a closer examination of the facts (grounds) would reveal the following:

1. Last quarter's performance in contacts was indeed lower than the previous quarter's, but right at the average over the past three years. (It so happens that the previous quarter was a great one for contacting potential accounts, and this made last quarter look bad.)

2. Historically, the correlation between the number of contacts and the number of sales has been surprisingly low. Therefore, the claim that the drop in sales was caused by a drop in contacts is based upon a weak warrant.

3. The high number of complaints to the service department is very salient in this case. A closer examination of the log shows that during the previous

quarter the service department set a company record in complaints received. Furthermore, there is an historical correlation between the number of complaints received in one quarter, and the number of sales made in the next.

The next time you are perplexed by an assertion someone is making in speaking or writing, try using these concepts of claims, grounds, and warrants to map the argument.

ANALYSIS The Shoe War

Directions   The following case depicts the situation of a large manufacturer of athletic shoes in the mid-1970s. Although we have made the case hypothetical, in many ways it reflects what actually happened in the athletic shoe industry. George Cervantes and Ingrid Mueller, two fictitious characters, saw the course of history changing and tried to prepare their company for the change. They were right, but they failed. Mercury Shoes Inc. was hit by a wave of innovative, hungry companies such as the makers of Nike shoes, New Balance, and the old competitor, Pumas.

The shoe industry proved so turbulent, even the winner of the mid-seventies war, Nike, was temporarily thrown off balance by failing to respond to rapid changes in the market. By the end of 1981, Nike was rated by *Forbes* magazine as the number one company in profitability over the previous five years ahead of all companies in all other industries.

But the jogging craze peaked at about 1982 and left the industry competing for a smaller market. Nike virtually missed the aerobic dancing trend, a trend that dictated a need for a different shoe design. The athletic shoe war has been a fascinating and sobering chapter in marketing history, and a challenge to all involved in thinking critically and creatively.

Read the case and answer the questions at the end.

*A **Long Leash***   George Cervantes was a happy man in November 1983. He had landed one of the plum positions in the field for young market analysts in business. After completing an MBA in a part-time program for middle managers, George accepted a position with Mercury Shoes Inc., the premier athletic shoe manufacturer in the world.

The leaders at Mercury told George he had been hired for three reasons. He is an American, and Mercury, a German company, is looking more seriously at developments in the U.S. market for athletic shoes and peripheral products such as sportswear and related equipment such as footballs, soccer and baseballs, timing devices, and rackets.

Second, George is young and interested in athletics. An amateur tennis player, he is fighting to stay fit, and has a broad interest in sports and sports training. Many of Mercury's managers and specialists are or were professional athletes, but George has the passion and breadth of the well-rounded amateur, and something about him captured the interest of the people who interviewed him.

Third, George showed great promise as a marketing analyst during the three years he worked for a home products manufacturing company in the Midwest. He sold the company's leadership on several innovations in home improvement products, and he saw the explosive growth in the do-it-yourself market before most of the competitors. But rewards for his visionary work were slow in coming with his old company, so when Mercury responded to his résumé with an interview and an offer that doubled his salary, he was not slow to relocate to Mercury's U.S. headquarters in Chicago.

George had been promised a "long leash" by the Director of U.S. Marketing, Ingrid Mueller. Mueller, a 28-year-old Austrian, had been with the company since the year after the 1968 Olympic Games in Mexico City. Ingrid had run on the Austrian track team, and her background in sports medicine had made an ideal asset to Mercury. She was one of the first German speaking employees to be sent to the U.S. to study the market in 1971.

Where's the Market Running?   George Cervantes' job was to survey the territory and help Mercury bolster its slumping performance in the U.S. athletic shoe market. Mercury was pleased with the performance of its other product lines, especially sportswear which had been picked up by schools and professional athletic teams. Equipment and timing devices had become profitable, big ticket items in Mercury's product development efforts as well. But shoes, the mainstay of Mercury's history and market strength, had begun to slip. Many people in the company had explanations of their own, but the company was perplexed—at least some of the young people, like Ingrid Mueller in Marketing, were perplexed.

Mercury had made its fortune from, and continued to thrive, on the strength of its athletic shoes. Begun in the later 1930s, the company had devoted itself to meeting the needs of the professional athlete. Hans Reiniger, the company's founder, had studied the training activities of the German Olympic teams over the years. He was the first to develop interchangeable spike elements for running on various terrains, indoor and outdoor. Mercury was known for its performance studies of athletic shoes "in use."

The company had secured endorsements from world-class athletes from the days of the post-war Olympic games. In short, Mercury had, over the three decades of its history, held its position as the preeminent sports equipment producer in the world.

Worrying about Success   George was excited but uneasy. Even in his job interview he had made a pitch for greater innovation and diversity. George had some strong opinions about changes in the U.S. market, a market that, everyone agreed, would set the trend for athletic product consumption for years to come. He thought Mercury was falling behind, but he had some trouble explaining what he meant. His energy and reassuring style had landed him the job, but now he needed to present a plan.

George did a lot of talking to everybody he could find. He traveled, he listened, he watched. As the weeks went by, he was more convinced than ever that things were changing. He had read Kenneth Cooper's book on aerobics, a new concept in the fitness world. His own impressions that the book would be significant were confirmed in evening cocktail parties and morning tennis matches. People had read the book, and a couple of his friends had started putting on their old "tennis shoes" to jog around the park before work.

Cooper's book was not the only new force out there. Millions of Americans had watched Frank Shorter win the prestigious marathon and cheered as Dave Wottle beat the great Soviet sprinter Evgeni Arzanov in the 800 meters at the Munich Olympics in 1972. Something big was afoot, and it had more to it than keeping the attention of professional athletes who wanted the best shoes money can buy. Amateurs, George was saying to everybody who would listen, are getting into running.

George and Ingrid agreed that Mercury had some reasons to worry. The shoe business was too easy to get into. Mercury had learned in the 1960s that cheap labor was readily available in Eastern Europe and Asia, and plants were easy to site. The large orders could be contracted out to these plants. Inexpensive labor and new manufacturing methods were making it easier to diversify product lines and get things to market sooner.

George had taken a trip to Oregon to talk to distributors about Mercury's competition. Tiger shoes, made by a Japanese company, were showing up more frequently; and Blue Ribbon Shoes, a partnership formed by a former University of Oregon track star and his old coach, was making a shoe called "Nikes."

And there was always the issue of technology. When and where would the next breakthrough strike, and would Mercury be the leader when it did? Mercury had about 20 full-time research and development people, but George had some evidence to show that newer, smaller companies were spending a greater percentage of their capital on research than Mercury.

The U.S. market was changing, or at least George thought it was. The "baby boomers," to use a term that would eventually become commonplace, were leaving school and becoming consumers. They were young, more conscious of health and fitness issues, and had the money and leisure to spend on exercise.

The Proposal   After five months of doing homework, it was time to make a move. George and Ingrid wrote a 26-page proposal designed to capture the attention of Mercury's leadership, and get the go ahead to produce and market Mercury shoes more aggressively for the U.S. consumer.

The executive summary section of the report included a list of recommendations.

1. *Step up research and development.*   Mercury has lead the world in this field, but the gap may be closing. The new companies talked about in the report are spending a greater percentage of their profits on research and development than we are. The technology is volatile. Can we afford to be outrun by new developments?

2. *Apply sharper pricing practices, particularly with our lower-priced shoes.*   The

competition is lean, and we've lost market share steadily for the past 20 months. We need to use pricing to discourage entry by smaller, less capitalized companies.

3. *Expand our network of dealers.*   We believe our network is somewhat dated and moving too slowly. We need to foster partnerships with innovative and entrepreneurial retailers. Our study of markets such as Los Angeles, California, and Atlanta, Georgia, convince us that we will see more specialty sporting goods stores and even athletic shoe stores in the near future. Mercury shoes need to be the featured shoes in those stores.

4. *Introduce new products.*   We know this is a controversial recommendation. Broadening our product line will cost money, but the cost of losing out in new market niches for specialty shoes will cost far more. Unfortunately, we cannot yet recommend any specific new lines, but we're confident we can have specific ideas soon. We're arguing for a change in attitude and policy about product broadening in athletic shoes. We cannot allow our success in sportswear and timing devices and equipment to distract us from winning the "shoe war."

In April 1974, the report was submitted to the vice president of marketing in Frankfurt and discussed at the strategic planning meeting three weeks later. The discussion was lively and provocative, and Cervantes and Mueller gained instant visibility among all the vice presidents. There were several phone calls and talk about bringing the two American marketing experts to Frankfurt for a special briefing. But, in late May, a letter from Hans Letke, vice president of Marketing, drained the life blood out of .the proposal. Letke was an American-educated German (MBA Harvard, 1956), a track star in the 1940s, and probably the most influential person in the company.

A portion of his letter is as follows:

We are intrigued by the thrust of your proposal and are eager to thank you for a fine effort made recently in reviewing the American market for Mercury.

We have discussed your recommendations at length and agree that we must react quickly and wisely to a changing market. We have maintained our preeminence for three decades by leading that market, and there is no reason to believe that pattern will change in this decade.

Allow me to summarize our major positions vis à vis your proposal.

1. We will begin immediately to review pricing practices. We are not at this point able to reduce prices on any of our shoe lines, but we are willing to reconsider that policy.
2. We pride ourselves on our world leadership in research and development. What other shoe manufacturer in the world has 22 full-time specialists involved in research? Who has spent more time with professional athletes? When innovations come in shoe design and materials manufacturing, I'm confident most of them will come out of Mercury.
3. We agree that we must enhance our network of dealers. We have sensed a decline in the responsiveness and effectiveness of the organizations that carry our products, and here you folks have made a major contribution to our prospects in the American market. We will be relying on you both for direction in how to improve our dealer network.

4. We are uneasy about your recommendation to broaden our product line. As a person with a fresh degree in business administration, you surely realize, George, that the dangers of overdiversifying a product line can be fatal, even to a company our size. What would it cost us to offer, let us say, four new shoe models in the coming year—beyond what we have already planned?

This company was built on paying strict attention to the needs of the professional athlete. You and Ingrid seem to be recommending that we design and market our products more to the masses. I for one seriously question how much interest the masses will have in high-performance, expensive shoes, when the imitators can produce a good looking shoe for one third our costs, and market that shoe worldwide.

My point is, we use a formula, a formula that has worked for thirty years: make a shoe a professional athlete would want to wear; get endorsements from the most visible athletes in the world, and you are assured a demand for your product. We know shoes; we know who needs our shoes and how they are going to be used. And we're going to continue to make the best athletic shoes in the world.

Discussion Questions

1. What was good about the frame of reference with which Cervantes and Mueller were working? How do you evaluate the "evidence" they used to support their recommendations? What else could they have done to make their case more convincing? How effective was the channel they chose to use—the written proposal? How would you have presented the case if you had been in their place?
2. Obviously, history showed that Hans Litke was wrong, but in what sense was he wrong? What should Mercury Shoes Inc. have been doing that they weren't doing to keep abreast of nascent changes in the market?
3. What personal roadblocks to good thinking do you think got in Hans Litke's way?
4. Given what you know about the multibillion dollar athletic shoe industry, what should a company such as Reebok or Nike be doing right now to gain a better market share and secure a future in a turbulent environment?

PRACTICE   Argument Mapping

Directions

The following exercise includes two arguments on the same topic. Your job is to read these arguments and analyze them in terms of their plausibility, validity, and persuasiveness.

This is a group exercise. Break into groups of four. Two people should analyze one argument, and another team of two the other. Take 15 minutes to read and discuss the arguments, and then present your analysis to the other pair of classmates.

ARGUMENT 1

The National Scholarship Achievement Board recently revealed the results of a five-year study conducted on the effectiveness of comprehensive exams at Duke University. The results of the study showed that since the comprehensive exam has been introduced at Duke, the grade point average of undergraduates has increased by 31%. At comparable schools without the exams, grades increased by only 8% over the same period. The prospect of a comprehensive exam clearly seems to be effective in challenging students to work harder and faculty to teach more effectively. It is likely that the benefits observed at Duke University could also be observed at other universities that adopt the exam policy.

Graduate schools and law and medical schools are beginning to show clear and significant preferences for students who received their undergraduate degrees from institutions with comprehensive exams. As the Dean of the Harvard Business School said, "Although Harvard has not and will not discriminate on the basis of race or sex, we do show a strong preference for applicants who have demonstrated their expertise in an area of study by passing a comprehensive exam at the undergraduate level." Admissions officers of law, medical, and graduate schools have also endorsed the comprehensive exam policy and indicated that students at schools without the exams would be at a significant disadvantage in the very near future. Thus, the institution of comprehensive exams will be an aid to those who seek admission to graduate and professional schools after graduation.

ARGUMENT 2

The National Scholarship Achievement Board recently revealed the results of a study they conducted on the effectiveness of comprehensive exams at Duke University. One major finding was that student anxiety had increased by 31%. At comparable schools without the exam, anxiety increased by only 8%. The board reasoned that anxiety over the exams, or fear of failure, would motivate students to study more in their courses while they were taking them. It is likely that this increase in anxiety observed at Duke University would also be observed and be of benefit at other universities that adopt the exam policy.

A member of the board of curators has stated publicly that his brother had to take a comprehensive exam while in college and now is a manager of a large restaurant. He indicated that he realized the value of the exams since his father was a migrant worker who didn't even finish high school. He also indicated that the university has received several letters from parents in support of the exam. In fact, four of the six parents who wrote in thought that the exams were an excellent idea. Also, the prestigious National Accrediting Board of Higher Education seeks input from parents as well as students, faculty, and administrators when evaluating a university. Since most parents contribute financially to their child's education and also favor the exams, the university should institute them. This would show that the university is willing to listen to and follow the parents' wishes over those of students and faculty, who may simply fear the work involved in comprehensive exams.[4]

1. Discuss the strengths and weaknesses of the arguments in terms of the major claims being made, and the warrants and backings the authors provide to support those claims.
2. Do you find the arguments persuasive and compelling? Why?

[4]*From* R. Petty and J. T. Cacioppo, *Communication and Persuasion: Central and Peripheral Routes to Attitude Change.* New York: Springer-Verlag New York Inc., 1986, pp. 54–55, 57–58. Used with permission.

APPLICATION Implementation Plan

1. Recall an activity in school or at work that required critical thinking. It may have been a problem of deciding which school to attend or which major to declare. It may have involved the management of complex data or a search for information, such as securing the best loan or writing a major paper or doing a design project. The activity should be one that included lots of information—more than a few notes to yourself—and specific actions or recommendations made by you.

2. Analyze your own critical thinking *process*. Over the next three weeks, study and respond to the following questions by writing a brief report (three to five pages) which would include key information from each step. Submit the report to your instructor.

   ■ Describe the problem/situation as clearly as you can.
   ■ Describe the following categories of relevant information that were available to you.
   Quantitative: financial data, clinical.
   Political: interest groups, turf issues, sponsorship, financial or social liabilities, risks.
   Administrative: problems and issues in implementing staffing.
   ■ What priorities or relative weights did you assign to the issues or criteria with which you had to work?
   ■ Did you encounter conflicting information or advice? How did you deal with it?
   ■ What did you think about the situation? What were your initial impressions and hunches? Did anything have you perplexed or puzzled?
   ■ Was there a shortage of information or an overload? Looking back, could you have done anything about that shortage or overload?

Competency 3 Presenting Information; Writing Effectively

ASSESSMENT That'll Show 'Em

Directions The following example[5] has some problems. Try your hand at revising it. You can take liberties with the details, or you can invent a few facts if necessary. After you've written your version, please share with your group why you think it's more effective than the original.

TO: All Employees
FROM: Samuel Edwards, Department Manager
SUBJECT: Abuse of Copiers

[5] *Adapted from* Marvin H. Swift, "Clear Writing Means Clear Thinking Means . . . ," *Harvard Business Review* (Jan.–Feb. 1973). Copyright © 1973 by President and Fellows of Harvard College; all rights reserved.

It has recently been brought to my attention that many of the people who are employed in this department have taken advantage of their positions by availing themselves of the copiers. More specifically, these machines are being used for other than department purposes.

Obviously, such practice is contrary to department policy and must cease and desist immediately. I wish, therefore, to inform all concerned—those who have abused policy or will be abusing it—that their behavior cannot and will not be tolerated.

If there are any questions about department policy, please feel free to contact this office.

Interpretation   1. What was your chief problem in rewriting this memo?

2. What do you think your primary purpose was in writing the memo?

3. Did other members of your group come up with solutions you hadn't thought of?

LEARNING   Presenting Information

Barry Tarshis, a popular writing consultant, sometimes begins his seminars with this quip: "If I gave you folks your choice between spending five days in solitary confinement, living on bread and water, and being confined to a desk for five days, allowed to do nothing but write, about half of you would ask what kind of bread they were serving in solitary this week." (Tarshis 1985, 7) Writing does not top the charts for preferred entertainment, but take heart. Many of the problems we have with the writing we do at work can be alleviated. You can learn to write more efficiently.

WRITING IN THE BUREAUCRACY

Writing in organizations differs from much of the writing we do in school. In school we are taught that we write in order to inform or persuade. But, once in an organization, we learn we sometimes write primarily to document a decision or action, not really to communicate a message. It's sometimes hard to identify the "audience" for bureaucratic documents because there isn't always an audience, other than the file into which the report is put.

To make things more difficult, a lot of ghost writing is done in organizations. You write a report for your department manager, who has been assigned to write a report for the vice president's signature. That report may also need a "sign-off" from other people up the line, with each person looking for something different. So we write documents for other people's signatures to audiences with whom we seldom communicate. We also do a lot of writing by committee, the least efficient process imaginable, but organizations have to work that way sometimes.

Finally, the communicating style of big institutions is often very conventionalized. It's difficult to make changes. Given these conditions, it's hardly surprising that organizations have trouble with writing.

DRAWING A BLANK

There are three major causes of the avoidance and anxiety managers and supervisors bring to a blank piece of paper. They feel they:

- Don't know how to begin.
- Struggle to find the right words.
- Worry about organization.

We'll present a three-stage process for writing documents, simple or complex. Variations of this process are used by hundreds of professional writers who face the same blocks and frustrations we all face. The three stages are (1) sketching a satellite outline, (2) fleshing out the outline with "automatic writing," and (3) revising that version until you have a polished draft.

DON'T KNOW HOW TO BEGIN

The biggest mistake you can make as a writer is to fixate on the polished version before you have done any sketching or mapping of what you need to say. People often start to mentally edit their work before they have even written a word. Keep the editor away from the composer. Let your mind work on the task uncensored. Most people, once they get used to it, like to begin their more complex writing tasks with a sketch or outline.

The term *outline* connotes the roman numeral method of I; A; 1, 2; a. b. This is the correct sequence, but few of us use it when given a choice. When required in school to write outlines to accompany papers, a lot of us wrote them *after* writing the paper. Classical outlining doesn't satisfy our needs because real topics have a way of not breaking into such symmetrical pieces. Increasingly, experts on the writing process advise us to use methods that are more organic and flexible.

This flexible method has been called "mind mapping." (Westheimer 1988, 52) or "satellite outlining" (Tarshis 1985, 65). Here's some instructions for making it work.

1. In the center of your paper draw a square or circle.

2. Inside the circle write the name of your project, subject of your correspondence, or item you intend to discuss.

3. Draw branches from the circle, like branches from a tree, to designate your main topics or concerns.

4. To help identify these topics, you might use the "five *w*s and one *b*." Ask yourself who, what, when, where, why, and how.

5. Branch off into smaller but related topics.

6. Don't worry about the organization of your branches; that comes later.

7. Use different colored pens or pencils to designate related topics. (Westheimer 1988, 52)

Beginnings and endings are a trap—the worst trap the writer faces. The best way to deal with beginnings and endings is not to, until you must. When you begin a memo or a major report, don't worry about what the first sentence or the first paragraph will be. The opening and closing will come.

Let's see how mind mapping or satellite outlining works. As the agent in charge of buying print and paper for a major metropolitan newspaper, you have just attended a briefing on the corporation's new policies for major purchases and for contracting out of the country. These policies were drafted quickly to respond to new federal trade legislation. You return to your office and start sketching a technical memo. You can build things around your target statement as shown in Figure 5.3.

TARGET STATEMENT

You'll notice that in Figure 5.3 we've added in the center of the satellite outline a statement of the writer's purpose. This is a **target statement** (Tarshis 1985, 57). A target statement is not a summary of what you want to say. It's a statement of your primary purpose. It's your idea of what you want the document to accomplish. You don't write your target statement in your document, but you may want to write it to yourself. Ask yourself before you write that memo, "What do I want?" I want them to know when and where the meeting is. I want them to stop taking the photocopy auditron from the copy room. I want them to turn in their requests for conference travel before the tenth of the month. I want Irene Woo to know how grateful I am for her work on the retirement banquet.

In our example in Figure 5.3, we show the target statement in a dotted box. If you can't write a target statement, you need to think more about your purpose.

MAKING MUD Automatic Writing

With a satellite outline finished, you're ready for the second stage, putting flesh on the bones. Al Switzler, a management consultant who has also written some excellent poetry, talks about this second stage as "making mud." When Switzler has talked through something, taken some notes, and perhaps tried a satellite outline, he turns to the keyboard and starts pounding away.

At this "mud-making stage" even a meticulous editor like Switzler doesn't yet care about word choices or organization. "This is the creative stage" says Switzler, "the critical stage comes later when you worry about grammar, punctuation, and transitions." Peter Elbow calls this process "automatic writing." Every

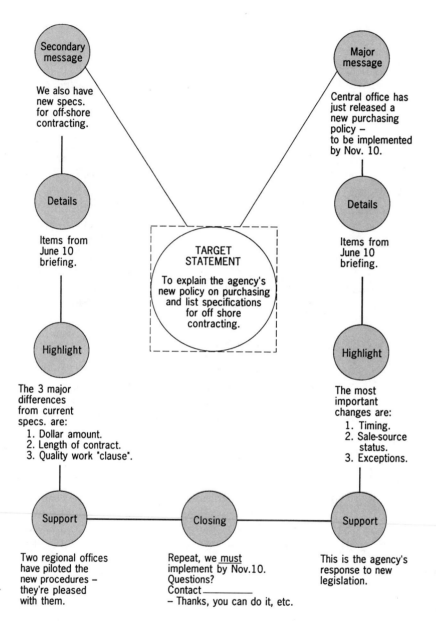

Secondary
message

We also have
new specs.
for off-shore
contracting.

Details

Items from
June 10
briefing.

Highlight

The 3 major
differences
from current
specs. are:
1. Dollar amount.
2. Length of contract.
3. Quality work "clause".

Support

Two regional offices
have piloted the
new procedures –
they're pleased
with them.

TARGET
STATEMENT

To explain the agency's
new policy on purchasing
and list specifications
for off shore
contracting.

Major
message

Central office has
just released a
new purchasing
policy –
to be implemented
by Nov. 10.

Details

Items from
June 10
briefing.

Highlight

The most
important
changes are:
1. Timing.
2. Sale-source
   status.
3. Exceptions.

Support

This is the agency's
response to new
legislation.

Closing

Repeat, we <u>must</u>
implement by Nov.10.
Questions?
Contact_____
– Thanks, you can do it, etc.

FIGURE 5.3 *An
example of mind-
mapping.*

writer has two roles to manage: the writer and the editor. Most of us allow the
editor to surface much too soon. The writer must be left to compose, to get
some things out, no matter how tentative or disorganized. Then, and only then,
should the editor be released with all of his or her critical scrutiny. Automatic
writing is like free association. It can ramble. Automatic writing is a tool for
discovery and clarification. Its purpose is to help you map the territory.

Remember, it takes courage and imagination to compose. When you write,
you create the trial balloon for people to shoot at. When all the committees

have met and groups have haggled and made their lists and voiced their opinions, the real hero is the person who grabs the pen or the keyboard and starts making mud.

FINDING THE RIGHT WORDS The Lard Factor

What are the major criticisms of bureaucratic writing? Too wordy and indirect. The "lard factor" (Lanham 1981, 2) is the problem. It's hard to tell "who's kicking who" in organizational writing because we like the passive voice, and we like to use the pseudoverb "is" instead of real action verbs with some kick to them. We also avoid sentences with real subjects that tell us who or what is doing the kicking. The passive voice is a major cause of wordiness.

The passive voice is a construction that makes the subject of a sentence the receiver of the action rather than the doer of the action. When we write "The decision was reached by the committee," the subject is "decision" and the subject is being acted upon. This is a passive voice construction. To make it active you make the subject the doer of the action: "The committee reached a decision." It's much clearer in the second sentence who is kicking whom. The committee is the kicker. It's kicking a decision. If we get rid of unnecessary passive constructions, we can cut the length of our sentences by almost 20%, and we can make them easier to read.

When you have to edit your own sentences, or someone else's, try using Lanham's formula for cutting fat.

1. Circle every form of *to be* (*is, was, will be, seems to be*).

2. Circle every prepositional phrase.

3. Now find out who's kicking whom and start rebuilding the sentence with that kicking action.

With a little practice, Lanham says, sentences like:

> *The role of markets is easily observed and understood when dealing with a simple commodity such as potatoes.*

will turn into:

> *Examining a simple commodity like potatoes shows clearly how markets work.* (*Lanham 1981, 5*)

The second sentence is 39% shorter than the first, and much easier to understand. Here's some other principles and strategies to remember when you edit your work.

1. Avoid the passive voice where appropriate.

2. Don't make nouns out of good, strong working verbs. Be wary of nouns ending in "ization," "tion," "ence," and "ance." Instead of "I am making the recommendation that she be promoted to Program Associate," write, "I recommend that she be promoted to Program Associate."

3. Be concise. Keep sentences short. If a sentence is longer than 20 words, you should look twice at it. The period is the most neglected form of punctuation.

However, you can avoid a choppy style by balancing a series of short sentences with a longer, more complex one.

4. Be specific. Use concrete terms instead of generalizations or vague phrases or terms. Instead of: "We should make such efforts as will ensure our coming closer to meeting the state's license issuance quota in the near future," write: "We should be certain we have met the state's quota for issuing licenses by the end of fiscal year 1991."

5. Don't hesitate to repeat words, phrases, or ideas when repeating increases clarity. "When the Department's computer network failed, the shift supervisor decided not to notify the Director of Operations, although he did activate the backup system. This caused great concern in the corporate office." Instead write: "When the Department's computer network failed, the shift supervisor decided not to notify the Director of Operations, although he did activate the backup system. *This first decision* caused great concern in the corporate office."

THE MEMO Workhorse or Dead horse?

Let's look at memo writing. The memo is the most common document produced in organizations. Entire books have been written just on the art of memo writing. (A couple of the best ones are listed in the references section at the end of this chapter.) Some memos are so simple they pose no problem for any of us, but as they become more complex, or more politically or socially sensitive, they represent an opportunity for failure.

Before we talk about how to write memos, let's say a few things about what a memo is. A memo is an internal document, one that stays within the organization. It is often written to an audience of more than one person (one of the things that distinguishes it from a letter) and focuses on one primary message or piece of information. A memo is usually a brief, concise document. The memo is supposed to make things easier for people. As they become complex, they become self-defeating

Read the two sample memos that follow.

VERSION A

SUBJECT: Meeting on Computer-Assisted Diagnostic Methods

Attached for your review is a packet on CAD methods. We will have Nelson Goodwin here from Mindread Inc. to give us a demonstration on their latest software.

This meeting is designed primarily for psychologists, but other members of treatment teams may wish to attend.

The meeting will be held on July 17, at 10:00 a.m., in Conference Room C, Administration Building. Hope you can attend.

VERSION B

SUBJECT: July 17 Meeting on Computer Assistant Diagnostic (CAD) Methods

You are scheduled to attend the CAD methods meeting we discussed at our retreat in June. The meeting will be held July 17, at 10:00 A.M., in Conference Room C, Administration Building. Nelson Goodwin of Mindread Inc. will give a presentation on his company's latest software. The enclosed packet gives you an overview of his presentation. You may want to think about questions to ask him.

As agreed at the June retreat, we're inviting all psychologists directly, but other treatment team members may also attend.

Which version do you prefer and why? Most people select version B because it presents the vital information first. In version A there is, or could be, confusion in the reader's mind about why the memo is being sent and what the main point is. Version A is written in what is called ascending order (Booher 1984). The vital information comes later in the memo. You have to wade through some introductory details and throat clearing to find the main point. Memos are practical documents. They are supposed to transfer information, not build suspense. That's why the experts recommend you write them in descending order. The main point comes first; support and explanation follow.

A pattern to remember for outlining memos in the first stage is:

1. Requests before justifications.

2. Answers before explanations.

3. Conclusions before discussions.

4. Summaries before details.

5. Generalities before specifics. (Westheimer 1988, 58)

MAKING YOUR MESSAGE ACCESSIBLE

Look at the following two memos.

TO: All Staff
FROM: Jason Bridge
SUBJECT: Travel Approval

We talked in the last staff meeting about travel approval, and the fact that some of the policies and procedures on travel might be changing. This month, we heard about some changes from central office. I want to share some of the major changes with you, and we can discuss them in the next staff meeting.

From now on, travel within state has to be approved before the travel. Apparently, we really do run the risk of not being reimbursed if we cannot demonstrate prior approval, or document "emergency status" if we did not have approval.

This means we will have to be more careful. Submit travel approval forms through your manager and be certain you have approval before incurring any expenses. If you have any questions, give me a call at 4567.

TO: All Staff
FROM: Jason Bridge
SUBJECT: New Policy on Travel Approval

The new policy on travel approval is here. Beginning August 30, we have to have prior approval for travel if we expect to be reimbursed.

Here's what you need to do.

1. Be certain you submit a travel approval form through your manager.
2. Be certain you have clearance before making a trip and incurring any expenses.

Apparently, we really do run a risk of not being reimbursed if we don't have prior approval.

The only exception is an "emergency trip," and that requires special documentation. We'll talk about that and other details at next Thursday's meeting.

If you have questions in the meantime, just call me at 4567.

Notice how much more accessible the message is in the second version? The writer, in addition to stating the message better, has also presented the message better. The second version uses white space much more effectively. Each key point is broken into a separate paragraph. Notice the one-sentence paragraph. You may have been taught that one sentence paragraphs are against the law, but they are permissible in memo writing, as long as you don't overdo it.

Notice also that the heading is better spaced for easier reading, and the subject line is more informative. The heading, "New Policy on Travel Approval" is more informative than the heading "Travel Approval."

ANALYSIS   A Look at Your Own Writing

Directions   Bring three samples of your own writing to the course. These samples can be from course work, or from practical writing tasks you have faced on jobs or in various organizations. Exchange these samples with a classmate and go through an informal assessment of what you think are some of the strong points of your writing, as well as those areas that might be improved.

Keep in mind that as editors or evaluators, you are just operating as readers reacting to each other's writing. There is no *one* way to do any of this. Except for the conventions we share on grammar, spelling, and punctuation, there is no best approach for saying what you need to say.

Put on a few different hats during the process. Be factual and honest, but also compassionate and supportive. Take a half hour for this exercise.

Discussion Questions   1. Did you discover weaknesses in diction and organization?
2. What would you change in your own writing? In the writing of others?

PRACTICE   Editing Exercise

Directions   Edit the following eight sentences. In some cases, you'll need to change from the passive to the active voice. Some sentences are too indirect or foggy. You don't have the context of these statements, and that limitation always makes editing more difficult. But you can improve all these sentences. You may have to assume a few facts and stretch the available information in order to make sense of some of them.

1. After completion of the application process, proceed to the interview section where you should submit your application and all other appropriate forms as required.

2. Individualization of treatment programs must become our top priority if we are to effect an ameliorated accreditation review.

3. Implementation of the new pricing guidelines should be put in place immediately.

4. From the assessment conducted recently, it was ascertained that a significant percentage of the auditors' time was consumed by the necessity of rescheduling previously arranged audits.

5. Pursuant to the requirements of our contract, we are herewith informing you of your right to request information on our bidder selection process.

6. It was the feeling of the committee that there was insufficient awareness on the part of the examiners of the importance of credential verification, particularly in the case of new applicants.

7. In running a large office, a willingness to delegate authority is essential.

8. The establishment of a state commission for the investigation of a growing trend of crimes against the elderly should receive our immediate support through both correspondence with the governor's office, and direct contact with other elected officials.

Discussion Questions   1. Did you have trouble making sense out of any of these sentences? Which ones? Why?
2. What major writing weaknesses were involved in these sentences?
3. Do you believe some sentences are purposely vague? Why?

APPLICATION   You Will Report to Work

You have a problem. You are vice president in charge of operations for Power Systems, the same company Christine Elm works for. You've just attended an emergency meeting of the company's executive board. An internal audit of the floor's inventory has revealed some dramatic shortages in material, such as copper wire, capacitors, and expensive testing equipment.

A "tip" about these shortages was made by an anonymous employee, but before the board had even met, the local paper printed a blurb on the "possible theft at Power Systems." Last evening, a local television reporter called the company's information office for details.

The board voted unanimously for an emergency inventory to be conducted this Saturday, May 19, beginning at 9:00 A.M. The plant's union representative was present and approved the inventory, but only after the board agreed to pay for overtime. The board also decided to provide lunch. As an "incentive," the board also voted to give priority to the vacation schedule requests of those employees who come to the inventory.

As the person in charge of operations, you were unanimously elected to write the memo to all employees. It's Wednesday afternoon. The inventory is this Saturday. Write the memo with the information provided.

REFERENCES

Booher, Dianna Daniels. *Send Me a Memo*. New York: Facts on File, 1984.

Boston, Bruce. *Stet!: Tricks of the Trade for Writers and Editors*. Alexandria, Va.: Editorial Experts Inc., 1986.

Browne, Neil M., and Stuart M. Keeley. *Asking the Right Questions: A Guide to Critical Thinking*. Englewood Cliffs, N.J.: Prentice Hall, 1986.

De Bono, Edward. *Six Thinking Hats*. Boston: Little, Brown, 1986.

Dumaine, Brian. "What the Leaders of Tomorrow See." *Fortune* (July 3, 1989): 48–55.

Eisenberg, Ronnie. *Organize Yourself*. New York: Macmillan, 1986.

Elbow, Peter. *Writing without Teachers*. New York: Oxford University Press, 1973.

Glueck, William F., and Lawrence R. Jauch. *The Managerial Experience: Cases, Exercises, and Readings*. New York: The Dryden Press, 1977.

Goldberg, Natalie. *Writing Down the Bones*. Boston: Shambala, 1986.

Goldman, Daniel. "Who Are You Kidding?" *Psychology Today* (March 1987): 24–30.

Guterl, Fred V. "Europe's Secret Weapon." *Business Month* (October 1989): 63–66.

Hogarth, Robin. *Judgement and Choice*. New York: John Wiley and Sons, 1987.

Imai, Masaaki. *Kaizen: The Key to Japan's Competitive Success*. New York: Random House, 1986.

Kaye, Sanford. *Writing under Pressure*. New York: Oxford University Press, 1989.

Lanham, Richard. *Revising Business Prose*. New York: Scribner's, 1981.

McCormack, Mark. *What They Don't Teach You at the Harvard Business School*. New York: Bantam Books, 1985.

Miller, Lawrence M. *American Spirit: Visions of a New Corporate Culture*. New York: Morrow, 1984.

Mitroff, Ian I., and Ralph H. Killman. *Corporate Tragedies: Product Tampering, Sabotage and Other Catastrophes*. New York: Praeger, 1984.

Neisser, Uric. *Memory Observed: Remembering in Natural Contexts*. San Francisco: Freeman, 1982.

Pirsig, Robert. *Zen and the Art of Motorcycle Maintenance.* New York: Bantam Books, 1974.

Schermerhorn, John R. *Management for Productivity*, (3rd ed.). New York: John Wiley and Sons, 1989.

Simmons, John, "The Painful Reeducation of a Company Man." *Business Month* (October 1989): 78–80.

Simon, Herbert A. *Reason in Human Affairs.* Stanford: Stanford University Press, 1983.

Sternberg, Robert. *The Triarchic Mind: A New Theory of Human Intelligence.* New York: Viking, 1988.

Tarshis, Barry. *How to Write without Pain.* New York: American Library, 1985.

Toulmin, Stephen, Richard Rieke, and Alan Janik. *An Introduction to Reasoning* (2d ed.). New York: Macmillan, 1984.

Wayne, Leslie. "Where Were the Accountants?" *The New York Times* (March 12, 1989): Section 3, pp. 11–13.

Westheimer, Patricia. *The Perfect Memo.* Glenview, Ill.: Scott, Foresman, 1988.

Winwood, Richard I. *Excellence through Time Management.* Salt Lake City: The Franklin Institute, 1985.

The Coordinator and Monitor Roles

Before we move on to the next two roles, let's put the coordinator and monitor roles into the context of the competing values framework. As with the other roles, these roles are appropriate in some situations, and not in others.

A BRIEF REVIEW

The coordinator and monitor roles are part of the the internal process model, in which the desired ends are stability and control. The assumed means to these ends have to do with routinization, measurement, and documentation. This model says that managers need to monitor and analyze the situation that surrounds them and use rational tools to plan, organize, and control the processes in the unit. The model assumes structure in terms of rules, procedures, norms, and values that constrain action, and the manager's job is to see that things stay in equilibrium.

WHEN THE COORDINATOR AND MONITOR ROLES ARE MOST APPROPRIATE

Again, the two axes show us when the internal process is appropriate. On the horizontal axis the model is defined by an internal focus, which suggests less external pressure for action and more internal pressures for communication, coordination, and conformity. On the vertical axis, it is defined by high control, which suggests situations where the basic problems are easily understood. When a situation does not require fast action (absence of external pressures) and the basic strategies are clearly known, things get routinized or programmed, and it becomes appropriate to monitor and coordinate. Others accept such behavior in this situation because it makes a great deal of sense. To innovate when there is no pressure to do so and when the appropriate means-ends strategies are clearly routine would be highly resisted.

COMPLEMENTARY ROLES

Because some people feel that the internal process model is inherently "right," they may tend to overuse it. In all situations they believe that they should be maintaining the status quo. At times, though, acting as a coordinator and monitor is not the best course that a manager can take. The failure to balance the director and producer roles with the other roles, particularly the innovator and broker roles in the open systems quadrant, can lead to problems. Consider the classic story of Henry Ford.

Ford was a determined entrepreneur with a vision. He wanted to build an automobile for the common man. He felt that if he could provide a dependable vehicle and sell it at a low price, he could become rich by selling the car in huge volume. His first big step was to produce the Model T. His second step was to apply the principles of scientific management to the production process, making great strides in efficient production. He, for example, reduced the assembly time for the automobile from many hundreds of hours to a little over 90 minutes. This very innovative man became very rich. While he continued to be innovative about production, his orientation to product became that of monitor and coordinator. In playing these two roles, he allowed no changes in the car. His philosophy, in fact, is reflected in the famous statement, "They can have any color they want, as long as it is black." The outcome was predictable and disastrous: Ford, the unquestioned leader in automobile production, soon fell behind General Motors and would never again match them in size. Later the company was forced to close for a year while they moved to the new Model A.

Clearly the roles in the internal process model must be seen in context. They must be balanced with other models.

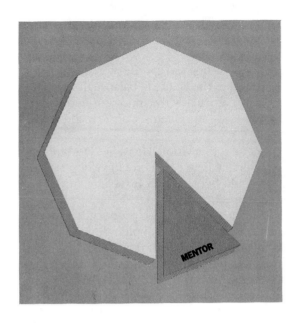

THE MENTOR ROLE

We now turn to the human relations model. In this model the focus is on individuals and groups. We will also discuss commitment, cohesion, and morale as indicators of effectiveness. A central belief in this model is that involvement and participation in decision making result in outcomes such as high commitment. The climate emphasized in this model is characterized by teamwork, and the key managerial-leadership roles are mentor and facilitator. The task is to establish and maintain effective relationships.

In Chapter 1 we pointed out that the **mentor** role might also be called the concerned human role. This role reflects a caring, empathetic orientation. In this role a manager is expected to be helpful, considerate, sensitive, approachable, open, and fair. In acting out the role, the leader listens, supports legitimate requests, conveys appreciation, and gives recognition. Employees are seen as important resources to be understood, valued, and developed. The manager helps them with individual development plans, and also sees that they have opportunities for training and skill building.

In Western society acts of caring and concern are sometimes seen as soft and weak. It is thought that to be a good leader one must be strong, powerful, and in control. Likewise, some individuals find that they have great difficulty with feelings and the expression of feelings. Given such societal and individual

| BOX 6.1   THE DERAILED EXECUTIVES

A comparison was made between 21 "derailed" executives and 20 "arrivers" to try to determine why some people succeed and others fail to reach their potential. Several characteristics of the derailed executives stood out:

1. Insensitive to others; abrasive and intimidating.
2. Cold, aloof, and arrogant.
3. Betrayed the trust of others.
4. Overly ambitious; always trying to move up.
5. Could not delegate or build teams.
6. Could not get along with people who had different styles.
7. Overdependent on others.

Source: Morgan W. McCall and Michael M. Lombardo, "What Makes a Top Executive?" *Psychology Today* (February 1983), pp. 26–31. Reprinted with permission from Psychology Today Magazine. Copyright © 1983 (PT Partners, L.P.)

however, is a mistake. Social science has clearly demonstrated the importance of this role in overall managerial effectiveness (Bass 1981). People who play the mentor role poorly do not fare well (see Box 6.1). The three competencies in this role are:

Competency 1   Understanding Yourself and Others
Competency 2   Interpersonal Communication
Competency 3   Developing Subordinates

Competency 1   Understanding Yourself and Others

ASSESSMENT   Managerial Orientation Measure

Directions   Circle the level of agreement or disagreement that you personally feel toward each of the following 10 statements.

Scale   SA = Strongly Agree   A = Agree   U = Uncertain   D = Disagree
SD = Strongly Disagree

1. People need to know that the boss is in charge.   SA (A) U D SD
2. Employees will rise to the occasion when an extra effort is needed.   SA (A) U D SD

3. Employees need direction and control or they will not work hard.   SA   A   (U)   D   SD

4. People naturally want to work.   SA   (A)   U   D   SD

5. A manager should be a decisive, no nonsense leader.   SA   (A)   U   D   SD

6. Employees should be involved in making decisions that concern them.   SA   (A)   U   D   SD

7. A manager has to be tough minded and hard-nosed.   SA   A   U   (D)   SD

8. A manager should build a climate of trust in the work unit.   SA   (A)   U   D   SD

9. If a unit is to be productive, employees need to be pushed.   SA   A   U   (D)   SD

10. Employees need the freedom to innovate.   SA   (A)   U   D   SD

Scoring and Interpretation

Items	SA	A ₁₁	U ₁	D ₁₁	SD
1, 3, 5, 7, 9:	1 point	2 points	3 points	4 points	5 points
2, 4, 6, 8, 10:	5 points	4 points	3 points	2 points	1 point

+++| : 20

To determine your score, add up the total points for all 10 items. Scores can be between 10 and 50. As we'll see next, high scores suggest managerial attitudes in line with "Theory Y," whereas low scores would indicate attitudes that fit with "Theory X."   :35

LEARNING   Understanding Yourself and Others

To be a successful mentor, managers must have some understanding of themselves and others. Although all members of a work group have something in common, each individual is also in some way unique. The challenge is to understand both the commonalities and differences and how these cause people to relate to one another in various ways. By being aware, you can better understand your own reaction to people and their reactions to each other. This understanding, should, in turn, make you more effective.

The relationship between self-understanding and personal effectiveness is illustrated in an incident from the career of Jane Evans, who is currently president and CEO of InterPacific Retail Group. Earlier in her career, when she was announced as the new CEO of Butterrick/Vogue, seven division vice presidents, all male, immediately quit. What would your reaction be? The confident Evans met with the seven men and bet them that, within one year, they would agree that she was the best boss they ever had. Using her highly developed skills in the mentor role, she won the bet.

VALUES AND ASSUMPTIONS

The assessment activity you just completed is based on the work of Douglas McGregor (1960). He argues that people tend to make two very different sets of assumptions about the world. The first orientation, called **Theory X,** reflects a classical view of management that emphasizes control and close supervision. It assumes that people are predisposed not to work. The manager's job, therefore, is to control, push, and prod people into action. In contrast, the **Theory Y** approach assumes that people want to work, they want control over their own activities, and they want ever-increasing levels of responsibility. It views people as entirely capable of being innovative and of making important contributions to the organization. The manager's job is to listen, respond, inspire, and reward. A low score on the assessment activity you just completed suggests a Theory X orientation, whereas a high score suggests a Theory Y orientation.

In understanding ourselves and others, we start by looking at people's values and assumptions because of their great influence on behavior. Someone who has a Theory X view of the world, for example, will do very different things than someone who has a Theory Y view. Moreover, each will probably have difficulty understanding and working with the other.

Values are basic—the fundamental standards of desirability by which we choose between alternatives. They are our assumptions about the nature of reality. They differ from attitudes, traits, or needs. An *attitude* is a feeling about an object. A *trait* is a regularly occurring pattern of individual action. A *need* is a sensed lack of something desired. Values precede each of these.

Values are learned early and continue to develop throughout our lives. They are acquired and developed through relationships, initially with parents and family members, and later, outside the family.

Research (Rokeach 1973) identifies two types of values: *instrumental values* (how you think things should be done) and *terminal values* (what your goals are). Instrumental values include such things as hard work, openmindedness, competence, lightheartedness, and forgiveness. Terminal values include such things as a prosperous life, accomplishment, peace, and self-respect.

Although people tend to hold the same general values, research shows that people vary widely in how they prioritize the values they hold. A study by Clare and Sanford (1979), for example, found that managers tend to value sense of accomplishment, self-respect, a comfortable life, and independence more than others. Their highest instrumental value for managers was ambition, and their highest terminal value was sense of accomplishment. Clearly most managers tend to be very achievement oriented. Naturally, these values affect their view of the world. If you were a manager of people who had values such as these, your job would be more different than if you were a manager of people who rejected these same values. A major challenge then is to know your own values and to know the values of other people. The more you do this, the more likely you are to choose the right strategy with the right person at the right moment.

VALUES AND UNDERSTANDING YOURSELF

The importance of understanding your own values and behaviors is obvious. If you don't understand yourself, it is nearly impossible to understand others. Yet there is evidence to suggest that many managers have considerable difficulty understanding themselves.

William Torbert (1987) uses a developmental model of behavior which suggests that people progress through a series of stages. In each stage they take on different values and assumptions. One of these stages is what he calls the technician stage. It represents the most prevalent style of managing; 47% of senior managers and 68% of first-line managers fall into this category.

People in the technician stage are concerned with expertise. They focus on technical logic and on efficiency, often setting standards of perfection. They tend to work closely but impersonally with others. They are constantly checking up on details and do not hesitate to take over in an emergency. In terms of learning about themselves, they are very slow, perhaps resistant to taking feedback about their behavior. The feelings of others are simply not interesting or valid. People in this stage feel that technical facts rather than the norms and values of the group should guide behavior.

If so many managers are in fact in the technician stage, then learning about and understanding themselves is no small problem. For this reason it is useful to know about a concept called the Johari window.

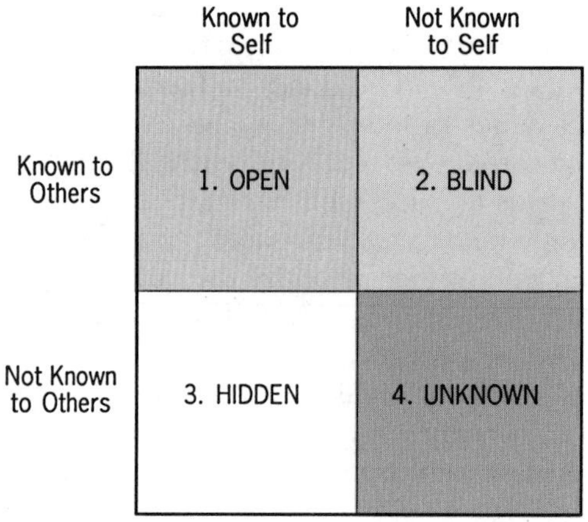

FIGURE 6.1 *The Johari window.*

The Johari window, developed by Luft and Ingham (1955), is a simple but helpful concept. As shown in Figure 6.1, it has four quadrants. In the upper left is the open area which represents the values, motives, and behaviors that are known to one's self and to others. In the upper right is the blind area. Here are the values, motives, and behaviors that are seen by others but are not recognized by you. In the lower left is the hidden quadrant. These are the things that you know but do not reveal to others. Finally, in the lower right is the unknown quadrant. Here are the motives and behaviors of which neither you nor others are yet aware; they exist, but no one has yet observed them or their impact on the relationship. Later, when they are discovered, it becomes obvious that they existed previously and did have impact.

The sizes of the four quadrants change over the course of time. In a new relationship, quadrant 1 is small. As communication increases, it grows large and quadrant 3 begins to shrink. With growing trust, we feel less need to hide the things we value, feel, and know. It takes longer for quadrant 2 to shrink in size because it requires openness to honest feedback. As we saw in Torbert's research, many people are not open to feedback about their blind spots. They feel defensive and use a variety of behaviors to close off feedback.

Quadrant 4 tends to change most slowly of all. It is often a very large quadrant that greatly influences what we do. Yet many people totally close off the possibility of learning about quadrant 4.

Some important lessons can be learned from the Johari window. People use a great deal of energy in order to hide, deny, or be blind to their own values, motives, and behaviors, particularly their inconsistencies and hypocrisies. As a result quadrant 1 begins to shrink and the others begin to enlarge.

When quadrant 1 increases in size, however, the others shrink: More energy, skills, and resources can be directed towards the tasks around which the relationship is formed. The more that this occurs, the more openness, trust, and learning there is and the more the positive outcomes begin to multiply.

VALUES AND UNDERSTANDING OTHERS

The Johari window informs us not only of our own blind, hidden, and unknown areas, but it also makes us aware that these areas exist in others. If we appreciate that others have these three covert areas, then it is likely that they also will be defensive about them. And if we point out things in the three areas, it is likely that they will reject us and that the relationship will grow less trusting.

How then do we help others to learn? How do we build trust? How do we come to better understand others?

The paradoxical problem brings us back to ourselves. A key to positive change is not in focusing on others but on ourselves. In fact we need to be sensitive and respectful of the need of others to be defensive. The secret of overcoming defensiveness in others is to overcome defensiveness in ourselves.

TABLE 6.1 Rules for Practicing Empathy

Empathy: The Ability to Experience the Feelings of Others
1. You must first examine yourself. If you do not truly want to understand others, if you are insincere, empathy will not work.
2. Communication is more than words. You must be sensitive to times when expressed thoughts and feelings are not congruent. You must read the nonverbal signals as well as the verbal ones.
3. Do not react too quickly to inaccurate statements of fact; listen carefully for the feelings beneath the statement before rushing in to correct facts.
4. You must allow the person to tell the emotional truth, which may include negative feelings about you. You must be ready to openly explore such negative feedback.
5. Use reflective listening (see Competency 2 in this chapter).

If we provide a role model of sensitivity, openness, and learning, we increase the probability of sensitivity, openness, and learning on the part of the other.

To provide such a role model, we need to feel secure enough to be open. Security, however, only comes by being open with ourselves. In other words, the key to understanding and helping others is to continuously increase our own awareness of those things we least want to know about ourselves, through openness to external feedback, and through sensitivity and respect for the defensiveness of others.

Integrity, security, and self-acceptance increase the ability to practice empathy, the key skill in helping others to grow. **Empathy** is truly putting yourself in the position of others and honestly trying to see the world as they see it. Table 6.1 lists five rules for helping you to practice being empathetic.

ANALYSIS   The Sherwood Holmes Case

Directions   Your role for this activity is that of Sherwood Holmes, the American cousin of that famous detective. Although you are not as well known as your cousin, you are lucky to have inherited the same skills that have inspired numerous novels and films.

After reading the case, carefully study the room diagram. Then construct and complete the Sherwood Inference Sheet. In your small group compare your observations and inferences; a large discussion will follow.[1]

Last month your department instituted the placement of suggestion boxes at all work sites. You came up with several suggestions, one of which was brought to the attention of your CEO. You have been called into the CEO's office to discuss how your suggestion could be implemented.

[1]*Adapted from* J. W. Pfeiffer and John E. Jones (Eds.), *A Handbook of Structured Experiences for Human Relations Training,* Vol. VI, San Diego, CA.: University Associates, Inc. 1977. Used with permission.

Always prepared, you reviewed your cousin's notes that stated:

> *Observation, knowledge, and induction and deduction are all any private investigator needs. Observation is what you see, hear, and so on. Knowledge consists of the meanings, facts, and information that is available to you. Induction is the process of reasoning from the specific to the general. For example, every tree I have seen has roots; therefore, all trees have roots. Deduction, on the other hand, is the process of reasoning from the general to the specific—all trees have roots; this is a tree; therefore, this tree has roots.*

When you arrive at the office, the secretary tells you that.the CEO will arrive in about 15 minutes. You are shown into the office to wait. Knowing you have several minutes alone in the office, your native curiosity becomes overwhelming. You begin to look around.

The office is carpeted in a short shag in blending colors of olive green, brown, and orange. You sit in one of the two orange club chairs to the left of the doorway. Between the chairs is a low wooden table on which there is an empty green glass ashtray. Next to the ashtray are two books of matches; both are from a local restaurant. On the wall behind you is a picture of an old sailing ship in blues and browns. A rubber plant set in a brown and green woven basket sits against the side wall next to the other chair.

Across from where you are sitting is a large wooden desk, with a black leather deskchair. An art print of the bicentennial celebration hangs on the wall behind the desk, and below that sits a closed briefcase. The black waste basket next to the wall by the desk chair is full of papers.

You can see most of the objects on the desk. A matching pen-and-pencil stand and a letter opener sit at the front of the desk. To one side of them is a calculator, and next to that is a brass desk lamp. In front of the lamp is a double metal photograph frame with photographs in it. It is of an attractive woman in her thirties with a young boy about eight years old. The other photograph is of a dalmation in a grassy field. In front of the frame is a stack of green file folders. On the desk, in front of the desk chair, are a few sheets of paper and a felt-tipped pen.

On the other side of the desk is a yellow stoneware mug. In front of it are a leather tabbed book and a legal-sized yellow pad. The book looks as if it is either an address book or an appointment calendar. Beside the yellow pad lies a pile of unopened mail—envelopes of many sizes. And partially on top of the pile and in back of it are half-folded newspapers: *The Wall Street Journal* and *The New York Times.*

Behind the desk and to one side is a credenza on which seven books are lined up. They are *Roget's Thesaurus,* the *Random House Dictionary, Basic Principles of Management, Marketing for Today, Intergroup and Minority Relations, People at Work, You Are What You Eat,* and last year's *World Almanac.* On the far end of the credenza sits a bronze statue; it appears to be of a man sitting with his legs folded in a Yoga position, but it is slightly abstract. In the corner next to the credenza is a philodendron sitting in a brown basket.

There is a window on the far wall, and you get up and go over to look out. Directly in front of the window is a sofa covered in an orange, olive green, and beige print. Two woven throw pillows in brown and beige lie against the arms of the sofa. The draperies at the window behind the sofa are a light beige woven material with an olive green stripe. The view from the window is pleasant: a few tidy shops bordering a small park.

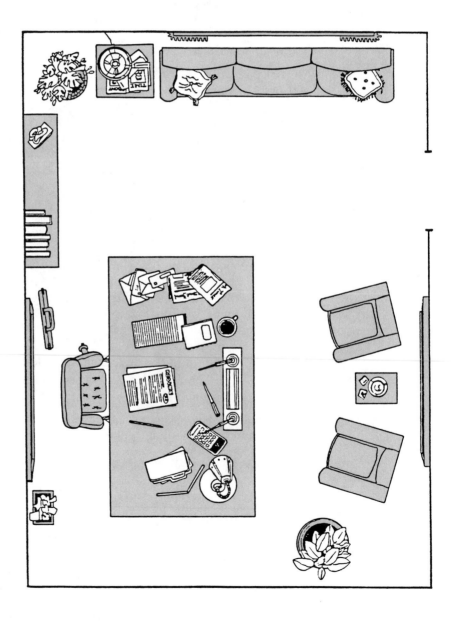

Your gaze turns to the square wooden table next to the sofa. Magazines are scattered in front of a brown ceramic lamp with a beige shade. The magazines are varied: two recent editions of *Time,* and one copy each of *Sports Illustrated, The New Yorker, Psychology Today,* and *Ebony.* Next to the table is the philodendron.

As you turn to walk back to your chair, you notice that the papers on the desk in front of you are from your personnel file, and that a statement of your sex has been circled with the felt-tipped pen. Since the CEO may return at any moment, you sit in the orange chair to wait.

Directions for inference sheet

Read the description of the CEO's office and study the room diagram carefully. Construct the Sherwood Inference Sheet by drawing three columns on a piece of paper.

1. In the left-hand column (Observation) note data from your reading that you think are important clues about the kind of person who occupies the room.

2. In the middle column (Knowledge) note any experiences that you may have had that influence your observation.

3. In the right-hand column (Inference) note whatever conclusions you reach as a result of your observations.

PRACTICE The Marvins Are Missing, Again

10/23

Directions

Read the case of each of the three Marvins. They are all absent from work, but for very different reasons. The performance of your unit is suffering as a result of these absences. Your manager is beginning to ask why you have so many reported absences in your unit.

Marvin Lowrey

Marvin Lowrey was one of your best workers until his wife was killed in a car accident several months ago. He asked for, and you approved, a two-week leave so that he could "think things out." *Counseling, Support, performance organizational impact*

When he returned, it was obvious that this was not the same Marvin you knew several weeks before. He seemed absentminded, irritable, and was nearly injured in a shop accident because of his carelessness. He also has called in sick several times. You called him at home to see how he was doing, and he said it was just the flu. He has also used up all his vacation time. In the past, Marvin has been a good employee, and you are concerned with the situation.

Marvin Fletcher

Marvin is absent from work again today. He called in to say he would be a half hour late because he had to run his daughter off to school. Marvin's wife also works, and running the kids around often falls under Marvin's responsibility.

In Marvin's favor is the fact that his performance doesn't suffer from these short absences. When he is at work, he works harder than anyone else. His overall productivity is at least as good as anyone else in your unit. The problem is that you feel it doesn't look good to have people coming in whenever they want. Other employees also want increased flexibility "because Marvin gets to you." You feel you need to talk to Marvin, but feel a little guilty about it. Just last week your son was sick and you had to stay home with him. Marvin knows about it too. *Flexitime; can't give too much slack to one employee*

Rita Marvin *age responsibilities ; compromise*

Rita Marvin is also absent from work today. Rita has a degenerative bone disease that causes her a great deal of pain. The pain seems to occur in bouts that prevent her from coming to work.

Rita has volunteered to do some work at home, but union agreements and insurance regulations do not allow it. She is a fine worker and has a great sense of humor. She is a real morale booster in the unit. Unfortunately, in the past couple months Rita has been missing too much work. Her illness is getting worse. You have overheard some of the other workers say she should go on disability. You have mentioned the possibility of disability to Rita, but she pleads with you to keep her on. The job gives her life meaning, and all her friends are from work. *part-time ?*

check w/ personnel

Discussion Questions

1. How would you deal with the Marvins' absences?
2. What strategy could you use in a discussion with each Marvin?

APPLICATION   Understanding and Changing Relationships

1. Identify three people with whom you have to relate regularly.
2. Specify your first impression of each one.
3. List ways in which your perceptions have changed or been reinforced.
4. If there are problems in any of the relationships, identify ways in which you may have contributed.
5. Specify how you might use the concepts in this section to improve these three relationships.

Competency 2   Interpersonal Communication

ASSESSMENT   Communication Skills

Directions   Analyze the communication in two of your relationships: one that is very painful and one that is very pleasant. Next, analyze how your communication behavior varies in the two relationships and what areas of communication you might need to work on. Answer the questions by using the following scale.

Scale   Minimal Problem   1   2   3   4   5   6   7   Great Problem

	Painful		*Pleasant*	
Other	*Self*	*Other*	*Self*	
1	1	1	1	1. Expresses ideas in unclear ways.
2	2	1	3	2. Tries to dominate conversations.
4	1	1	1	3. Often has a hidden agenda.
2	1	1	1	4. Is formal and impersonal.
2	1	1	1	5. Does not listen well.
1	1	1	1	6. Is often boring, uninteresting.
1	2	2	1	7. Is withdrawn and uncommunicative.
1	1	1	1	8. Is overly sensitive, too easily hurt.
1	1	1	1	9. Is too abstract and hard to follow.
3	2	1	2	10. Is closed to the ideas of the other.
18	13	10	13	Total score

10/23

Interpretation   Now go back and reexamine your answers. What patterns do you see?

1. How do you think your own communication behavior varies in these two relationships?
2. On what specific problems in the painful relationship do you most need to work?

LEARNING   Interpersonal Communication

Interpersonal communication is perhaps one of the most important and least understood competencies that a manager can have—and vital to playing the mentor role. As the research literature suggests, knowing when and how to share information requires a very complex understanding of people and situations (Eisenberg and Witten 1987).

An outstanding example of communication skill can be seen in Kenneth T. Kerr. In 1984, after Chevron bought Gulf Oil, Kerr was put in charge of integrating the two entities. Given the number of failures that occur around such merger efforts, the results were impressive. In fact some would call it a textbook case of doing it right. What skills do people most speak of when they reflect on Kerr's miracle? They talk about his ability to communicate, to listen and create an honest sense of dialogue. Kerr is now the company's vice chairman and a likely candidate to become the next CEO. The ability to communicate effectively is no small asset.

Communication is the exchange of information, facts, ideas, and meanings. The communication process can be used to inform, coordinate, and motivate people. Unfortunately, being a good communicator is not easy. Nor is it easy to recognize your own problems in communication. In the exercise you just completed, for example, you may have easily ignored your own weaknesses in communicating and may have given yourself much lower scores than you gave to the other person in the painful relationship. Although most people in organizations tend to think of themselves as excellent communicators, they consider communication a major organizational problem, and they see the other people in the organization as the source of the problem. It is very difficult to see and admit the problems in our own communication behavior.

Despite this difficulty, analyzing communication behavior is vital. Poor communication skills result in both interpersonal and organizational problems. When interpersonal problems arise, people begin to experience conflict, resist change, and avoid contact with others. Organizationally, poor communication often results in low morale and low productivity. After all, organizing *requires* that people communicate—to develop goals, channel energy, and identify and solve problems.

A BASIC MODEL OF INTERPERSONAL COMMUNICATION

The exchange of information may take a variety of forms including ideas, facts, and feelings. Despite the many possible forms, the communication process may be seen in terms of a general model (Shannon and Weaver, 1948). See Figure 6.2.

The model begins with the communicator encoding a message. Here the person who is going to communicate translates a set of ideas into a system of symbols such as words or numbers. Many things influence the encoding process including the urgency of the message, the experience and skills of the sender, and the sender's perception of the receiver. The message is transmitted through a medium of some sort. A message, for example, might be written, oral, or even nonverbal. Once it is received, it must be decoded. This means that the message

FIGURE 6.2 *A basic model of communication.*
Source: *Developed from C. Shannon and M. Weaver,* The Mathematical Theory of Communication (*Urbana: University of Illinois Press, 1948*). Used with permission.

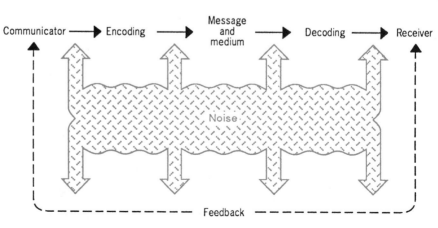

must be interpreted by the person who receives it. Like the encoding process, the decoding process is subject to influence by a wide number of factors.

The model includes a feedback loop between the receiver and the communicator. The **feedback** can take three forms: informational, corrective, or reinforcing. Informational feedback is a nonevaluative response that simply provides additional facts to the sender. Corrective feedback involves a challenge to, or correction of, the original message. Reinforcing feedback is a clear acknowledgment of the message that was sent. It may be positive or negative (Kreitner 1977).

The final aspect of the model is noise. **Noise** is anything that can distort the message in the communication process. As indicated in Figure 6.2, it can occur at any point in the process. A sender may be unable to clearly articulate the ideas to be sent. In the medium, a document may leave out a key word. In the decoding process, the receiver may make wrong assumptions about the motive behind the message.

PROBLEMS IN INTERPERSONAL COMMUNICATION

Interpersonal communication problems occur in organizations for several reasons.

- *Defensiveness.* As indicated in the first competency of this chapter, people have defenses that prevent them from receiving messages they fear. All people have some insecurities, and there are certain things they simply do not want to know. This is especially true of issues that impact values, assumptions, and self-image. You, for example, may have been somewhat defensive in responding to the two questions at the end of this section's communication assessment.

- *Inarticulateness.* Communication problems may arise because the sender of the message has difficulty expressing the concept. If the receiver is not aware of the problem, completely inaccurate images may arise and result in subsequent misunderstandings.

- *Hidden agendas.* Sometimes people have motives that they prefer not to reveal. Because the sender believes that the receiver would not react in the desired way, the sender becomes deceptive. The sender seeks to maintain a competitive advantage by keeping the true purpose hidden. Over time, such behavior results in low trust and cooperation.

- *Status.* Communication is often distorted by perceptions of position. When communicating with a person in a position of authority, individuals often craft messages so as to impress and not offend. Conversely, when communicating with a person in a lower hierarchical position, individuals may be unnecessarily cold or insensitive to that person's needs, causing the receiver to reject or distort the message that is actually sent.

TABLE 6.2 Rules for Effective Communication

1. *Be clear on who the receiver is.*   What is the receiver's state of mind? What assumptions are brought by the receiver? What is he or she feeling in this situation?
2. *Know what your objective is.*   What do you want to accomplish by sending the message?
3. *Analyze the climate.*   What will be necessary to help the receiver relax and be open to the communication?
4. *Review the message in your head before you say it.*   Listen to the practice message from the point of view of the receiver. Then say it.
5. *Communicate in the language of the other person.*   Use examples and illustrations that come from the world of the receiver.
6. *If the receiver seems not to understand, clarify the message.*   Ask questions. If repetition is necessary, try different words and illustrations.
7. *If the response is seemingly critical, do not react defensively.*   Try to understand what is happening in the receiver. Why is he or she reacting negatively? The receiver may be misunderstanding. Ask clarifying questions.

- *Environment.*   The nature of physical space can greatly influence communication. Some environments may be too hot or too noisy. Others may provide an inappropriate setting for a particular type of message. Informal messages may be inappropriate in a setting that is highly formal, and formal messages may be inappropriate in settings that are highly informal.
- *Hostility.*   In many cases the receiver is angry at the person who sends the message. When good will is lost in a relationship, all messages tend to be reframed in a negative way. Hostility makes it most difficult to send and receive accurate information. When trust is low and people are angry, no matter what the sender actually expresses, it is likely to be distorted.

Given the number and intensity of some of these barriers, how do people communicate effectively? Table 6.2 gives seven basic rules that will increase the quality of communication.

REFLECTIVE LISTENING

Managers often need to counsel a subordinate. Here effective communication is particularly important. Of all the skills associated with good communication, in such a situation, perhaps the most important is reflective listening. Most people fail to realize just how poorly they tend to listen.

Reflective listening is based on empathy (see Table 6.1). Reflective listening is a sincere attempt to experience the thoughts and feelings of the other person. In using empathy and reflective listening, instead of directing and controlling the thoughts of the other, you become a helper who tries to facilitate the other's expression. Instead of assuming responsibility for another's problem, you help him or her to explore it on his or her own. Your job is not to talk but to keep the other person talking. You do not evaluate, judge, or advise; you simply reflect on what you hear. In fewer words, you descriptively, not evaluatively, restate the essence of the person's last thought or feeling. If the person's statement is factually inaccurate, you do not immediately point out the inaccuracy. Instead of interrupting, you keep the person's flow of expression moving. You can go back later to correct factual errors.

The reflective listener uses open-ended questions like, "Can you tell me more?" or "How did you feel when that happened?" Evaluate questions and factual, yes-or-no, questions are avoided. The key is to keep the conceptual and emotional flow of expression. Instead of telling, the reflective listener helps the other person to discover. The practice exercise (below) will particularly help to illustrate this.

To the first time reader, reflective listening sounds very strange. Experience shows, however, that it can have major payoffs. Trust and concern grow with an ever-deepening understanding of interpersonal issues. More effective and lasting problem solving takes place, and people have a greater sense of impact. In short, communication greatly improves.

Reflective listening is not, however, a panacea. It is time consuming to really listen. It requires confidence in one's interpersonal skills and the courage to possibly hear things about one's self that are less than complimentary. There is also a danger that the sender will get into personal areas of life with which the listener is not comfortable and for which a professional counselor would be more appropriate. It is, nevertheless, a vital tool that is seldom understood or employed.

ANALYSIS One-Way, Two-Way Communication

Directions

10/23

The following activities focus on several aspects of communication, including active listening, speaking, and one- and two-way communication. Choose a partner, with whom you will work. One of you will act as the speaker, giving instructions verbally, and the other will be the listener, drawing the figure on paper according to the information the speaker provides. Your instructor will provide the figure. You will remain in these roles for both activities. Sit so that you cannot hear the interaction between other participants. A large group discussion will follow.

Activity A
Objective: To have the listener draw the described figure. Time: 5 minutes.

1. *Speaker.*   Sit back-to-back with the listener and describe one of the drawings you have chosen. You are to give drawing instructions *without* allowing the listener to see you or the figure. Do not answer any questions.

2. *Listener.*   Sit back-to-back with the speaker and draw the figure as it is described to you. Correct your drawing as you think necessary. Do not look at the speaker; *do not ask any questions.*

Activity B

Objective: To have the listener draw the described figure. Time: 5 minutes.

1. Speaker and listener remain in the same roles.

2. *Speaker.* Sit facing the listener and describe the second drawing you have. You are to give drawing instructions while looking at the listener and at his or her drawing. Be careful not to show the drawing to the listener. You may shake your head and use your arms and hands. You may not touch the listener or the drawing he or she is doing. You may not draw the figures on a board or in the air.

3. *Listener.* Sit facing the speaker and draw the second figure as directed. Do not allow the speaker to touch the drawing; you may ask questions.

Discussion Questions
1. What problems did you experience?
2. What were your major impressions?
3. What do these activities show you about communication?

PRACTICE   Reflecting Feelings and Ideas

Directions   Reflecting is demonstrating to the other person that his or her communication has been heard and understood. Read the following remarks and as the listener, select the response that best reflects the feelings or ideas of the speaker. A large group discussion will follow.[2]

Remark

1. The employee has been on a new crew for three months. During a counseling interview, he said, "I don't know why it is, but I just don't feel as though I'm one of the gang. They are all nice enough guys, but somehow they seem to have a closed circle and make me feel like an outsider. Maybe it's me; I don't know."

Possible Responses to Reflect

a. Why don't you use the first chance you get to do the crew a favor?

b. It seems to you that the group doesn't accept you.

c. It seems that the others dislike you for some reason.

d. You don't think they will accept you, even if you give them some more time to learn that you are a nice fellow.

Remark

2. A manager with 10 years' experience missed a chance for a promotion because of a low score on a promotion exam. "I'm just going to do the minimum to get by until retirement," she told a co-manager.

[2]*Adapted from Developing Managerial Skills,* by David A. Whetten and Kim S. Cameron. Copyright © 1984 by Scott, Foresman and Company. Used by permission.

Possible Responses to Reflect

    a. You are discouraged about missing the opportunity for promotion.

    b. You deserve to be upset. I would be too.

    c. Those exams don't measure your ability correctly.

    d. Your attitude had better change or you'll lose everything.

Remark

3. A clerical employee with 10 years' experience told his manager, "I've been doing this job for years now and nobody had ever complained. Now you send my work back and tell me to do it over. It isn't fair, and it doesn't make sense. Maybe I do make mistakes now and then, but nobody is perfect. And I don't know why I should get all the blame for what goes on around here."

Possible Responses to Reflect

    a. You don't think it's fair to ask you to correct your own mistakes.

    b. Suppose you check your work before you bring it to me.

    c. You think you are being blamed for not being perfect.

    d. You feel that I am too strict.

Remark

4. During an interview with his manager, an employee states, "I don't want to work with Jake anymore. He's lazy and is always taking a superior attitude, complaining about the rest of us not helping him as much as we should. He thinks he is too good for this kind of work and too good to work with the rest of us, and I'm sick of being around him."

Possible Responses to Reflect

    a. You feel that Jake ought to be disciplined in some way.

    b. Jake doesn't want to cooperate, is that it?

    c. You feel Jake's attitude makes the work unpleasant.

    d. You think Jake might fit in better somewhere else.

Remark

5. A young man whose work showed a sudden drop in quality was sent to the employment manager for an interview. One of the things he said on arriving was, "I don't know why I should be asked to talk to you about my work. I haven't complained and haven't time for this kind of chitchat. So give me what help you have in mind and I'll be on my way."

Possible Responses to Reflect

    a. You came to see me because you were sent, not because you believe you have any need for help.

b. Don't you feel that with my experience in the company I might be of some help?

c. You feel irritated for coming here because you don't think I can help you.

d. You mustn't jump to conclusions. Often people need help when they are unaware of this need.

Remark

6. A manager met with her superior to report on a difficult performance appraisal meeting. "I hated to terminate that probationary employee but I had no other choice."

Possible Responses to Reflect

a. I hate doing those meetings myself.

b. How did the employee respond?

c. It was uncomfortable for you to fire someone.

d. It gets easier over time.

Remark

7. In the middle of a counseling interview with her boss, a 58-year-old woman said, "You don't want me here; you just want young women. I'm getting old; so I guess I should get out."

Possible Responses to Reflect

a. It's not true that I favor the young women employees.

b. You believe I'd like to have you leave because of your age.

c. You feel you have reason to believe that I prefer young girls.

d. I can see that I must have done something to hurt your feelings.

Remark

8. A manager was discussing the work of a young man who has been out of high school about a year. The manager was trying to determine why important details on procedures were often overlooked or clearly violated. Suddenly the young man shouted, "You're the worst manager I've ever had. If a person shows initiative, you work him over. I refuse to follow silly rules."

Possible Responses to Reflect

a. Why don't you check with me before you make a change in procedure?

b. You resent me for criticizing your work.

c. Perhaps it's my fault that I didn't train you on the correct procedure.

d. You feel I should have someone else go over your work.

Remark

9. In a conversation with a co-worker, a young woman talked at length about her husband's lack of consideration, going into considerable detail to justify why she should divorce him. After a pause she remarked that she never had long-term relationships with anyone. "Other people seem to have old friends, but I get tired of them after I get to know them. Maybe I expect too much of people."

Possible Responses to Reflect

   a. You feel a divorce may be the solution to your problem.

   b. You think perhaps you should reconsider your divorce.

   c. After you get to know people, they cease to be exciting and fun.

   d. You believe that expecting too much of friends may interfere with long-term relationships.

Remark

10. Manager, age 35, says to a friend, "I'm determined to get ahead. I'm not afraid of hard work. I am not afraid to take a few hard knocks—if I can see my goal out there in front. And I'm not adverse to climbing over a few people who get in my way, because this means a lot to me. I can't be satisfied with just a mediocre job. No, I want to be somebody."

Possible Responses to Reflect

   a. You feel that you just have to be out on top no matter what you may do to others.

   b. You see yourself as a deeply ambitious person, is that it?

   c. What do you suppose is behind this strong determination of yours to get ahead?

   d. Strong ambition can be a real asset to anyone. Are you really sure, though, that you mean it when you say you're not adverse to climbing over those who get in your way? Couldn't that turn out to do you more harm than good?

APPLICATION   Active Listening

You will be working with two other people for this activity.[3] Assign yourselves the roles of *A*, *B*, and *C*. Then, follow these steps:

   1. Participant *A* will be the first speaker and should choose the topic to be discussed from the list that follows. If none of the topics is appealing,

[3]*Adapted from* J. William Pfeiffer and John E. Jones (Eds.), *A Handbook of Structured Experiences for Human Relations Training,* Vol. I. San Diego, CA.: University Associates, Inc., 1974. Used with permission.

additional topics may be substituted. Choose the topic about which you feel most strongly.

2. Participant *B* will be the first listener.

3. Participant *C* will be the first referee.

4. The speaker will then discuss the chosen topic for about 3 to 4 minutes. It is important to be sensitive to the needs of the listener. You can establish nonverbal cues for pacing the discussion.

5. The listener will summarize the speaker's point of view in his or her own words and without notes (time: about 2 minutes).

6. If the summary is thought to be incorrect, both the speaker and the referee are free to correct any misunderstanding.

7. The referee is to make certain that the listener does not omit, distort, add to, respond to, or interpret what the speaker has said.

8. The total process of speaking and summarizing should take about 7 to 8 minutes in each round. The instructor will indicate when time is up.

9. In the second round, participant *B* becomes the speaker, participant *C* the listener, and participant *A* the referee. The new speaker should choose a topic and begin discussing that topic. Round 2 should also take 7 to 8 minutes.

10. In the final round, participant *C* becomes the speaker, participant *A* the listener, and participant *B* the referee. Again, this round should take 7 to 8 minutes.[3]

Possible Topics

Capital punishment	Two-career couples
A memory from childhood	The AIDS epidemic
Drug use and abuse	All-volunteer army
Health care problems today	Vacation plans
Foreign policy	Soaring real estate prices
What I like about my job	Today's education system
What I dislike about my job	The open classroom
Rising food prices	The profit motive
Nuclear plant disasters	Expectations for this day
Slanted news stories in the press and on TV	The responsibility of the news media
	Tax reform
Raising children	U.S. involvement in Central America

1. What difficulties and barriers were encountered?

2. What did you learn about listening effectively?

3. How can you apply the principles in this section to your real-world problems?

Competency 3 Developing Subordinates

ASSESSMENT Assumptions about Performance Evaluations

Directions Check off the statement in each of the following pairs of statements that best reflects your assumptions about performance evaluation.

Performance evaluation is:

_____ 1 a. A formal process that is done annually.
___✓___   b. An informal process that is done continuously.
_____ 2 a. A process that is planned for subordinates.
___✓___   b. A process that is planned with subordinates.
_____ 3 a. A required organizational procedure.
___✓___   b. A process done regardless of requirements.
___✓___ 4 a. A time to evaluate subordinate performance.
_____   b. A time for subordinates to evaluate the manager.
___✓___ 5 a. A time to clarify standards.
_____   b. A time to clarify the subordinate's career needs.
___✓___ 6 a. A time to confront poor performance.
___✓___   b. A time to express appreciation.
___✓___ 7 a. An opportunity to clarify issues and provide direction and control.
_____   b. An opportunity to increase enthusiasm and commitment.
_____ 8 a. Only as good as the organization's forms.
___✓___   b. Only as good as the manager's coaching skills.

Interpretation 1. As you review your eight answers, do you see any patterns in your assumptions or in the assumptions you did not choose?

2. As you review the statements, can you explain why the performance evaluation process is disliked by most employees in the United States? *subjectivity / relational*

3. How would you design an effective process?

LEARNING Developing Subordinates

In a literal sense, *mentor* means a trusted counselor or guide—a coach. In this section we turn to this particular aspect of the role. It is interesting to note that the two previous competencies in this chapter did much to focus on the building of trust. Now we turn more specifically to coaching, or the notion of developing people by providing performance evaluation and feedback.

Feedback on performance is one of the most potentially helpful kinds of information that a person can get. It is critical to improvement, growth, and development. Yet, as implied in question 2 of the preceding exercise, performance evaluation is one of the most uniformly disliked processes in organizational America. Before we talk about how to do a performance evaluation, it might be useful to consider why performance evaluations so often fail.

THE MANY USES AND PROBLEMS OF PERFORMANCE APPRAISAL

In the mentor role performance appraisal is seen as a tool to facilitate the development of subordinates, to clarify expectations, and to improve performance. This is not, however, the only view. A study of why organizations do performance appraisals revealed that high percentages of large organizations report other reasons for performance appraisal (Locher and Teel, 1977).

Compensation	62.2%
Performance improvement	60.6%
Feedback	37.8%
Promotion	21.1%
Documentation	10.0%
Training	9.4%
Staffing planning	6.1%
Discharge	2.2%

Although performance appraisal may serve some developmental functions for the individual, it is also an organizational tool. It is often used to make systemwide decisions about rewards such as compensation and promotion. It may be used in cases of discharge. It may be used as a research base for developing selection and training strategies. Because of the importance of these formal functions, the organization is open to legal challenge. An employee, for example, may sue because of a given promotion decision. Hence issues of accuracy and fairness become increasingly critical, and much of the literature focuses on methods of forms design, statistical techniques, and sources of error. The objective, with good reason, is to build a generalized system that fits every situation in the organization and that is fair and defensible. This, of course, is a tall order, and in many organizations, performance appraisal becomes a source of high frustration or meaningless game playing. Often the result of the confrontation is a fairly meaningless procedure that is of little benefit to anyone.

In addition to the organizational problems, many personal pressures make performance appraisal difficult. The process often makes both managers and subordinates very uncomfortable. How well a person has performed over the past year is seldom as clear as the human resources staff would like to believe it is, and the form is seldom able to capture the complexity of real life. Subordinates sense that the quantitative evaluations are really a cover for subjective judgments and sometimes challenge what they are told. Managers feel uncomfortable admitting that the evaluation process often reduces to subjective judgment and they usually feel uncomfortable in the role of a "judge."

Both parties tend to fear being challenged with questions that they may not be able to answer. Managers often become frustrated when an angry subordinate becomes hostile or passive. In either case, they may lack the skills to know how to handle the problem. Because doing performance evaluation properly requires constant observation, recording, and feedback, it is seen by many managers as too time consuming to do right.

PERFORMANCE EVALUATION

In the assessment exercise at the beginning of this competency, you chose between options in eight pairs of assumptions about performance evaluation. In each pair of statements answer *a* reflected traditional control values—those normally associated with the evaluation process. Answer *b*, on the other hand, reflected values reflecting involvement, communication, and trust. In this section we will consider performance evaluation as a two-step process, one that mixes the *a* and *b* views of the world. Although the mixed view presented here differs from what is designed and practiced in most organizations, you may find it to be of some value.

PREPARATION

Performance evaluation starts long before the actual evaluation session. If you have the organizational freedom to do so, and if your situation is appropriate, you might even invite subordinates to join you in designing a program that will work. Their wisdom may surprise you. You might begin the planning session by discussing what program, if any, is currently in place and what is positive and negative about the system. You might review the value of feedback to individuals and the group and then consider the reasons that most programs fail. With these things in mind, you might as a group specify some guidelines that will work in your situation. Some samples are given in Table 6.3.

Giving and receiving feedback requires some self-confidence, trust in subordinates, and many of the skills and competencies discussed in the first two competencies of this chapter. If you feel uncomfortable, it may not be a good idea to try such a procedure. In any case, whether you generate your own guidelines or use existing ones, be sure, over time to regularly observe the performance of subordinates and make notes of concrete incidents that would be useful to discuss at evaluation time. Feedback, however, should not be a one-time experience. There should be no surprises at the evaluation meeting. In fact, coaching sessions should be considered along the way, before a formal performance evaluation takes place.

TABLE 6.3 Guidelines for Giving and Receiving Feedback

Giving Feedback

■ Before giving feedback, examine your motivation and make sure the receiver is ready and open to hear you.
■ While giving feedback, use "I" statements rather than "you" statements to indicate that these are your perceptions, thoughts, and feelings.
■ Describe the other person's behavior and your perceptions of it.
■ Ask the other person to clarify, explain, change, or correct.
■ After giving feedback, give the receiver time to respond.

Asking for Feedback

■ Before asking for feedback, make sure you are open to hearing information that may alter your perception.
■ Be aware that the person giving you the feedback is describing his or her own perception of the situation, but realize that his or her feelings are real.
■ Check your understanding of the feedback: Ask questions or give examples and share your reaction(s). Clarify issues, explain your actions, and correct perceptions people may have of you.

Instead of walking into the evaluation cold, you may want to try another unique twist. At some specified time before the evaluation, exchange with the subordinate a written evaluation of the subordinate's performance. Spend some time reading the person's self-evaluation and use empathy to put yourself in the person's place. Use this process to prepare yourself for the evaluation session. In scheduling the session, be sure to set aside enough time and be sure that you have a private setting where you will not be interrupted.

In the actual evaluation, be sure that your own objective is clear. Know what you want to accomplish. Get into an appropriate frame of mind. Ask yourself how you really feel about the person, and most importantly, if you really want to help the person. Few managers enter the process in such a frame of mind.

Begin by focusing on positive behaviors. Ask the person to list the things that he or she has done well and contribute to the list as much as possible. When you turn to areas that might need improvement, again ask the person to begin, and in a supportive way, continue together until you agree on a list. At this point, if you have the skills discussed in the last two sections, you might ask how you as a manager are contributing to this person's problems. For example, you might suggest going through the list and asking what you could do differently. As the person responds, you might use reflective listening to explore the person's claim in an honest way. Make commitments to change your behavior where possible. Hence you are modeling the behavior in which you would like the subordinate to engage. After doing this you might again go through the list and ask the subordinate what changes he or she might make.

At the conclusion of the session, summarize what each of you might do differently during the next few months. Ask to see the person's career development plan. Review what progress has been made and what each of you can do to speed progress in the next period. If there is no such plan, one of the assignments should be to write a plan. You may need to help the person. After this, do an overall review and check the person's understanding of each action step. Do a final summary, and set a time for future reviews.

ANALYSIS   United Chemical Company

Directions   This exercise gives you a chance to analyze the principles of supportive communication and supportive listening you have read about in this chapter. Read the case and then answer the questions that follow.[4]

The United Chemical Company is a large producer and distributor of commodity chemicals with five chemical production plants in the United States. The operations at the main plant in Baytown, Texas, include not only production equipment, but also the company's research and engineering center.

The process design group consists of eight male engineers and the manager, Max Kane. The group has worked together steadily for a number of years, and good relationships have developed among all members. When the work load began to increase, Max hired a new design engineer, Sue Davis, a recent master's degree graduate from one of the foremost engineering schools in the country. Sue was assigned to a project involving expansion of one of the existing plant facilities' capacity. Three other design engineers were assigned to the project along with Sue: Jack Keller (age 38, with 15 years with the company), Sam Sims (age 40, with 10 years with the company), and Lance Madison (age 32, with 8 years with the company).

As a new employee, Sue was enthusiastic about the opportunity to work at United. She liked her work very much because it was challenging and it offered her a chance of apply much of the knowledge she had gained in her university studies. On the job, Sue kept to herself and her design work. Her relations with her fellow project members were friendly, but she did not go out of her way to have informal conversations during or after working hours.

Sue was a diligent employee who took her work seriously. On occasions when a difficult problem arose, she would stay after hours in order to come up with a solution. Because of her persistence, coupled with her more current education, Sue usually completed her portion of the various project stages a number of days before her colleagues. This was somewhat irritating to her because on these occasions she went to Max to ask for additional work to keep her busy until her fellow workers caught up to her. Initially, she had offered to help Jack, Sam, and Lance with their part of the project, but each time she was turned down tersely.

[4]*Adapted from Organizational Behavior and Performance,* 3d ed., by Andrew D. Szilag; and Marc J. Wallace, Jr. Copyright © 1983, 1980 by Scott, Foresman and Company. Used by permission.

About five months after Sue had joined the design group, Jack asked to see Max about a problem the group was having. The conversation between Max and Jack was as follows.

> *Max:* Jack, I understand you wanted to dicuss a problem with me.
>
> *Jack:* Yes, Max. I didn't want to waste your time, but some of the other design engineers wanted me to discuss Sue with you. She is irritating everyone with her know-it-all, pompous attitude. She just is not the kind of person that we want to work with.
>
> *Max:* I can't understand that, Jack. She's an excellent worker whose design work is always well done and usually flawless. She's doing everything the company wants her to do.
>
> *Jack:* The company never asked her to disturb the morale of the group or to tell us how to do our work. The animosity of the group can eventually result in lower-quality work for the whole unit.
>
> *Max:* I'll tell you what I'll do. Sue has a meeting with me next week to discuss her six-month performance. I'll keep your thoughts in mind, but I can't promise an improvement in what you and the others believe is a pompous attitude.
>
> *Jack:* Immediate improvement in her behavior is not the problem, it's her coaching others when she has no right to engage in publicly showing others what to do. You'd think she was lecturing an advance class in design with all her high-power, useless equations and formulas. She'd better back off soon, or some of us will quit or transfer.

During the next week, Max thought carefully about his meeting with Jack. He knew that Jack was the informal leader of the design engineers and generally spoke for the other group members. On Thursday of the following week, Max called Sue into his office for her midyear review. One portion of the conversation was as follows:

> *Max:* There is one other aspect I'd like to discuss with you about your performance. As I just related to you, your technical performance has been excellent; however, there are some questions about your relationships with the other workers.
>
> *Sue:* I don't understand—what questions are you talking about?
>
> *Max:* Well, to be specific, certain members of the design group have complained about your apparent "know-it-all attitude" and the manner in which you try to tell them how to do their job. You're going to have to be patient with them and not publicly call them out about their performance. This is a good group of engineers, and their work over the years has been more than acceptable. I don't want any problems that will cause the group to produce less effectively.
>
> *Sue:* Let me make a few comments. First of all, I have never publicly criticized their performance to them or to you. Initially, when I was finished ahead of them, I offered to help them with their work, but was bluntly told to mind my own business. I took the hint and concentrated only on my part of the work. What you don't understand is that after five months of working in this group I have come to the conclusion that what is going on is a "rip-off" of the company. The other engineers are "goldbricking" and setting

a work pace much slower than they're capable of. They're more interested in the music from Sam's radio, the local football team, and the bar they're going to go to for TGIF. I'm sorry, but this is just not the way I was raised or trained. And finally, they've never looked on me as a qualified engineer, but as a women who has broken their professional barrier.

Discussion Questions   1. What are the key problems?
2. How would you use the information in this chapter to redesign the meeting between Max and Sue?

PRACTICE Giving and Receiving Feedback

Directions   Review the guidelines for giving and receiving feedback that were presented in Competency 3. Then read the two roles that follow. At the indicated time, conduct a meeting, initiated by the person playing Schultz, that allows you to practice the guidelines.

Role for Klaus Schultz, Manager

You are a parks maintenance manager at Winsome River State Park Campground. You are in your early forties and have been involved in campground maintenance since you were a child working summers at your parents' campground. You enjoyed those summers, so it seemed only natural to continue in this line of work.

Eight years ago you were made a manager. Your staff consists of eight full-time parks maintenance assistants. You have worked hard in this job and feel that you have had considerable success in building up your park's reputation over the past eight years. In fact, Winsome River has become the most popular campground in the state.

You are about to have a coaching session with one of your parks maintenance assistants, Martin LeFete. Martin also has had a lot of experience in the outdoors. He has done extensive backpacking and white-water rafting. He is a hard worker and very committed, but recently you have had several complaints from campers.

It seems that Martin has scolded several campers for littering and leaving fires unattended. Although these are fairly common occurrences in state parks, and they should be corrected, Martin's approach has been somewhat aggressive.

For example, a few days ago Martin followed a littering family, picking up their trash as they dropped it. When he arrived at their campsite, he threw the garbage in their tent. The campers were quite irate about the incident.

Although you do not think any severe action, such as firing Martin, is presently justified, you do feel the problems you have identified must be resolved.

Role for Martin LeFete, Parks Maintenance Assistant

After you were graduated from high school, you moved to Colorado to live with your older brother. You worked part-time but spent as much time as possible hiking through the Canadian Rockies. You also found time to raft down rivers in Colorado. When you money ran out, you decided to move back to New York. You applied for and got your present job at Winsome River State Campground. One of your goals in taking this job was to show ordinary citizens how wonderful the outdoors really are.

You like your boss, Klaus Schultz, and believe he respects your work. But workers at the park have been a little anxious lately. There has been little rain this season, and fire is a major danger. There have also been reports of bears lurking around the campground.

This is why it really angers you to see people being careless about fires and trash. They are endangering the safety of other campers, not to mention the spotless safety record built up by Klaus.

You realize you probably overreacted when you poured water all over a campfire blazing out of control last week. The camper complained that you ruined his steaks, but he could have ruined the entire campground. When you arrived, the flames were almost as high as the bottom branches of the pine trees.

You understand Klaus' position, but you do wish he would give you more backup support on this. Klaus has asked to talk with you this afternoon, and you are planning to bring the matter up.

Discussion Questions
1. At the conclusion of the role play, discuss each guideline. How well was each guideline implemented?
2. What did you learn from this role play?

APPLICATION   The Coach at Work

1. Select a parent, friend, teacher, or other associate with whom you spend time.
2. In what areas of life did the person coach you?
3. How well did he or she receive and give feedback? How did he or she think about objective setting? What were his or her strengths and weaknesses as a coach?
4. In a group of four to six students, make a list of the most common coaching mistakes made by people.
5. From the list you've made, choose the mistakes that also might be made by a manager.
6. Indicate what can be done to avoid such mistakes.

REFERENCES

Bass, Bernard M. *Stodgill's Handbook of Leadership: A Survey of Theory in Research.* New York: Free Press, 1976.

Bennis, W. G., D. E. Berlew, E. H. Schein, and F. I. Steele. *Interpersonal Dynamics: Essays and Readings on Human Interaction* (3rd ed.). Homewood, Ill.: Dorsey Press, 1973.

Burack, E., and N. J. Mathys. *Career Management in Organizations.* Lake Forest, Ill.: Brace-Park, 1980.

Carnegie, D., and D. Carnegie. *How to Win Friends and Influence People.* New York: Simon & Schuster, 1981.

Carroll, S. J., and C. E. Schneier. *Performance Appraisal and Review Systems.* Glenview, Ill.: Scott, Foresman, 1982.

Clare, D. A., and D. G. Sanford. "Mapping Personal Value Space: A Study of managers in four organizations." *Human Relations* 32 (1979): 659–666.

Dalton, G. W., P. H. Thompson, and R. L. Price. "The Four Stages of Professional Careers— A New Look at Performance by Professionals." *Organizational Dynamics* 6 (Summer 1977): 19–42.

Eisenberg, Eric M., and Marsha G. Witten. "Reconsidering Openness in Organizational Communication." *Academy of Management Review* 12, no. 3 (1987): 418–426.

Fournies, F. F. *Coaching for Improved Work Performance.* New York: Van Nostrand Reinhold, 1978.

Hall, D. T. *Careers in Organization.* Pacific Palisades, Calif.: Goodyear, 1976.

Helmstetter, S. *What to Say When You Talk to Yourself.* New York: Pocket Books, 1986.

Hunt, R. G. *Interpersonal Strategies for System Management: Applications of Counseling and Participative Principles.* Monterey, Calif.: Brooks/Cole, 1974.

James, M., and D. Jongewood. *Born to Win.* Reading, Mass.: Addison-Wesley, 1977.

Kotter, J., V. A. Faux, and C. C. McArthur. *Self-Assessment and Career Development.* Englewood Cliffs, N.J.: Prentice-Hall, 1978.

Kreitner, R. "People Are Systems Too: Filling the Feedback Vacuum." *Business Horizons* 6 (December 1977): 54–58.

Locher, Alan A., and Kenneth S. Teel. "Performance Appraisal—A Survey of Current Practices." *Personnel Journal* 56, no. 5 (May 1977): 245–247, 254.

Luft, Joseph, and H. Ingham. "The Johari Window, a Graphic Model of Interpersonal Awareness." University of California, Los Angeles Extension Office, Proceedings of the Western Training Laboratory in Group Development (August 1955). Group Processes: An Introduction to Group Dynamics, by Joseph Luft, Mayfield Publishing Co., 1963, 1970.

Maslow, A. *Motivation and Personality* (2d ed.). New York: Harper & Row, 1970.

McCormick, E. J. *Job Analysis: Methods and Applications.* New York: AMACOM, 1979.

McGregor, D. *The Human Side of Enterprise.* New York: McGraw-Hill, 1960.

Nierenberg, G. I., and H. H. Calero. *How to Read a Person Like a Book.* New York: Pocket Books, 1973.

Progoff, I. *At a Journal Workshop: The Basic Text and Guide for Using the Intensive Journal.* New York: Dialogue House Library, 1975.

Reece, B. L., and R. Brandt. *Effective Human Relations in Business.* Boston: Houghton Mifflin, 1981.

Rogers, C. R. *On Becoming a Person*. Boston: Houghton Mifflin, 1961.

Rogers, C. R., and B. Stevens. *Person to Person: The Problem of Being Human*. Lafayette, Calif.: Real People Press, 1967.

Rogers, Carl R., and Richard E. Farson. *Active Listening*. Chicago: Industrial Relations Center, University of Chicago, 1976.

Rogers, Carl R., and F. J. Roethlisberger. "Barriers and Gateways to Communication." *Harvard Business Review* 30, no. 4 (July–August 1952): 46–50.

Rokeach, M. *The Nature of Human Values*. New York: Free Press, 1973.

Rusk, T., and R. Reed. *I Want to Change but I Don't Know How*. Los Angeles: Price/Stern/Sloan, 1986.

Sashkin, M. *Assessing Performance Appraisal*. San Diego, Calif.: University Associates, 1981.

Shannon, C. and W. Weaver, *The Mathematical Theory of Communication*. Urbana, Ill.: University of Illinois Press, 1948.

Schein, E. H. *Career Dynamics: Matching Individual and Organizational Needs*. Reading, Mass.: Addison-Wesley, 1978.

Schoen, S. H. and D. E. Durand. *Supervision: The Management of Organizational Resources*. Englewood Cliffs, N.J.: Prentice-Hall, 1979.

Sheehy, G. *Passages: Predictable Crises of Adult Life*. New York: Dutton, 1976.

Sher, B. *Wishcraft: How to Get What You Really Want*. New York: Ballantine, 1983.

Torbert, W. R. *Managing the Corporate Dream: Restructuring for Long-Term Success*. Homewood, Ill.: Dow Jones-Irwin, 1987.

Watzlawich, P., J. Bearin, and D. D. Jackson. *Pragmatics of Human Communication*. New York: W. W. Norton, 1967.

Whetten, David A., and Kim S. Cameron. *Interpersonal Skill Development for Managers*. Lexington, Mass.: Ginn Custom Publishing, 1981.

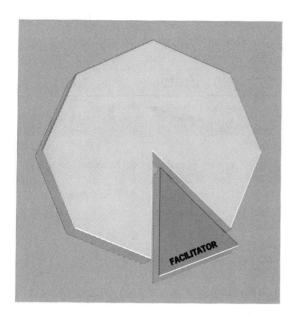

THE FACILITATOR ROLE

We have all spent a great deal of time working (and playing) in groups. Some of these groups seem to work very well together, and we sense that the group is able to accomplish something that none of the individuals could have accomplished on his or her own. Other groups, however, seem to function less effectively.

In this chapter we will focus on the role of the facilitator. The **facilitator role** falls in the human relations model of the competing values framework. In this role, the manager fosters collective effort, builds cohesion and morale, and manages interpersonal conflict. The facilitator uses some of the same competencies as the mentor, such as listening and being empathetic and sensitive to the needs of others. The role of facilitator, however, centers around the manager's work with groups.

In this chapter we will focus on three key competencies of the facilitator:

Competency 1 Team Building
Competency 2 Participative Decision Making
Competency 3 Conflict Management

Each of these competencies require the manager to balance individual needs with group needs in order to create and maintain a positive climate in the work group.

Competency 1 Team Building

Directions The following assessment instrument asks you to examine your behavior as a team member in organizational settings. For each pair of items, place a check mark in the space in the column that best identifies you at school, in clubs or student groups, or on your job.

	Very like me	Somewhat like me	Both describe me	Somewhat like me	Very like me	
Flexible in own ideas		✓				Set in my own ideas
Open to new ideas	✓					Avoid new ideas
Listen well to others	✓					Tune out others
Trusting of others	✓					Not trusting of others
Readily contribute in group meetings	✓					Hold back from contributing in group meetings
Concerned for what happens to others	✓					Not concerned for what happens to others
Fully committed to tasks	✓					Have little commitment to tasks
Share leadership with group	✓					Maintain full control of group

[1] *Adapted from* training materials for Income Maintenance Supervisors, Special Topics Workshop: "Motivation, Teambuilding, and Enhancing Morale," Professional Development Program, Rockefeller College of Public Affairs and Policy, University at Albany, State University of New York. Used with permission.

| Encourage others to participate | $\checkmark$ ___ | ___ | ___ | ___ | ___ | Expect others to participate without encouragement |
| Group needs come before my individual needs | ___ | $\checkmark$ ___ | ___ | ___ | ___ | My individual needs come before group needs |

Interpretation   1. In what ways do the preceding items agree with your concept of team membership?
2. What strengths do you think you have working on a team? Weaknesses?
3. Based on your responses, how do you evaluate yourself as a team member?

LEARNING

In his recent book on team building, William G. Dyer (1987) told a story about a management conference he had helped run. At the conference he asked approximately 300 managers whether they felt that teamwork and cooperation were essential in their organization and in their work unit. Without exception, managers reported that teamwork was essential. Dyer then asked how many conducted programs to ensure that their team was working effectively—fewer than 25% reported having conducted such a program. Finally, Dyer asked how many had ever been involved in a program of team building conducted by their boss. The response fell to between 10% and 15%. If teamwork is so essential to the proper functioning of the work unit, why are team-building programs so scarce in organizations?

Formal team building is not regularly practiced in organizations for many reasons. Some of these will be discussed later in this chapter. Before we talk about team building, however, we need to examine work groups and work teams and see how they function.

WORK GROUPS AND WORK TEAMS

We have all experienced times when we felt that we were working on a "team." That team may have been a sports team, a work-related group, or a group within some community organization. What were the characteristics of that group that made it a "team?" Probably, the group was well coordinated, everyone had a role to play, and there was a commitment to a common goal. Four key elements differentiate teams from other types of groups (Reilly and Jones 1974, 227):

1. The group must have a charter or reason for working together.
2. Members of the group must be interdependent—they need each other's experience, ability, and commitment in order to arrive at mutual goals.
3. Group members must be committed to the idea that working together as a group leads to more effective decisions than working in isolation.
4. The group must be accountable as a functioning unit within a larger organizational context.

Of these four key elements, perhaps the most important to a manager is that the "members of the group are interdependent—they need each other's experience, ability, and commitment in order to arrive at mutual goals." When the effective functioning of the work unit depends on individuals working together and using each other's experiences, abilities, and commitments, the work group must become a work team.

In some teams, such as golf teams or gymnastics teams, individuals function quite independently. Although they may practice together and give each other pointers on how to improve their performance, there is no real need for coordination of effort. Other teams, such as basketball teams or volleyball teams, require a great deal of interaction and coordination among team members. Players must be in constant communication with each other; each player must be able to "predict" the next player's moves.

ROLES OF TEAM MEMBERS

In teams requiring interaction and coordination, team members usually have specific, and sometimes very specialized, roles. A **role** is a set of expectations held by the individual and significant others about how that individual should act in a given situation. For example, in basketball, the point guard is expected to bring the ball down the court and set up the play; the center is expected to get under the basket and to rebound.

In work teams, there are also often specialized roles. For example, in a factory there are production managers, machine operatives, and repair persons. In addition, there are health and personnel specialists, accountants and financial managers, maintenance staff, secretaries, and office clerks. Each of these individuals has a specialized role. The manager also has a specialized role, one that we see as consisting of eight subroles, which were set forth in Chapter 1.

ROLE CLARITY AND ROLE AMBIGUITY

One of the responsibilities of the facilitator is to provide role clarity for his or her employees—to make it clear what is expected of an individual performing in a given job title and job position.

Role clarity implies the absence of two stressful conditions: role ambiguity and role conflict. Role ambiguity occurs when an individual does not have enough information about what he or she should be doing, what are appropriate ways of interacting with others, or what are appropriate behaviors and attitudes. Consider the following story about four people: Everybody, Somebody, Anybody and Nobody.

There was an important job to be done and Everybody was asked to do it. Anybody could have done it, but Nobody did it. Somebody got angry about that because it was Everybody's job. Everybody thought Anybody could do it, but Nobody realized that Everybody wouldn't do it. It ended up that Everybody blamed Somebody when actually Nobody asked Anybody.

New employees, who are not familiar with the work unit's norms and procedures, often experience role ambiguity if their manager does not clarify for them what is to be expected in their job. New managers, making the transition from worker to manager, also often experience role ambiguity because the role expectations for that individual have changed.

Role conflict occurs when an individual perceives information regarding one's job to be inconsistent or contradictory. For example, if manager X tells employee Y to perform task A, and then manager X's boss tells employee Y to stop what he or she is doing and to perform task B, the employee is likely to experience role conflict.

There are several potential sources of role conflict. Role conflict may occur when one or more individuals with whom an employee interacts send conflicting messages about what is expected. It can occur when an individual plays multiple roles that have conflicting expectations. For example, first-line managers represent their organization to their employees, informing them of rules and regulations or new policies and procedures. Managers, however, are also employees. In the employee role they may disagree with an organizational policy or directive. Role conflict can also occur when an individual's own morals and values conflict with the organization's mission or policies and procedures. For example, an environmental activist may find it difficult to work for Dow Chemical or any company that produces toxic or nuclear wastes as a side effect of its primary production of goods. Finally, role conflict can occur when the expectations for a given role exceed the available time to complete those tasks. This is sometimes referred to as role overload (Gordon 1987).

One of the major purposes of team building is to clarify roles so that everyone in the work unit understands what others expect. Later in this chapter team-building techniques that focus on the clarification of roles will be presented. First, however, we present some roles that employees play in their work groups.

TASK AND GROUP MAINTENANCE ROLES VS. SELF-ORIENTED ROLES

Task and group maintenance roles are roles that focus on two necessary components of effective team functioning. In a task role, one's behaviors are focused on *what* the team is to accomplish. Performing in a task role is sometimes referred to as having a task orientation, or being task oriented. In a group maintenance role, one's behaviors are focused on *how* the team will accomplish its task. Performing in a group maintenance role is sometimes referred to as having a group maintenance, or process, orientation, or being process oriented.

Just as there are several managerial subroles, there are several subroles associated with task and group maintenance orientations. We can identify six primary subroles associated with a task orientation (Benne and Sheats 1948).

1. The *initiator* gets the group moving by offering new ideas and suggesting ways to approach a task or a problem. In this role the group member reminds others that there is a task to be performed.

2. The *information giver* raises or clarifies important facts and opinions based on personal knowledge and experiences.

3. The *information seeker* encourages others to raise or clarify important facts and opinions based on their knowledge and experiences.

4. The *coordinator* brings together, schedules, and combines the activities of others.

5. The *evaluator* helps the group to assess the quality of its suggestions or solutions, testing to see if the ideas will work in reality.

6. The *summarizer* pulls together the range of ideas discussed in the group and restates them concisely, offering a decision or conclusion for the group to consider.

Likewise we can identify six primary subroles associated with a group maintenance orientation.

1. The *encourager* supports team members, helps build cohesiveness and warmth, and encourages and raises others' ideas.

2. The *harmonizer* alleviates tension and helps members find ways to see past their differences so that they can continue to work together. A person performing in this role will try to reduce tension in a group with humor and friendliness.

3. The *gatekeeper* maintains an "open gate" to others' participation, ensuring that all group members have sufficient opportunities to share their ideas and feelings.

4. The *standard setter* helps the group set appropriate goals and evaluate the quality of the group process.

5. The *follower* agrees with others and pursues their ideas and suggestions.

6. The *group observer* monitors the group process and provides feedback on group functioning.

In addition to the task and group maintenance roles, there are self- or individual-oriented roles. These roles tend to be counterproductive to effective group functioning, and they draw attention away from the group to personal needs that are not germane to the group's task or process. Here are four roles associated with this orientation:

1. The *blocker* opposes other members' ideas and suggestions, using hidden agendas to hinder group movement.

2. The *recognition seeker* tries to draw attention to himself or herself, boasting of personal accomplishments and acting in ways that indicate a feeling of superiority over other group members.

3. The *dominator* tries to take over the group by manipulating the group or individual members and by interrupting others.

4. The *avoider* separates from the group and maintains a distance from other group members. This behavior is sometimes used as a strategy to attract the attention of other group members.

TEAM DEVELOPMENT AND INFORMAL APPROACHES TO TEAM BUILDING

When a new work group forms, or an established work group undertakes a new task or problem, the group experiences different stages of team development as it transforms into a team. During the different stages of team development, the team requires a differing emphasis or focus on the various task and maintenance behaviors. The leader of a group must be aware of these stages of development and encourage group members to perform specific task and group maintenance behaviors at the different stages. These stages are summarized in Table 7.1.

STAGE 1: TESTING

At stage 1 the goals of the group are established and the task is defined. Group members ask themselves what is the purpose of this team and whether they want to be a member. (Of course, in most work-related situations, group members do not have a choice about their membership.) To create a climate where people can share ideas and feelings and build team spirit by encouraging co-operation, the group leader should encourage group members to take on the initiator, information-giver, information-seeker, encourager, and gatekeeper roles.

TABLE 7.1 Task and Group Maintenance Roles Needed at Each Stage of Team Development

1. Testing	Initiator Information giver Information seeker	Encourager Gatekeeper
2. Organizing	Coordinator Evaluator	Group observer Harmonizer Standard setter
3. Establishing interdependence	Information seeker Summarizer	Harmonizer Follower Encourager
4. Producing and evaluating	Initiator Evaluator	Gatekeeper Group observer

STAGE 2: ORGANIZING

At stage 2 the group establishes a structure. The group leader must emphasize the common purpose (task) and establish norms and standards. If the group has no appointed leader, one of the group members will often emerge as an informal leader in this stage. So that group members may ask more specific questions about what the group will do and how they will do it, the leader should encourage group members to take on the coordinator, evaluator, standard-setter, group-observer, and harmonizer roles.

STAGE 3: ESTABLISHING INTERDEPENDENCE

Individual talents are drawn out and used and attention is focused on how to coordinate individual efforts in stage 3. The group leader should focus on member interdependence, discourage competition, and encourage individuals to take on informal leadership roles. The key question group members ask themselves concerns how they can work together to accomplish the group's goals. Important task and group maintenance roles to encourage are information seeker, summarizer, harmonizer, follower, and encourager.

STAGE 4: PRODUCING AND EVALUATING

At stage 4 the group has transformed itself into a team and is working together smoothly. Group members are evaluating the product of the team effort and also how well the group worked together as a team. To solicit input from all group members in evaluating goals, task output, productivity, and team process, the leader should encourage group members to take on the initiator, evaluator, gatekeeper, and group-observer roles.

INFORMAL APPROACHES TO TEAM BUILDING

In addition to the specific task and maintenance behaviors discussed, a manager can do informal team building in several other ways. For example, a manager may encourage group interaction by suggesting that the group meet for a meal after work, or during a meal break, where possible. Other forms of group social interaction also promote team spirit. Recognizing and rewarding teamwork among group members can provide a model for other group members to follow. Once a norm of teamwork is established in a work group, group members often monitor their own behaviors and actively work to maintain a team spirit.

If the group is generally performing well as a team, but one or two individuals are exhibiting self-oriented behaviors, the manager should meet with those individuals privately and give them feedback on their behaviors. Recall from Chapter 6 that feedback should be specific, descriptive, and focused on how these behaviors affect others' feelings and actions, which in turn affect the overall effectiveness of the group.

FORMAL APPROACHES TO TEAM BUILDING

Informal day-to-day team building approaches are usually effective when the work group has a long, established track record of team functioning. Most work groups, however, experience frequent, if not constant, change. Sometimes these changes are associated with new group members; sometimes the changes are associated with new tasks and responsibilities. At this point it is often important to "stop the action" and involve the group in formal team-building activities.

You may have heard the expression, "When you are up to your hips in alligators, you forget that you came to drain the swamp." Sometimes it is important to step out of the swamp and think. Formal team-building activities allow the group to put aside the work of the day, to evaluate how well the group is performing as a team, and to make any necessary changes. At Goodyear Tires' radial tire plant in Lawton, Oklahoma, work teams meet regularly to discuss goals, problems, and improvement ideas (Robbins 1989).

When team members are interdependent, there is a need for effective communication among the team members. Periodic meetings that focus on information exchange may be the most effective way to enhance communication among team members. Many managers hold periodic off-site meetings to help keep employees enthusiastic and energized. The key is to encourage input from everyone regarding problems they are experiencing and questions or concerns they might have. Managers can also bring information about anticipated changes to these meetings. Sometimes it is important to clarify how much and what types of information individuals need in order to effectively perform their job. A group meeting to examine current information flows, and whether these flows meet each individual's needs, can enhance team functioning. (The section on participative decision making in this chapter will provide more information on how to conduct effective meetings.)

As mentioned earlier, one key to effective team functioning is for each team member to know his or her role, and how that role fits into the larger team effort. Several techniques are available. *Role analysis technique* (RAT) focuses one-by-one on the various roles in the group. This technique was first used by KP Engineering Corporation, a manufacturer of welding electronics, and is useful when team members are performing different functions (Dayal and Thomas 1968). In this activity the person performing in the role to be analyzed states his or her job as he or she sees it. Other group members then comment on and make suggestions for changes in this job description. The individual in that role then lists expectations of other members who affect how the job is performed. There is open discussion until agreement is reached on a job description and the associated expectations of others. This process is then repeated until everyone has had his or her job analyzed.

A similar technique is *role negotiation technique* (Harrison 1972). Here all members list simultaneously what expectations they have of others in the work group, focusing on what they feel others should do more or better, do less or stop doing, and maintain as is. Lists are exchanged, and individuals negotiate with each other until all team members agree on those behaviors that should be changed and those that should be maintained. A master list of agreements is later circulated to the group.

Responsibility charting (Beckhard and Harris 1977) involves creating a large chart that lists the group's decisions and activities along the left side of the chart and each employee's name along the top of the chart (see Figure 7.1). Codes

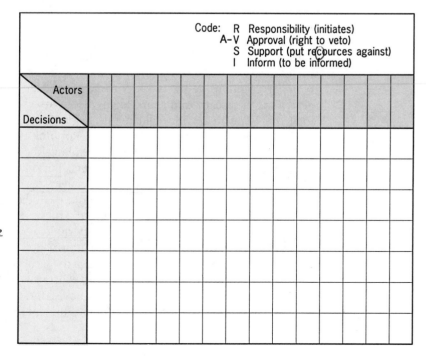

FIGURE 7.1
Responsibility chart.
Source: *R. Beckhard and R. T. Harris,* Organizational Transitions: Managing Complex Change *(Reading, Mass.: Addison-Wesley Publishing Company, 1977), p. 78, Figure 6.1. Used with permission.*

that indicate whether the individual has the responsibility for the activity or decision (R), has the right to approve or veto a decision (A-V), provides support or resources for the activity or decision (S), needs to be informed of the activity or decision (I), or has no role in the activity or decision (−) are then inserted into the boxes. The chart allows the group to see explicitly if some members of the group are overloaded and some could be given additional tasks and responsibilities.

BARRIERS TO TEAM BUILDING

One important reason why team building programs are not more widely used in work organizations is time. Often the need to get the job done leads work groups to focus on specific tasks, rather than on planning and coordination. Further, when group members focus on their own parts they sometimes find it difficult to see the whole picture, or to recognize that one is not currently seeing that picture.

A second reason is organizational climate. Effective team building requires an atmosphere that values differing opinions and open resolution of conflict (see the last competency in this chapter on conflict management). In an organization where there is mistrust or negative feelings among co-workers, it is difficult to establish a team spirit. In cases such as these, one should consider bringing in an objective outside consultant to do formal team-building or organization development activities.

A final reason may be a lack of knowledge about how to build a team. Some people assume that "team" is something that does or does not happen. They may not realize the many and varied techniques that can enhance team functioning. It is a manager's responsibility to examine the need for team building in his or her work unit, and if such a need exists to determine whether formal or informal approaches would be most effective.

ANALYSIS   Stay-Alive Inc.[2]

Directions   Read the case study and respond to the questions that follow.

Stay-Alive Inc., a small not-for-profit social service agency, hired Jean Smith to design, implement, and coordinate halfway house living programs for young adults.

---

[2] *Adapted from* Judith R. Gordon, *A Diagnostic Approach to Organizational Behavior* (Boston: Allyn and Bacon, 1983), pp. 304–305.

When Jean arrived, the agency had an informal organization with little hierarchical structure and extensive participative decision making. The prevailing ideology that shaped virtually all decisions and interpersonal relationships was that a democratic system would be most effective and would lead to a higher level of job satisfaction for workers than would a more rigid hierarchical structure. The staff members attended at least five meetings weekly. Incredibly, the group devoted the majority of time at each one to exploring interpersonal problems.

Most staff people were young and had recently finished college. They often remarked that they sought a place to belong and feel accepted. Stay-Alive met that need in many ways; the group acted as a surrogate family for many employees. Even their life outside of work revolved heavily around activities with other Stay-Alive members. Salaries were low, and so the agency hired inexperienced people. Although the employees were bright, enthusiastic, and motivated, they lacked the skills needed for effective performance in their jobs. Organizational leaders, therefore, defined success on the job in terms of the employees' ability to relate well to others at work instead of their ability to work with clients.

Within three months of her arrival Jean submitted her plan for implementing the program. Her manager praised it, calling it a remarkable piece of work. Soon after the program was implemented, however, it became clear that it was not working. Still the agency members responded by patting her on the back and told her what a great job she was doing. Jean soon became frustrated and angry and left the agency.

Discussion Questions
1. Why wasn't Stay-Alive Inc. an effective team?
2. How were task and maintenance behaviors being performed in this agency?
3. In what stage of team development would you say Stay-Alive Inc. was? Why?
4. What suggestions would you give Stay-Alive to help them to improve?
5. What would Stay-Alive Inc. be like if the opposite emphasis from that which existed were espoused?
6. Which behaviors would you like to see kept?

PRACTICE   Ethics Task Force

Directions   The entire class will be divided into two groups. In the first part of the exercise, group 1 will be the ethics task force, and group 2 will be observers. If time permits, the groups should switch places.

Directions for Group 1

You are all members of a task force that has been called in to discuss and make suggestions for policies and procedures to deal with the use of work time (and telephone) for personal business. Recently, some employees have reported to their managers that they feel that some individuals spend a substantial amount of time doing personal business from work and that this affects their work load.

A few managers who have confronted employees have indicated that their employees argue that they can only do business with certain individual companies during office hours, and it is not fair to expect them to take personal leave for a "few minutes" here and there. Other managers have indicated that the amount of time lost is not sufficient to "make a big deal" about it. The division director has asked you to come up with a list of recommendations in which you recognize the need for optimum employee productivity, as well as the potential costs, both financial and personal, of monitoring and attempting to change such behaviors. During your discussion, group 2 will observe your task and group maintenance behaviors.

Directions for Group 2

Review the lists of task and group maintenance behaviors presented in this section. You may want to divide the specific behaviors to be observed among members of your group. As you observe these behaviors, make a note of the person demonstrating that behavior, and if possible the context.

APPLICATION   Team Building Action Plan

Think about a student group, a work unit, a task force, or a committee of which you are currently a member, where you could do some informal or formal team building.

1. Consider carefully which team-building activities are most appropriate. For example, you may decide to personally practice using task and maintenance roles in group meetings. If you are a group leader, decide whether it is appropriate to meet privately with individuals who have been exhibiting self-oriented behaviors. Try to be very aware of yourself and others as you use your new team-building techniques.

2. Write a three- to five-page report on your efforts, carefully describing what you did, what the result was, how other reacted, and so on. Also discuss what you learned from your attempts at team building that will help you next time. When you are describing an ongoing group, discuss also the stage of the group's development and how this affected your team-building effort.

Competency 2   Participative Decision Making

ASSESSMENT   Meeting Evaluation[3]

Directions   Think of a meeting of a student organization, a study group, or a meeting at work that you recently attended. If you have not attended any such meetings, think about the "meetings" of your groups when working on small group exercises in this or other classes.

Identify whether you felt the meeting was: (1) very effective, (2) moderately effective, (3) neither effective nor ineffective, (4) moderately ineffective, or (5) very ineffective. Then respond to the items using the following scale:

Scale	Strongly Disagree	Disagree	Undecided	Agree	Strongly Agree
	1	2	3	4	5

_5_ 1. I was notified of this meeting in sufficient time to prepare for it.

_5_ 2. I understood why this meeting was held (e.g., information sharing, planning, problem solving, decision making, open discussion) and what specific outcomes were expected.

_5_ 3. I understood what was expected of me as a participant and what was expected of the other participants.

_4_ 4. I understood how the meeting was intended to flow (e.g., agenda, schedule, design) and when it would terminate.

_4_ 5. Most participants listened carefully to each other.

_4_ 6. Most participants expressed themselves openly, honestly, and directly.

_4_ 7. Agreements were explicit and clear, and conflicts were openly explored and constructively managed.

_4_ 8. The meeting generally proceeded as intended (e.g., the agenda was followed, it ended on time) and achieved its intended purpose.

_4_ 9. My participation contributed to the outcomes achieved by the meeting.

_4_ 10. Overall, I am satisfied with this meeting and feel that my time was well spent.

Scoring and Interpretation Add your responses to each of the questions and divide the sum by 10. The closer your score was to "5," the more your meeting could be considered a very effective meeting; the closer your score was to "1," the more your meeting could be considered a very ineffective meeting.

1. How close was your initial evaluation of the meeting to your rating based on the questions in the meeting-evaluation scale? *Close*
2. Review the meeting-evaluation scale. What were the meeting characteristics that made the meeting more effective? Less effective? *Parameters, agenda*
3. What were the specific events at the meeting that made the meeting more effective? Less effective? *Interup*
4. How can you make your next meeting more effective?

³*Adapted from* J. W. Pfeiffer and John E. Jones (Eds.), *The 1981 Annual Handbook for Group Facilitators.* San Diego, CA.: University Associates, Inc. 1981. Used with permission.

LEARNING   Participative Decision Making

The concept of democracy assumes that citizens should be able to have input into decisions that affect their lives. Similarly, at work, you are probably aware that important decisions should involve those individuals whose work lives are affected by the decision outcome. Not all decisions, however, directly affect employees' work lives. Managers need to be aware of when it is appropriate to involve employees and when it is not.

Over the past 20 years, thousands of managers have gone to seminars and workshops where they have learned that the most effective leaders are those who use a participative style of leadership. In their desire to put into practice what they have learned, many of these managers have returned to their work sites and tried to involve their employees in decisions affecting their work unit. In some cases, these managers have been successful. In others, the managers have failed miserably. Why the difference?

The truth is that participative decision making is not a single technique that can be universally applied to all situations. As we are about to see, a manager can involve employees in making decisions in a variety of ways. Which way is appropriate to use depends on the manager, the employees, the organization, and the nature of the decision itself.

A RANGE OF DECISION-MAKING STRATEGIES

Managers constantly encounter situations for which they must make decisions about their work units and their employees. Most often, the manager has the option of involving or not involving employees in these decisions. In reality, the choice is not simply between involvement and no involvement. Rather, there are a wide range of options available to the manager.

Tannenbaum and Schmidt (1958) were among the first to consider the process of participative decision making. They proposed that decision-making processes vary with respect to the amount of authority held by the boss and the amount of freedom held by employees; an increase in the authority held by the manager, by definition, results in a decrease in the amount of freedom held by employees. (See Figure 7.2.)

At one extreme of the continuum are processes that are considered to be boss-centered. In these situations, the manager makes the decision and announces it, or maybe tries to sell the decision. At the other extreme are processes that are considered to be subordinate-centered. In these situations, employees make decisions, usually within limits set by the manager. Between these two extremes are a series of options for which the manager may elicit input from employees, asking them for ideas and suggestions.

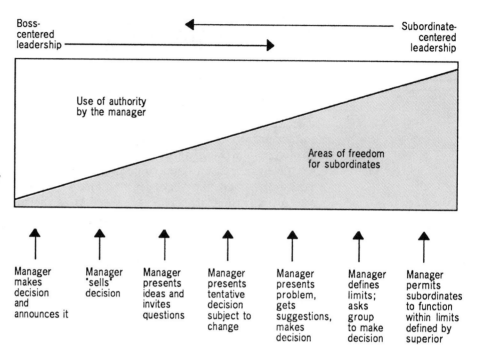

Boss-
centered
leadership

Subordinate-
centered
leadership

Use of authority
by the manager

Areas of freedom
for subordinates

Manager
makes
decision
and
announces it

Manager
"sells"
decision

Manager
presents
ideas and
invites
questions

Manager
presents
tentative
decision
subject to
change

Manager
presents
problem,
gets
suggestions,
makes
decision

Manager
defines
limits;
asks
group
to make
decision

Manager
permits
subordinates
to function
within limits
defined by
superior

How do you know which of these options to choose? Clearly there are both advantages and disadvantages associated with involving employees in the decision-making process.

Advantages

1. Groups tend to have greater knowledge or expertise than a single individual.

2. Group discussions tend to generate a wider range of values and perspectives, representing the range of issues and concerns at stake in the decision. Involving employees in the decision-making process, increases the probability that important issues affecting the decision will surface.

3. Employees have a greater commitment to implementing a decision in which they were involved, because they understand the reasons behind the decision.

4. Employees involved in the decision-making process will often be able to identify potential obstacles to implementing the decision, as well as ways to avoid them. James Houghton, chairman of Corning Glass Works, says, "If there is one thing our company and others like us have learned from our efforts to enhance quality, it is that the person on the job knows more about the job and how to improve it than anyone in the organization" (*The New York Times* 1987).

5. Involving employees in the decision-making process enhances their skills and abilities and helps them to grow and develop as organizational members.

Disadvantages

1. Participative decision making takes time. As the number of people who are involved in a decision increases, so does the time it takes to reach a decision.

2. If the group is involved in a decision for which it does not have the proper expertise, participative decision making will likely result in a low-quality decision.

3. If group meetings are not well structured, individuals with the appropriate expertise may fail to contribute to the discussion, whereas those with little or no knowledge may overcontribute and dominate the discussion.

4. When group members are overly concerned with gaining consensus in participative decision making, *groupthink* occurs (Janis 1972). Recall from Chapter 5 that groupthink is a situation where group members avoid being critical of others' ideas and thereby cease to think objectively about the decision at hand.

WHO SHOULD PARTICIPATE—AND WHEN

Given the numerous advantages and disadvantages to participative decision making, a decision to involve employees in any decision should be a function of the relative importance of these advantages and disadvantages in each situation. Vroom and Yetton (1973) created a model that allows managers to examine the questions of *when* to involve employees in the decision-making process; and when they decide to do so, *how* to do it most effectively. This model is the basis of Kepner-Tregoe's TELOS, a two-day management development program. The model identifies five decision-making strategies that can be classified as autocratic (A), consultative (C), or group decision making (G). The five strategies are:

AI   You solve the problem or make the decision yourself, using information available to you at the time.

AII   You obtain any necessary information from subordinates, then you decide on the solution to the problem yourself. In getting the information from them, you may or may not tell subordinates what the problem is. The role played by your subordinates in making the decision is clearly one of providing specific information which you request, rather than generating or evaluating solutions.

CI   You share the problem with the relevant subordinates individually, getting their ideas and suggestions without bringing them together as a group. Then *you* make the decision. This decision may or may not reflect your subordinates' influence.

CII   You share the problem with your subordinates in a group meeting. In this meeting you obtain their ideas and suggestions. Then, *you* make the decision which may or may not reflect your subordinates' influence.

GII   You share the problem with your subordinates as a group. Together you generate and evaluate alternatives and attempt to reach agreement (consensus) on a solution. Your role in much like that of chairperson, coordinating the discussion, keeping it focused on the problem, and making sure that the critical issues are discussed. You do not try to influence the group to adopt "your" solution and are willing to accept and implement any solution which has the support of the entire group. (Vroom and Jago 1974, 745)

Problem Attributes

A. Is there a quality requirement such that one solution is likely to be more rational than another?
B. Do I have sufficient information to make a high-quality decision?
C. Is the problem structured?
D. Is acceptance of the decision by subordinates critical to effective implementation?
E. If I were to make the decision myself, is it reasonably certain that it would be accepted by my subordinates?
F. Do subordinates share the organizational goals to be attained in solving this problem?
G. Is conflict among subordinates likely in preferred solutions?
H. Do subordinates have sufficient information to make a high-quality decision?

Decision Tree

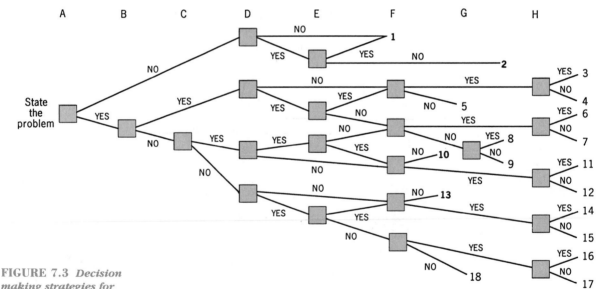

FIGURE 7.3 *Decision making strategies for group problems. From Victor H. Vroom and Arthur G. Jago, "Decision Making as a Social Process: Normative and Descriptive Models of Leader Behavior,"* Decision Sciences *1974, 5, 745. Reprinted by permission of the Decision Sciences Institute, Georgia State University, Atlanta, Georgia.*

Alternatives

1. AI, AII, CI, CII, GII
2. GII
3. AI, AII, CI, CII, GII
4. AI, AII, CI, CII, GII
5. AI, AII, CI, CII
6. GII

7. GII
8. CII
9. CI, CII
10. AII, CI, CII
11. AII, CI, CII, GII
12. AII, CI, CII, GII

13. CII
14. CII, GII
15. CII, GII
16. GI
17. GII
18. CII

Selecting the appropriate decision-making strategy requires the manager to ask eight questions that focus on (1) the required quality or rationality of the decision, (2) the necessity of group acceptance or commitment to the final decision, and (3) the time available to make the decision.

Figure 7.3 shows a decision tree with the eight questions displayed across the top. In deciding which decision-making strategy to employ, a manager asks the eight questions sequentially, following the appropriate path to a set of feasible decision-making strategies. The set of feasible strategies are shown at the bottom of Figure 7.3. Each set of feasible strategies is arrayed so that, reading from left to right, the strategies require an increasing commitment of time and allow for an increasing involvement of subordinates in the process. Thus, if you have great time constraints, you would likely choose the first strategy presented in the feasible set. If you have fewer time constraints, but are concerned about group commitment to the solution and therefore want to maximize input from the group, you should choose from the latter strategies within the feasible set.

In deciding whether or not to involve employees in the decision-making process, time plays a critical role. You should be careful, however, not to avoid group decision-making strategies because you believe that meetings tend to be inefficient and wasteful of both your own and your employees' time. Although a meeting may take a greater amount of employees' time overall, it may be possible to reach a decision within a shorter time period by bringing everyone together. Jack Stack, CEO of Springfield Remanufacturing Corporation, was faced with a decision that could have resulted in layoffs of 100 employees. After almost three months of trying to make the decision on his own, he held "town meetings" at all company sites and found that his employees were willing to work to bring on new products and jobs, rather than see fellow workers laid off. He later commented, "The neat thing about it was to realize that I couldn't make the decision myself. It was not a manager's decision. It was their future and their company" (*INC* 1988). The key to this dilemma involves learning to run meetings effectively.

INCREASING MEETING EFFECTIVENESS

No doubt you have attended some pretty horrible meetings in your life. You have also attended some good meetings. What characteristics differentiate good meetings from bad meetings? First, good meetings accomplish the desired task. Second, in good meetings there is appropriate input from group members, and everyone feels that he or she contributes in an important way.

Note the similarity of these characteristics to the task and group maintenance roles, played in transforming a work group into a work team, discussed in the first competency. This is no accident! One key to effective meeting management is the ability to balance the focus between task and group maintenance roles—making sure the group stays on track, while ensuring that everyone has an opportunity for appropriate participation. Here are some guidelines for effective meeting management; the guidelines focus on preparing for the meeting, running the meeting, and following up on the meeting.

Preparing for the Meeting

1. *Set objectives for the meeting.*   If you are not clear about the purpose of the meeting, it is unlikely that you will feel that you have accomplished something at the end of the meeting.

2. *Select appropriate participants for the meeting.*   Invite individuals who are affected by, or have an important stake in, the outcome of the decision. Where appropriate, choose participants with the intent of maximizing knowledge and perspective diversity.

3. *Select an appropriate time and place to meet.*   Choosing the appropriate time depends on individuals' work schedules, the amount of time required for the meeting, and what time of day is most appropriate: the fresh early morning or the work-focused end of day. Choosing an appropriate location depends on how large the group is, whether you will need special equipment (such as a blackboard or flip chart), and how much privacy or formality is necessary. Holding a meeting in your office will carry a very different message to your employees than holding the meeting in a conference room.

4. *Prepare and distribute an agenda in advance.*   Like setting the objectives for the meeting, preparing and distributing an agenda in advance increases the likelihood of accomplishing the objectives of the meeting. Include the time and place of the meeting and an estimated time for dealing with each major item on the agenda. Sequence the items so that there is some logic to the flow of topics. This gives participants a better sense of direction for the meeting. It also allows individuals to gather whatever information or resources they may feel will be important for the meeting.

Running the Meeting

1. *Start on time.*   Starting on time allows for the best use of everyone's time.

2. *Make sure that someone is taking minutes, where necessary.*

3. *Review the agenda and check if there are any necessary adjustments.*   Again, this provides a sense of direction for the meeting and will increase the likelihood of task accomplishment.

4. *Make sure that participants know each other.*   The atmosphere in the meeting will be much more pleasant when people know others with whom they are meeting.

5. *Follow the agenda.*   Pace the meeting. Make sure that each topic is carefully discussed; individuals should not go off on tangents or take the focus away from the item at hand.

6. *Be aware of everyone's contributions.*   Encourage participation by all. Remember, you selected the participants because you felt they had something to contribute to the decision. If some individuals dominate the discussion,

politely ask them to give others an opportunity to contribute. If some are reticent to contribute, try to ask for their opinions or suggestions without embarrassing them.

7. *Conclude the meeting by reviewing or restating any decisions reached and assignments made.*   In order to ensure agreement and to reinforce decisions, it is helpful to review or restate all decisions at the conclusion of the meeting. Clarification of decisions and assignments will increase the likelihood that the next meeting will be productive. You may also want to schedule the next meeting at this time.

Following Up on the Meeting

1. *If minutes have been taken, distribute them in a timely manner.*   This reminds people (or informs them, if they were unable to attend the meeting) of what happened in the meeting and what the group accomplished, as well as what their responsibilities are for the next meeting.

2. *If assignments have been made, periodically check with individuals as to their progress.*   It is best not to wait to the next meeting to find out that someone has been delayed in completing an assignment.

ANALYSIS   Decision by the Group[4]

Directions   Read the following story and answer the questions that follow.

John Stevens, plant manager of the Fairlee Plant of Lockstead Corporation, attended the advanced management seminar, conducted at a large midwestern university. The seminar, of four weeks duration, was largely devoted to the topic of executive decision making.

Professor Mennon, one of the university staff, particularly impressed John Stevens with his lectures on group discussion and group decision making. On the basis of research and experience, Professor Mennon was convinced that employees, if given the opportunity, could meet together, intelligently consider, and then formulate quality decisions that would be enthusiastically accepted.

Returning to his plant at the conclusion of the seminar, John decided to practice some of the principles which he had learned. He called together the 25 employees of department B and told them that production standards established several years previously were now too low in view of the recent installation of automated equipment. He gave the employees the opportunity to discuss the mitigating circumstances and to decide among themselves, as a group, what their standards should be. John, on leaving the room, believed that the em-

[4] *Source:* Reprinted with permission from John M. Champion and John H. Jones, *Critical Incidents in Management* (Homewood, Ill: Richard D. Irwin, Inc., 1975 ©).

ployees would doubtlessly establish higher standards than he himself would have dared proposed.

After an hour of discussion, the group summoned John and notified him that, contrary to his opinion, their group decision was that the standards were already too high, and since they were given the authority to establish their own standards, they were making a reduction of 10 percent. These standards, John knew, were far too low to provide a fair profit on the owner's investment. Yet, it was clear that his refusal to accept the group's decision would be disastrous. Before taking a course of action, John called Professor Mennon at the university to ask for his opinion.

Discussion Questions

1. What went wrong? *Group think; no goals/commitment.*
2. Was John's style of participative decision making appropriate for the situation? Why or why not? *No*
3. What style of participative decision making would you have advised John to use initially? *Share problem w/ group, CI he makes decision*
4. What would you suggest that John do now? Be specific in your suggestions! *Ask for rationale Explain profit def[...]*
5. Given the current situation, what advice would you give John about using participative decision making with his employees in the future? *Be more selective*

PRACTICE   The Sexual Harassment Case

Directions   Divide into groups of approximately six persons. Each group will compose an organization's civil rights review board. The review board examines evidence in civil rights cases, including sexual harassment incidents, and makes recommendations regarding appropriate action. Today, it will examine the evidence of a sexual harassment complaint and make a recommendation.

Each review board should begin by choosing a temporary chairperson. The review board should then read the Civil Rights Review Board Policy Guide on Sexual Harassment. Members of the review board should then read the statements by Mary Flaherty and Mike Blaggard.

The review board's charge is to review the evidence and make a decision whether action should be taken against Mike, and if so, what action.

Civil Rights Review Board Policy Guide on Sexual Harassment

Every employee is entitled to a working environment that is free from sexual harassment and its harmful economic, psychological, and physical effects. Sexual harassment in the workplace is not merely offensive; it is a form of discrimination in violation of federal law, as well as many states' laws. Harassment on the basis of sex is a violation of Section 703 of Title VII of the Civil Rights Act of 1964.

The costs of sexual harassment are considerable in both human and financial terms including replacement of personnel who leave their jobs, increased use of health plan benefits resulting from emotional and physical stress, absenteeism, and decline in individual and work group productivity.

In this organization, sexual harassment at the workplace is considered a form of employee misconduct. Moreover, sanctions may be enforced against supervisory and management personnel who allow such behavior to continue, as well as those individuals engaging in sexual harassment. Although the majority of incidents of sexual harassment involve a male supervisor or co-worker harassing a woman, the law also covers women harassing men, women harassing women, and men harassing men.

Official Definition of Sexual Harassment

"Unwelcome sexual advances, requests for sexual favors, or other verbal or physical conduct of a sexual nature constitute sexual harassment when:

1. Submission to such conduct is made either explicitly or implicitly a term or condition of an individual's employment; or
2. Submission to or rejection of such conduct by an individual is used as the basis for employment decisions affecting such individual; or
3. The conduct has the purpose or effect of unreasonably interfering with an affected person's work performance or creating an intimidating, hostile or offensive working environment."

Statement From Complainant, Mary Flaherty

I have worked in this division for three years. I like my job and am good at it. Mike Blaggard became my unit's manager a year and a half ago. Since his first day on the job, I felt something was wrong. He was always telling dirty jokes when he knew I could hear them. Then he would point me out and remark how I was blushing. It was embarrassing, but I got used to it after a while.

Then he asked me to help him with some materials in the storage closet. I agreed to and followed him. The closet door is hinged so that it closes automatically. After a few minutes we had taken care of the job, and he remarked that he thought I looked especially pretty today. I thanked him and went to leave the closet. He blocked my way, placing his hand on my shoulder. When I asked him to remove it, he smiled and tried to kiss me. I quickly moved past him and went back to my work area.

A little while later, Mike came over and apologized, saying that he hadn't meant to offend me. I told him not to worry about it and went back to work.

The next Thursday, I was one of the last to leave, and Mike again approached me. He asked if he could buy me a drink or something. I told him no, I had other plans. Then he grabbed me and started to kiss me again.

I slapped him and told him I was pressing charges. He "reminded" me that I was still in my probationary period, and this incident could reflect on his evaluation of me.

I am divorced and am raising two children on my own. I felt trapped and went out with him. The next day I told a friend what happened and she referred me to the people in personnel.

Statement from Defendant, Mike Blaggard

I was pretty new to the area and this division of the corporation. I had requested a transfer from another part of the country to work here. Right away I was attracted to Mary. She is very pretty and fun to talk to. She is also somewhat of a flirt. She would often come into my office and make a point of leaning over my desk. I never could tell if she was coming on to me.

When we would sit down to lunch she would sometimes touch me on the arm or hand when she talked to me. She always looked directly in my eyes when she talked to me. When that happens, I assume the girl is interested in me.

I asked her to help me with some stuff in the storage closet. She eagerly agreed. While we worked we talked about people we had been going out with and the problems we'd been having. Mary and I just seemed to click. When I tried to kiss her, she backed off and went back to work. I didn't know she was upset. If I had, I wouldn't have approached her a week later.

We were the last two to leave. Her flirting seemed to be more pronounced that day. At the end of the day, she seemed to be taking her time in getting her things together. Usually she is the first person out the door. But that night, her slowness seemed almost deliberate. I thought she was inviting me to ask her out.

When I asked, she acted real disappointed and said she had just made plans. She started to walk past me and brushed against me. There was plenty of room for her to walk by without touching. Her brush was deliberate, and I interpreted it to mean she was interested in me. I started to kiss her, and she slapped me and said she was going to file a complaint. That made me angry. I had not forced myself on her.

I told her that unless there was a change in her dress and demeanor, I would be unable to give her a favorable performance evaluation. I realize now that I should have waited for another time to tell her that, but I was angry.

She apologized, explaining the stress of raising her kids alone, and I apologized for any misunderstanding. We then agreed to go out for one "makeup" drink, and it ended up more like a date. But there was definitely no coercion.

The next day she initiated formal grievance procedures. I am confused over the entire episode.

Discussion Questions

1. What happened during the meeting of the civil rights review board?
2. Did you feel prepared for the meeting? If not, what additional information or material would have been helpful?
3. Did all review board members participate in the meeting?
4. Did the discussion stay on track, or was there a tendency to go off on tangents?
5. Did your group discuss any necessary follow-up measures?
6. What suggestions would you make to the meeting chair about running future meetings?
7. What suggestions do you have for yourself for the next time you chair a meeting?

During the next few weeks, try to attend and observe meetings of several groups with which you are involved. Ideas for meeting that you might attend are student organization meetings, sports team meetings, dorm meetings, and meetings where you work. After you have attended several meetings, choose one and write a three- to five-page paper describing the following aspects of the meeting:

1. What decisions were made at the meeting?
2. Were these decisions appropriate for group or participative decision making? Why or why not?
3. Who led the meeting?
4. Was an agenda distributed prior to, or at the beginning of, the meeting? Were specific time parameters set for the meeting?
5. Were people properly prepared for the meeting?
6. Was participation of all members encouraged?
7. Did the discussion remain focused on the main issues?
8. Was there proper closure to the meeting (i.e., summarizing accomplishments and allocating follow-up assignments)?
9. If this was a meeting you called, how well did you do at implementing new skills for participative decision making? If it was a meeting called by someone else, what advice can you give the group leader for future meetings?

Competency 3   Conflict Management

Directions   Think of some disagreements you have had with a friend, relative, manager, or co-worker. Then indicate how frequently you engage in each of the following described behaviors. For each item select the number that represents the behavior you are *most likely* to exhibit. There are no right or wrong answers. Please respond to all items on the scale. The responses from 1 to 7 are:

Scale

Always	Very often	Often	Sometimes	Seldom	Very seldom	Never
1	2	3	4	5	6	7

___4___   1. I blend my ideas to create new alternatives for resolving a disagreement.

[5]*Adaptation of* the Organizational Communication Conflict Instrument (OCCI), Form B, developed by C. Wilson and M. Waltman, in *Management, Communication Quarterly* 1(3), Feb. 1988, pp. 367–388, copyright © 1988 by Sage Publications, Beverly Hills, CA. Reprinted by permission of Sage Publications. Copyright © by Sage Publications, Beverly Hills, CA. Used with permission.

16
14
13
14
————
57/12 = 4.8 =

_6_ 2. I shy away from topics which are sources of disputes.

_2_ 3. I make my opinion known in a disagreement.

_4_ 4. I suggest solutions combine a variety of viewpoints.

_5_ 5. I steer clear of disagreeable situations.

_4_ 6. I give in a little on my ideas when the other person also gives in.

_5_ 7. I avoid the other person when I suspect that he or she wants to discuss a disagreement.

_4_ 8. I integrate arguments into a new solution from the issues raised in a dispute.

_4_ 9. I will go 50-50 to reach a settlement.

_4_ 10. I raise my voice when I'm trying to get the other person to accept my position.

_4_ 11. I offer creative solutions in discussions of disagreements.

_5_ 12. I keep quiet about my views in order to avoid disagreements.

_4_ 13. I give in if the other person will meet me halfway.

_4_ 14. I downplay the importance of a disagreement.

_5_ 15. I reduce disagreements by making them seem insignificant.

_4_ 16. I meet the other person at a midpoint in our differences.

_2_ 17. I assert my opinion forcefully.

_4_ 18. I dominate arguments until the other person understands my position.

_4_ 19. I suggest we work together to create solutions to disagreements.

_3_ 20. I try to use the other person's ideas to generate solutions to problems.

_4_ 21. I offer trade-offs to reach solutions in disagreements.

_3_ 22. I argue insistently for my stance.

_4_ 23. I withdraw when the other person confronts me about a controversial issue.

_4_ 24. I sidestep disagreements when they arise.

_5_ 25. I try to smooth over disagreements by making them appear unimportant.

_4_ 26. I insist my position be accepted during a disagreement with the other person.

_4_ 27. I make our difference seem less serious.

_5_ 28. I hold my tongue rather than argue with the other person.

_5_ 29. I ease conflict by claiming our differences are trivial.

_3_ 30. I stand firm in expressing my viewpoints during a disagreement.

20
11
12
——
43

Scoring and Interpretation

Three categories of conflict-handling strategies are measured in this instrument: solution oriented, nonconfrontational, and control. By comparing your scores on the following three scales, you can see which of the three is your preferred conflict-handling strategy.

To calculate your three scores, add the individual scores for the items and divide by the number of items measuring the strategy. Then subtract each of the three mean scores from 7.

> *Solution-oriented:* Items 1, 4, 6, 8, 9, 11, 13, 16, 19, 20, 21 AVG $4 = 3$
>
> *Nonconfrontational:* Items 2, 5, 7, 12, 14, 15, 23, 24, 25, 27, 28, 29 2
>
> *Control:* Items 3, 10, 17, 18, 22, 26, 30 $= 22/7 = 3 = 4$

Solution-oriented strategies tend to focus on the problem rather than the individuals involved. Solutions reached are often mutually beneficial, where neither party defines himself or herself as the winner and the other party as the loser.

Nonconfrontational strategies tend to focus on avoiding the conflict by either avoiding the other party or by simply allowing the other party to have "his or her way." These strategies are used when there is more concern with avoiding a confrontation than with the actual outcome of the problem situation.

Control strategies tend to focus on winning or achieving one's goals without regard for the other party's needs or desires. Individuals using these strategies often rely on rules and regulations in order to "win the battle."

Discussion Questions

1. Which strategy do you find easiest to use? Most difficult? Which do you use most often?
2. How would your answers to these items have differed if you had considered a different person than the one you chose?
3. How would your answers have differed for other work-related situations? Non–work-related situations?
4. What is it about the conflict situation or strategy that tells you which to use in dealing with a conflict situation?

LEARNING   Conflict Management

Over the past two decades, the topics of conflict and conflict management have become increasingly important to managers within organizations of all sizes. Research on organizational conflict suggests that managers spend between 20 and 50 percent of their time dealing with conflict; those at the lower levels of the organizational hierarchy report more time than those at the higher levels (Lippitt 1982). Although these statistics may seem disheartening at first, you will see in this chapter that conflict is not always negative. In fact, many people believe that constructive use of conflict keeps us from falling into the groupthink mode of decision making.

DIFFERENT PERSPECTIVES ON CONFLICT

The word *conflict* generally carries with it negative connotations. In both work- and non–work-related situations, people often try to avoid conflict because it creates bad feelings among people and can create a negative atmosphere in which to work or play. This view of conflict, sometimes called the traditional view of conflict (Robbins 1974), assumes that the most effective approach to conflict management is the elimination of the sources of conflict. Thus, if two employees in a work unit tend to engage in conflict consistently, the solution is to separate them and structure their work so that they do not have to interact.

A second view of conflict, sometimes called the behavioral or human relations view of conflict (Robbins 1974), views conflict as inevitable. Given the differences in individuals' personalities, needs, goals, and values, there is bound to be conflict; it simply cannot be avoided. Strategies for conflict management under this scenario focus on recognizing conflict when if surfaces and attempting to resolve whatever issues caused the initial conflict in a way that recognizes the different personalities, needs, goals, and values of the parties in conflict. Interestingly, people who hold this view see the process of conflict management positively, but still tend to see the actual conflict as a negative force in an organization.

In this section we will assume a third view of conflict. This third view, sometimes referred to as the interactionist view (Robbins 1974), differs from the first two because it does not view conflict as either good or bad, but as appropriate or inappropriate, functional or dysfunctional, for the particular situation. This view of conflict recognizes that not only is conflict inevitable, but it should sometimes be encouraged in order to allow new ideas to surface and to create positive forces for innovation and change.

In the remainder of this section, we will examine the sources of conflict in organizations and see how conflicts develop. We will then look at strategies for managing conflict that increase the likelihood that positive outcomes will result from the conflict.

LEVELS AND SOURCES OF CONFLICT

In order to use conflict constructively, it is important to understand how conflicts arise and how they develop. Although the primary focus in this chapter is on conflicts that arise between individuals or between groups (and that is, in fact, where most conflicts of consequence to organizations arise), it is important to recognize that conflict occurs at all levels of the organization. For example, conflicts may occur between two different organizations, or between units of an organization, when the first organization or unit senses that the second organization or unit is working against the goals or interests of the first.

In addition, individuals often experience internal, or intrapersonal, conflicts. Lewin (1935) identified three types of intrapersonal conflict.

1. Approach-approach conflicts occur when an individual must choose between two desirable outcomes or courses of action, such as when a manager must choose between two good job candidates.

2. Approach-avoidance conflicts occur when the same goal or outcome has both positive and negative consequences, such as when you choose a new job because it potentially has more promotional opportunities, but it also requires leaving the security of your present job.

3. Avoidance-avoidance conflicts occur when an individual must choose between two negative outcomes or courses of action, such as during a fiscal crisis when management must decide whether to totally eliminate a single project or program or to cut the budget across the board.

Although this chapter does not discuss at length conflicts at the intrapersonal or interorganization levels, it is important to be aware of their existence because of their potential impact on interpersonal or intergroup conflicts.

Conflicts in organizations develop for a wide variety of reasons. Often conflicts develop because of individual differences, such as differences in values, attitudes, beliefs, needs, or perceptions. Conflicts also develop between individuals when there are misunderstandings or communication errors, which lead individuals to believe that there are differences in values, attitudes, beliefs, needs, or perceptions.

Organizational structures may also create conflict within or between groups. For example, when two or more units perceive that they are in competition with each other for scarce resources, there is likely to be conflict among the units. Similarly, conflicts can arise when two or more units have different goals. For example, in large organizations, units associated with cost or quality control, or with setting organizational policies and procedures, often find themselves in conflict with other organizational units. This is a natural consequence of the differing focus or mission of the units.

STAGES OF THE CONFLICT PROCESS

Regardless of the level or the source of the conflict, conflicts usually follow a set sequence of events or stages. In the first stage, the conflict is latent. Neither party senses the conflict, but the situation is one in which individual or group differences or organizational structures have created the potential for conflict.

When the potential conflict situation is perceived by one or more of the parties, the conflict moves into the second stage. In this stage, individuals become cognitively aware of the differences and often experience an emotional reaction to the conflict, as well. Emotional reactions may take the form of anger, hostility, frustration, anxiety, or pain.

In the third stage the conflict moves from a cognitive or emotional awareness to action. It is in this stage that the conflict becomes overt, and individuals implicitly or explicitly choose to act to resolve the conflict or to escalate it. Actions to escalate the conflict include various forms of aggressive behaviors, such as verbally (or physically) attacking the person, acting in ways that purposefully frustrate the other person's attainment of goals, or attempting to engage others in the conflict by getting them to take sides against the other party. Actions to resolve the conflict generally require both individuals to take a positive problem-solving approach that allows both parties' needs and concerns to be heard and handled.

The fourth stage of conflict is the outcome or aftermath. Actions taken in the third stage directly affect whether the outcomes are functional or dysfunctional. Functional outcomes include a better understanding of the issues underlying the conflict, improved quality of decisions, increased attention to the use of creativity and innovation in solving and resolving future problems, and a positive approach to self-evaluation. Dysfunctional outcomes include continued anger and hostility, reduced communication, and a destruction of team spirit. More important, conflicts that result in dysfunctional outcomes often snowball, setting the stage for new conflicts that will potentially be more difficult to resolve because their source will be more complex.

CONFLICT MANAGEMENT STRATEGIES

In the assessment activity, you identified your preference among three conflict-handling strategies. These three strategies can be represented along two dimensions that show how individuals think and act in approaching situations where there is conflict (Thomas 1976). The first dimension represents *cooperativeness*, or the extent to which you are willing to work in order to meet the other party's needs and concerns. The second dimension represents *assertiveness*, or the extent to which you are willing to work in order to meet your own needs and concerns. Figure 7.4 shows how these two dimensions define five

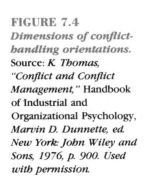

FIGURE 7.4
Dimensions of conflict-handling orientations.
Source: *K. Thomas, "Conflict and Conflict Management,"* Handbook of Industrial and Organizational Psychology, *Marvin D. Dunnette, ed. New York: John Wiley and Sons, 1976, p. 900. Used with permission.*

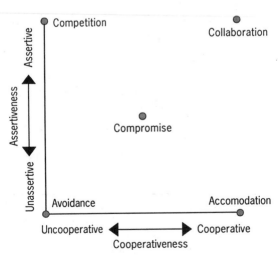

conflict management approaches. Nonconfrontational strategies are associated with avoiding and accommodating approaches; control strategies are associated with a competing approach; solution-oriented strategies are associated with collaborating and compromising approaches.

1. *Avoiding approaches.*   Avoiding approaches are those for which individuals recognize the existence of a conflict but do not wish to confront the issues of the conflict. In avoiding the issues, they work neither to satisfy their own goals nor to satisfy the other party's goals. Individuals may avoid by withdrawing and creating physical separation between the parties, or by suppressing feelings and attempting not to discuss the issues of the conflict. This approach is often useful when some time is needed to allow two parties engaged in a conflict to "cool off." In the long term, however, if the conflict is not dealt with, it is likely to surface again. Moreover, avoiding conflict can lead to avoiding important management issues. For example, the bankruptcy of the Penn Central Railroad has been attributed to mismanagement and a tendency by the company's board of directors to avoid conflict and to not question management's actions (Binzen and Daughen 1971).

2. *Accommodating approaches.*   Accommodating approaches are those for which individuals do not act to achieve their own goals, but rather they work only to satisfy the other party's concerns. This approach has the advantages that it preserves harmony and avoids disruption. In the short term, this approach is useful when the issue is not very important to you, or when the other party is much stronger and will not give in. In the long term, however, individuals may not always be willing to sacrifice their personal needs so that the relationship can be maintained. In addition, accommodating approaches generally limit creativity and stop the exploration for new ideas and solutions to the problem.

3. *Competing approaches.*   In direct contrast to accommodating approaches, competing approaches are those for which individuals work only to achieve their own goals. In these cases, individuals often fall back on authority structures and formal rules to win the battle. Although competing approaches are appropriate when quick, decisive action is necessary or when you know that certain decisions or actions must be taken for the good of the group, these approaches often result in dysfunctional outcomes. Competing behaviors set up a win-lose confrontation, for which one party is clearly defined as the winner and the other as the loser. In addition, like accommodating approaches, the use of competing behaviors generally limits creativity and stops the exploration for new ideas and solutions to the problem.

4. *Compromising approaches.*   Compromising approaches are the first of the solution-oriented strategies. Individuals using these approaches are concerned both with their own interests and goals and with those of the other party. These approaches usually involve some sort of negotiation during which each party gives up something in order to gain something else. The underlying assumption of compromising strategies is that there is a fixed resource or sum that is to be split, and that through compromise, neither

party will end up the loser. The disadvantage to this approach, however, is that neither party ends up the winner, and people often remember what they had to give up in order to get what they wanted.

5. *Collaboration approaches.*   The second solution-oriented strategy is collaboration, which is similar to the compromising approaches. Individuals using collaborating approaches are concerned with their own interests and goals as well as those of the other party. The difference is that there is no underlying assumption of a fixed resource that will force everyone to give up something in order to gain something else. Rather the assumption is that by creatively engaging the problem, a solution can be generated for which everyone is the winner and everyone is better off. Clearly these approaches have great advantages with respect to cohesion and morale; the great disadvantage is that they are time consuming and may not work when the conflict involves differences in values.

ADVANTAGES AND DISADVANTAGES OF CONFLICT MANAGEMENT APPROACHES

Each of the conflict management approaches has advantages and disadvantages that make it more or less appropriate for a given situation. Table 7.2 presents the five approaches and the appropriate situations for using each. Clearly your approach will also depend on your own comfort in using the various approaches.

TABLE 7.2 When to Use the Five Conflict Management Approaches

Conflict Management Approach	*Appropriate Situations*
Competing	1. When quick, decisive action is vital.
	2. On important issues where unpopular actions need implementing.
	3. On issues vital to the organization's welfare, and when you know you are right.
	4. Against people who take advantage of noncompetitive behavior.
Collaborating	1. To find an integrative solution when both sets of concerns are too important to be compromised.
	2. When your objective is to learn.
	3. To merge insights from people with different perspectives.
	4. To gain commitment by incorporating concerns into a consensus.
	5. To work through feelings which have interfered with a relationship.

TABLE 7.2 When to Use the Five Conflict Management Approaches (*Continued*)

Conflict Management Approach	*Appropriate Situations*
Compromising	1. When goals are important, but not worth the effort or potential disruption of more assertive modes.
	2. When opponents with equal power are committed to mutually exclusive goals.
	3. To achieve temporary settlements to complex issues.
	4. To arrive at expedient solutions under time pressure.
	5. As a backup when collaboration or competition is unsuccessful.
Avoiding	1. When an issue is trivial, or more important issues are pressing.
	2. When you perceive no chance of satisfying your concerns.
	3. When potential disruption outweighs the benefits of resolution.
	4. To let people cool down and regain perspective.
	5. When gathering information supersedes immediate decision.
	6. When others can resolve the conflict more effectively.
	7. When issues seem tangential or symptomatic of other issues.
Accommodating	1. When you find you are wrong—to allow a better position to be heard, to learn, and to show your reasonableness.
	2. When issues are more important to others than to you—to satisfy others and maintain cooperation.
	3. To build social credits for later issues.
	4. To minimize loss when you are outmatched and losing.
	5. When harmony and stability are especially important.
	6. To allow subordinates to develop by learning from mistakes.

Source: Kenneth W. Thomas, "Toward Multi-Dimensional Values in Teaching: The Example of Conflict Behaviors," *Academy of Management Review* 2, no. 3 (1977): p. 487. Used with permission.

Research has shown, however, that collaborating approaches are associated with such positive outcomes as decision-making productivity and organizational performance (Thomas 1976). In addition, as we discussed in the beginning of this section, the interactionist perspective suggests that a certain amount of conflict is to be encouraged to allow new ideas to surface and to create positive forces for innovation and change. Collaborating approaches are, in fact, the most effective of the conflict management approaches for allowing new and creative ideas to surface.

HOW TO USE COLLABORATIVE APPROACHES TO CONFLICT MANAGEMENT

Collaborative approaches to conflict management fall under the solution-oriented strategies. This should indicate to you that these approaches require the parties to work together to find a solution, or multiple solutions, that meet both sets of needs.

The first step in collaboration is to face the conflict. One party must recognize that a conflict exists, face one's feelings about the conflict, and be willing to approach the second party to talk about his or her feelings about the conflict. This is often difficult because it requires you to put aside any anger or hostility you are feeling and to be willing to face the anger or hostility that may be presented by the second party. Think in advance about how to handle this situation.

It is often a good idea to meet with the other party in a neutral environment. This will promote the atmosphere that you are willing to work together on generating positive solutions. When you meet, it is important that you examine your feelings, as well as the actual source of the conflict. Each person should state his or her views in a clear, nonthreatening way. Make use of the reflective listening techniques presented in Chapter 6.

After both parties have had a chance to surface their personal feelings and views of the conflict, the parties should move to a mutual definition of the conflict in terms of needs. It is important that both parties share a definition of the conflict before attempting to resolve the conflict; otherwise, you may be focusing on two separate and distinct issues. Again, it is important that you use reflective listening to come to a mutual definition of the conflict.

The next step is to brainstorm solutions (see Chapter 8 for an explanation of the steps involved in brainstorming). Search for solutions that address the needs of both parties. Use creative thinking techniques to increase the likelihood of finding a solution that meets everyone's needs; avoid making judgments about any of the solutions.

After both parties have listed all possible solutions, it is time to select an alternative. Both parties should identify their preferred solutions and think about why these solutions best meet their needs. The two parties should then see if any of the preferred solutions coincide, or what sorts of compromises are required to allow the two parties to come to a mutually acceptable agreement.

Once the solution has been identified, decide who will do what and when it will be done. That is, make sure you have an action plan that outlines the steps to carry out the solution. You may also want to identify steps to evaluate your success in implementing your solution. As a final step, it may be appropriate for both parties to identify what they learned from this conflict and what they will do in the future to avoid having the same situation surface again.

When using a collaborative approach, it is important to keep in mind this maxim: Confront the conflict; confront the problem; do not confront the person.

That is, if the two parties in conflict can see the problem as their enemy, rather than each other, it will be easier to come to a mutually acceptable solution.

ANALYSIS   Zack's Electrical Parts[6]

Directions   Read the following case study and answer the questions that follow.

Bob Byrne's ear was still ringing. Bob was director of the audit staff at Zack's Electrical Parts. He had just received a phone call from Jim Whitmore, the plant manager. Jim was furious. He had just read a report prepared by the audit staff concerning cost problems in his assembly plant.

Jim, in a loud voice, said that he disagreed with several key sections of the report. He claimed that had he known more about the audit staff's work, he could have shown them facts that denied some of their conclusions. He also asked why the report was prepared before he had a chance to comment on it. But what made him particularly angry was that the report had been distributed to all the top managers at Zack's. He felt top management would get a distorted view of his assembly department, if not his whole plant.

Bob ended the call by saying that he'd check into the matter. So he called in Kim Brock, one of his subordinates who headed the audit team for the study in question. Kim admitted that she had not had a chance to talk to Jim before completing and distributing the report. Nor had she really had a chance to spend much time with Dave Wells, who headed the assembly department. But Kim claimed it wasn't her fault. She had tried to meet with Jim and Dave more than once. She had left phone messages for them. But they always seemed too busy to meet and were out of town on several occasions when she was available. So she decided she had better complete the report and get it distributed in order to meet the deadline.

That same day, Jim and Dave discussed the problem over lunch. Dave was angry too. He said that Kim bugged him to do the study, but her timing was bad. Dave was working on an important assembly area project of his own that was top priority to Jim. He couldn't take the time that Kim needed right now. He tried to tell her this before the study began, but Kim claimed she had no choice but to do the audit. Dave remembered, with some resentment, how he couldn't get Kim's help last year when he needed it. But the staff audit group seemed to have plenty of time for the study when he couldn't give it any attention. Jim said that he'd look into the matter and agreed that they had been unnecessarily raked over the coals.

[6] *Reprinted from* Henry L. Tosi, John R. Rizzo, and Stephen J. Carroll, *Managing Organizational Behavior*. New York: Harper & Row Publishers, p. 504. Copyright © 1986 Henry Carroll. Used with permission.

Discussion Questions
1. What were the sources of conflict between the staff audit group and the managers in the plant? *Competition*
2. What were the differences between the interpersonal conflict and the intergroup conflict in this case?
3. How would you describe the conflict in terms of the stages it went through?
4. What should Bob and Jim do now to resolve this conflict?
5. What might Bob do to avoid future conflict situations between the staff audit group and other line managers? *Collaborate*

PRACTICE   The Vacation Schedule[7]

Directions
This role-play activity is designed to help you explore and practice participative decision-making and conflict resolution strategies. For this activity, the class will be divided into small groups of five people. If there are participants left over, they will become observers.

The role play takes place in the accounting unit of a major insurance company that experiences an increase in activity in the summer months. Vacation scheduling has always been a problem in this unit of 20 people. To help the situation, in March the manager developed a vacation schedule with only two vacations each week.

Each member of your group will assume a role that will be described in a handout distributed by your instructor. There are five roles: the manager and four workers (Marge, George, Annie, and Sam). Decide which group member will play each role. When the roles have been distributed, read *only* your own role. Do *not* read anyone else's role.

As you play your role, try to remember the conflict management strategies that will help you to positively deal with the present situation. When you finish the role play, respond to the following questions.

Questions for Everyone
1. What were the inherent conflicts in this situation?
2. What, if any, additional conflicts arose during the role play?
3. How did the manager present the problem to the group? How did this help or hinder movement towards a solution?
4. What were the advantages and disadvantages of bringing the group together to discuss the scheduling problem?

Questions for Role Play Participants
1. What were your feelings about the situation as you "went into the meeting?"
2. As the meeting progressed, how did you feel about the situation in general? Your role in the situation?
3. Did you feel that your ideas and concerns were heard by the group?
4. Do you feel that you listened fairly to the ideas and concerns presented by others?
5. How do you feel about the solution reached by your group?
6. How do you think others in your group feel about the solution reached?

Questions for Role Play Observers
1. How did you feel observing the conflict situation? Were there moments when you felt uncomfortable or troubled by the interaction of the group?
2. Do you feel that all parties had the opportunity to express their ideas and concerns?

[7]*Adapted from* J. William Pfeiffer and John E. Jones (Eds.), *A Handbook of Structured Experiences for Human Relations Training,* Vol. VIII, San Diego, CA.: University Associates, Inc., 1981. Used with permission.

3. Were there crucial points in the discussion that you felt moved the role players in one direction or another?
4. What feedback can you give the role players on their behaviors during the role play?
5. How do you feel about the solution reached by the group?

APPLICATION   Managing Your Own Conflicts

Select a conflict situation that either exists for you or that you have dealt with in the recent past. If it is a conflict that currently exists, work on resolving the conflict; include a plan for reducing the probability that the same conflict will arise again. Analyze the conflict situation and how it was or is managed; use the concepts and skills learned in this chapter. Describe the conflict in a three- to five-page report. Make sure you address the following topics:

■ The source of the conflict.

■ Your feelings about the conflict.

■ Your behavior concerning the conflict.

■ The other party's (parties') behavior concerning the conflict.

■ The current stage of the conflict.

■ The conflict management strategies used by you and the other party (parties) and the appropriateness, advantages, and disadvantages of those strategies.

■ The outcome of the conflict.

■ Your plan for dealing with this type of situation in the future.

REFERENCES

Beckhard, R. and R. T. Harris. *Organizational Transition: Managing Complex Change.* Reading, Mass: Addison-Wesley, 1977.

Benne, Kenneth D., and Paul Sheats. "Functional Roles of Group Members," *Journal of Social Issues* 4, no. 2 (1948): 41–49.

Binzen, P., and J. R. Daughen. *Wreck of the Penn Central.* Boston: Little, Brown, 1971.

Dayal, I., and J. M. Thomas. "Operation KPE: Developing a New Organization," *Journal of Applied Behavioral Science* 4 (1968): 473–506.

Dyer, William G. *Team Building.* Reading, Mass.: Addison-Wesley, 1987.

"For Better Quality, Listen to the Workers," *The New York Times,* (October 18, 1987).

Gordon, Judith R. *A Diagnostic Approach to Organizational Behavior.* Newton, Mass.: Allyn and Bacon, Inc., 1987.

"Getting to Know You," *INC.* (1988): 167–169.

Harrison, Roger. "Role Negotiation: A Tough Minded Approach to Team Development," in *The Social Technology of Organization Development,* W. Warner Burke and H. A. Hornstein (eds.), La Jolla, Calif.: University Associates, 1972: 84–96.

Janis, Irving. *Victims of Groupthink.* Boston: Houghton Mifflin, 1972.

Lewin, Kurt. *A Dynamic Theory of Personality.* New York: McGraw-Hill, 1935.

Lippitt, Gordon L. "Managing Conflict in Today's Organizations," *Training and Development Journal* (July 1982): 67–74.

Reilly, A. J., and John E. Jones. "Team Building," in *The 1974 Annual Handbook for Group Facilitators,* J. William Pfeiffer and John E. Jones (eds.); San Diego, Calif.: University Associates, 1974.

Robbins, Stephen P. *Managing Organizational Conflict: A Nontraditional Approach.* Englewood Cliffs. N.J.: Prentice-Hall, 1974.

———. *Organizational Behavior: Concepts, Controversies, and Applications.* Englewood Cliffs, N.J.: Prentice-Hall, 1989.

Tannenbaum, Robert, and W. H. Schmidt. "How to Choose a Leadership Pattern," *Harvard Business Review* (March–April 1958): 95–101.

Thomas, Kenneth W. "Conflict and Conflict Management," in *Handbook of Industrial and Organizational Psychology,* Marvin D. Dunnette (ed.), Chicago: Rand McNally, 1976: 889–935.

Thomas, Kenneth W. "Toward Multidimensional Values in Teaching: The Example of Conflict Management," *Academy of Management Review,* 1977 484–490.

Vroom, Victor H., and Arthur G. Jago. "Decision-making as a Social Process: Normative and Descriptive Models of Leader Behavior," *Decision Sciences* 5 (1974): 743–769.

Vroom, Victor H. and Philip W. Yetton, *Leadership and Decision-Making.* Pittsburgh: University of Pittsburgh Press, 1973.

The Facilitator and Mentor Roles

Before we move on to the next two roles, let's put the facilitator and mentor roles into the context of the competing values framework. As with the other roles, these roles are appropriate in some situations and not others.

A BRIEF REVIEW

These two roles are part of the human relations model, in which the desired ends are commitment and morale. The assumed means to these ends have to do with discussion, participation, and openness. This model assumes that individuals are unique, all with their own needs, values, and assumptions. The manager's job is to build these unique individuals into a cohesive team. This requires the skills of the mentor and facilitator roles.

WHEN THE FACILITATOR AND MENTOR ROLES ARE MOST APPROPRIATE

To understand when this model is appropriate, let's review the two axes that define the model. On the horizontal axis the model is defined by an internal focus, which suggests less external pressure for action; time is available before action needs to be taken. The vertical axis is defined by high flexibility, which suggests situations where the basic problems are ambiguous and not easily understood. In such situations, it is appropriate to bring people together to share their observations and opinions, to air all the different perspectives, and then to try to develop an action strategy that people believe in. This process is often time consuming and may cause conflict, so many people feel uneasy about entering such processes. However, to rush in, take charge, and make command decisions (as someone who operated in the rational goal model might), when it is clear that no one person has sufficient information about the situation and time is available before the decision must be made, is to lose credibility and engender resistance.

COMPLEMENTARY ROLES

Because some people feel that the human relations model is inherently "right," they may tend to overuse it. In all situations they believe that they should be process oriented. At times, though, acting as a facilitator and mentor is not the best course that a manager can take. The failure to balance the facilitator and mentor roles with the other roles, particularly the director and producer roles in the rational goal model, can lead to problems.

Some managers become so concerned about the feelings and desires of their subordinates that they become permissive, allowing almost total freedom. This well-intentioned strategy sometimes has disastrous results. In an organization, a managerial leader may build a productive team by skillfully blending the competencies from the human relations model and the rational goal model. On the other hand, by ignoring task concerns, and overresponding to human concerns, a productive team orientation can easily become a nonproductive "country club" orientation.

This is what happened a few years ago at Honeywell. They introduced the need to practice participative decision making. Managers interpreted this practice to mean that managers simply abdicate all decision authority to subordinates. The result was organizational chaos. A major intervention was necesssary in order to teach managers how to balance participation with direction.

Clearly the roles in the internal process model must be seen in context. They must be balanced with other models.

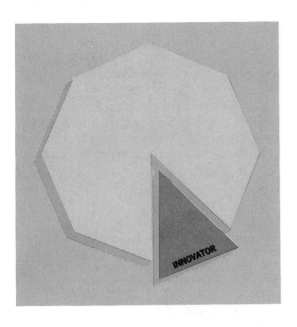

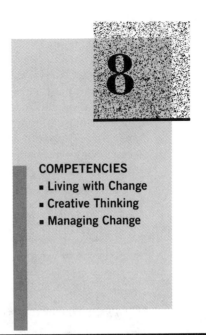

COMPETENCIES
- **Living with Change**
- **Creative Thinking**
- **Managing Change**

THE INNOVATOR ROLE

The **innovator role** is one of the most compelling, and yet least understood, of the eight leadership roles. It is the first role of the open systems model, which, you will recall, stresses adaptability and responsiveness to the external environment. The innovator role involves the use of creativity and the management of organizational changes and transitions, and provides a unique opportunity for managers to affirm the value of individual employees within the organizational setting.

When people think of the words *innovator* and *innovation,* they tend not to think in terms of large established organizations. Rather, they associate the terms with new entrepreneurial business endeavors or with specific corporate divisions related to such things as new product development, new design, or new advertising lingo. In fact, given the many rules and procedures that must be followed in large organizations, they often assume that managers in these organizations have little opportunity to be innovative or to create flexible, risk-taking environments.

You should be aware, however, that change is inevitable in all aspects of organizational life today. Moreover, in many cases change and innovation are desirable. They are indispensable to the function, growth, and survival of organizations. The issue today is not whether organizations will experience change, but how they will manage that change. In his book *Thriving on Chaos,* Tom

Peters states, *"No skill is more important than the corporate capacity to change"* (author's emphasis) (1987, 333).

Innovation and managed change make readiness and adaptability possible in society's increasingly changing conditions and accompanying demands. Today, managers play an important role both in the initiation and the implementation of organizational change. In this chapter the three key competencies of the innovator are:

> ***Competency 1*** Living with Change
> ***Competency 2*** Creative Thinking
> ***Competency 3*** Managing Change

Each of these competencies require the manager to be flexible and open to new ideas, new ways of thinking, and new challenges that the managerial role presents.

Competency 1 Living with Change

ASSESSMENT Personal Acceptance of Change

Directions The following questionnaire will help you assess your personal acceptance of change. Consider carefully the following list of changes. List any others that are applicable. Which of these changes have occurred in your life in the past five years? As you consider each change, recall your resistance to change when it happened.

In column A, place a number reflecting your resistance at the time of the change. Next, in column B, place a number reflecting your current level of acceptance of that change. If you did not experience the change, place a "0" in both blanks.

Scale A

No resistance				Strong resistance
1	2	3	4	5

Scale B

No acceptance				Strong acceptance
1	2	3	4	5

A	B	
—	—	1. You were married or engaged.
___	___	2. There was a death in your immediate family.
1	5	3. You moved to a new location.
1	5	4. You enrolled in a college or university.
___	___	5. You had a personal health problem.
1	3	6. You began work at a new job.
?	___	7. An important relationship in your life changed.
2	2	8. Your income level changed by over $10,000 a year.
—	—	9. You were divorced or separated.
1	5	10. A close friend or relative was divorced or separated.
___	___	11. Other (List):

Interpretation   What do your responses reveal about how you deal with change? As you look at each item, note the difference between the number you placed in column A (resistance to change) and the number in column B (acceptance of change). A large difference (4 is the maximum possible) indicates that your ability to accept change is strong.

1. Which changes did you strongly resist at first, but now accept? Think of as many reasons as possible why you now accept these changes. Identifying these reasons may help you identify your strengths in acceptance of change.

2. Based on your responses, do you consider yourself to be open to change, or do you find change difficult to deal with?

3. Are there any events which you strongly resisted, and which you now have difficulty accepting? Seek to identify the reasons for your nonacceptance. As you compare strongly resisted events which you accept with those you do not, you may find valuable clues to your ability to cope with change in your life.

LEARNING   Living with Change

One of the greatest challenges to the manager in the innovator role is that of living with changes that are unplanned and sometimes unwelcome. As a manager you must often deal with a difficult dilemma when experiencing such change: on the one hand, you need personally to adjust to an unplanned change that you may not welcome, and at the same time you must present the change to your employees in a manner that helps them to make the adjustment as well. Both cases may require a shift in attitude towards change and a conscious effort to eliminate psychological resistance to change.

In studying change in organizations, it is helpful to recognize that people do not just work in organizations—people live in organizations. In fact, people who work full time generally spend more time at work than they do engaged in any other activity, with the possible exception of sleep.

We recognize that changes take place in life, and although we may resist, we also know that we must adjust to these changes. The same is true of changes in the workplace. What can we learn about change in our lives in general that will help us respond to changes in the organization? Let's consider several differences between planned and unplanned change in life, and relate those findings to the workplace.

PLANNED AND UNPLANNED CHANGE

In our lives we frequently experience planned changes. Generally we plan beneficial changes, and thus we welcome those changes. Some planned changes have only minor impacts on our lives, such as planning a change in hairstyle or wardrobe. Other planned changes are major and can potentially change the course of our lives, such as plans to go to college, plans to have children, and plans to buy a home. Our plans may not always have the intended results, but we usually plan changes with the intent of benefiting ourselves.

From time to time, though, we may find ourselves resisting changes that we have planned for ourselves. Why? We may resist change when we have ambivalent feelings towards those changes. For example, although we work towards graduating, we may still wonder if we can make it on our first job. We also resist changes that involve a lot of work. Moving to a new house can be exciting, but it can also be very stressful and difficult. Likewise, we resist changes that involve unknowns. Many people plan their retirement years in advance, but when the time draws close, they resist because they do not know what it will be like.

The fact that we plan change reflects the needs we have to exercise control over our lives and to know, with some certainty, what the future holds. Sometimes the need to feel in control is stronger than the reaction to the actual change. Even changes that are beneficial to you may be resisted if someone else has planned them. For example, if someone else planned what courses you should take or for what new job you should apply, you would probably find yourself resisting those plans—even if the plans exactly matched your own.

In addition, people have a need to know what will happen next. All of us are more comfortable when we can predict what will happen and how others will respond to us. Anxiety and stress increase when we find ourselves in situations where we do not know how to behave or what to expect from others. For example, if you were invited to attend religious services for a religion with which you are totally unfamiliar, you might try to contact someone who knows more about the religion to find out what to expect. With that information, your ability to predict the behavior of others, and your ability to behave appropriately, increases and you are more comfortable.

Let's turn now to unplanned change, or changes that are not anticipated—changes that are sudden, imposed upon us, and largely unwelcome—and compare these to planned changes. Five important differences between planned change and unplanned change are presented here. Table 8.1 summarizes these differences.

First, planned change usually carries a more positive connotation than does unplanned change. We plan changes in our lives that are intended to benefit us. Unplanned changes, however, are painful, difficult, or present us with per-

---

TABLE 8.1 Differences Between Planned and Unplanned Change

1. Planned change carries a more positive connotation than unplanned change.
2. Planned change tends to involve a sense of gain; unplanned change tends to involve a sense of loss.
3. Planned changes can be anticipated; unplanned changes are sudden.
4. We are active participants in planned changes; we see ourselves as passive receivers of unplanned changes.
5. Planned changes are usually less stressful than unplanned changes.

sonal crises. Examples of painful unplanned changes include the death of a loved one, the loss of a friend, the loss of a job, and divorce. Although unplanned changes sometimes bring long-term benefits, the short-term pain of unplanned changes is often difficult to cope with.

Second, planned change tends to involve a sense of gain, whereas unplanned change tends to involve a sense of loss. Sometimes we do lose something. For example, we may lose contact with co-workers whose promotions take them to a new location, or there may be a loss of flexibility in the organization after a reorganization. We may experience the loss of a sense of security, a sense of control, our ability to anticipate what is going to happen to us, or a sense that everything is fine.

Third, planned change can be anticipated; unplanned change is sudden. With planned change, we have time to adjust and to think about alterations that will accompany the change. Time to adjust translates into assistance with coping and adaptation. In dealing with unplanned change, however, we do not have the benefit of time. Adaptation is more difficult, and the suddenness comes as a stark reminder of how little control we actually have over our lives.

Fourth, we usually welcome planned change, but see unplanned change as imposed upon us. When we welcome change, we are active participants in the event; when change is imposed, we are passive receivers of others' actions. Within organizations, change may happen by chance, or as a result of forces beyond our control, but we usually perceive unplanned change as imposed by an organizational hierarchy. This sense of imposition is not pleasant and understandably people generally resist. Once again, unplanned change reminds us that we have little control over our lives.

Finally, planned change is usually less stressful than unplanned change. Although both types of changes may require coping and adaptation, the positive aspects of planned changes can enhance the coping process. Unplanned events are often stressful because they disturb our equilibrium, our sense of comfort with the predictable nature of life, and our sense of control over our existence.

HELPING OURSELVES AND OTHERS TO DEAL WITH UNPLANNED CHANGE

The first step in living with change is to learn about individual response to change. The more we know, the better we will be able to manage it—both at work and in our personal lives.

Understanding the roots of resistance to unplanned change in yourself and in others is most important for the manager. As a manager your challenge is twofold:

Challenge 1   To assist yourself in adapting to unplanned changes which you may not welcome and with which you may, in fact, strongly disagree.

Challenge 2   To assist your employees to do the same.

To deal with these changes you need to ask yourself, "What can I do to adjust? How can I deal productively with change, while at the same time assisting employees in doing the same? Are there things that I can initiate before a change occurs that will help my work unit adjust to unplanned changes when they occur?" The strategies that help you to cope with unplanned change can also assist others in doing the same, because you are able to offer these same strategies to your employees. Any strategy will need to be directed at reducing resistance, both yours and that of your employees. The ability to redirect resisting energy to positive work energy is an important skill of the innovator.

Here are three general guidelines for coping with unplanned change in the innovator role. These steps should be taken concurrently.

1. Recognize that you experience additional stress during times of adjustment to unplanned changes. Study the recommendations in the section on stress management in Chapter 3 and incorporate them into your life.

2. Identify strategies that have helped you deal with the stress of unplanned changes in the past. Ask yourself, "When I have been faced with unplanned changes in my life, in or out of the workplace setting, what has been helpful to me?" Here are three frequently reported sources of strength for individuals facing unplanned change in their lives.

   ■ A supportive environment where people around you understood your difficulties and provided a setting where you did not have to defend or justify your feelings. Adjustment to unplanned change involves emotions. Some people are very uncomfortable with dealing with their emotions, especially in the workplace. The relief and positive energy that is given to individuals when they realize that it is acceptable to express their emotional responses without being negatively evaluated should not be underestimated.

   ■ A feeling from others that you are accpted and respected for your strengths. People often feel vulnerable during times of unplanned change. Concern for how others view you may prevent you from expressing emotions about unplanned change. At these times it is important to be the recipient of respect from other people.

   ■ A hopeful belief in the potential benefit, or gain, from successfully dealing with the change. An attitude of optimism about the future and in its improvement over today can give you impetus to face changes with renewed vigor.

3. Seek ways to replicate the conditions in step 2, and any others which you can identify, when you need the assistance. In your managerial position, you need to encourage the expression of these conditions in your work unit as well.

Once you have met the challenge of establishing your personal coping strategy, your second challenge is to assist your employees in adjusting to unplanned changes. Consider the situations that you experience outside the workplace when helping friends and others deal with unplanned changes in their lives. What do you usually do to be helpful to others during trying circumstances? Most likely, you may try to do for others what you have identified as helpful for you. Within the organization, can you help your employees to deal with unplanned changes? In this situation you have two major tools at your disposal: (1) the organizational culture and (2) your leadership style.

USING THE ORGANIZATIONAL CULTURE TO DEAL WITH UNPLANNED CHANGE

In many ways, organizations mirror society. One striking way in which this takes place is that, like societies, organizations have cultures. An organizational **culture** is a collection of meanings, values, beliefs, expectations, and attitudes that are shared by members of the organization. It is seen in the taken-for-granted assumptions about how individuals behave and how the work is to be done. Organizational cultures are powerful entities that influence the members of the organization.

An organization's culture reflects its philosophy and mission. It influences the way organizational members perceive events and situations. Cultures also influence the way in which members of the organization interact with one another and with outsiders in job-related responsibilities. For example, at each of the Disney theme parks, the culture reflects a strong emphasis on customer service; employees are expected to "go the extra mile" to ensure that the customer is satisfied. Similarly, an organization's culture may reflect a strong emphasis on human resources, individual development, and training. In addition, how an organization deals with planned change is reflected in its culture. Note, however, that organizational cultures are not engraved in stone; they change and interact with the values and beliefs of members, as well as with the society from which the members come.

How can your organizational culture help you in your efforts to assist employees in dealing with unplanned change? If the culture is one which embraces values of inflexibility and resistance to change, or if the culture promotes the belief that the way things have always been done in the past is the only way to do things in the future, then the culture may be a hindrance. IBM had such a culture, but current efforts by CEO John Akers has changed the culture into a flexible one. As you examine your organizational culture, identify those elements of the organizational culture that reinforce resistance to change, and try to reduce their strength. Also identify those elements of the organizational culture that are consistent with a supportive environment, and seek to strengthen those elements. As a member of the organization, and as a manager, you have a great deal of influence over the organizational culture, especially within your work unit.

Moreover, *before* the crisis of an unplanned change occurs, begin now to reduce the strength of the resistant forces and strengthen the supportive elements of your organizational culture so that you are more prepared for change as it occurs. Three ways for using your organizational culture to deal with unplanned change are as follows.

First, support an organizational (work unit) culture that values flexibility and adaptability. If necessary, take opportunities to raise the issue of change for discussion in your work unit. Advance the notion that change is in the nature of things, and that change should be expected. Let your employees know that opportunities for change are opportunities for learning and growth, and that these can be welcomed. Reflect this belief in your reactions to change as it occurs.

Second, encourage employee participation in work unit changes. Wherever possible, when implementing change, allow employees to suggest alternative methods of implementation that are respectful of their attitudes, values, and concerns. Again, by encouraging employee involvement, you are reducing resistance to change and thus engaging in cultural change. At American West, chairman of the board Edward Beauvais and president Michael Conway have created a culture that strongly encourages employee participation by maintaining an open-door policy for all employees.

Finally, think of employees as creative resources. Tapping employees' creativity helps them see their value and unique strengths. Such encouragement will undoubtedly assist them when coping with unplanned changes.

USING YOUR LEADERSHIP STYLE TO DEAL WITH UNPLANNED CHANGE

The second tool available to you in helping employees to deal with unplanned change is your own leadership style. The phrase *leadership style* refers to the way managers treat and interact with employees. How one treats and interacts with employees is likely to affect whether employees resist unplanned change, or are open and flexible to suggestions.

There are two types of leadership styles: the manager as conductor and the manager as developer (Bradford and Cohen 1984). In the manager-as-conductor style, the manager is boss and gives instructions to employees, who are simply expected to carry out the instructions. The second leadership style is the manager-as-developer style. This is also known as the "empowerment" leadership style because managers take the posture of supporting employees in the performance of their responsibilities.

The manager-as-conductor style is perhaps the most familiar, and it is what we tend to think of when we consider management in hierarchical organizations. In this model, there is a formal hierarchy of authority, which also describes approved lines of communication. The manager using this style figures out how best to coordinate the work efforts, and how to get subordinates to do things properly. Using the orchestra as a metaphor, the manager-as-conductor literally orchestrates the situations being faced in the most productive way possible. The manager-as-conductor style, however, potentially can lead to resistance because employees feel no sense of control and see no credit or reward for successful implementation of change. They feel that although they have performed well in getting the work accomplished, the manager-as-conductor takes total responsibility for the success; after all, without someone there to coordinate and motivate, the work would not be done.

In contrast, the manager-as-developer seeks ways to "empower" subordinates, helping them to realize their potential. The manager-as-developer engages employees in the decision-making process and delegates responsibilities without necessarily telling individuals how to do it. The manager-as-developer focuses on the unit's work as a joint venture, a team effort. Under this leadership style, employees often feel that "their brains are being tapped" and that their views and creative ability are welcomed and valued. Employees of the manager-as-developer learn and grow from the work experience. John Carlzon, of Scandinavian Airline Systems, has as one of his mottoes, "Run through walls." His employees know that they are allowed to make the wrong decisions, and that the right decisions will lead to praise and rewards.

To be successful, the manager-as-developer gives credit to employees for their accomplishments, rather than taking credit for the work done in the unit. The manager-as-developer is not threatened by the talent and success of employees, but rather welcomes employees' abilities and seeks ways to use their strengths. Figure 8.1 summarizes the characteristics of both leadership styles.

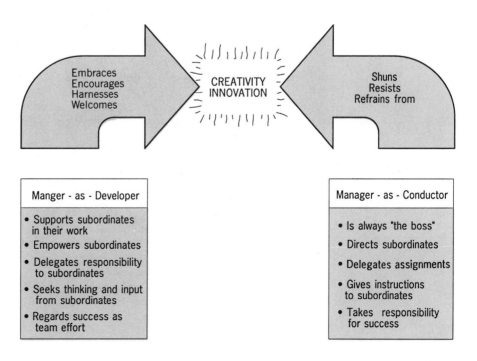

FIGURE 8.1
Innovation and leadership style.

One advantage of using your own leadership style as a tool for helping to deal with unplanned change is that it is within your control. Although it may be the case that others around you engage in the manager-as-conductor leadership style, you can still embrace the manager-as-developer style for yourself and your work unit. Moreover, managers who adopt the manager-as-developer leadership style can expect to experience less resistance to change from employees than those who adopt the manager-as-conductor leadership style.

ANALYSIS   Resistance to Change

Directions   Read the following paragraph, and think of yourself as the manager in this organization. In the questions that follow, analyze how you would react to these changes. Try to be as honest as possible in considering your reactions.

You are a manager in a relatively small division of a large corporation. The division employs approximately 600 people. You have been with this organization for 12 years. You have come up through the ranks and consider yourself well regarded by your boss and others in upper management. You are responsible for a work unit of 35 employees. Suddenly and with no warning you find that major organizational changes are about to occur: your division will be structurally reorganized and moved to a larger and more spacious building. You will maintain your same title and salary, but other things will change: you will now be responsible for managing 25 people. The office space for your unit will be more desirable (higher floor, more windows), but the space is smaller in proportion to the decrease of the staff. Because of the larger parking lot, you and a number of other managers will now have your own assigned parking space. Currently there is no assigned parking owing to space limitations. You will report to another manager, who in turn reports to your current boss. Although you have nothing against this newly hired manager, this change does require an unexpected adjustment; you have come to regard your current boss as a good friend.

Discussion Questions   1. How would you describe your feelings? Check all that apply:
_____ I feel hurt.
_____ I feel angry.
_____ I feel less valued by the organization.
_____ I feel demoted even though the salary and title remain the same.
_____ I feel like getting another job somewhere, if personal circumstances permit.
_____ I feel like I would like to talk this out with someone in higher levels of management, but I feel powerless to do so.
_____ I feel that others in the organization are looking on me and my work unit differently, and that they may be regarding my work unit as less important to the organization's purpose.
_____ I feel less pride in my work.

_____ I feel unappreciated by the division manager and others in upper management.

_____ I feel a decreasing sense of accomplishment.

_____ I feel as if I have been abandoned by my boss.

2. Do you have other feelings? Elaborate.

3. What are the sources of your resistance to this change? Analyze the situation and write down three factors that may account for your feelings.

PRACTICE   Resistance to Change Revisited

Directions   Refer to your responses to the preceding analysis activity. In that activity you analyzed your feelings with regard to a hypothetical situation of unplanned change at work. Now switch roles: Pretend that you are in upper management, and you are the change agent for these same changes. Identify how you would handle the change by responding to the following statements:

1. I expect the positive responses of my employees to this change will be

   _____.

2. I expect the negative responses of my employees to this change will be

   _____.

3. Sources of their resistance to the move include _____.

4. My employee's questions about the move will be _____.

5. The areas and issues I will have to address concerning the move are _____.

6. I can help defuse some of my employee's resistance and negative responses by using the organizational culture to _____.

7. I can help defuse some of my employee's resistance and negative responses by using my leadership style to _____.

8. To initiate this change, my three most important actions will be _____.

APPLICATION   Diagnosing Your Organizational Culture

Write a brief case study on the culture of an organization in which you are, or have been, involved. After a careful description, respond to the following questions:

1. What are some of the shared meanings, values, beliefs, expectations, and attitudes that are reflected in your organization's culture?

2. What are some unquestioned basic assumptions in the organizational culture?

3. Based on your answers to questions 1 and 2, would you describe your organizational culture as supportive or nonsupportive of employees in dealing with unplanned change? Why?

4. What specific steps would you take to enhance the way that your organization deals with unplanned change? Choose at least two of these steps, and write an action plan that indicates how you would implement these changes if you could.

Competency 2   Creative Thinking

Directions   Listed are a series of statements describing individual behaviors or attitudes that have been found to be related to creative thinking ability. Read each statement and place a check mark next to those items that you are surprised to see related to creativity. Then review the list, and circle the number of those statements that you think describe you.

_____ ① In a group, voicing unconventional, but thought-provoking opinions.

✓ _____ ② Sticking with a problem over extended periods of time.

_____ 3. Getting overly enthusiastic about things.

_____ 4. Getting good ideas when doing nothing in particular.

_____ 5. Occasionally relying on intuitive hunches and the feeling of "rightness" or "wrongness" when moving toward the solution of a problem.

_____ ⑥ Having a high degree of aesthetic sensitivity.

_____ 7. Occasionally beginning work on a problem that could only dimly be sensed and not yet expressed.

✓ _____ 8. A tendency to forget details, such as names of people, streets, highways, small towns, and so on.

_____ 9. Sometimes feeling that the trouble with many people is that they take things too seriously.

_____ 10. Feeling attracted to the mystery of life.[1]

Interpretation   1. Which of these behaviors and attitudes did you previously think of as reflective of creative ability? Which surprised you? Was there any pattern to the items that surprised you? What might that be?

2. Are any of the items you checked behaviors or attitudes you think of as undesirable? If so, think about why you see them as undesirable. How might you redefine these behaviors or attitudes so that you could channel some of your untapped creative energies into productive use?

3. Overall, how creative do you think you are?

[1] Reprinted by permission of the Putnam Publishing Group from *How Creative Are You?* by Eugene Raudsepp. Copyright © 1981 by Eugene Raudsepp.

LEARNING

When we think about who is creative, our popular notions of creativity tend toward individuals who we regard as singularly unique, gifted, talented, and just different from the rest of us. In the arts and sciences we think of people like Bach, Handel, Einstein, and Rembrandt. In business we think of people like Steve Jobs (co-founder of Apple Computers), Jack Welch (General Electric), and Donald Peterson (Ford Motors). People rarely think of creative ability existing in the general population. More importantly, we are rarely encouraged to think or learn about being creative. It is not surprising, then, that many people underestimate their creative abilities.

In fact, a very wide range of behaviors and personality traits have been found to be associated with creative ability. More important, creative thinking is a skill that each person can develop.

Creativity is a way of thinking that involves the generation of new ideas and solutions. More specifically, it is the process of associating known things or ideas into new combinations and relationships. Illustrations of this definition of creativity are found in many diverse areas, from science to humor.

Louis Pasteur's discovery of vaccines against disease provides a good example of creative thinking. The idea of vaccination had been widespread since the mid-1700s, but it had been only associated with cow-pox and small-pox disease. It was not until 1879 that Pasteur discovered the prevention of infectious diseases by inoculation, quite by accident. Previously no one had applied the idea of vaccination to other diseases because it involved two different frames of reference: vaccination and the concept of disease being caused by microorganisms. Pasteur had knowledge of both; Pasteur brought the two together.

In much the same way, researchers at 3M who know about adhesive and that people often use small pieces of paper for notes, brought the two ideas together to create Post-it note pads.

These two examples illustrate how creative thinking often involves utilizing information that is already known, and discovering new associations, rather than, as many people think, generating new ideas out of nothing. In Pasteur's words, "Fortune favors the prepared mind."

How can we increase our ability to engage in creative thinking? First, we need to recognize that all of us have assumptions and thought patterns that we use, but do not question. As we learn to think more creatively, we break away from these thought patterns. In a classic and telling statement, Koestler (1964, p. 96) referred to creativity as "an act of liberation: the defeat of habit by originality." Many creative thinking skill exercises are designed to assist us in developing different ways to look at things, and specifically, to look beyond our assumptions.

Second, we need to recognize that the information used in generating new relationships among things and ideas is already in the mind. Creative thinking is the act of combining those pieces of information in new and unique ways.

Thus, although there is a great deal of evidence that <u>creative thinking is not linked to intelligence, creative ability in certain areas is often linked to knowledge and expertise in those areas.</u> For example, one could say that any biologist could have invented penicillin, but not any person.

How does creative thinking differ from critical thinking? Because critical thinking is discussed in Chapter 5, it would be useful to compare them briefly now. Generally, <u>critical thinking is analytical, logical, and results in few answers</u>; <u>creative thinking is imaginative, provocative, and generates a wide variety of ideas.</u> Critical thinking is often described as vertical, logically moving up until you arrive at a correct answer. In contrast, creative thinking is described as lateral, spreading out to find many possible solutions (de Bono 1970). Figure 8.2 summarizes these differences.

For example, suppose that you, as a marketing specialist, have been assigned to join a special citizen's task force in your community. The task force is considering the problem of how to persuade families and tourists to take their vacations in your home state this year. Notice that there is not merely one answer to this; there are perhaps hundreds or thousands of ways to persuade people to take their vacations in your state. Notice, too, the need for imagination, and the prospect of generating many ideas.

By contrast, consider any mathematical problem whose solution has a single answer. Such a problem involves critical thinking; information is analyzed to determine the one best or correct solution. If your task force has generated a large number of suggestions, it will need to use critical thinking in order to decide which ones would be best to implement. Further, critical thinking skills will be necessary in order to arrive at a viable plan of action.

The two modes of thinking are complementary; the findings of the creative thinking process can be analyzed for usefulness by critical thinking. Although our Western culture has traditionally emphasized critical thinking skills, the value of creative thinking has become increasingly recognized, within organizations and in society as a whole. Moreover, there is a growing assumption that both creative and critical thinking skills will be needed to meet the challenges of the twenty-first century.

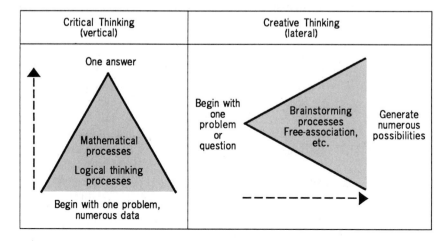

FIGURE 8.2 *Critical and creative thinking.*

DEVELOPING CREATIVE THINKING SKILLS IN YOURSELF AND OTHERS

People often underestimate their own creative ability. Research indicates, however, that there is one major difference between people who exhibit creative tendencies and people who don't: <u>personal belief in creativity.</u> That is, those who engage in creative thinking tend to regard themselves as creative; the others see themselves as noncreative.

Since many people simply do not see themselves as creative, the manager has an opportunity to affirm employees as individuals by recognizing their creative potential and encouraging the use of creative thinking. In this way subordinates are strengthened both on the job and as individuals. By empowering employees to think creatively, managers increase the probability that new and better ways will be found to do things.

To focus on developing creative thinking skills, both in yourself and in others, consider the three dimensions of creativity: domain-relevant skills, creative-relevant skills, and task motivation (George T. Geis in Kuhn 1987).

DOMAIN-RELEVANT SKILLS

<u>Domain-relevant skills are associated with the basic and expert knowledge that is essential to creative thinking.</u> Increasing your domain-relevant skills primarily involves increasing your knowledge base. Not anyone could have discovered penicillin, but perhaps any biologist with the requisite expert knowledge could have. Remember that creative thinking is largely knowledge-based, using information already in the human mind.

Within organizations, some knowledge differs from area to area. For example, knowledge required for financial planning differs from that required for personnel management. Alternatively, knowledge of organization and management skills are relevant across various areas of an organization. In reading this textbook, you are increasing your domain-relevant skills for creativity in the managerial role. You can also increase your domain-relevant skills by learning how other organizations in the United States, in other Western cultures, and in non-Western cultures structure their work environments. For example, Japanese management differs in how manager-employee relationships are regarded, in the role of management in organizations, and in the role of organizations in society. Although the extent to which it is either possible or desirable to implement concepts of Japanese management in the United States will vary across organizations, exposure to these ideas may help you to think creatively about your own work environment and relationships with employees.

CREATIVE-RELEVANT SKILLS

Creative-relevant skills are those that enable individuals to associate previously unrelated concepts and to think differently. A vast array of techniques, often called "creativity heuristics," ranging from using analogies to mental imagery are available to enhance your creative-relevant skills. These techniques are individual strategies that will help you as an innovator to develop your personal creative thinking skills.

One key to enhancing your creative-relevant skills is the ability to break away from commonly held assumptions regarding the relationships between ideas and things, so that you are able to consider new relationships. It is especially important to recognize cultural barriers to creativity, those commonly held assumptions that are a part of our societal or organizational culture. For example, Western culture traditionally has embraced reason and logic to the exclusion of feeling and intuition. This emphasis on reason and logic has created several barriers to creative thinking, including:

1. A negative value on fantasy and reflection as a waste of time, a sign of laziness, or even a bit crazy.

2. The belief that only children should play and that adults should be serious.

3. The assumption that problem solving is serious and, therefore, humor is out of place.

4. A negative value on feeling and intuition, which are regarded as illogical and impractical.

Although we cannot change these societal-based cultural barriers, we can guard ourselves against their influence. If we are able to diminish our cultural barriers to creative thinking, we enhance our abilities to think differently and develop skills for creativity.

In addition to the barriers presented by our societal-based cultural assumptions, individuals often make assumptions that hinder their attempts to become more creative. Like cultural barriers, individual barriers can be overcome if we consciously seek change.

<u>Individual barriers frequently have an emotional basis</u>. These barriers result from personal beliefs and fears associated with taking risks, trying out a new idea, or trying to convince others of the value of our new ideas. Ten of the most common individual barriers to creative thinking are:

1. *Resistance to change.*   It is natural to become secure in the way things are and to resist change.

2. *Fear of making a mistake and the fear of failure.*   To counter this fear, the Limited clothing stores encourage mistakes by evaluating buyers on their failures as well as on their successes. They believe that if employees do not make mistakes, then they may not be taking initiatives and trying new ideas. Somerset Maugham once said, "You'll win some. You'll lose some. . . . Only mediocre people are always at their best" (Quoted in Miller 1987, 17).

3. *Inability to tolerate ambiguity.*   Our need for predictability nurtures our inability to tolerate ambiguity. We like to know the way things are, and to be able to categorize things, events, and people in our lives. Creativity requires flexibility in our thinking; inability to tolerate ambiguity is an inability to tolerate flexibility.

4. *The tendency to judge rather than to generate ideas.*   This is an expression of the culturally based preference of critical thinking over creative thinking. Many of us are trained to be critical in our thinking, and judgmental in our approach. To some extent, we may feel better about ourselves if we are able to critique another's work or action.

5. *Inability to relax or to permit any new idea to incubate.*   Many of us find a perverse comfort in having too much to do, and as a result, find relaxation uncomfortable and difficult. Some people report that they do not know how to relax. Others relax by engaging intensely in another demanding project. Research has shown, however, that freeing our conscious minds, through relaxation or repetitive activity (e.g., cutting the grass or cleaning the house) increases our ability to seek associations amidst old ideas.

6. *The tendency towards excessive self-criticism.*   Many of us are taught to be excessively self-critical. In this respect, some people are kinder to people they actively dislike than they are to themselves. Efforts to eradicate this self-defeating tendency can increase your creative abilities.

7. *Fear of looking foolish.*   This is the biggest barrier of all and the hardest to remove. No one likes to appear foolish to others. We find, however, that often we think we appear foolish when we actually do not. The development of a "so what?" attitude can be helpful in these instances. (Rawlinson 1981, 21).

8. *Conformity, or wanting to give the expected answer.*   This is very apparent in groups and organizations. Individuals may not want to rock the boat or present an unpopular argument (see the discussion of groupthink in the section on participative decision making in the Chapter 7). Managers should actively encourage employees to present different ideas or perspectives (Rawlinson 1981, 16).

9. *Stereotyping, or limiting the possibilities of objects and ideas to their "known" use.*   The inability to see a problem from various viewpoints is a function of mental stereotyping (for example, a chair is for sitting).

10. *Lack of information, or too much incorrect or irrelevant information.*   Lack of information may limit the creative handling of data.

Are you afflicted by any of these barriers? The extent to which you are is an indicator of how much your creative ability is hampered. Equally important for managers is that the encouragement of these barriers in employees will hinder employee creativity as well.

TASK MOTIVATION

Task motivation refers to the existence of a nurturing organizational environment for employee creativity. All individuals have the potential to be creative. The

TABLE 8.2 Task Motivation Checklist for Managers

1. Do not overdirect, overobserve, or overreport.
2. Recognize differences in individuals. Have a keen appreciation of each person's unique characteristics.
3. Help subordinates see problems as challenges.
4. Assess your employees regarding ways they think they are most creative or would like to be most creative, and what sort of creative contribution they would most like to make.
5. Allow more freedom for individuals to guide their own work.
6. Train yourself and others to respond to the positive parts of proposed ideas rather than react to the often easier-to-spot negative ones.
7. Develop greater frustration tolerance for mistakes and errors.
8. Provide a safe atmosphere for failures.
9. Be a resource person rather than a controller; a facilitator rather than a boss.
10. Act as a buffer between employees and outside problems or higher-up demands.
11. Enhance your own creative ability through special workshops and seminars, specialized reading, and practice of creative exercises and games. This sets an excellent example employees will want to emulate, and makes it easier for you to recognize and relate to the creative ability of others.
12. Make sure that innovative ideas are transmitted to your boss with your support and backing; then insist on a feedback mechanism. Without feedback, the flow of creative ideas dries up because innovators feel that their ideas are not given a fair hearing or taken seriously.

Adapted from Eugene Raudsepp, President, Princeton Creative Research, Inc. in R. L. Kuhn, *Handbook for Creative Managers* (New York: McGraw-Hill, 1987), pp. 173–182. Used with permission.

issues are: (1) will they and (2) what can managers/innovators do to increase the opportunities for their employees to use their creative thinking abilities.

The task of providing an environment which is conducive to creativity has many challenges. The individual and cultural barriers often decrease our abilities to create such environments. Managers must be aware of these barriers as they strive to enhance creativity in the workplace.

There are two types of organizational barriers which managers must overcome to increase employees' opportunities and abilities to use creative thinking. The first is inherent in the definition and structure of organizations; the second is associated with managerial style and attitudes and affords more of a chance to make changes.

Hierarchical, highly structured organizations inevitably create barriers to creative thinking. Set procedures, rules and regulations, specialization of work, criteria for employment evaluation, formal channels of communication, and the preference for status quo over change are inherent characteristics of large organizations. Since these organizational characteristics are unlikely to change, it is helpful for managers to recognize these barriers for what they are, and to anticipate that resistance to creative endeavors may take root in these barriers.

Other barriers, however, are within the manager's realm of influence. These barriers are attributable to managerial style, which is itself often fostered by the hierarchical, highly structured organization. As discussed in the previous section, the manager-as-conductor style (Bradford and Cohen 1984) is one that regards the manager as "boss." Inherent in this style are several characteristics that create obstacles to creativity in employees including authoritarianism (an inflexible, closed attitude) and "functional fixedness" (the attitude that there's only one way to do things). Alternatively, the manager-as-developer style empowers employees and helps them to do their jobs better. This style is conducive to innovation and creativity.

Table 8.2 is a checklist that may help you to assist your employees to become more creative. Review this checklist monthly, and assess yourself on each item. Ask yourself: (1) To what extent is change needed to help my unit be more creative? (2) To what extent is this within my control?

BRAINSTORMING AND THE NOMINAL GROUP TECHNIQUE

One of the most effective strategies for finding and encouraging employee creativity is **brainstorming.** Marshaling the skills, thinking, and knowledge of employees, brainstorming is a technique used for generating new ideas. In brainstorming sessions, group members are encouraged to contribute ideas, without regard for quality. Evaluation of ideas is withheld until all have been expressed. Nominal group technique (Delbecq, Van de Ven, and Gustafson 1975) is a process that uses brainstorming to generate new ideas and then uses group discussion and systematic voting to choose from among the ideas generated by the group. It is often used when the problem has a large number of potential alternative solutions.

Assume that 10 professional employees who depend very heavily on secretarial and clerical support report to you. Two secretaries have just left for higher paying jobs and one clerk will be out for several weeks for surgery. As time progresses, it is apparent that conflicts are about to develop over the need for support staff time. You have several options: You may devise a plan and issue memoranda to your employees regulating the use of the available secretarial and clerical resources (and hope they are pleased enough with your solution to happily go about their work in order to finish before the deadline); you may go to your boss for direction (risking, perhaps, the judgment that you cannot handle this yourself); or you can plan a nominal group technique session during which you will get ideas from your employees and, with them, arrive at a workable solution.

Before you hold a brainstorming session, you must first settle in your own mind that you genuinely want the ideas from your employees. Brainstorming sessions can be inadvertently sabotaged by well-meaning managers who have hidden agendas and use the session as a way to manipulate employees to accept an already formulated plan. Secondly, you must resolve that all ideas should be heard; you must provide a safe environment for the free flow of ideas from employees. You have to be able to accept good ideas from employees, and not feel that you have to be the one to generate all of the good ideas at work.

The following steps should be used for planning a nominal group technique session.

1. *Make sure that everyone agrees on the problem defintion.*   If there is not agreement on the problem definition, you may find that different members of the group are solving different problems.

2. *Have participants write down all their ideas.*   Even ideas that do not seem feasible may give other people ideas. During this time no one should talk, except to ask questions about the problem definition. This step may take anywhere from 10 minutes to one-half hour.

3. *Use a round-robin procedure to allow participants to share their ideas.*   Have each participant give one idea at a time. Record the ideas on a flip chart so that all ideas are visible to all participants. Again, do not allow discussion as the ideas are being recorded.

4. *After all ideas are recorded, review each idea one at a time.*   Allow participants to ask questions and share reactions regarding the feasibility and merits of the idea. Use your meeting management skills (discussed in Chapter 7, Competency 2) to ensure that you stay on track and that people are contributing appropriately.

5. *Have participants vote on their preferred alternative solution.*   Generally, the voting should be secret, and a rank vote should be used. That is, have participants individually identify their top five ideas, and then assign a score of five to their first-ranked idea, four to their second ranked idea, and so forth.

6. *Review the voting patterns.*   If one alternative stands out as the obvious preferred choice, then you are ready to decide how to implement that choice. If not, choose the top 5 to 10 alternatives and return to step 4, this time rank ordering only the top three choices.

THE IMPORTANCE OF CREATIVE THINKING IN ORGANIZATIONS

The use of creative thinking in problem solving allows organizations to access human resources that often go untapped. In comparing Japanese and American organizations, Deming (1986) has argued that "the greatest waste in America is failure to use the abilities of people." Managers should recognize that employees' abilities are a free resource. Although most resources have extra cost factors involved, creative thinking does not. From this perspective, one could argue that no organization—public or private—can afford to waste this resource.

Beyond the overall organizational benefits, managers should recognize the personal benefits of encouraging creative thinking among their employees. Creative thinking can increase the effectiveness of the unit through better problem solving. In addition creative thinking can be used as a motivational tool. In the work environment of large organizations, it is sometimes easy for employees to see themselves as a replaceable cog in the giant wheel and to become demotivated. When individuals are encouraged to be creative in their thinking and problem solving, they are more likely to feel unique, valued, and affirmed as important employees of the organization. Thus, not only are there benefits from the employees' good ideas, but individuals feel better about themselves as employees. In sum, the encouragement of employees' creative thinking can result in substantial benefits to the organization, to the work unit and to the individuals who exercise their creative skills.

ANALYSIS   Creativity and Managerial Style

Directions   Creative problem solving skills are not always tied only to your own thought processes. Often creativity involves knowing how to work with other people who are creative, and using techniques that will maximize the probability that those people will generate creative solutions.

As a manager, you can either encourage or discourage employee creativity. To examine your own managerial style, first reflect on the managers with whom you have worked. If you have not yet been employed, use this exercise to reflect on the skills of a parent, teacher, or anyone else who has evaluated your work. Choose one person for this exercise and analyze whether that person's style helped or hindered the tapping of your creativity. Check any of the following which applied to your situation:

_____ 1. Were you instructed to do things according to a set pattern?

___✓___ 2. Did this person seek your opinion regarding matters that affected you?

___✓___ 3. Did this person ever reconsider a decision in light of your input?

_____ 4. Did you have a tendency to fear that you may appear foolish to this person?

___✓___ 5. Did this person value your ideas and your thinking?

_____ 6. Did you ever feel that there was a better way to do something, but did not bring it to the attention of this person?

_____ 7. Did you feel that it was important for this person to like you?

_____ 8. Did you feel that this person would like you more if you tended to agree with him or her?

_____ 9. Did you feel as if this person was always evaluating you?

Discussion Questions   1. How did you feel about yourself in that situation?

2. From your responses, identify specific behaviors that helped you feel affirmed as a valued person, and those that did not.

3. How would you answer question 2 focusing on two other persons: one with whom you had a very positive experience, and one with whom you had a negative experience?

4. From your responses to the preceding items, which areas do you need to give special attention as you develop in your role as a manager?
5. What specific strategies would you use in order to encourage more creativity in a work unit?

PRACTICE   Creative-Relevant Skills

Breaking Established Thinking Barriers

1. *The Paper Clip.*   To assist in thinking differently about objects and concepts, list on a separate piece of paper as many uses as you can think of for a paper clip.
2. *The Restaurant.*   A new restaurant is opening adjacent to your campus. It will feature vegetarian food. Think of as many possible names for this restaurant as you can.

Developing Mental Imagery

One of the skills in developing one's creativity is to practice mental imagery. The following exercises are designed to assist you in improving your imagination. Translate each of the follow descriptions into a mental image. As you do, rate its clarity according to the following scale:

Scale   C = Clear   V = Vague   N = No image at all

Can you visually imagine:

__C__ 1. A familiar face.
__C__ 2. A rosebud.
__C__ 3. A body of water at sunset.
__C__ 4. The characteristic walk of a friend.
__C__ 5. A newspaper headline.

The following descriptions are intended to evoke other modes of sensory imagery. Can you imagine:

__C__ 1. A bird twittering.
__C__ 2. Children laughing at play.
__C__ 3. The prick of a pin.
__C__ 4. The taste of toothpaste.
__C__ 5. An itch.

Don't be discouraged if you were not able to create clear images. This was a skill developing exercise designed to fine-tune your mental imagery processes. Test yourself again in several months and note the improvement.[2]

Using Analogies

Identify three pressing problems which you currently have at school or work. Describe each one briefly in writing. Then review the following list of analogies. Try to apply an analogy from this list, or from your own thinking, to each problem.

1. A snowball rolling downhill, gathering speed, and growing rapidly.
2. Finding your way in the fog.
3. Trying to start a car on a cold winter morning.
4. Having a bath.
5. Frying potatoes.
6. Sending a letter.
7. Trying to untangle a ball of string.
8. Cutting the grass with a pair of scissors.
9. A child playing with a new toy.
10. A fish out of water.

Identify the feelings you have associated with each problem, and describe them with an analogy. The use of analogies should help you to see the problems differently. Describe the different perspectives which you now have on each problem. Use the perspectives to generate possible solutions to the problems.

APPLICATION   New Approaches to the Same Old Problem

Write a three- to five-page paper describing your plans to approach an old problem in a new way.

1. Start by writing a description of the problem. *Cat sleeps on bed*
2. Restate the problem in several ways. *Cat invades bedroom   Cat views bed*
   lives in bedroom   as pers. prop.
3. Write down as many facts related to the problem as possible. *The ultimate*
   Spend 23 hrs/day   *resting place*
   on bed
4. Identify advantages to this problem.
   Cat growing
   on bed
5. Identify as many new ways as possible to approach this problem.
6. Identify people who might be able to help you with this problem.
7. Determine which action you will take first in arriving at a solution to this

---

[2]*Adapted from* Robert H. McKim, *Experiences in Visual Thinking*, 2nd ed. Copyright 1980, PWS-Kent Publishing Company, a division of Wadsworth. Used with permission.

problem, and write down on your calendar the date and time that you will take that action.

8. Identify a strategy to help you increase your use of creative thinking skills whenever you face a problem that you always approach in the same way.

Competency 3 Managing Change

ASSESSMENT Changes in My Organization

Directions Think about two changes that have taken place in an organization with which you have been involved. The organization may be a work organization, a school-related organization, or a community group. On a separate piece of paper, carefully describe the following:

1. An implemented change which in your view was needed, implemented, and was successful long after implementation.

2. An unsuccessfully implemented change.

3. From what you have observed, why was the first change implemented successfully and not the second one? If you can distinguish the content of the idea from the methods for implementation, identify the extent to which the success (or lack of success) of the proposed changes was due to content versus the implementation strategies.

4. Write down *one* change that you would like to make in that organization. If you received approval to make that change, what is the most important thing you would do in your efforts to implement that change? Why?

LEARNING Managing Change

Our society is currently experiencing change at an exponential rate. Each day, the potential exists for advancements in technology and knowledge that could change the way we live. In addition, national and global social, political, and economic changes affect both our personal and organizational lives.

Changes are necessary in order to accomplish goals and objectives, such as improving efficiency, improving cost effectiveness, competing for money and resources, advancing technologically, meeting government regulations, enhancing services to clients, and addressing public pressure. Although we make these changes to respond to societal changes, these are not necessarily unplanned or imposed changes. Rather, these are changes and adjustments we choose to make in order to more effectively fulfill the mission of the organization in a nonstatic world.

Effectively planning for and managing organizational changes, however, can be a challenge for managers, as well as for others who are affected. In the 1980s, an ever-present change was the constant enhancement of computers and computing technology. Change happened, and continues to happen, so rapidly in this area that a person knowledgeable about the state of the art at one time could easily become out of touch with the state of the art in less than a year. Yet, as managers, it is necessary to have some familiarity with this changing technology and to consider the opportunities for enhancing your work unit's functioning using new computer technologies.

UNDERSTANDING RESISTANCE TO PLANNED CHANGE

Even changes that are necessary and even desirable are resisted. Like resistance to unplanned change, resistance to planned change often arises in response to the very fact of change, and not necessarily to the specific content of the change. For example, if everyone in your work unit enthusiastically agrees that there needs to be more communication with other work units, and you introduce a change that would increase this communication, you might still expect to encounter some resistance to that change simply because it involves changing the status quo.

In addition to resistance from people, you are also likely to meet resistance from the organization. Just as hierarchical organizations present barriers to creative thinking and innovation, they also offer many of the same characteristics as barriers to change. Organizational barriers include the power of existing organizational routines and organizational structure, resource limitations, an organizational cultural value that tradition is preferable to change, and so on.

<u>Five types of organizationally related change are likely to provoke employee resistance.</u> These changes cause resistance because employees perceive them as negatively affecting their expected job behaviors. As in the case of planned change, understanding these sources of resistance to change will better equip you to make appropriate changes and to implement them in such a way as to ensure their success.

1. *Changes that affect knowledge and skill requirements.*   Employees will resist changes (such as automation) that make their skills seem outdated or unnecessary.

2. *Changes associated with economic or status loss.*   Employees will resist changes that result in a demotion or loss of employment. The resisting employee does not have to be the person directly affected by the job changes. Resistance may also come from employees who perceive that the change may somehow ultimately affect them negatively. For example, when Kodak's CEO, Colby Chandler, cut 11,000 jobs in his first year, many of the remaining employees were demoralized, fearing that they would be the next to be fired.

3. *Changes suggested by others.*   Sometimes good ideas are resisted because they are not our ideas. (See Chapter 5 for a discussion of the "Not-Invented-Here" syndrome.) When one employee is jealous of the success of a fellow employee or perceives that one employee's success diminishes the esteem the manager has for the other employees, or when there is intense competition within a work unit, employees are unlikely to accept others' ideas.

4. *Changes involving risks.*   Risk taking sometimes results in mistakes. When an organization's culture does not value risk taking, individuals will not want to take the chance of making a mistake, and will probably be reluctant to suggest or embrace changes that involve risks.

5. *Changes that involve disruption of social relationships.*   Although organizations have public missions and purposes, they also provide a social environment in which people associate and form friendships. For many people, their work organization is a primary source of social interaction. When these patterns of interaction are disrupted, people often resist.

Resistance to change reminds us that change must be carefully planned. Resistance often forces us to consider carefully the impact of the change so that ill-advised changes may be avoided.

DESIGNING CHANGE AND DESIGNING HOW TO CHANGE

Once the decision has been made that a change in the work processes, procedures, or structure should occur, the manager must focus on two issues: (1) the design of the change, and determining what change needs to occur, and (2) the process of implementing the change.

DESIGNING CHANGE

Designing change involves considering various alternative courses of action, anticipating consequences of such actions, and choosing what specific course of action is appropriate.

The design of the change is the first issue that faces the manager. The manager must ask whether a change is necessary, and if so, what specifically should be changed. Kurt Lewin proposed a model called **force field analysis.** This model is based on laws of physics: An object at rest will remain at rest unless the forces on the object to move are greater than the forces for it to remain stable. For example, when your car is parked in the driveway with the emergency brake engaged, it will remain there, in a stable condition, even if your neighbor's nine-year-old son decides to push on the car to move it. The emergency brake is a stronger stabilizing force than is the boy's force. If the car is put into the neutral gear with the emergency brake disengaged, however, the forces for its stability are diminished, and it becomes more possible that the young boy could disrupt the equilibrium.

Similarly, there are forces within organizations that are pressures for change and forces that are resistances to change. When the forces for change are stronger than the resistant forces, change will occur; likewise, when the forces against change are stronger than the pressures for change, change will not occur.

Let's set up a force field analysis list to examine some of the pressures for organizational change, known as **driving forces,** and the pressures against organizational change, known as **resisting forces.**

Force Field Analysis of Change in Organizations

Pressures for Change *(Driving Forces)*	*Pressures Against Change* *(Resisting Forces)*
Social change in society	Perceived threats to power
Economic change in society	Routine and structure
Improved efficiency	Resource limitations
Improved cost effectiveness	Preference for tradition
Competition for money and resources	Changes in skill requirements
Technological advances	Economic or status loss
Compliance with government regulations	Nonsupport of others' ideas
Public pressure	Reluctance to take risks
Expansion	Disruption of social relationships
Improved effectiveness	
Administrative changes	
Availability of new products	

It is necessary to consider more than the length of the list; you must also look at the importance or relative force of the individual items. Some items may have more impact on a situation than others. To make the list more useful, you would need to assign weights or values to each item.

The following steps are necessary to set up a force field analysis:

1. List the driving forces and the resisting forces.
2. Examine each force and assess its strengths. Note the possible consequences of each force and its value. You may wish to assign a numerical value to each force.
3. Identify those forces over which you have some influence or control.
4. Analyze the list to determine how to implement the change. Your analysis will reveal several natural choices for action:
   - Increase the strength of driving forces.
   - Add new driving forces.
   - Decrease the strength of resisting forces.
   - Remove some of the resisting forces.
   - Determine whether any of the resisting forces can be changed into driving forces.

Research has shown that the last three strategies, which involve <u>diminishing the effect of resisting forces</u>, are more effective than the first two strategies. Increasing the effect of the driving forces often serves only to increase the resistance.

Once you have worked through this process, you have a chart of the driving and resisting forces to the proposed change, the relative weight of each force, and an assessment of which forces you can influence. Identifying the items over which you have some influence should tell you know where to direct your efforts and planning when implementing your changes.

IMPLEMENTING CHANGE

Implementing the change—designing how the change should occur—is just as critical for innovators as the process of designing what change should occur. Although a proposed change might objectively be the very best thing for the organization or for the work unit, careless implementation could potentially make the proposed change look foolish, resulting in the ultimate failure of the idea.

Unfortunately, the process of designing how to change is often given less attention than is necessary. First, we assume that once we have determined that a proposed change is necessary, appropriate, and beneficial, we are inclined to see its value as so obvious that we expect others to endorse it and work for it with vigor and enthusiasm! Since we have worked so hard at the analysis, we often assume that the hard part is over. A poorly implemented change, however, will reflect on the credibility of the proposed change, and careless attention to implementation of even the best idea will, more often than not, result in failure. Assuming that a given change is seen as desirable and beneficial to the organization, implementing the change will require the same thoughtful effort and consideration as the design of the change.

THREE APPROACHES TO MANAGING CHANGE

In attempting to manage change within organizations, as well as in their personal lives, individuals tend to use one of three general approaches: rational-empirical approaches, normative-reeducative approaches, and power-coercive approaches (Chin and Benne 1976).

RATIONAL EMPIRICAL APPROACHES

Rational-empirical strategies for change are based on two assumptions: (1) people are rational, and (2) once a proposal has been clearly explained, individuals see that it is in their best interest and subscribe to the change. This approach encourages the acquisition of knowledge and data to better understand the substantive aspects of change.

An important strength of this strategy is that it requires you to examine the pros and cons of a situation carefully and to present the logic of the decision. Generally, people respond more positively to change when the process and details are explained to them.

A major weakness of this strategy, however, stems from a flaw in the logic of the basic assumptions. It is incorrect to assume that if we explain to people the logic and benefits of a change, they will embrace it. Even when individuals understand that a change is in their best interest, we cannot assume that they will comply. How many times have we known, for example, that it is in our best interest to lose weight, to exercise, or to stop smoking? Quick reflection reveals that it is a rare individual who complies with a needed change simply because of the realization that it is needed.

Further, no matter how well we think we have explained something to an individual, we cannot assume that the individual understands it in the way we intend. If we want people to comply with a change, we need to also consider their perceptions of what we have said to them.

NORMATIVE-REEDUCATIVE APPROACHES

Normative-reeducative approaches to change consider the values, attitudes, meanings, and habits of individuals in the change process. This approach assumes that individuals are affected emotionally and personally by their work experiences. Normative-reeducative strategies for change also recognize the impact of the organizational culture as forces for or against change.

A strength of this approach is its usefulness in both the design and implementation of change. The normative-reeducative approach requires us to focus on the change in terms of how people will react, what the change means to them, and whether their needs are adequately met by the change. Normative-reeducative strategies tend to be most effective in overcoming individual resistances to change.

The major weakness with this approach is that it is slow; its effects are often detected only after considerable time has passed. One reason for this slowness is that sometimes people do not want to change. Furthermore, organizations often want change to occur faster than it does. Managers must exercise considerable patience and farsightedness in order to plan change utilizing normative-reeducative strategies.

However, the normative-reeducative approach is the most respectful of the individuals involved in the change process, and as such it is highly successful in the long term.

POWER-COERCIVE APPROACHES

Power-coercive approaches to change are based on the assumption that the individual desiring the change has more power than the individual who is expected to comply with the change. The latter individual will change because of fear of punishment or the withholding of some valued reward. In organizations, we tend to think of those higher up in the hierarchy as having the power to create a negative situation, (e.g., by giving poor performance evaluations or demotions, or by making the work environment more difficult). Employees, however, can use power-coercive strategies as well. For example, employees may slow down their work efforts in order to get managers to comply with their wishes.

Strategies associated with the power-coercive approach focus on two types of power. First is power which accompanies the hierarchical position of the individual, along with the implicit threat of economic sanctions against individuals who do not comply. Second is the use of moral power, where guilt and shame are used in order to initiate compliance to change.

A strength of this approach for organizational change is its recognition of the importance of legitimacy of the upper administrative levels. Sometimes, when individuals are resistant, rules are required to implement mandated changes. For example, laws against sexual harassment may be required to change the behaviors of individuals who do not see such behavior as negative.

The major weakness of this approach is that the use of threats, guilt, and shame are not, in the long term, effective strategies of change. These are manipulative techniques which often work only in the short run. In the long run, they build resentment. Further, this strategy may provoke the sabotage of future proposed changes.

EFFECTIVE MANAGEMENT OF CHANGE

The three approaches to managing change in organizations provide helpful strategies for the design and implementation of proposed changes. With the recognition of the strengths and limitations of each strategy, managers can be more cognizant of the potential consequences of their efforts at change. Table 8.3 presents guidelines for effective management of change. Note that these steps incorporate elements from the empirical-rational approach, as well as from the normative-reeducative approach.

TABLE 8.3 Guidelines for Effective Management of Change

1. During the planning of the change, encourage participation of those affected by it. Encourage use of creative thinking by employees in problem solving.
2. Let employees experience the need for change.
3. Maintain open and frequent communication with employees.
4. Avoid a "we-they" mentality.
5. Consider needs of individual employees.

4/20

ANALYSIS   Reorganizing the Legal Division

Directions   Read the following case study and answer the questions that follow each section.

The Relocation and Reorganization Begins.   As part of a new relocation and reorganization plan for the legal division of a large corporation, the director, Paul Lindford, decided to set up a central paralegal pool. This pool would handle all of the research reports for the entire office, which consisted of 20 attorneys. In the old location, the paralegals had been located in offices adjoining those occupied by the attorneys for whom they worked. Several paralegals even had their own small private offices.

The nature of the office was such that many of the attorneys traveled a considerable amount and consequently were away from their offices for extended periods. During these absences the paralegal assistants had little to do.

Stop Reading   Respond to the following questions.

1. Based on the limited information, what advantages of the change approved by Paul Lindford can you identify? more consistent work for the paralegals
2. What might be the response of the paralegal assistants to this change? unhappy
3. What might be the response of the attorneys to this change? pos/neg
4. If you were Paul, what problems would you anticipate at this point?

The Case Continues   For some time, Paul had felt that establishing a central paralegal pool would result in a saving of personnel, as well as more efficient use of the paralegal staff. Paul had been reluctant to make this change in the old location, where the attorneys and paralegal assistants were accustomed to working in adjoining offices. But now, with the new office, he felt the time was right to try out the new arrangement.

Two weeks before the move, Paul asked Ashley Ricci to coordinate the move for the paralegal assistants, even though she was not the most senior paralegal. There were two others at higher ranks, with more experience than Ashley, but Paul felt good about his choice. Ashley had a lot of energy and was well liked by her co-workers. She seemed to best fulfill the requirements for the job as he saw it. She had worked on some special projects for Paul in the past, and she had been exceptional. At this point, Paul had not really given any thought to who would be directing the paralegal assistants when the move was complete.

Stop Reading   Respond to the following questions.

1. Paul has chosen to implement this change when the general office moves into a new location. Why does he see this timing as advantageous? Do you agree?
2. If you were Paul, would you have chosen Ashley to coordinate the move? Why or why not?
3. What mistakes do you believe Paul has made so far in the implementation process?

The Case Continues Paul announced his plans for the new central paralegal pool one week before the move. It was received with little enthusiasm. Several assistants objected and threatened to leave rather than accept the change. Some insisted they could not work for more than one person; others complained they would be unable to work in a small cubicle office in a large room. Many of the attorneys affected by the new policy were resentful as well. They believed that a personal paralegal assistant was essential for efficient conduct of their respective offices.

Although Paul knew this change was unpopular, he believed that feelings of the attorneys would change as the benefits of the more efficient service became apparent. Although many of the attorneys probably felt the loss of a personal paralegal assistant as something in the nature of a "demotion," Paul felt they should understand and help make the new plan work. He felt that the few die-hards should not be pampered.

When the change was made, Ashley did everything she could to maintain the workload at a high level and hoped that, as a result, the complaints from the attorneys would decrease. Their complaints centered around: (1) errors made by paralegal assistants who were unfamiliar with the attorneys' caseloads; (2) the slowness of the paralegal staff in bringing back final drafts of the reports that had been assigned to them; and (3) the excessive time they themselves had to spend in minor research efforts that had previously been handled by their personal paralegal assistant.

Stop Reading Respond to the following questions.

1. What are the specific sources of resistance from the paralegal assistants and the attorneys? Do you see these resisting forces as unreasonable or legitimate?
2. Do you think that Paul is correct in his prediction that the complaints will decrease after the change has been in operation for a while and its benefits are noted? Why or why not?
3. What type of change strategy is Paul using? How well is it working? What should Paul do at this time?

The Case Continues Ashley also listened to complaints from the paralegals. They felt very strongly that: (1) the work they were getting was neither challenging nor generally very interesting; (2) they were not able to consistently work on a particular caseload, and, therefore, the quality of their work was decreasing; and (3) they were tired of taking abuse for the changes they themselves had not instituted.

After the new system had been in operation for six months, Ashley suggested to Paul that perhaps some of these complaints might be eliminated if each attorney were allowed to have priority claim on the time of one paralegal assistant. This arrangement would allow the paralegal to become familiar with the particular work of one attorney, including the issues and current caseload of that attorney. The paralegal could then be asked to work elsewhere when not busy with the work of the attorney. Paul, however, felt that such a move would defeat the very purpose for which the central paralegal pool had been established.

Stop Reading   Respond to the following questions.

1. What are Paul's sources of resistance? Are they legitimate?
2. If you were Paul, what would you do at this point? Why?

The Case Concludes   After much prodding by Ashley, Paul finally agreed that something had to be done to make things run more smoothly. Paul admitted that he shared some of her doubts about the success of the new arrangement and wondered if perhaps the change had not been managed well. More important, he wondered if something could be done to regain the full support and cooperation of the attorneys and paralegals. He even considered returning the office to its old method of operation, allowing each attorney to work solely with one paralegal assistant.

Discussion Questions
1. What do you think Paul may have learned about this experience regarding implementation of change?
2. Do you think the change was well designed? Why or why not?
3. What strategies could Paul have used in the beginning to help him sort out the aspects of the proposed change, and to help him plan?
4. If you were a consultant and Paul commissioned your professional expertise, what advice would you give him about what he should do now and how to do it?

PRACTICE   Force Field Analysis

Directions   Examine the preceding case study, "Reorganizing the Legal Division," and pretend that you are Paul. Do a force field analysis, listing the driving forces and the resisting forces of the case. Weigh the value of each force with a number from 1 (least forceful) to 10 (most forceful). Also, identify your level of influence over those forces using the following scale:

Scale
> IS = able to influence strongly   IM = able to influence moderately
> NI = unable to influence

Discussion Questions
1. What forces for change did you identify? What are the forces against change?
2. Which are the strongest forces over which you have the most control?
3. How could each force be altered?
4. Which actions are most feasible?
5. What should be the plan of action?

Directions   In the assessment activity at the beginning of this third competency, you were asked to write down one change that you would make in an organization in which you had been involved. Do a force field analysis for this situation, listing the driving forces and the resisting forces of the change. Again, weigh the value of each force with a number from 1 to 10 and identify your level of influence over those forces using the scale on page 269. Also answer questions 1 to 5 (see above) for this situation.

In the assessment activity, you were also asked to identify the most important thing you would do in your efforts to implement that change. Do you agree with your earlier thinking? If not, why? Write down any changes to your original assessment and the reasons you have for your views.

APPLICATION   Planning a Change

On a separate sheet of paper, write today's date. Then describe a change which you wish to make—either at work or in your personal life. Determine when you would like to begin implementing the change. The format should be as follows:

Today, write:	Today's date.
	Description of a change you wish to make.
	Implementation target date.
	Design of the change.
	Strategies for implementing the change.
On the implementation target date, write:	Description of your experience to date and an evaluation of your plans.
	Target completion date.
On the target completion date, write:	Description of your experience, evaluating the strategies you used.

Now, answer the following questions.

1. How did you feel once you identified the change and the implementation date? Many people feel vaguely dissatisfied with themselves when they want to change something and often think the dissatisfaction will remain until the change is completed. However, as you probably experienced in this activity, when we take action towards change, the dissatisfaction with ourselves often diminishes, and we are thereby encouraged to continue our plans.

2. What difference do you note in writing down your proposed change, with its accompanying dates, rather than merely having these ideas in your head? Writing down the proposed change is a clarifying effort, and by so doing you tend to increase your belief that it will happen.

REFERENCES

Bradford, David L., and Allan R. Cohen. *Managing for Excellence.* New York: John Wiley and Sons, 1984.

Chin, Robert, and Kenneth D. Benne. "General Strategies for Effecting Changes in Human Systems," in *Organization Development,* Wendell L. French, Cecil H. Bell, Jr., and Robert A. Zawacki (eds.). Plano, Texas: Business Publications, Inc., 1983.

De Bono, Edward. *Lateral Thinking: Creativity Step-by-Step.* New York: Harper & Row, 1970.

Delbecq, Andre L., Andrew H. Van de Ven, and David H. Gustafson. *Group Techniques for Program Planning.* Glenview, Ill.: Scott, Foresman, 1975.

Deming, W. Edward. *Out of the Crisis.* Boston: Massachusetts Institute of Technology Center for Advanced Engineering Study, 1986.

Kiel, John M. *The Creative Mystique: How to Manage It, Nurture It, and Make It Pay.* New York: John Wiley and Sons, 1985.

Kimberly, John R., and Robert E. Quinn. *Managing Organizational Transitions.* Homewood, Ill.: Richard D. Irwin, Inc., 1984.

Koestler, Arthur. *The Act of Creation.* New York: Macmillan, 1964.

Kuhn, Robert Lawrence (ed. in chief). *Handbook for Creative Managers.* New York: McGraw-Hill, 1987.

Lewin, Kurt. *Field Theory in Social Science.* New York: Harper and Row, 1951.

McKim, Robert H. *Experiences in Visual Thinking.* Monterey, Calif.: Brooks/Cole Publishing Co., 1972.

Miller, William C. *The Creative Edge: Fostering Innovation Where You Work.* Reading, Mass.: Addison-Wesley, 1987.

Nierenberg, Gerald I. *The Art of Creative Thinking.* New York: Cornerstone Library, 1982.

Pascale, Richard T., and Anthony G. Athos. *The Art of Japanese Management.* New York: Simon and Schuster, 1981.

Peters, Tom. *Thriving on Chaos.* New York: Harper & Row, 1987.

Rawlinson, J. Geoffrey. *Creative Thinking and Brainstorming.* New York: John Wiley and Sons, 1981.

Whetten, David A., and Kim S. Cameron. *Developing Management Skills.* Glenview, Ill.: Scott, Foresman, 1983.

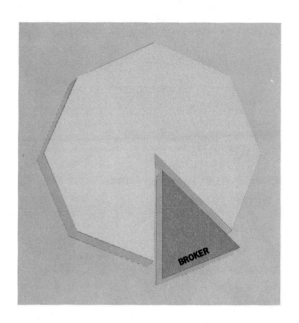

COMPETENCIES

- **Building and Maintaining a Power Base**
- **Negotiating Agreement and Commitment**
- **Presenting Ideas: Effective Oral Presentations**

THE BROKER ROLE

*T*he competing values framework helps us see that leadership at any level is a social activity as well as a technical activity. It is a job that requires the human relations competencies of the coach and mentor, as well as the analytic and take-charge competencies of the monitor and director. This chapter focuses on the broker role. With the innovator, the broker occupies the upper right quadrant of the competing values framework. If the innovator envisions change and a better way of doing things, the broker presents and negotiates those ideas effectively. In organizations, good ideas only work if people can see a benefit to adopting them.

This chapter will focus on the broker role and the core competencies associated with it.

Competency 1   Building and Maintaining a Power Base
Competency 2   Negotiating Agreement and Commitment
Competency 3   Presenting Ideas: Effective Oral Presentations

Competency 1 Building and Maintaining a Power Base

Some sources of power and influence in your personal life, or in an organization with which you are affiliated, may have little direct impact on you. Others affect you a great deal. A good way to start mapping the complex network of power and influence that most affects you is to draw a diagram of the people and positions upon which you depend. On the surface, the network of dependencies may be quite simple, but it will probably become more complex the more you think about it.

Directions   Look at Figure 9.1. The case in point is a hospital manager. You'll notice the degree to which this manager (in the center of the diagram) depends upon other people and positions has been indicated.

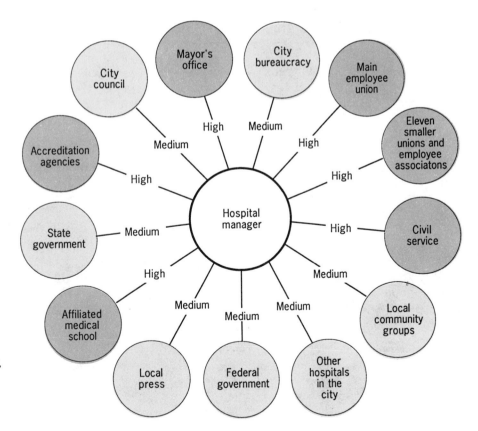

FIGURE 9.1 *A power/ dependency diagram. Reprinted from "Power, Success and Organizational Effectiveness," by John P. Kotter,* Organizational Dynamics (*Winter 1978*), *p. 29. Copyright AMACOM, a division of American Management Association, New York. All rights reserved.*

Now draw a diagram of your organization on a separate sheet of paper. You may choose to analyze your position as a student or a member of your family, or you may choose a position in an organization with which you have experience. When you have your diagram completed, answer the following questions, first to yourself, and then, if time permits, in small groups.

Interpretation

1. Whom do you really depend on in the position you're analyzing? How important is each dependency? What is the basis of each dependency?
2. Are any of these dependencies inappropriate or dysfunctional? What can you do about that?
3. How do you maintain your own base of influence in each of these dependencies? Do you feel you have a base of influence in each of them?
4. What kinds of power and influence do you think you need to develop further? What resources can help you?

LEARNING   Building and Maintaining a Power Base

POWER   Why Are We Ambivalent?

Our perceptions of power are very revealing. They tell us as much about ourselves as they do about power. How do you feel about the role power plays in the organizations you have observed? When you think of power, what people, experiences and memories are called to mind? Refer to Box 9.1 and ask yourself whether you share these misconceptions.

BOX 9.1   MISCONCEPTIONS ABOUT POWER

1. *I am the manager. I can do what I want.* Authority and power are not the same thing. People do not do what you want simply because of the position you hold. It takes more than position to effectively influence people.

2. *Power is something people in higher positions exercise upon people in lower positions.* Managers exercise power and influence on subordinates, but subordinates also exercise power and influence on managers. Power is something that exists when people are dependent on each other. Think of your peers. Do they ever influence your manager? Do some influence your manager more than others? Why is this so?

3. *Supervisors and middle managers are powerless.* This statement is partially true. Some are powerless. However, supervisors and managers are never powerless unless they choose to be. Claims of powerlessness are often forms of flight from responsibility. Because the organization is dependent on supervisors and managers, they do, in fact, have latent power. If you use power effectively, it increases; if you use it ineffectively, it decreases. The more you have to use it, the less you will have.

All of us have power, and all of us are influenced by others who have power. Some of our most painful memories revolve around someone else's misuse of the power and influence they held over us. As children, school may have brought us enough boredom, confusion, and fear to last a lifetime. As teenagers, the authority of our parents may have collided with our need for freedom. To handle power is to make mistakes, often at the expense of others. But to be powerless is to be frustrated and defensive. Thus, most of us have mixed feelings about power. We need it and want it, but we know we can easily abuse it, or create the impression that we are abusing it.

People often say power is a "necessary evil" in organizations. That statement assumes that power, in all its manifestations, is evil in itself. Power in organizational life is inescapable, but is it inherently evil? Organizations exist in order to get things done. Power clusters around the most important things an organization has to do, and around the people who have the greatest access to the resources required to do those things.

POWER AT THE INDIVIDUAL LEVEL

There are two levels from which to study power. First, the macro, or organizational level, and second the individual, or personal level. On the organizational level, power can be viewed as the ability to influence the flow of available energy and resources toward certain goals. This kind of power shows up in activities such as legislating policies and laws, setting rules and procedures, and making goals and plans. On the second, more personal level, power can be seen as person *A*'s capacity to influence person *B*'s behavior so that *B* does something he or she would not do otherwise. This focus on power and influence stresses interpersonal relationships and the resources we bring to bear in those relationships. In this chapter we will deal primarily with power and influence at the individual level, because it's the level we can influence the most.

THE MYTH OF THE SOLITARY ENTREPRENEUR

In U.S. culture we value individualism and self-reliance. But we have become, particularly since the second world war, a society that does most of its work and play through formal organizations. That means we are much more interdependent than ever in our history. It also means that most power and influence must be channeled through intercommecting groups. Lee Iaccoca saved a foundering Chrysler Corporation, but he could not have saved it without the support of the U.S. government, the United Auto Workers, and the patience of Chrysler's suppliers who were owed hundreds of millions of dollars. In fact, the Iaccoca "miracle" is a good example of successful negotiation, diplomacy, and persuasion, rather than the exercise of raw power.

GOOD POWER, BAD POWER, AND NO POWER

Power can be manipulative and coercive. Power can and has corrupted many people who could not resist using it for personal gain at others' expense. People can use the power contained in their professional positions to get personal gain beyond their entitlement; people can use their access to information to extort or blackmail others; they can use their ability to reward or punish others unfairly, to escape blame, or recieve underserved credit. Power, like energy, is neither good nor bad. It is tempting. But the moral or immoral use of power is the product of motives, decisions, and thinking—not the fault of power itself.

Power is necessary in using resources to meet goals and to get things done. Not using power when you need to can be as bad as abusing it. For every person who has dealt in bad faith, broken the law, and played fast and loose with influence, there may be three people who are guilty of not pushing hard enough, not exerting enough influence and gumption to gain the power necessary to accomplish a worthwhile goal.

When we put ourselves on the line, we want strong, solid people in our corner. We don't want to entrust the things we cherish to weak and passive leaders. Managers who have no power base are not doing their jobs. Part of their job is to effectively and appropriately build a base of legitimacy, information, and influence from which to serve the needs of their unit and their organization.

FIVE SOURCES OF POWER

Where does power come from? First, and perhaps most obvious, is position. If you are director of finance for a large firm, you have power by virtue of that position. That position carries a good deal of legitimacy and influence. **Position power** is also known as "legitimate power."[1]

Personal power comes from the shape and impact your presentation of self has on others—the personal characteristics that people find attractive or influential or persuasive. These resources include attributes such as articulateness, physical stature and appearance, dynamism and spontaneity, intelligence, humor, and the ability to empathize with others. Your personal power is also rooted in the overall impressions you generate in other people—impressions of being trustworthy, reasonable, modest, or courageous.

Expert power is based on the expertise that you may have in a special

[1]*Adapted from* "The Bases of Social Power," by F. R. French and B. H. Raven from *Group Dynamics*, 3rd ed., edited by D. Cartwright and A. Zander. Copyright © 1968 by Dorwin Cartwright and Alvin Zander. Reprinted by permission of Harper & Row Publications, Inc.

field or knowledge area. Notice that expert power is not the same as the personal resource of intelligence. It is tied to valuable, specialized skills or abilities. The in-house computer expert has more power when the computer system crashes than when the system is working. When the United States suddenly has vital interests at stake in the Persian Gulf, people who speak the languages of that region have more power and influence than they had before.

Opportunity power is related to expert power, but it deals more with being in the right place at the right time. One of the rules of success is to be lucky, and lucky people are around when opportunities and resources are being handed out. However, not everyone recognizes an opportunity when it surfaces. In written Chinese, the word *crisis* is expressed with two characters, one meaning "opportunity" and the other "danger." Most people don't see opportunities in crises or the potential benefits offered by problems. Often, the differences between a leader and a merely competent administrator is the ability to seize an opportunity.

Information power depends upon access to information and is, of course, tied directly to expert power. But information about a particular event or an individual is also a source of power. The employee who has just become aware of a scandal within a department or a corporation has just picked up a lot of information power and will have to make some moral and professional decisions about how to use it.

INFLUENCE STRATEGIES

In Chapter 1 we talked about the importance of "cognitive complexity," the ability to see things in more than one way or solve a problem in more than one way. Most managers are too limited in their choice of strategies to influence people. The master broker knows that effective leadership requires a broad base of approaches and strategies. Too many leaders are asssertive or insistent when they need to be open and flexible. Others are passive and deferential when they need to be confrontational and firm.

Roger Smith, very late in his tenure as CEO of General Motors, decided he needed to "soften" his personal management style, though he still needed to make some very tough decisions for the good of the company. Smith said in an interview with *Business Week* Magazine:

> *I sat down and figured out that, for the good of the corporation, I was going to have to change the way I did things. I used to just make up my mind to do something and tell somebody that's the way I wanted it done. Now I sit down and we make team decisions . . . . I spend a lot more time working at participative management. But I have to admit we get better decisions out of it* (Business Week *1989, 78*).

But Smith's new, participative style did not mean the decisions reached were easy. General Motors, in the midst of its restructuring and streamlining, laid off over 40,000 employees. Smith says he had to be very tough about the necessity of some trimming in the work force, and the need for all GM employees to be more flexible and productive. Some individuals would win and others would lose, but GM would be around to see the 21st century. In short, Roger Smith had to broaden his base of influence strategies in order to manage better.

Read the following list of influence strategies, and make note of how many you use. Which do you seldom or never use? Which strategies are practical in your work environment? Are there any you would feel uncomfortable using? Why?

Eight Influence Strategies[2]

Influence Strategies	*Outcome*
1. Involve the person in the decision process.	Identifies with and accepts the decision.
2. Control the information. Be the expert.	Needs you for direction.
3. Enginer the situation. Control tasks, schedules, where people work, and so on.	Does what you want without knowing you wanted it.
4. Rely on your position. Make formal requests within your realm of authority.	Complies with your request if it is seen as legitimate.
5. Use rational persuasion. Show people that it is in their best interest.	Complies because the request leads to accomplishment.
6. Offer desired rewards.	Complies to get a particular resource.
7. Generate hope of a better future; show a higher good is being accomplished.	Complies because it is "morally right."
8. Increase your dependence on the other person.	Responds to informal expectations because of growing trust.

INFLUENCE VERSUS MANIPULATION

Of course, the column labeled "outcome" may look simplisitc, or naïve. When you choose to appeal to a higher good, people don't always comply "because it is right." They may think your approach is ridiculous, or they may suspect that you have an ulterior motive. You have to decide what your motives are and have the integrity and authenticity that make your strategies genuine. And, as you have probably learned from your own experience, you'll have to brace yourself to be misunderstood in spite of good intentions. The people who work

[2]*Adapted from* Thomas Bonoma and Gerald Zaltman, *Psychology for Managemetn.* Boston: PWS-Kent Publishing Company, 1981. Used with permission of the authors.

with you daily usually know where your values and interest are, and they watch what you do at least as much as what you say.

These eight strategies listed are not designed to encourage you to manipulate people. They suggest that there are avenues of influence that habits or cultural norms may have kept you from considering. If you consistently appeal, even in subtle ways, to the authority of your position in order to get people's cooperation, you should probably try strategies that will increase your dependence on your subordinates or offer them more personal support by expressing appreciation or taking time to listen carefully to how things are *really* going for them. A common belief in U.S. management philosophy is that learning from subordinates is a sign of weakness. But learning from others is really a sign of being secure and authentic, and so is the habit of listening carefully (Macobby 1988, 118). The master broker knows what other people need and how they feel. Most of that information comes from listening and observing, not from talking.

INCREASING INFLUENCE WITH SUPERIORS, PEERS, AND SUBORDINATES

Here is an additional list of specific modes of influence tailored to the role and level of the person you are trying to influence. These methods of influence must, of course, be adapted to your situation.

SUPERIORS

- Look for ways to solve problems that your superiors are facing.
- Show appreciation to superiors for things they do to help.
- Encourage superiors to discuss their problems. Listen carefully. Give understanding and support.
- Provide constructive feedback on things superiors do.
- Point out new ways superiors can use your skills.
- Be loyal, even when it's difficult (unless some ethical principle or legal issue is at stake).
- Be clear about the balance of exchange between you. If you feel you are being used or exploited in any way, try bargaining and negotiating. If this does not help, look for another manager.

These are powerful and practical modes of influence. However, there are roadblocks to using them. A major roadblock is the norms of the organization (see the discussion of norms in Chapter 5). Norms are unwritten expectations about how work will be done, how people will act, and so on. Your work unit may have a "them and us" norm about relating to superiors. It may not be socially acceptable to show appreciation to your manager, or to be loyal, or to give encouragement to the people you manage. Suggesting new methods or solutions may be taboo. If so, you may want to consider how much these norms are costing you in your professional and personal development. You may not only need a new manager, but you may also need a more positive work climate. Moreover, as a leader in your work unit, you may have to address those norms specifically and try to change them for everyone's benefit. Think about what modes of influence you could use in that effort.

PEERS

- Find ways to help peers reach their goals and look and feel successful.
- Try to understand their problems and share useful information.
- Look for common goals you can mutually pursue.
- Form informal problem-solving groups between units.
- When a peer becomes a problem, get others to exert pressure to get the person back in line.

Influencing peers is a tremendous challenge. Often organizations have norms that prohibit rocking the boat or going beyond the job description. Efforts to become more influential can be mistaken for power plays or a vote of no-confidence toward your colleagues. Building influence with peers takes a long time, and a lot of patience. But people ultimately respond when they see that you are determined to do good work and want to share the credit and stimulation with them. Remember, credit is not a zero-sum commodity. Stephen Covey, a management consultant, encourages people to create a "mentality of abundance," an attitude that there is plenty of credit and opportunity to go around. This attitude is often self-fulfilling. When people are generous and encouraging, opportunities increase in an organization. The paradox of selfishness is that it usually results in a net loss of resources. When people start hoarding and hiding information, recognition, physical resources, and their own energy, the work unit begins to wilt.

SUBORDINATES

- Consciously try to increase their trust in you.
- Give them recognition for good performance.
- Give them credit for their ideas when talking to your superiors.
- Help them solve problems that may be beyond their ability or experience.
- Keep current on new information and trends in your field.
- Provide training. Champion the cause of professional development.
- Never pretend to know something you don't know.
- Hold regular performance appraisals.
- Do not be afraid to talk about the ways you depend upon each other.
- Clarify your responsibilities to them and theirs to you.

ANALYSIS   "I Hope You Can Help Me Out": Don Lowell Case Study

Directions   In your small groups, read the following case study and answer the discussion questions individually. Record your answers on a flip chart, and be prepared to report on your discussion in the large group.

Don Lowell is a mental hygiene therapy aide in a psychiatric center. He has been in his present position for 13 years, having worked his way up from the bottom. He thoroughly enjoys his job, but he missed being chosen for a promotion twice in the last two years. He was one of the top three on the list but was not able to get the promotions he wanted. He has been working very hard to make himself known in the right circles and has volunteered to serve on various county and private committees, boards, and task forces over the past few years.

Don also works three nights a week and weekends at the Rosewood Home, a well-known, highly rated nursing facility. Don serves as one of the two part-time activity coordinators. With his oldest daughter about to enter college, he can certainly use the money. He also enjoys the work and gets to meet a number of people in the community. He's been thinking for some time now that at some point in the future he would like to return to school and complete the degree which he began years ago. Right now, however, he enjoys working with the patients and feels the added experience will help him in the future.

Last week Don received a phone call from Frank Calvin, the chief of service in his division at the development center. Frank's 69-year-old mother is in the hospital recovering from a broken hip. Frank has applied to the Rosewood Home primarily because of its reputation in the area of physical therapy and rehabilitation. The home, however, has a very long waiting list (from six months to a year) and Frank understands that unless his mother receives physical therapy immediately upon release from the hospital, her chances of returning to her former mobility level are quite low. Moreover, Frank's sense of the situation, after meeting with the home's intake social worker, was that his mother was not going to be given priority consideration.

In dicussing the situation with Sarah Anderson, Frank's assistant, he was reminded of Don Lowell. Sarah told Frank that Don is working as a part-time activity director at the home. He remembered Don's name from some paperwork that came across his desk. Frank decides to call Don to see if there was any way around normal procedures and asks if Don can help.

During the conversation, Frank mentions that if Don were able to assist him with this, he (Frank) would try to help him when he could. In addition, Frank said that he would put a note in Don's file stating the cooperation he received from Don in placing his mother in the appropriate health facility. "I just don't know where to turn with this problem," said Frank, "and I really hope you can help me."

Don told Frank that he would see what he could do. He told Frank that he didn't know all that much about the admissions process and really didn't have that kind of "pull" at the facility, but he would give it his best shot.

Don made some informal inquiries around the home concerning the admissions procedures (of which he knew very little). He found out that the director of the intake department, Sheila Hogan, is someone he knows slightly, because he worked with her on a couple of committees. He remembered her as being very focused and knowledgeable, and one who usually plays everything by the book. However, he had found her to be accommodating when necessary.

He also remembered an item in the Rosewood newsletter stating that the intake department was severely short staffed and was looking for volunteers or other staff coverage. Don had some ideas that he thought would work very well at providing coverage at no additional cost to the home. He decided to arrange a meeting.

Discussion Questions
1. What power strategies does Don have available to him?
2. If you were Don, what action would you take?
    a. Would you decide not to try to influence the admission process? If not, why?
    b. Would you decide to help only by clarifying the mother's need for admission?
    c. Would you decide to do everything within your power to get the mother admitted?
3. Using the concepts and skills presented in the learning activity, what are the consequences of your decision and what you could do to maximize your options?
4. What strategy and techniques is Frank using on Don?
5. What options or strategies should Don use with Frank?
6. What should Don's next steps be?
7. What positive and negative role does power and influence play in a situation like this? Do you believe power and influence can be used effectively in a positve, ethical way? Explain.
8. Have you ever encountered a similar situation? What strategies, if any, did you use? What steps did you take?

PRACTICE   The Big Move[3]

Directions
In small groups of six participants, role play a task force in a financial services unit of a large firm. First read the background and instructions, and choose one of the roles indicated. Then prepare yourself by reading only your own role description sheet (*not* those of the other people in your group). Put on the name tag describing the role you are going to play. Start the role play and discuss the issue at hand for about 45 minutes. Further instructions will follow.

Background

Department X, a financial services unit of a large health care system, is currently located in Albany, New York. The department has come under pressure to move

[3] *Adapted from* J. William Pfeiffer and John E. Jones (Eds.). *A Handbook of Structured Experiences for Human Relations Training*, Vol. VII. San Diego: University Associates Inc., 1979. Used with permission.

its headquarters from Albany to Weschester County, an area closer to New York City. Many of the hospitals and clients served by the unit are located around Westchester County, and the system has recently acquired a building large enough to house the entire financial services unit under one roof. The relocation would allow the system to cancel a very expensive building lease in Albany. The current offices in Albany are now inadequate, and expansion would be very expensive and pose some legal difficulties with zoning. The board of directors has created an interunit task force to discuss the possibility of the move. This task force has to come up with a recommendation to the board. The department must move as a whole or not at all.

The task force consists of managers from the following areas:

1. Client Financial Services
2. Accounting
3. Purchasing
4. Stock and Bond Transfer
5. Policy Development
6. Personnel

Each role description sheet outlines an initial position or opinion as to the advisability of the move: for, against, neutral. This is only an initial position, however, and you should feel free to switch sides and/or be influenced by the others. Assume and display the power-personality characteristics outlined in your role description.

A secret ballot vote will be taken at the end of the meeting, and the results will be announced. The board has asked for a recommendation from a task force of managers. You should assume that the recommendation of the group will strongly influence the final decision of whether or not to relocate. At the conclusion of the role play, you will all be asked to complete a questionnaire on your assessment of each character's effectiveness.

Role Description Sheets

Manager: Client Financial Services

You have been with the department since its founding and have worked your way up from your original job. During the 10 years that you have been a manager, you have been committed to the success of the department, have carried it through the lean years, and have contributed enormous energy toward making it the success it is today. You understand the possibilities for expansion and growth that the move to a new location could offer the department; however, you are getting older and definitely feel reluctant to undertake the relocation of your family, the sale of your beautiful home, and the separation from friends that the move would require. Also, although you have not announced it yet, you intend to retire in a couple of years, and the department's move could force you to retire before you had intended.

Your Power Personality. Past experience has shown that your positional power and the weight of your seniority can be used effectively to influence and control others. Your long years of experience make you a credible authority on a variety of matters. You know the workings of the department inside and out.

You use occasional unpredictability as your ace in the hole, catching others off guard by either saying or doing what they least expect. You tend to be calm and soft-spoken most of the time but have found that occasional outbursts of simulated anger (and a penchant for spicy language) can often shock people into compliance.

Manager: Accounting

You have been with the department for several years, and you are in favor of the move because of the positive effect it will have on the distribution of services. Going to a new office space will be much less expensive than trying to expand, even if you could find the available land. The operating budget has increased in the past few years, but lack of expansion space will put a ceiling on the provision of services within a very short time. The strength of the department's financial position and the growth potential of the relocation would really be a boost to the department.

Your Power Personality. You are very careful to have the hard facts about any question before you enter a discussion. You are willing and able to research those facts to enable you to use them to counter emotional arguments. You have a great deal of financial information at your disposal. Since almost every activity in the department affects the bottom line, your auditor's examination of every unit has given you a great deal of information about the efficiency of these units as well as an awareness of a number of skeletons in various closets.

You are soft-spoken, which requires others to listen carefully when you speak. Your power tactic consists largely of strategic use of information, both financial and your own personal experience. Typically, you will let an opponent expound his or her views, then submit your information, pointing out that his or her argument is based on opinion whereas yours is based on hard facts.

Manager: Purchasing

You have been with the department for 25 years and are reluctant to leave the Albany area where you have family and social ties. You think that many others in the department feel the same way you do about leaving Albany. With only a few years left until retirement, you do not want to make any drastic changes in your life.

In terms of logistics, a new location could lack easy access and efficient facilities for shipping equipment and materials. You think that these increased transportation costs are a legitimate argument against moving to the new location.

Your Power Personality. You are personally very suspicious of change. You like the feeling of power you get by, at least initially, saying "no" to any proposal that involves making changes from the traditional way of doing things, regardless of well-supported arguments for the change. You have found that intransigence on your part can produce the desired effect of stopping the proceedings and can prompt others to placate you. When others demand reasons for your refusal, you know you can always blow up any small legitimate objection to defend your position. You are not afraid to let your tone of voice and bodily posture convey that you think people are picking on you unduly. You have often found that if you complain long enough and persistently enough, you will get your way.

Manager: Stock and Bond Transfer

You joined the department not too long ago, and the relocation plan is your brainchild. You feel strongly that the move will be good for the department and that services can be expanded only if some kind of move is made soon. You would like to start influencing the department's future in the most obvious way possible: by ushering in a new era of expansion. The move is bound to force some early retirements and resignations among management personnel who want to remain in the Albany area. You feel that this will revitalize the organization, especially with some of the go-getter replacements you have in mind.

Your Power Personality. You have found that few opponents can withstand the force and high energy level of your arguments. You are not afraid to criticize someone or to interrupt at strategic points in a discussion. In fact, you are rather rude. You are not above instilling a little fear in others by reminding them that you control one of the important units of the department and have access to all evaluation data that point toward the need for expansion.

You are quick to pick out another's weakness and capitalize on it. Emotional arguments or personal considerations are very easy to attack. You single-mindedly intend to get your way.

Manager: Policy Development

You can say with pride that the fact that the department can even consider the proposed expansion move is a direct result of the changes in policy since you took over as manager of the policy development unit three years ago. Your innovative approach has been successful in the department's offering of more service options to clients.

Moving to another location would open up new areas to be served. You personally look forward to moving away from Albany; however, you are afraid that the proposed relocation of the department would mean the loss of some of its best people. Move or no move, you are confident that the department's accomplishments in providing excellent services will continue.

Your Power Personality. You enjoy using your skills as a conciliator, a mediator of different points of view, to get questions settled quickly. You have confidence that your cheerful, humorous, positive, "let's-get-things-settled-to-everyone's-advantage" approach will gain you prestige as the one who engineered the solution to the problem. Periodically during the meeting, you take it upon yourself to summarize the various positions expressed by the members of the task force and to keep the discussion on track.

Manager: Personnel

The department created a personnel unit some years ago, and you became its manager eight months ago. You are in favor of the move because there could be a wealth of semiskilled and trainable people in the area surrounding the new location. You know that restaffing will be an enormous job, but this very requirement could be an opportunity for you to increase your somewhat tentative power position in the department by demanding that you unit's staff be increased to handle the big job of hiring and firing caused by the move. You personally look forward to moving away from Albany.

Your Power Personality. You try to appear calm, cool, and level-headed. One way to get your point across in a debate is to repeat your statement or position over and over, never raising your voice, and looking your opponent straight in the eye. You counter the arguments of others by an appeal to logic: The most rational alternative must be the best one. You do not attack your opponents directly but, rather, attack the logic of their arguments by questioning their research methods and basic assumptions. You are open-minded to the extent that a more logical solution than your own may sway you.

Improving Power-Oriented Behaviors

Observation Sheet

Directions   Make notes on the power-oriented behaviors used by the different people in the role play.

> Manager: Client Financial Services
>
> Manager: Accounting
>
> Manager: Purchasing
>
> Manager: Stock and Bond Transfer
>
> Manager: Policy Development
>
> Manager: Personnel

Assessing Power-Oriented Behaviors

Questionnaire Sheet

Directions   In the two spaces provided on the power scale that follows, first write the number that best represents your perception of the degree of power each of the department managers had in this meeting. Second, indicate the source of each manager's power, that is:

Position (POS)   Personal (P)   Expert (E)   Opportunity (O)   Information (I)

Scale | No power | 1 2 3 4 5 6 7 8 9 10 | Very powerful |

Power Scale   *Power Source*

_____   _____ 1. Manager: Client Financial Services

_____   _____ 2. Manager: Accounting

——— ———3. Manager: Purchasing
——— ———4. Manager: Stock and Bond Transfer
——— ———5. Manager: Policy Department
——— ———6. Manager: Personnel

APPLICATION Changing Your Power Base

This activity is designed to help you further develop and maintain your own power base with your subordinates, colleagues, superiors, and other power systems, if applicable, in your organization.

1. From your power/dependence analysis, determine which dependencies need more power-oriented behaviors from you. For each dependency, identify some of the issues in which you could become more involved right now and, using the ideas and skills discussed in this unit, take some definite action in those areas. (You may need to relate this assignment to your work in a volunteer organization, or a social unit such as a fraternity or sorority. You may have to choose a hypothetical organization if you are not currently affiliated with one to which this exercise could apply.)

2. In a three- to five-page report, describe your plans and actions to further develop and maintain a firmer power base in your organization. Turn in the report to your instructor by the agreed-upon date.

Competency 2 Negotiating Agreement and Commitment

ASSESSMENT Are You a Novice or Expert Negotiator?

Directions Think about some experiences you've had with negotiating—as a consumer, an employee, or a partner in a relationship you value. Ask yourself questions such as those listed, and add any you think are significant.

After answering the questions to your own satisfaction, discuss those you feel comfortable discussing in small groups (of about six people). Take 30 minutes for the discussion, and be prepared to report to the rest of the class on any themes or insights that surfaced in your group.

1. Have you ever returned a damaged product and negotiated for a refund, even though, technically, the warranty had lapsed, or was somehow invalid?

2. Have you ever bargained for a shift change, a raise, or an adjustment in working conditions with a manager or employer?

3. Have you ever gone around normal channels to secure items such as season tickets, or a discount, or passes to a concert or play, after initially being told they were unavailable?

4. Do you press for more information or clarification when listening to a sales pitch, or do you hesitate to ask questions for fear of appearing uninformed or unsophisticated?

5. In a personal relationship, do you ever tolerate negative behavior in the other person because (a) you feel incapable of broaching the issue effectively, (b) you fear being misunderstood, or (c) you don't want to hurt the other person's feelings, even though the behavior is causing you serious problems?

6. As a rule, do you feel you have a reputation among your peers and members of your family for being a tough bargainer or as someone who is easy going and deferential in presenting his or her needs and conditions?

LEARNING	Negotiating Agreement and Commitment

READING YOUR ORGANIZATION'S CULTURE

The first competency in this chapter dealt with building and maintaining a power base. However, we can't exert influence in an organization without knowing what kinds of influence the organization is ready to accept. The rest of this chapter will deal with negotiating agreements and selling ideas.

All members of an organization have a credit rating. That rating goes up or down depending on how supportive, cooperative, and competent people perceive us to be. We do a balancing act. We have to be concerned about the needs of others, and we have to get our jobs done as well. Support is not automatic. Amateur brokers believe that their assigned duties guarantee them support. The expert broker never takes such support for granted.

The balancing act between looking after the needs of others and getting the things we need leads us to the topic of negotiation. Just as we are ambivalent about power, most of us have mixed feelings about negotiation.

Expert brokers are solid negotiators. They have a clear sense of what their needs are, but they also know that the people they deal with have needs as well. Good brokers take these needs into account early in the process. The salesperson to whom you return your broken stereo, the ticket seller at the box office, the partner in a significant relationship—all these people bring to the situation a set of needs, values, procedures, rewards, and goals they are trying to meet. In an organizational setting, these forces and values and procedures make up a culture. Organizational cultures have three dimensions:

1. *Tasks and procedures.* These include not only the way people act, but what the organization actually has them do. Organizational culture is shaped by

the technology, processes, and procedures the organization uses to do its work. For example, a coal mine has a dramatically different culture from a bank, because the nature of the work is dramatically dissimilar.

2. _Sense-making_.   This is everything people go through to clarify and understand why they do what they do. For instance, an outsider could not understand how miners feel about mining without perceiving how they make sense of the discomforts, the risks, and drudgery of their work.

3. _Norms._   These are unwritten assumptions that groups have about what is important or acceptable or forbidden. For example, bank tellers would not value physical courage in their day-to-day work as much as coal miners. A bank teller's dress might be much more scrutinized than that of coal miners.

The negotiation style recommended in this book is somewhat on the soft and "reasonable" side, but it also recognizes the need for tough mindedness, particularly around the issues you're trying to champion. This reasonable approach tries to be tough on principles and gentle on people.

FOUR PRINCIPLES FOR GETTING TO "YES"

Roger Fisher and William Ury, in their influential book *Getting to Yes* (1986), offer four basic principles they believe should guide any negotiation. These are:

1. Separate the people from the problem.
2. Focus on interests, not positions.
3. Generate a variety of possibilities before deciding what to do.
4. Insist that the result be based upon some objective standard.

SEPARATE THE PEOPLE FROM THE PROBLEM

The natural tendency, when there are misunderstandings or bruised egos, or struggles over credit or blame, is to make personalities the focus. This is a mistake. The problem is the thing that needs solving.

Once people feel threatened or criticized, their energy goes into defending their self-esteem, not into solving the problem. Keep the focus on the problem, even if you feel another person is at fault.

It is important to realize that the other person may be constructing the situation in a totally different way. Ask yourself, "How does the other party see the situation?" A good way to find out is to ask questions and then lean forward and listen—really listen. Talk to the other person about his or her perceptions. Don't assume them. Talk about them, and then feed them back to be certain you have heard correctly. "If I understand what you're saying, you feel my request for attending this conference is unreasonable because of the current increase in our case loads. Am I on track?"

Another key is to establish rapport. We'll talk about rapport in the section on effective oral presentations, but rapport is important in any approach to negotiation. Take the time to be in touch with the person you're dealing with before you begin dealing with the issue. Everyday we see doctors treating patients without first establishing rapport. In medicine it's called "bedside manner," and there is enough research and common sense to prove that bedside manner is vital to the healing process. We see teachers begin their classes before connecting with their students. We see managers giving directions but not relating to the people they are talking to.

When you focus on problems and not personalities, you are more able to let people blow off steam without your taking it personally. There's an old German proverb that says, "Let anger fly out the windows." It's good advice, because it saves both parties from that chain reaction of one person's anger feeding off another. The next time someone at work or at home unloads on you, do yourself a favor and imagine yourself opening a window and letting the heat of that anger out. In the meantime, collect yourself to deal with the problem behind the anger. All professional negotiators seem to agree. *Don't react to emotional outbursts*.

FOCUS ON INTERESTS, NOT POSITIONS

Fisher and Ury (1986) begin their discussion of positions as traps with an example from the negotiations between the Soviet Union and the United States on strategic arms limitations. The U.S. team was committed to a position of allowing for at least six missile base inspections per year by each side. The Soviets dug in for a maximum of three. Negotiations were stalemated for weeks over the magic numbers six and three.

The problem was that no one had really thought through the needs and concerns behind the positions they had taken. Both parties had hunkered into their positions. Someone needed to ask, "What is an inspection? One person walking around a missile site for one day, or a team of eight people spending a week?" The United States was apparently concerned about sufficient frequency and thoroughness in inspections, and the Soviet Union was anxious about how intrusive the inspections would be. But on reflection, it became obvious that the number of inspections was not the major issue.

Remember, you are not your position. Focus on the goals and principles behind your position, and separate those goals from your own ego (as best you can). There may be other ways of reaching your goal than those offered by the first position you develop. Thus, the next rule of thumb: Generate other possibilities.

GENERATE OTHER POSSIBILITIES: MAKE THE PIE BIGGER

When people are arguing over how to divide a pie, most of them never consider the possibility that the pie could be made bigger. Often it can. Good negotiators try to think of options that are of low cost to them but of high benefit to the other party. This strategy is often called "dovetailing" or collaborating. In order to dovetail your needs with the needs of the other party, you have to probe what those needs are, and not take the other party's position at face value. When a fellow manager says that he or she must have control of the training rooms in your facility every Friday afternoon, his or her position may be based more on a need for power and control than a practical need for those rooms at that time. It may also be that he or she needs guaranteed space over time, but not necessarily every Friday afternoon. The trap is in reacting to that manager's position before uncovering his or her real needs. That act of questioning and probing will usually enable you to come up with alternatives.

For example, in negotiating over price with a box supplier, a purchasing agent from a small company saw an opportunity. The agent learned from the discussion that the supplier was in a cash-flow squeeze after purchasing a very expensive fabrication machine. The supplier had taken a rigid position on price, and now the purchasing agent knew why. Seizing the opportunity, the agent offered to prepay the supplier for the entire job in exchange for a faster turn-around time *and a major price reduction* (Calano and Salzman 1988, 76). These opportunities for win-win agreements are too often overlooked because negotiators fail to solve the other side's problems first. Dovetailing your needs with that of the other party requires you to separate your needs from your position, but also to separate the other party's needs from its position.

If alternatives don't come to mind right away, don't panic. Take some time. Huddle with a few associates and friends you trust and do some brainstorming. Come up with creative alternatives based on everything you know about your needs, the needs of the other party, and the facts of the situation at hand.

As a manager, you may need to use your negotiating skills in helping others resolve problems or reach compromises. This process is called *mediation*. Expert brokers think twice before intervening in a dispute or disagreement between colleagues or subordinates. It's usually best to wait to be invited, but this is not always possible. For example, if two people have to work together, and a disagreement is making it impossible for them to work effectively, their manager may need to become involved. As their manager, you would have to decide if you want to deal with the people individually or together, and determine how willing they are to solve the problem. For cases in which you decide it's necessary to function as mediator, here are some principles to help you develop a strategy:

1. Acknowledge to your people that you know a conflict exists, and propose an approach for resolving it.

2. In studying the positions of both parties, maintain a neutral position regarding the disputants—if not the issues.

3. Keep the discussion issue oriented, not personality oriented. Focus on the impact the conflict is having on performance.

4. Help your people put things in perspective by focusing first on areas where they might agree. Try to deal with one issue at a time.

5. Remember, you are a facilitator, not a judge. If you assume the role of judge, each person will focus his or her energy on trying to persuade you, rather than on solving the problem and learning something about negotiation. Judges deal with problems; facilitators deal with solutions.

6. Make sure your people fully support the solution they've agreed upon. Don't stop until both parties have a specific plan, and if you sense hesitancy on anyone's part, push for clarification: "Tom, I sense you're less enthusiastic than Carol about this approach. Is there something about it that bothers you?"[4]

GIVE ME A REASON: INSIST ON USING OBJECTIVE CRITERIA

Fisher and Ury (1986) advise us to make negotiated decisions based on principles, not pressure. Often negotiators make the process a contest of wills: It's my stubbornness and assertiveness against yours. Some people call this "yes we will, no we won't" cycle "efficient disagreement." A way around this trap is to find some objective standards or criteria that will help the parties test the reasonableness of a position. For example, your car is totaled in an accident and you refuse to argue with the insurance adjuster over a price based upon sentimental value: "My father gave me that car!" or "I've owned that care since I was in high school!" You would have to refer to some standard, like market value as indicated in the "blue book," or some other objective that both parties could consider reasonable.

It's smart to look for the theories and assumptions behind the position. If your bureau chief unveils a plan for deciding how to award release time for training, you may want to know more about the criteria behind the procedures. It's not a matter of trust or professionalism; it's a matter of knowing what criteria are behind the position the person is taking. Fisher and Ury use the following example from a colleague whose parked car was totaled by a dump truck. It was time to settle with the insurance company through an adjuster (Fisher and Ury 1986, 96–98).

Adjuster:	We have studied your case and have decided the policy applies. That means you are entitled to a settlement of $3300.
Tom:	I see. How did you reach that figure?
Adjuster:	That was how much we decided the car was worth.
Tom:	I understand, but what standard did you use to determine that amount? Do you know where I can buy a comparable care for that amount?
Adjuster:	How much are you asking?
Tom:	Whatever I'm entitled to under that policy. I found a second-hand car just about like mine for $3850. Adding sales and excise tax it would come to about $4000.
Adjuster:	$4000! That's too much!

---

[4] *Adapted from* David A. Whetten and Kim S. Cameron, *Developing Management Skills.* (New York: Scott, Foresman, 1984), pp. 425–426. Used with permission.

Tom:	I'm not asking for $4000, or 3 or 5; I'm asking for fair compensation. Do you agree it's only fair I get enough to replace the car?
Adjuster:	Okay, I'll offer you $3500. That's the highest I can go. Company policy.
Tom:	How does the company figure that?
Adjuster:	Look, $3500 is all you'll get—take it or leave it.
Tom:	$3500 may be fair. I don't know. I certainly understand your position if you're bound to company policy, but unless you can state objectively why that amount is what I'm entitled to, I think I'll do better in court. Why don't we study the matter and talk again?
Adjuster:	Okay, Mr. Griffith, I've got an ad here for a 1978 Fiesta for $3400.
Tom:	I see, what does it say about the mileage?
Adjuster:	It says 49,000. Why?
Tom:	Because mine had only 25,000 miles. How much does that increase the value in your book?
Adjuster:	Let me see, $150.
Tom:	Assuming the $3400 as possible base, that brings the figure to $3550. Does the ad say anything about a radio?
Adjuster:	No.
Tom:	How much extra for that in your book?
Adjuster:	That's $125.
Tom:	What about air-conditioning?[5]

A half hour later, Tom walked out with a check for $4100. Notice how unemotional Tom was? He was working from a need to ground their discussion of price on objective criteria acceptable to both parties. He didn't lose control, and he didn't cave in to personal pressure. He knew his appeal to objective criteria was fair and reasonable. Negotiating can be an emotional ordeal, but good negotiators don't lose control.

The tough part is dragging an emotional discussion back to the issues. Bob Purcell, a corporate attorney, was defending his clients, two partners in a small business, in a lawsuit. The clients describe the scene:

> *During the negotiation, the opposing lawyer began ranting and raving, attempting to intimidate Purcell into accepting a lesser deal. This guy was down right nasty, raising all kinds of superfluous issues and insulting Purcell's competence. We sat there incensed [we weren't allowed to say a word], and it was all we could do not to stand up and shout, "To hell with you buddy, we'll see you in court!"*
>
> *Purcell's response? He ignored the other side's offensive behavior and kept restating our bottom-line settlement offer. After a few rounds it became obvious that we weren't going to budge, emotionally or substantively. Our opponent instructed his attorney to accept our offer.*
>
> *Afterward we asked Purcell how he had managed to keep cool. He gave us the long suffering look one gives young innocents, which we were, and said simply, "Oh, it's all part of the game." On the way out of the courthouse, we passed the opposing attorney in the hall. The two of us wanted to run to him an jeer, "Nyah, nyah, nyah." But Purcell beat us to the punch. He said, "See you around, Mike" The other attorney smiled and said, "OK, Bob, have a good weekend." What a game!* (Calano and Salzman 1988, 96)

[5] Excerpts from *Getting to Yes* by Roger Fisher and William Ury. Copyright © 1981 by Roger Fisher and William Ury. Reprinted by permission of Houghton Mifflin Company.

THE FREEDOM SCALE: NEGOTIATING EXPECTATIONS UP AND DOWN

One of the greatest sources of stress in organizational life is caused by unclear expectations. We want the people who manage us to be more explicit about what they want, and how they want us to operate with them. And as managers we are often confused by the people we manage. "Didn't I explain how I wanted her to report to me on that project? Why is she bugging me with questions on all these details?" The problem can be solved in part by negotiating your position on what Oncken calls the "freedom scale" (Oncken 1984, 106). The freedom scale describes the degree of freedom or discretion you want to enjoy in your working relationships: up, down, and across the organization. You are the person who has to take the initiative to negotiate, or discuss your position on the scale with your boss and with those you manage. Your position will change over time and with various projects and assignments you work on. Here's the scale.

Level 5   Act on your own, routine reporting only.
Level 4   Act, but advise at once.
Level 3   Recommend; then take resulting action.
Level 2   Ask what to do.
Level 1   Wait until told.

The most critical role to work out is that in which you are the mana*gee*, the person being managed. You may be operating at a level 3 with your manager, but feel a need to move to level 4 on most (not all) projects. Your manager may, when presented with the idea, be delighted to give you more discretion and room in which to operate. This change would save your manager time and energy. Of course, the freedom scale is like an insurance policy. You can save your manager time and energy by taking out a very cheap policy—one that allows your manager to let you make the decisions and report routinely. The risk, however, is that if something goes wrong, your manager will be only distantly involved and may take a great deal of blame if things get out of control. That is why your position on the freedom scale will vary, depending upon your manager's anxiety level and personal interest in various projects and responsibilities in which you are involved. The most expensive policy a manager can have is to be surrounded with people who are waiting to be told what to do (level 1). This means that the manager is essentially micromanaging everything, taking very little risk, but paying too much for his insurance policy. The manager is working too hard, and the people he or she manages are probably frustrated beyond belief.

Think about your future role as mana*ger*. If a consulting team talked to the people you supervise, would they be able to clearly explain where they feel they are on the freedom scale in their working relationship with you? Have you ever made your employees' role and level of discretion explicit? This is a simple but powerful tool that you can put to work immediately with your superiors, peers, and subordinates.

ANALYSIS   Conflict in the Cafeteria: The Broker as Mediator[6]

Directions   Now it's time for you to practice some mediating and negotiating strategies of your own. Remember, the same principles of negotiating apply to mediation, but as mediator, you're trying to help other parties resolve their differences. This three-person simulation can be used to demonstrate both ineffective and effective approaches to mediation.

Role for Tony Lodge

You manage 10 people in Production Supply. You've been with the department almost two years now and are quite pleased with your job.

Three months ago your unit was assigned to a new project. It required your people to work a lot of overtime and change vacation plans. Now the project has been expanded and another unit, headed by Billie Deore, a woman in her mid-thirties who has transferred recently from another branch office, has been brought in to help. Employees will still need to work overtime for at least two months.

The people in your unit are tired and are complaining that they haven't seen much of their families during the past three months. You feel Billie's people should assume the major portion of the overtime to give your employees a rest. Your people are burned out and morale is slipping. Billie's people, on the other hand, are fresh and could really give you a rest. You have heard, however, that Billie intends to have her unit pick up only half the overtime.

Your manager has told you that he expects you and Billie to settle the overtime issue and then inform him of your joint decision. On the way to get a cup of coffee, you meet Billie Deore. You decide to bring up the issue.

Role for Billie Deore

You manage 10 people in Production Supply. You've been with the agency just over one year and are generally happy with your job.

Your unit has been assigned to help Tony Lodge on a recently expanded project. The project has required and will continue to require people to work overtime. The project is expected to last at least two months.

Your manager has asked that you and Tony work out the distribution of overtime. You like Tony and look forward to working on this project with him. You feel the overtime should be evenly split between your two units. That way, there will be minimal disruptions in people's schedules as vacations near.

However, you have heard through the grapevine that Tony expects your unit to assume all the overtime. It is his feeling that someone else has to take up the slack because his people have done it for the past three months. You can sympathize, but you don't want your people to take on all the overtime. Your manager has told you that he expects the two of you to work out the details and inform him of your decision. One the way to get a cup of coffee, you meet Tony Lodge. You decide to bring up the issue.

Role for Leslie MacIntosh

You're a friend of Tony and Billie and a unit manager in Production Supply. You've been with the department for seven years and are quite happy in your job.

As you walk into the coffee lounge this morning, you notice the two managers, Tony and Billie, seemingly engaged in some kind of argument.

This disturbs you because you depend on their cooperation to meet production demands. If they fail to reach an agreement on the staffing for the special project, the entire department will be disrupted.

You decide to sit down with them and see if you can help them. You want to do whatever you can to help Tony and Billie work through the problem.

Instructions for "Failure" Third Party (Leslie)[7]

Your instructor has assigned you to demonstrate how to fail as a mediator. You're going to play the part of a person who has the best of intentions but the worst possible approach to mediating. Please follow the instructions as closely as possible. In real life, of course, you would not do as badly as in this demonstration. Remember, you're very serious about helping the two parties, but you're going about it in all the wrong ways.

1. Listen to the discussion for a short time.
2. Begin to communicate nonverbally your discomfort with the discussion (sit back, fidget a bit, shake your head).
3. Intervene in the discussion. Some possible actions you might take are:
   - Agree with one of the people but not the other—take sides.
   - Say that they shouldn't be talking about this kind of thing at work or where others can hear them.
   - Suggest that their discussion would be better held later when they've cooled off.
   - Talk about the fact that they're both wrong.
   - Say that you think the boss ought to be handling this.
   - See if you can get both of them to attack you.
   - Get up, wash your hands of the whole affair, and leave.

Instructions for "Success" Third Party (Leslie)

Your instructor has assigned you to demonstrate how one might effectively help two people who are engaged in a heated argument to listen to each other. Please follow the following directions as closely as possible.

[7]Adapted by permission from *Organizational Behavior in Action* by W. C. Morris and M. Saskin. Copyright © 1976 by West Publishing Company. All rights reserved. Instructions for "Failure Third Party," p. 180.

1. Listen to the discussion for a short time.

2. Begin to lean forward intently to listen to both persons. Show your interest by physical movements.

3. Intervene in the discussion, attempting to use the following process.

   - Say something like, "It may be we're not clear on what either of you is saying. I'd like to ask you to try something with me."

   - Do some checking with one of the people, asking that person to feed back what he or she thinks the other person has said. The other can then comment on it—a check to see if communication has been clear.

   - Quickly, before the first person starts the check, tell the second that you want him or her to do the same thing when the first person has finished. This should convey to both of them that you are not taking sides, but only trying to facilitate communication.

   - If they have trouble during the process, help them; continue to be active and be positive about what you want them to do.

PRACTICE   The Copy Machine Problem

Directions   In this activity you'll have the chance to practice some negotiation on a work-unit level. Work in pairs. Each of you will seek a compromise using some of the strategies and principles discussed in the course material. *Note:* If you are unable to solve your problem, you may call upon another mediator from the class.

The Situation

There is a problem with the use of the copying machine. In the last two weeks, members of two work units have been fighting for use of the machine they share. Yesterday the conflict erupted into an argument with yelling and name calling between workers from each unit. Managers, Doyle Buchanan and Mary Caputo, have decided to meet and try to solve the problem.

Doyle Buchanan

Your unit has extensive contact with the public. You have 10 workers who need to use the machine for routine documentation of their work. Most of the copies are photocopies of signed documents that must be returned to the signer. The original is filed.

Your unit's work flow is regular, not sporadic, and in the past workers made their single copies throughout the day and returned to their workstation. Your workers need access to the machine throughout the day.

Mary Caputo

Although your unit has less direct contact with the public, your unit is responsible for periodically mailing important documents to citizens throughout the state. You have three workers who use the machine for larger work orders.

They need one to two hours at a time to complete the copying. Your unit's work flow is sporadic and not predictable, but you have tight deadlines when you do get work.

APPLICATION   Negotiating Positions on the Freedom Scale

Choose one of the following exercises to work on over the next two weeks. Write the results of your work in a memo to your instructor.

1. Go to the library and research a recent management-labor negotiation. What were the issues involved? What were the bargaining chips used? What did each side give up? What was the final resolution? Did the parties reach a commitment? In your opinion, how effective were the negotiators, and why?

2. Take an issue in your life—buying a VCR or some other expensive item, scheduling shifts in a summer or part-time job, or solving a problem in a personal or family relationship. Describe the issue in terms of the negotiating techniques you have learned in this chapter.

3. Describe your efforts at working with William Oncken's freedom scale. You may choose to focus on the levels of initiative you pursue with your own manager, with the levels you have negotiated with those whom you manage, or with both. The freedom scale is a powerful concept. You may wish to talk explicity about it with your staff, or your manager. If you feel that approach would be inappropriate, you may want to take a more casual approach and focus on a particular task you have been assigned (if you're dealing with your manager), or one you have recently assigned to someone on your staff.

The idea behind this assignment is to come to a clear and supportive agreement with the other party on what level of initiative the two of you can expect. What level are you now on? Do you agree about the current level? If not, why? Where do each of you want to be? If you want to work on level 4 and your manager wants you on level 3, what do you do?

Write a two-page discussion of your experiences in negotiating positions on the degree of freedom scale. Address such questions as:

1. What were your biggest challenges in implementing this principle?

2. Was your manager or your co-workers threatened by this idea, or encouraged by it?

3. Were your discussions about mutual expectations positive and productive, or awkward?

4. Did you feel comfortable with the process?

5. What do you need help with, and how can you get that help?

Competency 3 Presenting Ideas: Effective Oral Presentations

The Presenter's Touch: You May Have It and Not Know It

Directions   Teachers are constantly discovering students who are superb oral presenters, but who have little idea of how good they are. They also encounter people who are convinced that they are poor communicators, but who have the presenter's touch. React to the following questions[8]

Yes	No	
____	____	1. Do you get a kick out of helping other people solve their problems?
X	____	2. Do you use the word "you" more than "I"?
X	____	3. While watching TV panel shows, do you sometimes answer the questions before the experts do?
____	____	4. Can you cut through a rambling, foggy conversation—dig out the main point—and say it so that everybody understands and agrees?
X	X	5. Do you have a high energy level? Do other people seem to be talking slowly to you?
____	X	6. Is there a bit of the cheerleader in you? Do you usually lead the applause?
X	____	7. Do you like to tell people what you've learned? Would you make a good teacher?
X	____	8. Are you a good editor? Can you digest lots of material into simple, clear language?
X	____	9. Do you like the feeling of being "in control"?
X	____	10. Can you handle pressure without blowing your top? Can you deal with provocative questions without flaring up?
X	____	11. Do you like to demonstrate what you're talking about? Do you tend to "act out" what you're describing.
X	____	12. Do you look people in the eye when you talk to them, and when they talk to you?
____	____	13. Do people turn to you when it's time for the meeting to be summed up?

Scoring and Interpretation   If you answered "yes" to half of these questions, you are probably a very strong presenter right now. If you scored less than that, don't be discouraged. Your honesty will be a great asset in improving your ability to communicate. You need to believe you really can improve, which is possible by applying some of the principles presented in this third competency.

[8]These questions are adapted from *I Can See You Naked* by Ron Hoff. Copyright © 1988 by Andrews, McKeel and Parker Publishers. Used with permission of the author.   *good book*

LEARNING Presenting Ideas: Effective Oral Presentations

Public speaking is the number one phobia of people in this country. In surveys asking people what they most dread, giving a speech is invariably first on the list. For most of us, there is no way around the requirement, because our jobs bring us in front of people regularly. In organizational life, we do most of our work in groups. This is why communication is vital to every role you play as a manager.

Steve Jobs, in his efforts to launch his Next computer, forged a partnership with IBM, the company he competed so aggressively against during his days with Apple Computers. Jobs and IBM entered into an agreement to use the "NextStep" software, developed by Jobs' company, to facilitate IBM's own software development for computer workstations. The communication skills Jobs mobilized to ice the deal were, according to industry watchers, extraordinary.

Jobs' first move came at a party when he risked chiding IBM chairman John Akers for relying so exclusively on Microsoft software for IBM's mission to capture more of the workstation market. Akers responded with interest and asked, "How would you like to help us?" Jobs then agreed to bring Bud Tribble, his Next cofounder and chief software engineer, to IBM headquarters in Armonk, New York for a formal presentation. (Notice the communication forum has changed from the informal cocktail party setting to a stand-up presentation before a group.) Jobs and Tribble decided to lay aside the secrecy about the workings of their Next computer and their new NextStep software and show the IBM executives everything. IBM liked what they saw.

A few weeks later it was time to negotiate. In April of 1989, Jobs and IBM officials met for a bargaining session at the Dallas offices of Texas billionaire Ross Perot, an investor in the Next computer. They struck a secret deal which gives IBM permission to evaluate the NextStep software, and pay royalties to Jobs' company if IBM decides to offer it. That partnership with IBM has allowed Jobs to woo other software developers into working agreements. It has also made it easier for Jobs to capitalize his projects. Without Jobs' ability as a communicator, his team's technical creations would never have been supported (Schlender 1989).

In this final section, we will discuss presentations, and give you some practice on giving them and evaluating them. However, everything discussed will also apply to all communication tasks: writing, interviewing, negotiating, mediating, coaching, and so on.

For this brief discussion of effective presentations, we will use Al Switzler's framework for effective communication.[9] Switzler says that our strategies and

---

[9]This discussion is based on conversations with Al Switzler, May 1989.

choices for how to communicate with a group should be driven by three considerations:

1. Our purpose.
2. Our audience.
3. Our resources.

We have to know our purpose and not assume our audience will automatically share that purpose. We also have to know as much as possible about our audience. We can learn a lot about an audience just by looking at them and listening to them talk among themselves. We can ask lots of questions about a group if we're invited to speak to them. This information will guide our choices. Do these people know a lot about this topic, or very little? Are they likely to agree with the position or advice or approach we plan to use?

Finally, resources are time, money, energy, and information. All are finite and in limtied supply, but we often have more than we think. What resources do you have available in making a presentation? Can you get some additional advice on a topic or some help with graphics? How much is the presentation "worth" to you? How much time can you spare for preparation? Can you risk giving a mediocre performance? What does the situation require?

SSSAP

The other elements of Switzler's framework are known as **SSSAP.**

SET

Set deals with an audience's initial impressions and expectations. Good communicators connect with their audiences early to prepare them for the journey they are about to take. Good presentations are audience centered, not speaker centered. Most poor presentations are built on weak set. Set does three things: It assures the listener that you are worth listening to, it creates a mood and tone favorable to listening and acceptance, and it maps the journey you are asking the listener to take with you. Switzler calls these three functions of set the credibility set, climate set, and content set.

Credibility set is the assurance you provide the audience that you are informed and legitimate as a speaker—that you know what you're talking about because of your experience, credentials, interest, special expertise, and so on. Often the credibility set is offered by the person who introduces you. However, in less formal settings, you may need to provide the set yourself. Obviously, when speaking to a group you know very well, you may not need to provide a credibility set. But sometimes the briefest comment will suffice: "I had the opportunity last summer to spend three weeks at the FBI's National Training

Academy in Virginia. Susan Grace asked me to share some of the things I learned at their forensic sciences lab."

Don't assume people know why you are qualified to take their time. Without boasting, you need to think about your credibility set every time you address a group that doesn't know you well.

Climate set is the effort you make to establish rapport with the audience and cue them to a mood or style appropriate to the presentation. Climate set is frequently neglected, and at great cost. First, consider the speaker's task: establishing rapport. *Rapport* is a French word meaning to bring back or refer. In English it has come to mean having an accord or harmony with another person. We tend to feel a rapport, or lack of it, when we speak to people individually, but rapport is equally important in speaking to groups. Without rapport, you will not be allowed to communicate.

As a way of improving your ability at gaining rapport, try to apply some of the following principles at the next meeting you are required to conduct.

1. Be in the room first and greet each person.

2. Make eye contact. Notice the facial expressions and energy level of the people coming in. Does Kay look tired or distracted? Is Craig irritable or bored before the meeting even begins? Don't ignore these cues. Use them to establish rapport by helping you key in on the group's mood and energy.

3. As you begin the meeting, make eye contact with every person present.

4. Be positive and pleasant, but don't press too much energy onto a resistant group, especially at first. Try to mirror their energy level close enough so as not to turn them off. You can show more energy and enthusiasm as you go. Most groups will resist abrupt jumps between their energy level and that of a speaker.

5. Be positive and supportive. Improve your "climate set" by being positive, even if you have unpleasant or difficult business to conduct. If you aren't positive, what is your justification for being in charge? When this advice is given to people, some react, "But this is just another dumb meeting. Everybody knows that. I'd feel like a jerk trying to get people to enjoy it." That's the point. Even perfunctory, routine meetings are much more bearable when the person in charge is positive and professional. Grand occasions are often less challenging to our skills than routine ones. Try it and see. Don't be dramatically different, but push up your level of energy and optimism, and you'll be pleased to see how contagious those qualities are.

Content set is the road map you provide your audience. Most of us are uncomfortable with ambiguity. We want to know what's going on. When you talk to a group, let them know where you're about to take them, early in your presentation. "I want to talk for 10 minutes about why I think our record in work-related accidents is rising, and make some suggestions on how to turn the corner on the problem. When I've done that, I would like your questions and suggestions." With that "set" the audience can understand what is coming because you've given them a map to follow. A good communicator remembers what it's like not to know much about the topic in question (Wurman 1989, 130). The more we know about a topic, the more inclined we are to overestimate how much our audience knows about it. Define terms and avoid jargon as much as possible. People appreciate a clear and candid style in speaking as well as writing. William Zinsser, a gifter writer and engaging speaker, shares an example of how not to do it:

> *A few years ago, I was shanghaied on to an advisory panel at Time Inc., and at our first meeting someone asked the chairman what our committee had been formed to do. He said, "It's an umbrella group that interacts synergistically to platform and leverage cultural human resources companywide." That pretty much ended my interest in the committee. And when it later experienced "viability deprivation" (went down the tubes) I was overjoyed. (Wurman 1989, 118)*

Think about what people need to know up front so that they can relax and pay attention. Will you give people a chance to ask questions? What major themes will you cover? Without the answers to these questions, people might interrupt just before you get to the point they are interested in, or stop listening because they assume you are not covering the topic about which they want to hear. The road map you give your audience will keep their understanding and attention on track.

SEQUENCE

May I Pray While I Smoke?   Remember from the discussion of writing that certain "positions" have more prominence in messages than others. For example, beginnings and endings are the more prominent positions. An audience is more likely to remember the opening and closing comments you make in a talk than the things that go in the middle.

If your content set gives the audience a map of the journey, the sequence you choose is more like the journey itself. Do you go to the store first or the bank? Do you talk about the new security policy from central office, or the events that led to the policy?

Sequence is the order or flow or linear arrangement of your talk, or the agenda you are building if you're conducting a meeting. You may have superb content, but if you present it in the wrong order, you may be misunderstood or ignored. Sequence is vital, but we often pay little attention to it. Look at these two sentences.

> *Carol is a superb systems analyst, but she is not good at dealing with people.*

> *Carol is not good at dealing with people, but she is a superb systems analyst.*

These sentences do *not* mean the same thing. Each gives us a different impression of Carol. In the first sentence, the emphasis is on Carol's purported weaknesses in interpersonal relationships. The second stresses her strengths as systems analyst, allowing for her poor performance with people. Gordon Allport, a prominent social scientist, used to tell his students about two monks who argued often about the appropriateness of smoking and praying at the same time. They decided independently to ask their superior to settle the question. One monk asked, "Father, may I smoke while I pray?" "Heavens no, my son. Prayer is a serious matter," was the answer. Later, the second priest, knowing the power of sequencing asked, "Father, may I pray while I smoke?" He was told, "My son, it is always good to pray."

Spill the Beans. In most presentations or briefings, the best approach is to "spill the beans." Unveil your most important message first, and then support the point with elaboration and details. This approach is the same as the "descending" order of presentation talked about in Chapter 5 for the monitor role. A good memo tells the reader up front what its main point is. A good presentation spills the beans at the beginning and provides backup later. We love suspense when we're reading a novel or watching a film, but not when we're listening to a presentation at work.

There are exceptions to this rule. If you have bad news, you usually need to "buffer" the jolt by verbally placing the arm on your listener's shoulder.

> *I think most of you know I've been meeting frequently with our director over office space. I've played all the chips I had to win a resource for what I think is the best staff in this agency. I appreciate your support and your patience. Unfortunately, we've lost this one. We won't be moving into the new wing when it's finished. We need to talk about what that means, and how best to live with it.*

The worse the news, or the tougher the topic, the more the need for a buffer. However, don't overdo putting off the bad news. People know what's going on. They don't want to be patronized; they usually just want to be treated civilly and professionally.

Deciding on Sequence. Sometimes it's hard to decide what sequence to use. Do you present things in the order in which they happened (chronologically)? Do you go from the known to the unknown, or the simple to the complex? Any of these approaches might work, but you have to decide in each particular case. Think about your purpose and the audience's needs. You may need to persuade a group that your approach to tracking inventory is most accurate, but your audience may need to be assured that it will not take more time to implement than the current system. Remember, audience-centered communication is your goal.

A very helpful strategy is to use the magic number three. The number three is a very important number in our culture. Think about the advice in Chapter 5 about each message needing a beginning, a middle, and an end. "People are comfortable with things that come in threes" (Hayden-Elgin 1987, 181). You can capitalize on that comfort by using three elements in your presentations, particularly if you have little time to prepare and little time to make the points you wish to make. Suzette Hayden-Elgin recommends this formula:

1. State or present the problem or situation.
2. Provide three supporting items: *a*, *b*, and *c*.
3. Conclude with a summary.

For example:

1. I'm very pleased to introduce Fawn Ashton.
2. Because:
   - She is the person who organized the first Concerned Citizens for Clean Air chapter in the state.
   - She is recognized as one of the best authorities in the country on air pollution and its effects on children with respiratory disorders.
   - She is a friend I have known and admired for over 20 years.
3. The best thing I can offer my associates in this cause is to give them a chance to hear Fawn Ashton.

This model of three things within a framework of three will seem familiar, logical, and nonthreatening to your audience, because we deal with this kind of structure all the time. When you think about sequencing, think about the number three, and then decide the best order in which to put those three items.

SUPPORT

For help with principles of support, refer to the Toulmin model of argumentation discussed in Chapter 5. **Support** is the substance of your presentation: the facts, the major arguments, the reasons you argue for doing one thing rather than another. Support is the bones of your presentation. Switzler says that the support you provide in any presentation should be correct, concrete, complete, relevant, and logical, and he gives this hint about checking on the effectiveness of your support. Ask yourself these questions:

1. What do I mean? Do I define things adequately?
2. Am I specific? Do I use illustrations?
3. How do I know? Do I invoke appropriate authorities?
4. So what? Do I make my message relevant?

Try, whenever possible, to anticipate objections to your position, or points of misunderstanding, and address them as you go. For example:

> *Our field tests have shown that this new compound forms a better bond for broken pipe joints than any we've used. Admittedly it's less effective in very cold temperatures, so we will be limited to three-season use,* but *new batches are being developed that promise to be effective year-round.* Some of you pointed out *in your field reports that the compound dries much slower,* but *most of us who have used it think the greater durability is really worth it.*

If you are speaking to your colleagues or members of a unit attached to your organization, use your knowledge of that culture to help you support your points. How does that organization process information? What passes for a "good reason" in this culture? Laborde (1987) talks about a colleague who was told by his manager that, in the wake of a reorganization, his office would be the smallest one in the unit. After thinking for a few days, this person went to his boss and told her that the new situation would hamper his productivity, and in fact had already gotten in the way of several important negotiations. This argument struck a chord because his boss was more concerned at that point about productivity than she was about equity, or fairness, or appearance, or any other value he could think of. There were several real and honest reasons the person could have laid on the table for getting his office changed, but he felt this one would have the most impact. It correlated more closely with the values and interests of the person with whom he was dealing. In another situation, another reason would have been more effective.

In speaking, try to use the support that has the greatest relevance, validity, and impact. Don't load too many reasons into the hopper. This tactic will weaken your arguments overall.

ACCESS

Some presentations are interesting, but the points they make are hard to pinpoint. **Access** deals with making information accessible to the listener. When you write, you improve access by using boldface type, white space, headings, borders, numerals, and color. When you give a presentation, you can improve access by using good visual aids and making clear transitions from one point to the next. You can also make things more concise by stating them in fewer words, or summarizing them.

Words, Numbers, Pictures.   Visuals are extremely important to access. We live in a visual age. We are children of the media, and we process most of our information visually. A talking head is death in the media industry. Most network programming will not keep the camera on a person talking for more than 15 seconds. They break up the "talking head" with graphics or footage illustrating what the person is talking about. We know all this from our own experience, but time and again we see people pull their captive audiences through long, tedious presentations, glutted with details, and void of visual enrichment.

Most of the visuals used in presentations are very ineffective. Typically, the more time, money, and effort spent on visuals, the worse they are. Here are some of the reasons why. Most of us prepare a lot of word/number visuals when we give presentations. These are usually overhead transparencies with lots of words and or numbers on them. The transparencies are easy to make because of computer graphics; they are striking and professional looking, but are usually too detailed and hard to follow. Here are some guidelines for using visuals.

1. Visuals are the tail. You, as presenter, are the dog. Don't let visuals control your presentation.
2. Visuals do enhance audience comprehension and improve your credibility. Most speakers need to think more visually. When you have to talk to a group, try to translate from words into pictures. Even if you choose not to use visuals, your talk will be more vivid.

3. Visuals help you by providing a reason for moving, pausing, and pointing. This movement gives your audience the variety they need, and makes you easier to listen to.

4. Visuals need to be simpler than we usually make them. We should use line drawings, sketches, and photographs more, and be careful about flashing columns of numbers on the screen. Sometimes you have to use lots of numbers. If so, highlight the most significant ones with a colored marker, or bracket the figures in some distinct way.

5. Visuals are primarily for the audience, not the speaker. Make every choice based upon their need to understand, not your need to dwell on fine points or impress them with how much homework you've done.

6. Visuals can make a fool of you if you don't rehearse with them. Practice the pacing and sequence of your visuals, and become comfortable with handling them.

7. Visuals made from reports or other "page size" documents are usually unreadable. If your audience is 18 feet away, the lettering on your charts or overheads must be one-half inch (as the audience sees it on the chart or screen); from 32 feet they should be at least one inch.

8. Visuals need lots of white space. For word visuals, use no more than five items per visual, and no more than six words per item.

The overhead projector is now a fixture in most conference and board rooms across the world, but people are sometimes too eager to use it. Transparencies are easy to carry and very easy to produce, but the projector is noisy, and in small groups, covers too much of your audience's field of vision. Don't underestimate the effectiveness of the flip chart. You can draw lists and simple charts on them, and prepare them ahead of time and flip to them as you present. Now, electronic boards enable you to write notes or simple graphs, and then copy them with a push of a button. Flip charts and electronic boards are ideal in groups of not more than 15 people. Flip chart paper is fragile, and doesn't travel well, so for repeat presentations have your visuals mounted on poster board and placed on an easel.

POLISH

Polish is the finish you put on anything that represents you or carries your reputation with it. It is the added and extra attention to details and little things. It is having your notes in order, having good visuals arranged at the overhead projector, dressing in such a way that you do not draw too much attention to yourself, but need not worry about your appearance. Polish is arranging the environment for maximum effectiveness. People can hear you. They can see the screen. The room isn't stifling or chilly. You can't control all the aspects of the environment, but you can do some things, and these make a huge difference. Polish is the extra attention to detail that tells the audience that the topic is important, they are worth the effort, and they are not wasting their time. Polish is giving a presentation you want to have your name on.

ANALYSIS   Applying SSSAP

Directions   Within the next week, take special note of a presentation in which you are part of the audience. A live presentation would be better than a televised one. Use the SSSAP principles and your own experience and expertise as a communicator to evaluate the presentation. Consider these questions:

1. Was it effective? Why or why not?
2. How could the presenter have improved his or her performance?
3. What do you think the presenter's main purpose was? Was that purpose clear?
4. Did the presenter prepare the audience with climate, credibility, and content sets?
5. Was there a good summary?
6. Was the presentation vivid? Were visuals used? If not, should they have been used?

PRACTICE   You Be the Speaker

Directions   Prepare a six-minute presentation on a topic of your choice. It may involve a problem or project at work, but it may also be taken from another class or your personal experience. Think carefully about the SSSAP principles, and tailor your presentation to your audience. You will share your presentations in groups of eight to ten and give each other feedback and recommendations on things that worked well, and things that could be improved.

APPLICATION   You Be the Critic

Write an assessment of a presentation you have given recently at work, in a class, or in any organization or group with which you are affiliated. Ideally, this presentation should be given since you've been exposed to the principles we've discussed in this chapter. Talk about the context of the presentation. Your presentation could be for a class, or a church or service group, or an agenda item in any kind of meeting.

Discuss in writing how successful and effective you think your presentation was and why. Did your exposure to the SSSAP principles help you as a communicator? What do you need more work on in oral communication? Write your evaluation and give it to your instructor by the assigned date.

REFERENCES

Calano, Jimmy, and Jeff Slazman. "Tough Deals, Tender Tactics," *Working Woman* (July 1988).

Dimbleby, Richard, and Graeme Burton. *More Than Words: An Introduction to Communication.* New York: Methuen, 1985.

Ekman, Paul. *Telling Lies: Clues to Deceit in the Marketplace, Politics and Marriage.* New York: Berkley Books, 1985.

Fisher, Roger, and William Ury. *Getting to Yes: Negotiating Agreement Without Giving In.* New York: Penguin, 1986.

Goodmand, Gerald, and Glenn Esterly. *The Talk Book: The Intimate Science of Communicating in Close Relationships.* Emmaus, Penn.: Rodale Press, 1985.

Hamlin, Sonya. *How to Talk So People Listen.* New York: Harper & Row, 1988

Hayden-Elgin, Suzette. *The Last Work on the Gentle Art of Verbal Self-Defense.* New York: Prentice-Hall, 1987.

———. *More on the Gentle Art of Verbal Self-Defense.* New York: Prentice-Hall, 1983.

Hoff, Ron. *I Can See You Naked: A Fearless Guide to Making Great Presentations.* Kansas City: Andrews and McMeel, 1989.

Kirkpatrick, Donald K. *How to Plan and Conduct Productive Business Meetings.* New York: McGraw-Hill, 1987.

Kuhn, Robert L. *Dealmaker: All the Negotiating Skills and Secrets You Will Ever Need.* New York: John Wiley and Sons, 1988.

Laborde, Genie. *Influencing with Integrity:* Palo Alto, Calif.: Syntony Publishing, 1987.

Maccoby, Michael. *Why Work: Motivating and Leading the New Generation.* New York: Simon & Schuster, 1988.

Mayer, Kenneth R. *Well Spoken: Oral Communication Skills for Business.* New York: Harcourt Brace Jovanovich, 1989.

Oncken, William, Jr. *Managing Management Time: Who's Got the Monkey?* Englewood Cliffs, N.J.: Prentice-Hall, 1984.

Pfeffer, Jeffrey. *Power in Organizations.* Marsfield, Mass.: Pitman Publishing, 1981.

Pfeiffer, William J., and John E. Jones. *A Handbook of Structured Experiences for Human Relations Training.* vol. VIII. San Diego: University Associates, Inc., 1979.

Raiffa, Howard. *The Art and Science of Negotiation.* Cambridge, Mass.: Belknap Press of Harvard University, 1982.

Schendler, Brenton R. "How Steve Jobs Linked up with IBM," *Fortune* (October 9, 1989): 48–61.

Simmons, John. "Reeducation of a Company Man," *Business Month* (October 1989): 78–80.

Tannen, Deborah. *That's Not What I Meant: How Conversation Style Makes or Breaks Relationships.* New York: Ballantine Books, 1986.

3M Management Group. *How to Run Better Business Meetings.* New York: McGraw-Hill, 1987.

Whetten, David A., and Kim S. Cameron. *Developing Management Skills.* Glenview, Ill.: Scott, Foresman, 1984.

Wilder, Lilyan. *Professionally Speaking.* New York: Simon & Schuster, 1986.

Wurman, Richard Saul. *Communication Anxiety.* New York: Doubleday, 1989.

Zartman, William I. *The Practical Negotiator.* New Haven: Yale University Press, 1982.

The Innovator and Broker Roles

We have just completed our discussion of the innovator and broker roles. Before we leave these roles in the competing values model, let's put them in a larger context.

A BRIEF REVIEW

These two roles are part of the open systems model, in which the desired ends include external support, resource acquisition, and growth. The assumed means to these ends have to do with insight, innovation, and adaptation. This model assumes that the environment is always changing and that organizations must adapt to the changes. To facilitate such change, managerial leaders must play the innovator and broker roles.

WHEN THE INNOVATOR AND BROKER ROLES ARE MOST APPROPRIATE

To understand when this model is appropriate, let's review the two axes that define the model. On the horizontal axis the model is defined by an external focus and thus a greater sensitivity to the pressures for action. The vertical axis is defined by high flexibility, which suggests situations where the basic problems are ambiguous and not easily understood. When a situation is characterized by high pressure to act and high ambiguity, someone must take action based on intuition and values. Managerial leaders must act before they know what the right answer is—a risk, but a necessary one. Sensing the urgency and developing an educated guess about the right strategy requires the skills of the innovator and broker.

COMPLEMENTARY ROLES

Because some people feel that the open systems model is inherently "right," they may tend to overuse it. In all situations they believe that they should be intuitive and creative. At times, though, acting as a innovator and a broker is not the best course that a manager can take. The failure to balance these roles with the other roles, particularly the monitor and coordinator roles in the internal process model, can lead to problems.

People who excel at the innovator and broker roles are often entrepreneurial, and they may start a new organization around their vision of a new product or service. They successfully develop their idea by securing resources and hiring an increasing number of people into the new system. Interestingly, the ever-increasing number of new people causes a problem. As the organization becomes larger and more complex, the need for predictability and control increases. People begin to ask for job descriptions, organizational charts, information systems, and other structures. Often the founders of such organizations resist engaging these internal process values. They believe that the monitor and coordinator roles are antithetical to good management. Some founders are actually forced to leave their organizations as a result. One famous example is Steve Jobs, who was forced to leave Apple Computer. Some lead their unit to organizational death: the organization actually ceases to exist. Such was the case with Don Burr, the founder of People Express Airlines (his story appears in Chapter 10).

Clearly the roles in the internal process model must be seen in context. They must be balanced with other models.

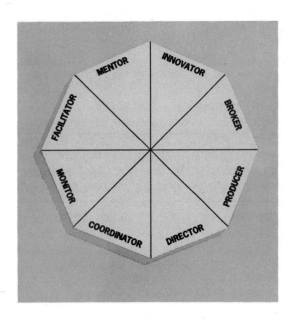

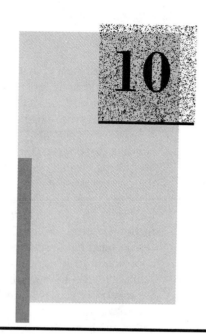

INTEGRATION AND THE ROAD TO MASTERY Understanding the Developmental Process

W e have now presented all eight roles in the competing values framework. You have had the opportunity to work on many of the 24 competencies, and you may have experienced some significant change. If you completed the competing values self assessment instrument at the outset of the course (the assignment at the end of chapter 1), it may now be useful to return to the instrument and again assess yourself.

ASSESSMENT Reexamining Your Profile

Again answer the questions and examine your profile. Based on the latest profile, answer these questions: *Mentor, Facilitator, Broker*

Teamwork building

1. What were my greatest strengths and weaknesses at the outset?

2. How do I see myself differently at this time?

Portions of this chapter are adapted from *Beyond Rational Management: Mastering the Paradoxes and Competing Demands of High Performance* (Quinn 1988). Used with permission.

LEARNING   Integration and the Road to Mastery

You have had the opportunity in the course to work on the skills presented in this book. The mastery of management, however, requires more than just the development of skills alone. It requires the ability to enter a situation, to see it from contrasting perspectives, and to call upon contrasting competencies. It often requires the blending of contrasting competencies. This is not easy. Consider, for example, the following story that might have taken place in your own class.

> *This week in my introductory class the topic was groups, and the students were assigned to engage in several group activities. I began my lecture on the topic by pointing out that groups evolve through predictable stages and that if this evolutionary process is managed correctly, the group can become one of the manager's most powerful tools. In "turned on" groups people get inspired and work productively without much need for intervention or control on the part of the boss. After presenting several concrete examples, I noted that few managers ever experience the phenomenon because they destroy the evolutionary process in its early stages. I presented a list of task functions and a list of process functions that must occur in order for the group to evolve.*
>
> *As we discussed task functions such as initiating structure, giving information, clarifying, summarizing, and evaluating, they had little difficulty understanding. When we turned to process functions such as processing observations, empathizing, participating, surfacing rather than smothering conflict, and managing interpersonal tension in positive ways, they seemed more challenged.*
>
> *After class, one of the students wanted to talk. He said he had noticed when his group first met that one of the members was not involved. After the first meeting he concluded that he would try to include that student. This is what he told me. "I totally failed. When you assigned the second exercise, I noticed that this guy was again sitting around and not saying anything. But I decided that I could not do anything about it. We had only so much time and the work had to get done. I do not think it is possible to get the work done and also do those other things you were talking about. You cannot think about both at the same time."*

A DYNAMIC PERSPECTIVE

Many managers are like the student in the preceding story. They excel in some competencies, but they find that integrating them with others is difficult. They perform well in some situations, but they fail or are awkward in others. The objective of this chapter is to put all the competencies into a dynamic perspective and to show how they are interrelated. Understanding this aspect of the model may help you to avoid some pitfalls and to move, with practice, toward mastery. As a result, you will see that you can *develop* competencies as you go through different stages in your career. The earlier you understand the need for different competencies, the more effective you will be as a manager.

THE DEVELOPMENT OF MASTERY

Mastery of an activity involves a learning process that takes place over time. Dreyfus and Dreyfus (1986) provide a five-stage model that describes the evolution from novice to expert (see Figure 10.1).

Stage 1: The Novice.   As a novice, you learn facts and rules. The rules are learned as absolutes, which are never to be violated. For example, a beginning chess player learns the names of the pieces, how they are moved, and their value. He or she is told to exchange pieces of lower value for pieces of higher value. In management this might be the equivalent of reading a textbook. The student in the story was still at the novice stage in trying to perform the maintenance functions in a group.

Stage 2: The Advanced Beginner.   Experience becomes critical. Performance improves somewhat as real situations are encountered. Understanding begins to exceed the stated facts and rules. As you observe certain basic patterns, you begin to recognize factors that were not stated in the rules. A chess player, for example, begins to recognize certain basic board positions that should be pursued. The new manager discovers the basic norms, values, and culture on the first job. Technical procedures, types of relationships, appropriate dress, and typical career paths are among the things that may vary dramatically from what the novice learned in textbooks. The student in the story was just beginning to experience real-world challenges in terms of doing both task and maintenance functions.

Stage 3: Competency.   Here you begin to appreciate the complexity of the task and recognize a much larger set of cues. You develop the ability to select

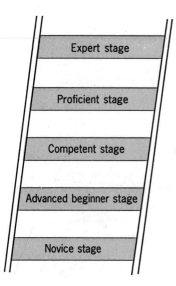

FIGURE 10.1 *Five steps to mastery.*

and concentrate on the most important cues. With this ability grows competence. Here the reliance on absolute rules begins to disappear. You engage calculated risks and complex trade-offs. A chess player may, for example, weaken board position in order to attack the opposing king. This plan may or may not follow any rules that the person was ever taught. The manager may experiment with going beyond the technical rules taught in school as he or she experiments with new behaviors. You may begin to take risks and suggest new approaches. These may occasionally result in successful outcomes. Here the trial-and-error process is critical to continued development. The student, in the original illustration may begin to experiment with stopping the group process to check what quiet members are feeling, or he may experiment with raising conflicts that are being avoided. Slowly we will learn when and how to best make such interventions.

Stage 4: Proficiency.   Calculation and rational analysis seem to disappear. The unconscious, fluid, and effortless performance begins to emerge, and no one plan is held sacred. You learn to unconsciously "read" the evolving situation. You notice cues and respond to new cues as the importance of the old ones recede. New plans are triggered as emerging patterns call to mind plans that worked previously. Your grasp of the situation is holistic and intuitive. We are talking, for example, about the top 1 percent of all chess players, the people with the ability to intuitively recognize and respond to change in board positions. The manager has become effective, capable of meeting a wide variety of demands and contradictions.

In the proficiency stage our student would be able to manage both task and maintenance functions in a seemingly effortless way. But this would be deceiving. Proficiency does not come easily. Consider, for example, John Sculley of Apple Computer. He arrived at Apple in 1983 after leaving PepsiCo as a marketer. He knew nothing about personal computers. He immediately set about the task of learning a new business from the ground up. Although Sculley sees himself as essentially an intuitive leader, he regularly points out that a person can only be intuitive about something he or she really understands. Sculley's intuitive decisions have made Apple a highly successful company. He is proficient, perhaps expert, because he paid the price of moving through the first three stages and into the fourth.

Stage 5: Expert.   At this level people do what comes naturally. They do not apply rules but use holistic recognition in a way that allows them to deeply understand the situation. They have programmed into their heads multidimensional maps of the territory of which the rest of us are not aware. They see and know things intuitively that the rest of us do not know or see. They frame and reframe strategies as they read changing cues. This ability facilitates their engagement of the natural flow of events. Here the manager has fully transcended any natural blind spots and is able to shift roles as needed. The master seems to effortlessly meet the contradictions of organizational life.

THE PROFILE OF THE MASTER

The mastery of managerial leadership is composed of two elements. First is the ability to play all eight roles at least at a competent level. Second is the ability to blend and balance the competing roles in an appropriate way.

Does the notion of mastery really apply to the tasks of management? As we consider the eight roles and 24 competencies in the competing values framework, is it possible to perform all of these well? Is it possible to link the demands of one role with the demands of a role in an opposite area of the framework? In order to approach this question, let us briefly review a study of ineffective and effective managers (Quinn, Faerman, and Dixit 1987).

Using the competing values model, researchers have found that ineffective organizational leaders tended to have profiles that were badly out of balance.

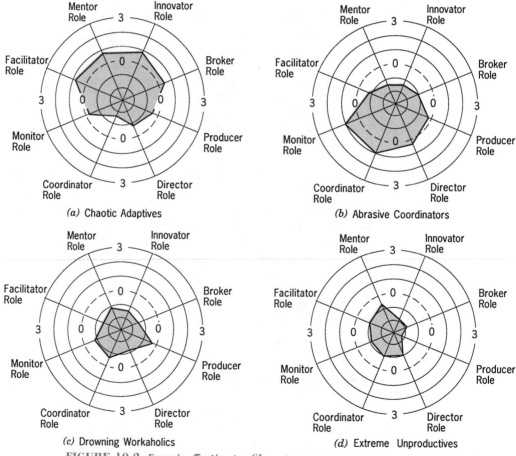

FIGURE 10.2 *Four ineffective profiles.* Source: *Robert E. Quinn,* Beyond Rational Management: Mastering the Paradoxes and Competing Demands of High Performance (*San Francisco: Jossey-Bass, 1988*), *pp. 98–99.* Used with permission.

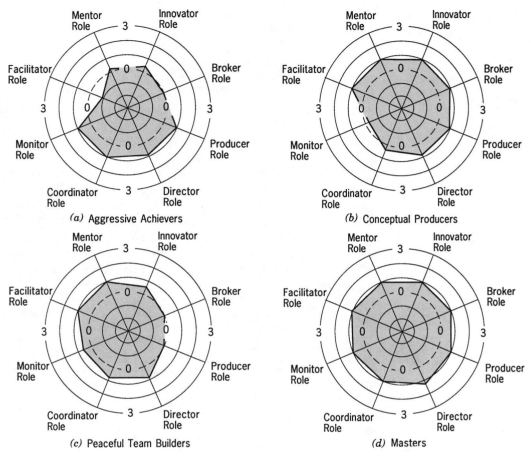

FIGURE 10.3 *Four effective profiles.* Source: *Robert E. Quinn,* Beyond Rational Management: Mastering the Paradoxes and Competing Demands of High Performance (*San Francisco: Jossey-Bass, 1988*), *pp. 101–102.* Used with permission.

Those leaders might be above average on the top four roles (mentor, facilitator, innovator, broker) and then be well below average on the bottom four (monitor, coordinator, director, producer). Such managers were seen by associates as impulsive and chaotic, spreading disorder everywhere. Some had the opposite profile. They were seen as narrowly focused on control and abrasive towards people. Among the ineffectives, there were several other profiles as well, but all were badly out of balance. Four of the ineffective profiles are shown in Figure 10.2.

Interestingly, most of the effective profiles also had some imbalance in them. But here there was a difference. In the effective profiles, people tended to have many roles upon which they were rated high. The scores on their weaker roles, however, tended to fall near the average. In other words, they did not neglect any of the roles. Nevertheless, they were not free of style. They tended to emphasize some areas more than others.

Figure 10.3 shows four types of effective profiles: aggressive achievers, conceptual producers, peaceful team builders, and masters. The aggressive achievers tend not to excel in the human relations quadrant. The conceptual producers tend not to excel in the internal process quadrant, and the peaceful team builders are near the average on the two roles to the right of the framework. Although each of these three clearly reflects a style, all are effective.

The fourth profile is different from the others. The masters have a profile that is big and round. They seem to have transcended style because they can appreciate the underlying values in each quadrant and can also employ the behaviors that are represented in each one. Hence, they have far more flexibility than others.

How do masters come to round out their profiles? The answer is experience. Masters tend to be in upper-middle and top-level positions. It is reasonable to suggest that these people are not born as masters. Although some people have years of experience and are still ineffective, masters tend to grow. They evolve; they go through transitions that are most challenging. If met successfully, they come out of these transitions with a wider array of competencies and are less tied to their natural styles. To understand this change process, we now turn to a case illustration.

THE TRANSFORMATION OF AN AGGRESSIVE ACHIEVER

Consider the case of a truly successful organizational leader whose journey towards mastery pivoted around a crucial crisis and transformation (Quinn 1988).

> *He had graduated from a five-year engineering program in four years and had taken a job with his current organization. Starting out in a brilliant fashion, he was promoted rapidly. He had an ability to take a complex technical problem and come up with a better answer than anyone else. He was also a hard-driving person who pushed his people to accomplish some impressive tasks. Initially he was seen as an action-oriented person with a bright future. His profile was that of an aggressive achiever (see Figure 10.3).*
>
> *After his last promotion, however, everything started to change. He went through several very difficult years. For the first time he received serious negative feedback about his performance. His ideas and proposals were regularly rejected, and for the first time he was passed over for a promotion. In reflecting on those days, he said:*
>
> *"It was awful. Everything was always changing and nothing ever seemed to happen. They would sit around forever and talk about things. The technically right answer didn't matter. They were always making what I thought were wrong decisions, and when I insisted on doing what was right, they got angry and would ignore what I was saying. Everything was suddenly political. They would worry about what everyone was going to think about every issue. Your appearance, attending cocktail parties, that stuff, to me was unreal and unimportant.*

"I went through five and a half terrible years. I occasionally thought I had reached my level of incompetence, but I refused to give up."

Finally, a critical incident occurred. Like many critical incidents in the transformational process, it may seem comical to an outside observer.

On several occasions, the engineer's boss commented that he was very impressed with one of the engineer's subordinates. Finding the comment somewhat curious, he, on one occasion, asked for an explanation. The boss indicated that no matter how early he, himself, arrived at work, the subordinate's car was always there.

The engineer went to visit the subordinate and indicated that he had noticed that no matter what time he came in, the subordinate's car was already in the lot. The subordinate nodded his head and explained,

"I have four teenagers who wake up at dawn. The mornings at my house are chaotic. So I come in early. I read for a while, then I write in my personal journal, read the paper, have some coffee, and then I start work at eight."

When the engineer left his subordinate's office, he was at first furious. After a couple of minutes, though, he sat down and started to laugh. He later explained, "That is when I discovered perception." He went on to say that from that moment everything started to change. He was more patient. He began to experiment with participative decision making. His relationships with superiors gradually improved. Eventually he actually came to appreciate the need to think and operate in more complex ways at the higher levels of the organization.

This story represents a learning process. The engineer was very adept in using the skills in the two lower quadrants. Here he was in the proficient or expert stages. Rapid promotions, however, put him into a new and more complex situation. At the higher organizational levels, skills in the top two quadrants were much required. Here he was in the novice or advanced beginner stage. He applied his old assumptions and governing rules only to see them fail. The resulting frustration and panic led him to try even harder. He intensified the use of his old skills. This, in turn, resulted in more failure and frustration. Fortunately for him, he did not quit. Eventually there was enough frustration to weaken his intensely held existing model, and an event occurred which gave him the critical, creative insight that he needed. This led to a reframing about what it means to be successful. The human and political domains (human relations and open systems models) began to become a part of his world view. He began to explore and experiment with new skills. This was eventually followed by a marked improvement in performance.

As a manager this man was not now perfect. Clearly he had his share of bad days. There were occasions when he got discouraged and there were times when his subordinates felt he was too harsh. Nevertheless, he had a wide range of capacities and most of the time displayed an ability to call upon them in successful ways. For the most part, he had become, with considerable effort, a master, a person with the capacity to both play and balance completing roles.

HOW MASTERS SEE THE WORLD

What is it that differentiates a master from others? The answer may have to do with how masters see the world.

Most of us, like the engineer in the preceding story, learn to think of the concept of organization in a very static and purposeful way. One reason we have this perception is because of our experience. At the lowest levels organizations are encountered as relatively stable, predictable patterns of action. They appear to be, or at least we expect them to be, the ultimate product of rational-deductive thinking. We think of them as static mechanisms designed to accomplish some single purpose.

One of the most difficult things for most of us to understand is that organizations are dynamic. Particularly as one moves up, things become less tangible and less predictable. A primary characteristic of managing, particularly at higher levels, is the confrontation of change, ambiguity, and therefore, contradiction. Organizational leaders spend much of their time living in fields of perceived tensions. They are constantly forced to make trade-offs. There are often no right answers.

The higher one goes in an organization, the more exaggerated these tensions become. One-dimensional guidelines (care for people; work harder; get control; be innovative) are simply half-truths representing single domains of action. What exists are contradictory pressures. Much of the time the choice is not between good and bad, but between good and good—or bad and bad. In such cases the need is for complex, intuitive decisions, and many people fail to cope successfully with the resulting tension, stress, and uncertainty. This is well illustrated by the initial failure and frustration of the engineer.

The people who come to be masters of management do not see their work environment only in structured, analytic ways. Instead, they also have the capacity to see it as a complex, dynamic system that is constantly evolving. In order to interact effectively with it, they employ a variety of different perspectives or models. As one set of conditions arises, they focus on certain cues that lead them to apply a very analytic and structured approach. As these cues fade, they focus on new cues of emerging importance and apply another frame, perhaps being very intuitive and flexible. At another time they may emphasize the overall task, and at still another they may focus on the welfare of a single individual.

Because of these shifts, masters may appear to be paradoxical. They engage the contradictions of organizational life by using seemingly contradictory frames. Viewed from a single point in time, their behaviors may seem illogical; they, themselves may seem to be contradictory. Yet these seeming contradictions come together in a fluid whole. Things work well for these people.

THE POSSIBILITY OF SELF-IMPROVEMENT

The engineer "stumbled" into a new paradigm. He was both determined and lucky. Many people who encounter his problem are defeated by it. Although you are also likely to encounter similar problems in your development, you have some major advantages. First, you have a framework to help you appreciate the necessity of performing in the areas that do not come naturally. Second, you have the self-confidence gained from the learning experiences in this course. You have already developed new competencies, and this should help you in your efforts to continue developing. Finally, you have a theory that helps you to understand the necessity to think complexly and to integrate diverse competencies. You have some tools to help you improve yourself.

Conscious self-improvement is possible. Many managers, however, excuse themselves from this responsibility:

- "I am simply not creative, and there is no way to change that."
- "I hate details, and I will never be a good monitor."
- "Being a hard-driving producer is fine, but it is not worth the effort—life is simply too short."
- "Different people have different talents, and working with people is not my thing."

In each case the statement is an excuse for not making changes. In each case the statement is untrue. It is always possible for someone to make improvements in his or her weak area. He or she may legitimately choose not to, since, as we learned in the last chapter, it is possible to somewhat neglect certain roles and still be effective. However, it is inaccurate to say, "It is not my style, I am not able." Although painful, it is in fact possible to make improvements in one's weak areas. Here we will outline a procedure for doing so.

AGENDA FOR SELF-IMPROVEMENT

Table 10.1 is an agenda for self-improvement that involves three general steps: learn about yourself, develop a change strategy, and implement the strategy.

Within these three steps are some key subpoints. This process has been used with many managers and graduate students. In the beginning of the process, many participants are cynical, and some make only half-hearted efforts. Needless to say, they show little achievement. But others attack the process with zeal, and they naturally achieve considerably more. The interesting thing is that the people who make progress do so in whatever quadrant they choose. It is possible to learn in any area.

Learn About Yourself.   The first step is to do a self-assessment. This involves filling out the competing values instrument, analyzing your skills in each role,

---

TABLE 10.1 Agenda for Self-Improvement

---

1. **Learn About Yourself**
   - Complete the competing values instrument.
   - Do a written self-evaluation of each role.
   - Have others evaluate you.
   - Discuss your skills with people who will be honest.

2. **Develop a Change Strategy**
   - Keep a journal.
   - Identify specific areas in need of improvement.
   - Identify role models for your weak areas.
   - Read appropriate books.

3. **Implement the Change Strategy**
   - Be honest about the costs of improvement.
   - Develop a social support system.
   - Constantly evaluate and modify your strategy.

---

and doing a written assessment of yourself in each role. In the written assessment, you should explain why you believe you are strong or weak in each area.

This step is a relatively painless but often misleading one. Many people assess themselves in a more positive way than do their subordinates, peers, and superiors. This leads to a more difficult and painful step—obtaining honest feedback from others. It involves having others assess your strengths and weaknesses.

Although most of us claim that we want to receive honest feedback from those around us, we in fact behave in ways that prevent such feedback. In one class students were assigned to not only improve themselves in the course of a semester but also to go out and improve a manager. They arranged to act as consultants to a practicing manager. Over the semester they analyze the manager's behavior and worked with the person to improve weak areas. This provided an important mirror that allowed the student to see the flaws and the resistances in themselves by seeing them first in another person. The following is a typical statement about feedback, written by one of our students.

> *Perhaps one of the most amazing things to me is that, not only the manager we worked with, but virtually every manager that was helped by one of the teams in the class, was so deeply interested in feedback from subordinates and others. They were simply unsure what others thought about them. In every case, it was the first time in their careers that they received such feedback. As I think about it now, it seems incredible that such a single thing could be so powerful.*

Feedback from others is indeed powerful. Sometimes it can be too powerful. Occasionally a person receives feedback suggesting that other people see him or her as less effective in a given area than the person sees himself or herself. Although most people can handle this negative message, some cannot, and this can be a cause of crisis. Some people get depressed and withdraw; others get angry and want to punish those who gave the feedback. Neither response is healthy.

When you get feedback that comes as a surprise, use it as a base for honest exploration and discussion. First, wait long enough to get in the proper frame of mind so that you are indeed ready to hear what people have to say. This may take some time and preparation. Go to those who know you best, ask questions, and then "listen" to what they have to say. This strategy takes maturity and self-esteem. If you feel unsure of yourself, you should wait until some future time to seek feedback. Be careful not to behave in ways that force people to say what you want to hear.

You may feel unable, for whatever reason, to approach particular people for feedback, but that should not be a cause for concern. In fact, it is a common occurrence. People should talk to those few others with whom they have a trusting relationship but who will nevertheless be honest in their feedback.

Develop a Change Strategy. A key element in developing such a strategy is to keep a journal. In this journal you should record the self-analysis as outlined. You should then employ the journal as you engage in the following steps.

Once you have sought feedback from others, you might then make a final assessment of what you think are your strong and weak areas. As you write a final assessment of your strengths and weaknesses in each role of the competing values framework, pinpoint the ones on which you most need to work. In doing so you should also identify someone who does very well in your weak role. This will help to make concrete the kinds of behaviors that are appropriate in this role. When you are in situations that call for behavior in the role, you can ask yourself: "What would the person do in this situation?"

This step sometimes makes you uncomfortable because you may not like the people who do well in your weak areas. For example, a student had a colleague who, in terms of the competing values framework, was an exact opposite in outlook, strategy, and behavior. Working with him was very difficult. There was conflict over nearly every decision. In a final paper the student wrote:

> *Although the costs of working with him have been high, I have also learned a great deal from him. In many situations I have watched him do the exact opposite of what I would have done. It sometimes has been shocking to see his strategies work far better than my own. Over time I have come to recognize certain situations in which his thinking might be better than mine. I am now able to stop before implementing my natural strategy and ask myself what he would do in this case. Often I am dissatisfied with the answer and proceed with my own approach. There are, however, times when I go against my instincts and follow his lead. Thinking about him as a role model in my weak areas enlarges my pool of possible strategies. Sometimes, following uncomfortable strategies results in the development of a wider array of behaviors and skills.*

Another key activity is to read literature that is related to your weak roles. At the end of this chapter you will find "A Competing Values Reading List." It is organized according to the eight roles in the competing values framework and lists approximately 15 to 20 books under each role. Some are self-improvement books, others are professional management books. Most are very basic.

Many managers have used the list as a source of ideas on how to better play a particular role.

You should select the most relevant books and read them very rapidly. Then briefly record any useful ideas in your notebook. On a regular basis, consolidate these ideas into strategies that you would like to try.

Implement the Strategy. After you finish analyzing your strengths and weaknesses, considering role models, reading for ideas, and consolidating insights into possible action strategies, it is time to experiment. The first step in the experimental process is to be honest about the costs of improvement. Many people simply are not interested in changing, whereas others are so idealistic and impatient that they quickly become disillusioned by the failures that they encounter. The improvement process involves some exertion.

Because it is not always easy to engage in this process, it's important to develop a social support system. The key is to find someone to talk to, perhaps a roommate, parent, or colleague. Many managers choose their immediate superiors to play this role; when appropriate, this can be a very significant and effective arrangement. But others feel uncomfortable with their superiors and select some other person at work. Still others choose a spouse. Regardless of whom you select, arrange a schedule that will allow you to regularly meet with that person to discuss your failures and successes. This person will often be able to provide encouragement and creative insights.

As you begin to experiment with new strategies, remember that getting off a plateau usually involves some risk. It sometimes means moving into a situation that requires assumptions very different from those with which you are familiar. Instead of trying to avoid failure, you may need to embrace failure and to see it as an indispensable part of the learning process.

As you engage in your intuitive experiments, constantly evaluate your progress. Keep your notebook close at hand. Record and analyze failures, record insights, modify your strategies. You will be impressed with the power of constant self-evaluation. One manager scored low on the broker role and was very concerned about his inability to make persuasive presentations. He worked through all the steps described here and reported a dramatic improvement in performance. Here is what he wrote about the process of self-evaluation:

> *I had never before kept a journal. It was very hard for me to get used to the idea. But I was intense about trying to improve, and it was clear that a journal was going to be important. I read everything I could get my hands on, and I made lots of notes. Whenever anyone made a presentation of any kind, a salesperson, a politician, a young kid in my Sunday school class, I would analyze what was effective and what was not. Each time I drew lessons for myself. Whenever I made a presentation, I would immediately find some time to do a self-analysis. I was a tough self-critic.*
>
> *Every so often, I would make notes of my notes. That is, I would reduce them to a list of those principles that seemed to be most important for me. I was, without knowing it, building my own personal theory of persuasive speaking. The important thing is that it was an applied theory. It told me "how to." After four months or so,*

I really started to show signs of progress. People told me they were amazed at how much better I was doing.

THE RESULTS

The improvement process is sometimes easier than one thinks it is going to be. The competing values profile of one manager suggested that she was very strong in all the roles except that of monitor. She saw herself as a visionary, and she thought that being a monitor was simply "not her style." Hence, it was with some dread that she undertook the implementation of the steps outlined earlier. Here is her report:

I picked a role model, read some books, made some notes, and designed a change program. It was really very simple. Basically it boiled down to setting times to do a whole raft of tasks that I normally ignored. That was all there was to it. I was amazed. It was not a matter of ability, it was actually quite easy. It is now hard to believe that I once thought I was incapable of doing the things in the monitor role.

In summary, it is possible to become a better manager, particularly to improve in those areas that seem far from your natural style. When the steps outlined herein are applied in a serious way, they can be very helpful in moving you forward along the road to mastery.

ANALYSIS   A Comparison of Two Managers

Directions   The following are the descriptions of two managers. Read the descriptions and then answer the questions.

Don Burr of People Express

One of the most interesting management stories of this decade concerns Don Burr and how he used his creative genius to build a spectacular company. But it is also a story of how he turned his strengths into a problem, how he got trapped in a negative zone, and how that led to the demise of the company.

People Express was incorporated in April 1980. It was driven by a unique vision. Among the key elements of this vision were the ideas of offering extraordinarily inexpensive fares made possible by large productivity gains, of focusing on the high-density eastern U.S. markets, and of operating out of the underutilized Newark International Airport. In a two-year period, the company grew to 1200 employees, owned 17 aircraft, serviced 13 cities, and carried 2 million passengers. But this was just the beginning of the company's growth. Before its demise in 1986, People's would become the fifth largest airline in the country.

Before starting the company, Don Burr had been the president of Texas Air. When he left to start People Express, more than 15 of Texas Air's top people followed him. At that time, although Burr was only 39 years old, he was the oldest member of the new company. Many of the people who followed him left their old jobs knowing little or nothing about even the most basic aspects of the new company. They came because of their trust in Burr and the opportunity to build a new system.

From the beginning, the driving beliefs were that people were trustworthy and that this was a chance to build an organization where people could maximize their abilities. Burr's people were ingenious in creating the new company. They developed a unique vision based on low fares and convenient schedules. The company's aircraft were redesigned for the most efficient use and maximum carrying capacity. Hiring and training practices drew on unique labor pools, and employees developed a deep sense of commitment and teamwork. Labor costs were kept low by maintaining lean staffs who were highly motivated and willing to do any job deemed necessary. New ticketing and collection procedures were worked out. Technologies and administrative hierarchies were kept simple.

At the core of this were Burr's enthusiasm and entrepreneurial leadership. Never satisfied with a plateau, he continually pushed for more growth and greater effort and creativity on the part of the staff.

Burr was clearly a very effective manager. Indeed, he has been one of the most creative managers of our time. But something went wrong. After five years of explosive growth his dream died. In September 1986, People Express was sold to its archrival, Texas Air. The death of People Express resulted in many post hoc analyses of what went wrong. Generally the analyses agreed on two themes. The first and most obvious theme concerned expansion, particularly People's well-publicized purchase of Frontier Airlines. Burr simply tried to expand the airline too rapidly.

The second theme had to do with the evolution of the company's infrastructure. Critics argued that Burr was unable to let the organization go through some necessary processes of formalization. They claimed that he failed to understand basic details, such as which routes were profitable and which were not. He was unable to let go of job rotation strategies, which were initially successful but eventually resulted in serious problems. He resisted the continually expressed need for more management and direction. The critics argued that Burr failed, in the end, because he had limited vision.

Bill Gates of Microsoft

Microsoft is the second largest software company in the world. Run by Bill Gates, who is still in his early thirties, Microsoft has been best known for its widely used MS DOS system. But in 1987 Gates was successful in convincing IBM to adopt its newest product, called Windows, for use in IBM's new line of personal computers. Upon completion of the agreement, analysts began to predict that within 12 months Microsoft would become the largest software company in the world.

In many ways, Gates, like Burr, is the stereotypical entrepreneur. He is a technical genius with a burning mission. He feels a drive to bring the power of computing to the masses. His company is marked by considerable flexibility and excitement. The median age of the work force is 31. People work long days, with Gates himself setting the example with an early morning to midnight routine. There are frequent picnics, programmers set their own hours, dress is casual, and the turnover rate is less than 10 percent.

The company has grown rapidly. From 1980 to 1981 Gates watched his company go from 80 to 125 employees and saw profits double to $16 million. The market value of the company now exceeds $2 billion. Given our earlier cases, all these indicators would lead us to worry about Gates and his ability to meet the demands for formalization.

In fact, however, Gates has already faced the formalization crisis and has come off well. What were the keys to this success? First, he made a very significant decision to bring in professional managers and to focus his own energies on technology. He seemed to grasp an important paradox that eludes most entrepreneurs: to have power means one must give up power. Maintaining a primary focus on technology, however, does not mean that he has abandoned the tasks of leadership. Instead, he has taken the time to learn the principles of law, marketing, distribution, and accounting and apply them in his work. He also has the paradoxical capacity of simultaneously caring and being tough. For example, dissatisfied with the performance of Microsoft's president, Gates removed him from office after only one year. But not long after, Gates was invited to be the best man at the wedding of the former president.

Discussion Questions   1. What strengths did Burr and Gates share?

2. In what ways did Burr and Gates differ?

3. What is mastery and how was it displayed in these cases?

PRACTICE   The Evaluation Matrix

Based on all you have learned in Chapters 1 to 9, and on the assessment exercise at the outset of this chapter, complete the following matrix, Table 10.2.

APPLICATION   Your Strategy for Mastery

Based on the material in this book, particularly the material in this chapter, write a final paper. In the paper do a self-analysis, an improvement plan for the coming year, and develop a long-term improvement strategy that will span your career.

TABLE 10.2 Evaluation Matrix

	Director	Producer	Coordinator	Monitor	Mentor	Facilitator	Broker	Innovator
1. In regards to this role, what do I know about myself?								
2. How could I more effectively play this role?								
3. Who are some people I could imitate?								
4. What books should I read?								
5. What objectives and deadlines should I set?								
6. With whom should I share my objectives?								
7. How will I evaluate my efforts?								

REFERENCES

Dreyfus, H. L., S. E. Dreyfus, and T. Athanasion. *Mind over Machine: The Power of Human Intuition and Expertise in the Era of the Computer.* New York: Free Press, 1986.

Quinn, R. E. *Beyond Rational Management: Mastering the Paradoxes and Competing Demands of High Performance.* San Francisco: Jossey Bass, 1988.

Quinn, R. E., S. R. Faerman, and N. Dixit. *Perceived Performance: Some Archetypes of Managerial Effectiveness and Ineffectiveness.* Working paper, Institute for Government and Policy Studies, Department of Public Administration, State University of New York at Albany, 1987.

A COMPETING VALUES READING LIST

This resource contains a reading list organized according to the competing values framework and designed to help you identify books that address the areas in which you need improvement. It is meant to suggest a few of the many readings that can expand your knowledge in each area. Readers are encouraged to send the author additional suggestions of books for inclusion.

Director Role

Albrecht, K. *Successful Management by Objectives: An Action Manual.* Englewood Cliffs, N.J.: Prentice-Hall, 1978.

Allison, G. T. *Essence of Decision: Explaining the Cuban Missile Crisis.* Boston: Little, Brown, 1971.

Behn, R. D., and J. W. Vaupel. *Quick Analysis for Busy Decision Makers.* New York: Basic Books, 1982.

Below, P. J., G. L. Morrisey, and B. L. Acomb. *The Executive Guide to Strategic Planning.* San Francisco: Jossey-Bass, 1987.

Benson, H., and M. Z. Kipper. *The Relaxation Response.* New York: Avon Books, 1975.

Drucker, P. F., *Managing for Results: Economic Tasks and Risk-Taking Decisions.* New York: Harper & Row, 1964.

Engel, H. M. *How to Delegate: A Guide to Getting Things Done.* Houston, Texas: Gulf, 1983.

Huber, G. P. *Managerial Decision Making.* Glenview, Ill.: Scott, Foresman, 1986.

Jenks, J. M., and J. M. Kelly. *Don't Do. Delegate!* New York: Ballantine, 1985.

Keppner, C. H., and B. B. Tregoe. *The Rational Manager: A Systematic Approach to Problem Solving and Decision Making.* New York: McGraw-Hill, 1965.

Mali, P. *MBO Updated: A Handbook of Practices and Techniques for Managing Objectives.* New York: John Wiley and Sons, 1986.

Selye, H. *The Stress of Life* (2d ed.). New York: McGraw-Hill, 1978.

Woolfolk, R. L., and F. C. Richardson. *Stress, Sanity, and Survival.* New York: New American Library, 1979.

Producer Role

Bain, D. *The Productivity Prescription: The Manager's Guide to Improving Productivity and Profits.* New York: McGraw-Hill, 1982.

Friedman, M. *Overcoming the Fear of Success: Why and How We Defeat Ourselves and What to Do About It.* New York: Warner Books, 1980.

Grove, A. S. *High-Output Management.* New York: Random House, 1985.

Kendrick, J. W. *Improving Company Productivity.* Baltimore, Md.: Johns Hopkins University Press, 1984.

Kushel, G. *The Fully Effective Executive.* Chicago: Contemporary Books, 1983.

Mandell, M. *1001 Ways to Operate Your Business More Profitably.* Homewood, Ill.: Dow Jones-Irwin, 1975.

Nash, M. *Making People Productive: What Really Works in Raising Managerial and Employee Performance.* San Francisco: Jossey-Bass, 1985.

———. *Managing Organizational Performance.* San Francisco: Jossey-Bass, 1983.

Phillips, J. J. *Improving Supervisors' Effectiveness: How Organizations Can Raise the Performance of Their First-Level Managers.* San Francisco: Jossey-Bass, 1985.

Sawyer, G. C. *Designing Strategy.* New York: John Wiley and Sons, 1986.

Stankard, M. F. *Productivity by Choice: The 20 to 1 Principle.* New York: John Wiley and Sons, 1986.

Vough, C. F. *Productivity: A Practical Program for Improving Efficiency.* New York: AMACOM, 1979.

Ziglar, Z. *Top Performance: How to Develop Excellence in Yourself and Others.* New York: Berkley Books, 1986.

Coordinator Role

Becker, F. *The Successful Office: How to Create a Workplace That Is Right for You.* Reading, Mass.: Addison-Wesley, 1982.

Bernstein, L. A. *Analysis of Financial Statements.* Homewood, Ill.: Dow Jones-Irwin, 1984.

Drucker, P. F. *Management: Tasks, Responsibilities, and Practices.* New York: Harper & Row, 1973.

Frame, J. D. *Managing Projects in Organizations: How to Make the Best Use of Time, Techniques, and People.* San Francisco: Jossey-Bass, 1987.

Kish, J. L., Jr. *Office Management Problem Solver.* Radnor, Pa.: Chilton, 1983.

Loen, R. O. *Manage More by Doing Less.* New York: McGraw-Hill, 1971.

Newman, W. H. *Constructive Control: Design and Use of Control Systems.* Englewood Cliffs, N.J.: Prentice-Hall, 1975.

Nickerson, C. B. *The Accounting Handbook for Non-Accountants.* Boston: CBI Publishing, 1975.

Oncken, W. *Managing Management Time: Who's Got the Monkey?* Englewood Cliffs, N.J.: Prentice-Hall, 1984.

Vollmann, T. E., W. L. Berry, and D. C. Whybark. *Manufacturing Planning and Control Systems.* Homewood, Ill.: Dow Jones-Irwin, 1987.

Wanat, J. *Introduction to Budgeting.* Boston: Duxbury Press, 1978.

Winston, S. *The Organized Executive: New Ways to Manage Time, Paper, and People.* New York: Norton, 1983.

Monitor Role

Adler, M., and C. Van Doren. *How to Read a Book.* New York: Simon & Schuster, 1972.

Brown, A. S. *Maximizing Memory Power: Using Recall to Your Advantage in Business.* New York: John Wiley and Sons, 1987.

Cascio, W. F. *Costing Human Resources: The Financial Impact of Behavior in Organizations.* New York: Van Nostrand Reinhold, 1982.

Eisenberg, R. *Organize Yourself.* New York: Macmillan, 1986.

Fockart, J., and D. W. Delong. *Executive Support Systems: The Myth and Reality of Top Management Computer Use.* Homewood, Ill.: Dow Jones-Irwin, 1987.

Posner, M. J. *Executive Essentials. Part II: Coping with the Information Explosion.* New York: Avon Books, 1982.

Reimold, C. *How to Write a Million-Dollar Memo.* New York: Dell, 1984.

Salerno, L. M. (ed.). "Catching Up with the Computer Revolution." *Harvard Business Review Executive Book Series,* New York: John Wiley and Sons, 1983.

Sloma, R. S. *How to Measure Managerial Performance.* New York: Macmillan, 1980.

Winston, S. *The Organized Executive: New Ways to Manage Time, Paper, and People.* New York: Norton, 1983.

Mentor Role

Carnegie, D. and D. Carnegie. *How to Win Friends and Influence People.* New York: Simon & Schuster, 1981.

Drake, J. D. *Effective Interviewing: A Guide for Managers.* New York: AMACOM, 1972.

Hall, D. T. *Careers in Organization.* Pacific Palisades, Calif.: Goodyear, 1976.

Helmstetter, S. *What to Say When You Talk to Yourself.* New York: Pocket Books, 1986.

James, M., and D. Jongewood. *Born to Win.* Reading, Mass.: Addison-Wesley, 1977.

Kotter, J., V. A. Faux, and C. C. McArthur. *Self-Assessment and Career Development.* Englewood Cliffs, N.J.: Prentice-Hall, 1978.

McGregor, D. *The Human Side of Enterprise.* New York: McGraw-Hill, 1960.

Maslow, A. *Motivation and Personality* (2d ed.). New York: Harper & Row, 1970.

Nierenberg, G. I., and H. H. Calero. *How to Read a Person Like a Book.* New York: Pocket Books, 1973.

Progoff, I. *At a Journal Workshop: The Basic Text and Guide for Using the Intensive Journal.* New York: Dialogue House Library, 1975.

Reece, B. L., and R. Brandt. *Effective Human Relations in Business.* Boston: Houghton Mifflin, 1981.

Rogers, C. R. *On Becoming a Person.* Boston: Houghton Mifflin, 1961.

Rogers, C. R., and B. Stevens. *Person to Person: The Problem of Being Human.* Lafayette, Calif.: Real People Press, 1967.

Rusk, T., and R. Reed. *I Want to Change but I Don't Know How.* Los Angeles: Price/Stern/Sloan, 1986.

Schein, E. H. *Career Dynamics: Matching Individual and Organizational Needs.* Reading, Mass.: Addison-Wesley, 1978.

Sheehy, G. *Passages: Predictable Crises of Adult Life.* New York: Dutton, 1976.

Sher, B. *Wishcraft: How to Get What You Really Want.* New York: Ballantine, 1983.

Torbert, W. R. *Managing the Corporate Dream: Restructuring for Long-Term Success.* Homewood, Ill.: Dow Jones-Irwin, 1987.

Facilitator Role

Beck, A. C., and E. D. Hillmar. *Positive Management Practices: Bringing Out the Best in Organizations and People.* San Francisco: Josey-Bass, 1986.

Blake, R., J. Mouton, and R. Allen. *Spectacular Teamwork: What It Is, How to Recognize It, How to Bring It About.* New York: John Wiley and Sons, 1987.

Doyle, D. S. *How to Make Meetings Work.* New York: Jove, 1982.

Dyer, W. G. Team Building. Reading, Mass.: Addison-Wesley, 1987.

Filley, A. C. *Interpersonal Conflict Resolution.* Glenview, Ill.: Scott, Foresman, 1975.

Fox, W. M. *Effective Group Problem Solving: How to Broaden Participation, Improve Decision Making, and Increase Commitment to Action.* San Francisco: Jossey-Bass, 1987.

Janis, I. *Victims of Groupthink.* Boston: Houghton Mifflin, 1972.

Lawler, E. E. III. *High-Involvement Management: Participative Strategies for Improving Organizational Performance.* San Francisco: Jossey-Bass, 1986.

Ouchi, W. G. *Theory Z: How American Business Can Meet the Japanese Challenge.* Reading, Mass.: Addison-Wesley, 1981.

Walton, R. E. *Managing Conflict: Interpersonal Dialogue and Third-Party Roles.* (2nd ed.) Reading, Mass.: Addison-Wesley, 1987.

Zander, A. *Making Groups Effective.* San Francisco: Jossey-Bass, 1982.

Zander, A. *The Purposes of Groups and Organizations.* San Francisco: Jossey-Bass, 1985.

Innovator Role

Ackoff, R. L. *The Art of Problem Solving.* New York, John Wiley and Sons, 1987.

Albrecht, K. *The Creative Corporation.* Homewood, Ill.: Dow Jones-Irwin, 1987.

Beckhard, R., and R. T. Harris. *Organizational Transitions* (2d ed.). Reading, Mass.: Addison-Wesley, 1987.

Brandt, S. C. *Entrepreneuring in Established Companies: Managing Toward the Year 2000.* New York: Mentor, 1986.

Gawain, S. *Creative Visualization.* New York: Bantam Books, 1978.

Hornstein, H. A. *Managerial Courage.* New York: John Wiley and Sons, 1986.

Kanter, R. M. *The Change Masters: Innovation for Productivity in the American Corporation.* New York: Simon & Schuster, 1983.

Keil, J. M. *The Creative Mystique: How to Manage It, Nurture It, and Make It Pay.* New York: John Wiley and Sons, 1985.

Kilmann, R. H. *Beyond the Quick Fix: Managing Five Tracks to Organizational Success.* San Francisco: Jossey-Bass, 1984.

Kirkpatrick, D. L. *How to Manage Change Effectively: Approaches, Methods, and Case Examples.* San Francisco: Jossey-Bass, 1985.

LeBoeuf, M. *Imagineering: How to Profit from Your Creative Powers.* New York: Berkley Book, 1980.

Martel, L. *Mastering Change: The Key to Business Success.* New York: Simon & Schuster, 1986.

Nayak, P. R., and J. M. Kettersingham. *Break-Through.* New York: Rawson Associates, 1986.

Peale, N. V. *The Power of Positive Thinking.* New York: Fawcett Books, 1956.

Pinchot, G. III. *Intrapreneuring: Why You Don't Have to Leave the Corporation to Become an Entrepreneur.* New York: Harper & Row, 1985.

Ray, M., and R. Myers. *Creativity in Business.* New York: Doubleday, 1986.

Tichy, N. M. *Managing Strategic Change: Organization Development Redefined.* New York: John Wiley and Sons, 1983.

Tichy, N. M., and M. A. Devanna. *The Transformational Leader.* New York: John Wiley and Sons, 1986.

Von Oech, R. *A Kick in the Seat of the Pants: Using Your Explorer, Artist, Judge, and Warrior to Be More Creative.* New York: Harper & Row, 1986.

————. *A Whack on the Side of the Head: How to Unlock Your Mind for Innovation.* New York: Warner Books, 1983.

Broker Role

Allen, R. W., and L. W. Porter. *Organizational Influence Processes.* Glenview, Ill.: Scott, Foresman, 1983.

Back, K., and K. Back. *Assertiveness at Work: A Practical Guide to Handling Awkward Situations.* New York: McGraw-Hill, 1982.

Bedrosian, M. M. *Speak Like a Pro: Building Visibility, Impact, and Profits Through Public Speaking.* New York: John Wiley and Sons, 1987.

Block, P. *The Empowered Manager: Positive Political Skills at Work.* San Francisco: Jossey-Bass, 1987.

Cohen, H. *You Can Negotiate Anything: How to Get What You Want.* New York: Bantam, 1982.

Culbert, S., and J. J. McDonald. *Radical Management: Power Politics and the Pursuit of Trust.* New York: Free Press, 1985.

Fisher, R., and W. Ury. *Getting to Yes: Negotiating Agreement Without Giving In.* New York: Viking Penguin, 1983.

Greenburger, F., and T. Kiernan. *How to Ask for More and Get It: The Art of Creative Negotiation.* New York: Doubleday, 1978.

Hegarty, C. *How to Manage Your Boss.* New York: Ballantine, 1982.

Jandt, F. E. *Win-Win Negotiating: Turning Conflict into Agreement.* New York: John Wiley and Sons, 1985.

Kenny, M. *Presenting Yourself.* New York: John Wiley and Sons, 1982.

Korda, M. *Power: How to Get It, How to Use It.* New York: Random House, 1975.

Leech, T. *How to Prepare, Stage, and Deliver Winning Presentations.* New York: AMACOM, 1982.

Nirenberg, J. S. *How to Sell Your Ideas.* New York: McGraw-Hill, 1984.

Pfeiffer, J. *Power in Organizations.* Marshfield, Mass.: Pitman, 1981.

Smith, M. J. *When I Say No, I Feel Guilty.* New York: Bantam Books, 1975.

Viscott, D. *Winning.* New York: Pocket Books, 1987.

Yates, D. T., Jr. *The Politics of Management: Exploring the Inner Workings of Public and Private Organizations.* San Francisco: Jossey-Bass, 1985.